Language Diversity in the Classroom

BILINGUAL EDUCATION & BILINGUALISM
Series Editors: Nancy H. Hornberger (*University of Pennsylvania, USA*) and Colin Baker (*Bangor University, Wales, UK*)

Bilingual Education and Bilingualism is an international, multidisciplinary series publishing research on the philosophy, politics, policy, provision and practice of language planning, global English, indigenous and minority language education, multilingualism, multiculturalism, biliteracy, bilingualism and bilingual education. The series aims to mirror current debates and discussions.

Full details of all the books in this series and of all our other publications can be found on http://www.multilingual-matters.com, or by writing to Multilingual Matters, St Nicholas House, 31–34 High Street, Bristol BS1 2AW, UK.

BILINGUAL EDUCATION & BILINGUALISM
Series Editors: Nancy H. Hornberger (*University of Pennsylvania, USA*) and Colin Baker (*Bangor University, Wales, UK*)

Language Diversity in the Classroom

John Edwards

MULTILINGUAL MATTERS
Bristol • Buffalo • Toronto

For Suzanne

Library of Congress Cataloging in Publication Data
A catalog record for this book is available from the Library of Congress.
Edwards, John
Language Diversity in the Classroom/John Edwards.
Bilingual Education & Bilingualism
Includes bibliographical references and index.
1. Education, Bilingual–United States. 2. Languages in contact–United States. 3. Children with social disabilities–Education–United States. 4. English language–Study and teaching–United States–Foreign speakers. 5. Teaching–Social aspects–United States. I. Title.
LC3731.E49 2009
370.117'50973–dc22 2009033459

British Library Cataloguing in Publication Data
A catalogue entry for this book is available from the British Library.

ISBN-13: 978-1-84769-226-9 (hbk)
ISBN-13: 978-1-84769-225-2 (pbk)

Multilingual Matters
UK: St Nicholas House, 31–34 High Street, Bristol BS1 2AW, UK.
USA: UTP, 2250 Military Road, Tonawanda, NY 14150, USA.
Canada: UTP, 5201 Dufferin Street, North York, Ontario M3H 5T8, Canada.

The policy of Multilingual Matters/Channel View Publications is to use papers that are natural, renewable and recyclable products, made from wood grown in sustainable forests. In the manufacturing process of our books, and to further support our policy, preference is given to printers that have FSC and PEFC Chain of Custody certification. The FSC and/or PEFC logos will appear on those books where full certification has been granted to the printer concerned.

Typeset by Datapage International Ltd.
Printed and bound in Great Britain by the Cromwell Press Group.

Contents

Chapter 1
Introduction

L'école est un curieux lieu de langage. Il s'y mélange les langues officielle, privée, scolaire, des langues maternelles, des langues étrangères, de l'argot de lycéen, de l'argot de la cité. À considérer toutes ces langues qui cohabitent, je me dis que l'école est peut-être le seul lieu où elles peuvent se retrouver dans leur diversité et dans leurs chevauchements. Mais il faut être très vigilants et justement tirer partie de cette belle hétérogénéité. (Steiner & Ladjali, 2003: 83–84)

A Brief Rationale

Among my other academic activities and duties, I have been giving talks to teachers and teachers' organizations since the early 1970s. These have typically dealt with the points of intersection among education, social class, ethnolinguistic status and group identity. Such topics, with all their many ramifications, have always been of great interest to teachers, since they are so obviously relevant to the daily life of an ever-increasing number of classrooms. Whether it is a matter of accepting or rejecting nonstandard dialects or foreign languages at school, of adapting classrooms to language diversity or attempting to maintain a strict monolingual regimen, of seeing school as a contributor to social change or as a supporter of some 'mainstream' status quo, of arguing the merits of 'transitional' versus 'maintenance' programs of bilingual education, of embracing multiculturalism or recoiling from it – in all these matters, the knowledge, sensitivities and attitudes of teachers are of no small importance.

And yet, over three decades or so, I have been amazed and disappointed at how ill-prepared teachers typically are with regard to linguistic and cultural variation in the classroom. The education of teachers generally involves very little exposure to this sort of hetero-geneity, and yet it is easy to see that it has made its presence felt in virtually every global setting. Even schools in 'traditional' and rural areas whose populations were historically both local and stable are now more and more confronted with children from many different backgrounds. The geographical spread of Spanish speakers throughout the USA – far beyond the initially adopted settlement areas of Florida and the southwest – is a case in point, as is the widening distribution and permanence of the European 'guest workers', as is the exploding mobility that has now brought hundreds of thousands of east Europeans, as well as African and Asian refugees, to countries in western Europe; and so on. I have also discovered that many jurisdictions have essentially denied a diversity that was always there, a reflection of a sort of socially imposed ignorance. Thus, for example, when I began research work in Nova Scotia, it was immediately clear that prevailing perspectives made little room for longstanding groups of low social status. In some schools, there were sizeable groups of African-Canadian youngsters, descendants of those who came to Canada during the American Civil War, along the 'underground railroad', or who had been given land grants in return for service in the British army; in others, there were Acadian children of French-speaking background. An inability or an unwillingness to see such groups as anything other than very minor aberrations in an essentially English/Celtic mainstream had the predictable consequences.

Even if there was *no* great likelihood of teachers encountering social or linguistic diversity in their classrooms (increasingly implausible as this would seem), I think that a good case could still be made for giving much more attention to such diversity. In this book, I will argue that *all good education worthy of the name is multicultural* and, if this is so, a logical implication is that any heightening of teachers' cross-cultural and cross-subcultural sensitivities must be a good thing.

Finally here, it is important to note that expanded sensibilities are not at all difficult to bring about. The matters under discussion in this book are not rocket science. To take one example: the evidence that Black English dialects are just as valid as any other English variants, that they are just as rule-governed, that their patterns of pronunciation and emphasis are just as regular, that they serve the cognitive needs of their speakers just as well as any other form of speech does – all this and more can be presented to, and understood by, anyone who has an open mind. I know, because I have made presentations to teachers and teachers-in-training, as well as to hundreds of senior students in language seminars. So much the worse, then, that so many are still left to labor under stereotyped, inaccurate and potentially harmful illusions. As I shall shortly point out, poor and socially disadvantaged children have very real burdens to bear; it is an unnecessary further tragedy that their linguistic and cognitive skills should be misunderstood or denigrated.

The consequences, in terms of impediments to learning, early curtailment of formal education and reduced chances in the world beyond the school gates can be enormous.

Sympathetic Voices

There have been several contemporary calls for the sort of attention I hope to highlight in this book, as well as earlier ones demonstrating the longstanding nature of the issue. There has, for instance, been a number of recent works arguing for greater and more precise attention to the teaching of foreign languages, and almost all these works stress the importance of the ideological framework within which this occurs. Unlike earlier and more linguistically focused treatments, these later ones encourage a broader sociolinguistic and sociocultural contextualization (e.g. Osborn, 2000; Reagan & Osborn, 2002). Their very existence, of course, testifies to a continuing need. In the American context, the need is particularly evident where Hispanic children are concerned: Flores (2005) presents a rather chilling chronological table in which the assessments of the 1920s – a time when Spanish speakers were sometimes judged to be mentally retarded – have now become condemnations of bilingual education programs that prevent the most efficient acquisition of English. (Flores' table can be interestingly set against another, provided by Baker [2006], which charts the rise and fall of language programs in the USA.) A recent small-scale example demonstrates the continuing tendency for alleged language deficiencies to be taken as evidence of underlying cognitive weakness (Commins & Miramontes, 1989). In another setting, Hélot and Young (2005: 242–244) show that, since the French educational system is still largely 'envisaged from a monolingual point of view... it is difficult for most teachers to view the different languages and cultural backgrounds of their pupils as other than problematic'. The authors suggest that, where linguistic diversity *does* seem to be mildly encouraged by the education ministry, this is 'mainly as a policy to counterbalance the hegemony of English'. This alerts us to the possibility that, in some contexts, concerns for 'small' languages and cultures are more apparent than real, often masking other agendas.

Work by McDiarmid (1992) and McDiarmid and Price (1990) reveals that multicultural training programs in America seem either to make little impact on teachers-to-be or, worse, they actually reinforce minority-group stereotyping. Drawing upon this, Deering (1997: 343) argues for more, and more effective, ways to encourage teachers' multicultural sensitivity towards other cultures, particularly among American teacher populations that he found to be less culturally sensitive than their UK counterpart; see also Noguera (1996) on insufficient teacher preparation for culturally heterogeneous classrooms. Several aspects of Deering's brief report are less than completely satisfactory, however, and Burton-wood and Bruce (1999) cast some doubt upon the allegedly greater UK sensitivity. Nevertheless, they concur with the general observations about the need for improvement. They also remind us that the Swann Report (1985), which had made an argument for just such improvement, was effectively overtaken by British educational reform legislation three years later, reform that stressed the importance of a national curriculum (and thus, in the eyes of many observers, made less room for diversity in the classroom).

Later work has confirmed some of the difficulties here. Zientek (2007) has written about the general shortcomings of teacher-preparation programs in America; more specifically, she discusses the inadequate information provided about cultural and linguistic diversity in the classroom. Some of the current diversity here involves, of course, black, Hispanic and Asian American pupils, and Tenenbaum and Ruck (2007) have demonstrated the varied expectations that teachers have of children in these groups: Asian pupils were expected to do best at school, followed by 'European American' children, then Hispanics and, finally, black children. Teachers were also found to be more encouraging in their interactions with those of whom they expected the most. The dangers of such stereotypic preconceptions are obvious, contributing as they easily can to self-fulfilling prophecies; see also Wiggan (2007).

There is even evidence that the more specific training of teachers for bilingual education programs has been less than adequate. Grinberg and Saavedra (2000) cite some representative comments that demonstrate how university courses leading to teacher certification are often of 'little relevance'. One trainee notes: 'In my preparation as a bilingual educator I was not prepared for the reality in the school' (Grinberg & Saavedra, 2000: 433). Another observation:

> Living here in the heart of New Mexico, we have very fertile grounds to develop strong, effective bilingual programs... [but] the university does not have a good program to prepare teachers... there is no rigor... the content of the classes is minimal, at a low level. (Grinberg & Saavedra, 2000: 434)

Grinberg and Saavedra discuss the emphasis upon language per se in training courses, and the lack of time devoted to cross-cultural education more broadly. The dissatisfaction noted by the first trainee teacher (above) is a particular problem: on the one hand, there is insufficient exposure to multicultural themes; on the other, the training that does exist under this heading is often inadequate. This may account for the reports of Martin (1995) and Zeichner (1994), who found that when teachers-to-be appeared uninterested in, or resistant to, multicultural training courses, *their* teachers characterized them as ill-prepared or, less charitably, as unrepentant possessors of racist and stereotyped views. It is not difficult to detect potential vicious circles here (see also McAllister & Irvine, 2000).

When discussing the 'culture' of the foreign-language classroom, the best of the recent books and papers give some attention to the language-dialect distinction and, more particularly, to the appropriate understanding of the validity of nonstandard dialect varieties. Siegel (2007: 76) provides a good example with a discussion showing just how little ground has been gained in this area. Describing creoles and nonstandard dialects in education, he points out that, despite several decades of sociolinguistic insight, accurate depictions of such varieties 'have not filtered down to many educators and administrators, or to the general public'; see also Zéphir (1997, 1999), who draws explicit parallels between the educational reception of creole and that of Black English. Such treatments touch upon the most important category here.

At 20-year intervals, the American Dialect Society (1943, 1964 and 1984; and Preston, 2003) published four works outlining 'needed research' in dialect studies. In the latest of these, several authors write about the important linguistic demonstrations of the validity of Black English and other nonstandard dialects, and about the useful developments in language-attitude research, 'perceptual dialectology' and 'folk linguistics' (see later chapters). They also acknowledge, however, that unenlightened stereotypes continue their baleful course. There is clearly much more to do, particularly in educational settings. In 1979, the Center for Applied Linguistics in Washington issued five booklets devoted to 'dialects and educational equity'; these were revised and updated in one short volume by Wolfram and Christian (1989). In a question-and-answer format, the authors deal with issues raised by teachers in workshops, in-service sessions and other similar venues; although there are obvious limitations and discontinuities in such an approach, most of the important matters are at least touched upon. Wolfram and Christian note that, while researchers and those who teach teachers agree on the importance of information about dialect variation in the classroom, they have been hindered by the lack of appropriate texts.

It is interesting, to say the least, that over the 20 years following Labov's (1969) classic demonstration of the 'logic of nonstandard English' – in an America where Black English was achieving a new visibility – no suitable teacher-training material was apparently developed. Cochran-Smith (1995: 493) was blunt, describing the American educational system as 'dysfunctional for large numbers of children who are not part of the racial and language mainstream'. She argues, as Stone (1981), Sleeter and Grant (1987) and others have done, that multicultural 'education' has often been trivialized by attention to 'foods, folkways and handiwork'. There are no broad strategies, Cochran-Smith asserts, for dealing with cultural and linguistic diversity at school. Virtually all those who have written in scholarly ways about Black English have, of course, argued for the greater sensitivity to black culture and lifestyles that should logically accompany demonstrations of the validity of black dialects; the work of Smitherman (e.g. 1981a, 2006) is noteworthy here (and see also my discussion of Ebonics, below). Thus, in a review of a book on Black English, Kautzsch (2006) points to the necessity for more open-minded and well-informed teachers, and for educational systems committed to 'difference' rather than 'deficit' stances on cultural and dialect variations. And Godley *et al.* (2007: 124) provide a very recent classroom demonstration of the continuing assessments that equate 'standard' with 'correct', and Black English with 'incorrect, ungrammatical English'. A collection by Nero (2006) is also concerned with nonstandard varieties in the classroom; in his foreword, Elbow points to the pivotal issue of reconciling an acknowledgement of the validity of all varieties with the effective teaching of more standard ones.

Overall, the monograph-length treatment most similar to mine here is that of Corson (2001). His title is similar, and so are the areas he focuses upon: standard and nonstandard dialects, language education in its several formats, and discourse 'norms' in relation to cultural and gender variation. In this book, I stress ramifications of the first two, and pay less attention to matters of gender and discourse (for reasons that will be made clear). And, like me, Corson aims at a comprehensive overview of those aspects of linguistic diversity most relevant in education. However, while his notes about the intended audience reveal a basic concern with advanced social-science students and 'experienced teachers', and while I hope and expect that *this* book will be of interest in those quarters too, my central focus is upon teachers-to-be, those who train them, and researchers in the area. That is, the material between these covers is meant primarily to contribute to the lessening of misinformation and stereotype, and to the breaking of the unfortunate circles that they maintain. There is ample evidence that the inaccurate language attitudes often held by beginning teachers – who are, after all, members of societies in which stereotypes abound – are reinforced in a school culture that, like the larger community outside its gates, has traditionally encouraged ('privileged' would be the word many use nowadays) what is 'standard'. These attitudes, it has been suggested, are often strong enough that new teachers will 'hear' minority-group children's speech as nonstandard even if, in fact, it is not. Finally here, to make matters a little more poignant, there is *some* evidence to suggest that *some* younger teachers are initially more inclined to believe the 'different-but-not-deficient' argument about nonstandard varieties: how sad, then, if that encouraging initial insight becomes overwhelmed by the existing culture of the school (see Corson, 2001; Edwards, 1986; Fasold, 1984; see also the fleshing-out of these matters in the chapters following).

Brouwer and Korthagen (2005) have discussed aspects of this in a lengthy review. They note, at the outset, that 'occupational socialization in schools is a known factor counteracting attempts at educating innovative teachers' (Brouwer & Korthagen, 2005: 153). This is one pole of the problem, as it were: teachers, like the rest of us, are very susceptible to the cognitive and emotional tone of their surroundings. It is not to be doubted that such susceptibility is correlated with vagueness or ignorance, so that the issues on which one is least informed are likely to be those most prone to influence. A corollary is that attempts to replace ignorance with awareness are likely to act as inoculations against later susceptibility. To make this more specific: providing new teachers with accurate linguistic information about the competence of their pupils may disrupt a chain of ignorance and misinformation that is otherwise likely to continue. This brings me to the second pole. As Brouwer and Korthagen (2005: 153) observe, some studies have shown that the 'effects of teacher education on the actual practices of teachers are generally meager'. The implication here, then, is that the provision of linguistic and psychological information must be done well in order to have any chance of becoming that 'inoculation'. Fortunately, as I have already noted, it is not especially difficult to present the relevant findings in a digestible manner. Fortunate, but again a little sad, inasmuch as so much more could have easily been accomplished already.

Corson draws attention to the need for improved teacher sensitivity and to the benefits of having more ethnic-group members as teachers; above all, however, he echoes one of my opening concerns here (or, more accurately, one aspect of a broader concern). He remarks that 'classroom-related work on non-standard varieties is still in its infancy' (Corson,

2001: 79). In fact, this is a little inaccurate: as the list of references in this book demonstrates, there is no shortage of relevant research, much of it deriving from, and meant to feed back into, the educational system. It is the lack of appropriate *synthesis*, and then of *application* – in teacher-training programs, for instance – that is the crux of the matter. This makes the second of Corson's broad observations rather more apposite: 'formal educational policies for the treatment of non-standard varieties in schools are conspicuous by their absence in most educational systems' (Corson, 2001: 68).

Like Corson before them, Quiocho and Rios (2000) consider the impact upon minority-group children of having teachers from their own group. They are undoubtedly correct in pointing out that there are fewer such teachers in America, the UK and elsewhere than we would like (see also Burtonwood & Bruce, 1999). They may also be right when they say that teachers who are from minority groups will be more likely to demon-strate multicultural sensitivity in the classroom. But it is important to point out that minority-group members who become teachers may, by that fact alone, be atypical of the group. Relatedly, the process of teacher training may tend to accelerate their middle-class socialization. (From a rather more polemical perspective, Grinberg and Saavedra [2000: 436] note that once Latinos and other minority-group members 'enter the system, internal processes of colonization take over'.) It is by no means clear, then, that increasing the number of teachers from particular sociocultural groups will lead to a commensurate increase in multi-cultural sensitivities in the classroom. And there is one fact here that never seems to be mentioned at all. When Quiocho, Rios and many other like-minded scholars call for educators and institutions to encourage more minority-group students to take up the profession of teaching, they may be encouraging a sort of self-imposed restriction that does not apply to 'mainstream' individuals. Over the years, I have had a number of Canadian native students in my university seminars, many of whom told me that they intended to become teachers. As I came to know them a little better, it was apparent that – as the (educated) minority within a socioeconomically depressed minority – they felt a duty to 'give back' to their community. Such altruistic motives are, of course, highly commend-able, but I came to realize that at least some of my students were charting their career course out of a sense of obligation, rather than on the basis of personal preference. And it struck me that this was, in some sense, yet another burden that they carried, yet another limitation that their white counterparts rarely had to consider at all.

This Book

This book is an attempt to bring under one roof some important matters – largely linguistic but also, inevitably, sociocultural – that, I believe, should have greater exposure. It is not any sort of handbook or 'how-to' manual. It does not outline specific activities or curriculum adaptations, and its coverage is not restricted to what might be seen as immediately relevant in the classroom. It deals, rather, with background information that could reasonably inform pedagogical activities and research. In short, this book does not tell teachers what to do in class, but it may provide some useful underpinnings. As implied above, good contextualization is central to the enhancement of cultural and linguistic sensitivities, but there is also a case to be made for some linguistic and sociolinguistic basics, as noted by Brumfit (2001). Some of these obviously relate to 'foreign' languages, and some to nonstandard dialects. And, as Ferguson (2006: 174) reminds us, there is a third category. In a world in which English is becoming more and more globalized, but where its apparently permanent incursions are spawning sturdy local 'Englishes', teachers' awareness of these could 'replace absolutist conceptions of what is proper and correct in language with greater flexibility and principled pragmatism regarding norms and models'. The teacher who has some awareness along these lines will surely have a better understanding of language varieties that, although they may exist as nonstandard in American or British classrooms, increasingly represent Englishes that are locally or regionally standard at their points of origin.

Andersson and Trudgill (1990: 179) make the point, too: 'teachers who are prepared to take an open-minded, unprejudiced attitude towards the varieties of language spoken by their pupils will be the ones who also succeed best in fostering and developing children's linguistic interests and abilities'. We could expand this, in fact, and say that such teachers are likely to succeed best in developing *all* of their pupils' potentials. But the observation also prompts us, of course, to consider how best we might facilitate the development of open-mindedness among teachers (and others). It is obvious that the most important factor here involves the presentation of the most up-to-date evidence bearing upon linguistic and cultural issues. This is the motivation for all the works cited in this chapter, as well as Andersson and Trudgill's discussion of 'bad' language, and Bauer and Trudgill's (1998) debunking of a score of language 'myths'. It is also the motivation behind many other works, most of them more focused; for some recent examples, see Beykont (2002), Pearce (2005) and Gaine (2005).

Information should be presented as a matter of course to teachers. Although it may have positively influenced subsequent programs of teacher education, I don't think that the judgment in the famous Ann Arbor Black English trial (see below) that *required* teachers to take courses in sociolinguistics (see Labov, 1982; Lanehart, 1998) was necessarily the best precedent for future procedure. Rather, I believe that careful and regular attention to basic language matters is the soil in which teacher sensitivities are most likely to grow and thrive. Of course, I also hope that the information here may be of some use across a range of specializations. Reagan (2006) has recently noted that educating language teachers has been made more difficult by the 'balkanization' of sub-fields, and his point is very well taken and in tune with my purposes here: there are 'artificial boundaries' that unnecessarily restrict the effective transmission of information that ought to be part and parcel of the training of *all* teachers. In a similar vein, I should say that my central focus here is not on specific matters – of linguistic and dialectal detail, say, or of teaching methods or the technicalities of bilingualism and bilingual education – for which many excellent treatises already exist. Rather, the emphasis here is upon the ramifications of social, political and linguistic interaction among ethnocultural groups, particularly between majorities and minorities, between the powerful and the powerless, between privilege and poverty.

This book should be of use and interest to students and researchers, as well as to teachers and educators. To that end, I have written it (I hope) in a direct and jargon-free manner, while also providing a great many references for those interested in further and more specialized enquiry. I have also taken particular care to re-present here some earlier research, studies that have either been rather neglected, or still have something to tell us, or both. It is clear, for instance, that the discourse-analysis emphasis that has taken over from more empirical investigations in several language areas often has less to say than (for example) some of the 'classic' work in language attitudes and stereotypes: less, at least, in terms of practical and generalizable information of immediate interest to teachers and others. I am heartened to find that the careful study of language beliefs and attitudes – improved, of course, from the studies of 30 years ago, often incorporating insights common to discourse analysis – has not quite capitulated. Collections by Milroy and Preston (1999), Kristiansen *et al.* (2005) and Garrett *et al.* (2003) are examples here. The first is noteworthy in its attempt, in five papers dealing with attitudes and stereotypes, to merge linguistic and psychological insights. The second is quite broad in scope, with reports from Britain, the United States and the Nordic countries. The third focuses on Wales, but its opening chapters deal with language attitudes in a general way; it is interesting to see just how many of the references cited there, are of the 1970s vintage (see below). Ladegaard's continuing series of studies in Denmark (Ladegaard, 1998a, 1998b, 1998c, 2000; see also Ladegaard & Sachdev, 2006) is also important.

Similarly, the new or renewed emphasis upon 'folk linguistics' and 'perceptual dialectology', which often represents a desire to get to grips with more fully fleshed language attitudes, is a vital modern sub-discipline; see the overviews provided by Preston (1999) and Long and Preston (2002). Finally here, I note that Rampton's (2006) ethnographic treatment of classroom discourse acknowledges that, while the attitudinal atmosphere at school with respect to the tolerance and treatment of dialect variation is not the same as it was in the 1960s and 1970s, perceptions of social class, its linguistic reflections and the attendant psychological stresses remain important. Writing of two pupils, Rampton notes that

> both Hanif and Ninnette had fairly clear images of the kinds of disadvantaged lives they wanted to avoid... working-class pupils might not be quite as fragile as sociolinguistics has sometimes implied, but everyday experience and a huge non-linguistic literature on class provides [sic] ample reason for taking class-related insecurities very seriously. (Rampton, 2006: 320)

Sensitive attention to the details of discourse and conversation can of course reveal many things of interest. Studies of gender differences in the classroom are a good case in point here, one in which a close analysis of verbal exchanges can be of the greatest value: variations in the question-and-answer patterns of girls and boys, for instance, or of differential attention provided by teachers (see Carr & Pauwels, 2006; Julé, 1984; Sommers, 2000). But even its most fervent advocates admit that, in many cases, discourse studies do *not* reveal much that is new (Stubbs, 1984) and the level of detail in which they often revel is unlikely to lead to ameliorative action. This is an important matter, important enough to justify fuller attention in the next chapter.

The broader message, to this point, is that I have tried to assemble here a useful and comprehensive combination of older work (some of it dating to the 1960s and 1970s: a time when, for instance, a great deal of attention was being given to describing and categorizing dialect variation) and the most recent insights. Apart from the continuing relevance of some earlier discussions, it is also the case that the problems arising from language diversity in the classroom have remained remarkably, if very regrettably, similar to what they were when those discussions were first published. This, of course, is the reason for the continued attention that this book represents. I focus most basically here upon 'macro'-level work, in the belief that a broad-brush knowledge has more chance of applicability than fine-grained analysis. What is more likely to be of service and usefulness: a 20-page analysis of 15-minute samples of the speech patterns of four Bangladeshi schoolchildren in Bradford, or an overview of the general nature of Bengali-English language contact and interference? And, to repeat, I am more interested here in sociolinguistics, or the sociology/social psychology of language than (with one or two exceptions) with linguistics itself. This is because the vast majority of issues that affect speakers of 'foreign' languages or of nonstandard dialects of indigenous varieties are psychosocial in nature: they have to do with perceptions and prejudice, with stereotypes and assumptions, with power and subordination.

Nonstandard-dialect and foreign-language speakers comprise the two main constituencies with which this book deals. There are relationships between them, of course, and these have allowed me some economy of description. An understanding, for example, of the social perceptions attaching to nonstandard English dialects of low social status will be found applicable to those associated with foreign languages, particularly those mother tongues of minority groups whose socioeconomic clout does not match that of the mainstream.

Some might initially imagine that speakers of foreign languages – more than those whose maternal varieties are nonstandard dialects – have quite specifically linguistic problems when they find themselves in classrooms where their language is not used. It is, of course, true that there are ways to improve or lessen the effectiveness of second-language learning, ways that will involve matters linguistic. But consider the social context in which such speakers must engage in that learning, consider their own attitudes and motivations, consider the sociopolitical questions that swirl around the provision (or not) of some sort of extra help for them at school. Should they be left entirely to their own devices? Should the school, on the other hand, make some adaptations for them? Should formal programs of bilingual education be put in place: if so, what sort? These are all matters that range far beyond linguistic beginnings. Ultimately, they have to do with people's sense of who they are and who they want to be, with the defence of some existing 'mainstream' or a willingness to see it evolve in the face of changing demographic circumstance, with tolerance and prejudice – in a word, with matters of individual and group *identity*.

Educational and social disadvantage underpinned by (among other things) inaccurate linguistic opinion and prejudice remains a great problem. Popular speech and language attitudes continue to hold certain dialects and accents as better or worse than others. There is no real difficulty, of course, in the possession of personal preferences, in the fact that I think Italian to be the most beautiful and mellifluous of languages, whereas you find the greatest music and poetry in Scottish Gaelic. But there are dangers when we imagine that we are arguing about substantive linguistic issues, about the inherent properties of one variety or another, or – worse still – about the cognitive attributes thought to accompany certain language forms. In all these ways, the so-called 'deficit' theory of nonstandard dialects and, indeed, of certain foreign languages continues to hold wide sway. The man or woman on the Clapham omnibus or the Bondi tram may not be able to articulate this theory, may indeed be quite unaware that they *have* a theory, but it is the easiest thing in the world to demonstrate the theory's influence: just ask people about 'correct' and 'incorrect' language (see Lippi-Green, 1997; Trudgill, 1975).

To conclude and to reiterate: my hope is that, while this book is clearly not a 'how-to' manual in any direct sense, it will prove a comprehensive guide to important language issues for students, teachers and research-ers. There are some parts of some discussions that are more tightly presented than others, of course – but none, I believe, is beyond the grasp of any intelligent reader. The audience will no doubt be largely an anglophone one, and it is certainly true that I draw most of the information here from literature in English. However, since the funda-mental issues of concern extend well beyond the anglophone world, the treatment has – *mutatis mutandis*, as they say – a broader scope.

Among the large number of references to other work that I make in this book, some may at first glance seem outdated. This is not so, however: the earlier publications I cite have been carefully chosen for their enduring value and salience. One of my chief contentions here is that the essential issues in the area remain much as they were when these seminal pieces of research first appeared. I have, of course, supplemen-ted them freely with more up-to-date work, but only when these later undertakings have in fact added substantially to what has already appeared. (Or, of course, when discussing matters that are, themselves, more recent: Ebonics, for example.) A more subtle point in all of this is my concern for historical and contextual embedding, a concern amplified upon reading some of the new research, where many old wheels are painfully reinvented and where, relatedly, little if any attention is given to important predecessors.

I should also point out here that, with the overall aim of providing a general guide, I have largely refrained from giving my own opinions. Since (I hope) most of the sections in most of the chapters achieve a certain degree of roundedness, I have not thought it necessary to make formal concluding observations at this level. I do, however, provide an initial chapter overview (in the next section), as well as a brief concluding statement (in Chapter 14) in which I draw together some of the main themes. It is here, perhaps, that my own assessments are given in clearest form. One final word here: it is natural in a book of this sort to emphasize negative or, at least, problematic areas and topics, to attempt to highlight issues of continuing concern, to point to matters that stand in need of attention. This posture suggests a scholarly detachment (I hope, again) rather than any personal sense of hand-wringing. In fact, there have been many interesting and favorable alterations in attitudes and practices relating to languages at school. But one does not intend a book like this to be an encomium, and my task here does not include the dispensing of laurel branches.

Chapter overview

In Chapter 2, I provide a critical survey of discourse analysis. I acknowledge that small-scale enquiries can illuminate broader matters and (at the beginning of Chapter 6) I also mention the implicit association between most of the contemporary work in the area and the 'difference' position on language; to their credit, discourse analysts of most stripes are highly sensitive to cultural and class variations, and most unlikely to cast matters in any better-or-worse perspective. Nonetheless, my general contention is that the micro-level perspective associated with discourse analysis is not of the greatest or the most immediate value for our purposes here. Further, I argue that discourse analysis and its various offspring have become very inward-looking, increasingly tricked out in noisome jargon and much given to the highly specialized theorizing and debate that one associates with weak disciplinary areas. There is promise here, but at the moment the area is essentially an incestuous preserve of little applied value.

Having begun with some necessary brush-clearing, in the next three chapters I turn to the topic of disadvantage. In the first of these, I suggest that 'disadvantage' is an accurate and useful term, provided that it is used properly as a reflection of group difference that is, itself, a product of social discontinuity and comparison. The knowledge, attitudes and inclinations that arise in one setting, and that may represent reasonable adaptations to it, may prove inappropriate in another setting – inappropriate and distinctly disadvantageous. Given the nature of stratified societies, it is obvious that poverty and social disadvantage often go hand in hand, but they are not synonymous. In terms of success in the wider society, for example, it is clear that there are many 'good' homes in the inner city, and many 'poor' ones in the more affluent suburbs. Still, variations in family 'culture' are likely to produce more difficulties for working-class and minority-group children at school than for their middle-class counterparts; and these may sometimes be seen as the 'third variable' that links poverty with social disadvantage.

I argue very strongly (in Chapter 4) that it is incorrect to see social and educational disadvantage as having a genetic underpinning. Over the long historical haul, this has been the most popular view, but it is wrong: it is shot through with prejudice and inaccurate knowledge of the causes and ramifications of class and cultural variations. Nonetheless, precisely because the genetic 'case' has been such a longstanding one and, indeed, such a continuingly attractive explanation for group disadvantage, I provide some detail about its more unpleasant consequences. Theories of mental and physical disability, of eugenic intervention and of immigration control have all sprung from assumptions of genetically 'fixed' inheritance. I also point out, in this chapter, how the genetic conceptions of the 19th and 20th centuries were essential foundation stones for the emerging disciplines of psychology and sociology, and for the testing ethos that is still so much a part of modern education and society. Well, if not nature, then perhaps nurture; if not heredity, then clearly environment. Chapter 5 thus introduces environmental factors as the other logically possible source of disadvantage. There have been two broad stances here: on the one hand, 'deficit' theorists argued that certain social contexts produced real and longstanding deficiencies. 'Cultural deprivation' was a phrase often used in the literature, even though a moment's thought reveals that it must imply that a group is being perceived as deprived of *another* group's culture; after all, it hardly makes sense to describe a community as being deprived of itself. The implication, in fact, was that poor and lower-class sociocultural settings were deficient precisely because they did not exhibit middle-class values and practices. Social difference was translated, in other words, into social deficit. In most writing in this vein, the deficit here was seen to be virtually as deep-seated as if it were genetic in origin.

The other environmental stance accepts the existence of important class and cultural differences, but it refuses to see them as deficits. Rather, it attempts to understand how environmental variations produce attitudinal and behavioral ones, and resists the temptation to make moral judgments from middle-class perspectives. I suggest that this environmental 'difference' position is the only logically tenable one, although the force of social pressure and prejudice that can turn difference into deficiency is admittedly very powerful. If potent 'mainstream' sentiments hold that class and cultural differences are actual defects, then academic conceptions of right and wrong may seem rather insignificant. Perception is everything, after all. But perception can be based upon misinformation – or worse – and so my argument here is that we should make the different-but-not-deficient argument wherever and whenever possible. Social prejudice may be inevitable in stratified societies, but it is not monolithic.

In Chapter 6, I turn to language matters, where the general deficit-difference debate has been played out in more specific terms. Indeed, the historically prejudicial perceptions that saw class and cultural variations as based upon real genetic or environmental deficits also saw language and dialect variations in the same way. I attempt to show how the work of the late Basil Bernstein – whether the 'real' Bernstein or Bernstein misinterpreted – unfortunately provided a contemporary reinforcement of these inaccurate perceptions. Working-class language 'codes' were seen to exemplify linguistic deficiency or deprivation, and their speakers to possess a repertoire distinctly inferior to that of their middle-class counterparts. The implications of this theoretical position involve justification for a continued disdain and rejection of dialectal variants, and for compensatory interventions aimed at replacing them with middle-class forms viewed not merely as more socially acceptable but, quite simply, intrinsically better.

I naturally spend some time in this chapter demonstrating that conceptions of linguistic deprivation and deficit are profoundly misguided. They ignore the fact, for instance, that no human grouping has ever been found with a language inadequate for its own social purposes. But we can easily see, again, that an acceptance of this point of view hardly rules out judgments of disadvantage when members of a particular community move beyond their own borders: the language that serves them perfectly well may not best equip them in altered circumstances. For this reason, it is entirely possible to wholeheartedly reject 'deficit' perspectives while simultaneously endorsing programs of language-repertoire expansion. These need not imply for a moment any intrinsic defect in the maternal variety; they simply acknowledge that different settings may call for different responses. No one will accuse a francophone executive of having an inherently flawed mother tongue just because she learns English when posted to Detroit. No one *should* consider American Black English as a flawed dialect just because it is not the sort of English that she will acquire when she gets there.

Old ideas die hard, and old prejudices are hard to dislodge, particularly when they continue to underpin quick and easy alternatives to real, disinterested or, indeed, compassionate understanding. So, while the preceding chapters led up to, and illustrated, the two central points of the argument – social disadvantage is a product of cultural *difference*, only exists where comparisons are drawn, and is not simply a synonym for deficiency; and there are no inherently deficient or substandard languages or dialects – Chapter 7 documents the persistence of deficit ideologies. Not only do these remain, at some implicit level, outside the academic cloisters, they also have a continuing existence within them. I dedicate some considerable space here to the formulations of John Honey. His writings, like the earlier ones of Bernstein, have unfortunately reinforced popular views and prejudices by seemingly providing a scholarly scaffolding for them. The sociological and linguistic debate occasioned by Honey's work serves to illustrate, once again, the pivotal features of the topic. In that sense, I suppose we might appreciate Honey's intervention, although, in a much larger sense, it is unfortunate that so much time and energy has had to be invested – again – in a fight against specters that many had hoped were rapidly fading. The chapter concludes with some examples of the persistent 'applied' influence of deficit theorizing.

In Chapter 8, I show that all languages and dialects – even those 'disadvantaged' ones that evoke negative attitudes – represent important aspects of group identity. All languages and dialects act as markers of solidarity and belonging and, as such, anchor group members in the collective. This being so, it is not difficult to understand that the attachment and affection felt for particular varieties may in fact be greater when those varieties, and their speakers, are socially stigmatized. After all, a sense of – and a desire for – the security that group membership affords is normally heightened in circumstances of external threat or discomfort. It is also the case that attempts to abandon a socially non-prestigious dialect are fraught with danger; consequently, even those who aspire to upward mobility, and who imagine that altering their language will contribute to this, run the risk of falling between stools. In this chapter, I also discuss the phenomenon of 'covert prestige', whereby working-class or 'disadvantaged' speech styles exhibit an attractiveness based upon their perceived qualities of toughness and directness. This sort of prestige obviously adds to the disinclination to shift dialects, but one of its more interesting features is its appeal to middle-class speakers as well.

Of course, covert prestige is largely a male phenomenon: where middle-class men have been found to adopt (and over-report their use of) working-class speech patterns, middle-class women tend to claim more standard-dialect usage. Indeed, some nonstandard-dialect speakers show evidence of 'hypercorrection', essentially an over-emphasis upon standard forms.

I also return briefly, in Chapter 8, to the important matter of teachers' attitudes, presenting the results of a number of studies investigating the various dimensions along which these attitudes are displayed. It is clear that speakers of low-status forms receive unfavorable assessments on many attitudinal dimensions, some of which probe far beyond the borders of the speech samples that are typically used to evoke judges' ratings. It is sobering to realize that teachers and others may draw very extensive conclusions from brief exposure to children's language – serious judgments (as I say in the chapter) based upon information that may be irrelevant to any accurate consideration of abilities and scholastic potentials. I conclude by noting the important difference between *attitude* and *belief*, and by suggesting that we need fuller and more detailed information about what lies behind the judgments and assessments made of speech and language varieties.

I devote Chapter 9 to Black English Vernacular (BEV). This continues the brief treatment of that dialect in Chapter 6 – where it served as an excellent counter to misguided notions of language deficit – but expands it considerably in the light of some important contemporary developments. The controversy swirling around 'Ebonics' highlights many important features of the sociology of language: pedagogical questions are revisited here of course, but so too are larger matters of the linkage between language and identity. Quite apart from the interesting debate about the essential nature of BEV – could the divergence of Ebonics from other forms of English be sufficient to warrant the label of a separate language? – the emotionally charged rhetoric here illustrates how a 'disadvantaged' variety of low prestige can be rejected by some of its own speakers. At the same time as scholars were trying to bring linguistic evidence to bear upon the discussions about Ebonics in school districts in Michigan, California and elsewhere, prominent figures within the black community were decrying what they saw as deficient and inappropriate language. This is perhaps a demonstration of that 'minority-group reaction' mentioned at the beginning of Chapter 8; in any event, it represented an unfortunate sort of solidarity between popular and ill-informed views of Black English in mainstream America, and those held by some black speakers themselves.

In the next chapter, I consider the ways in which schools have traditionally reacted to the presence of foreign languages in their classrooms. Just as it has often been thought right to work to eradicate 'incorrect' dialects and replace them with 'proper' standard ones, so schools have often considered – implicitly or directly – that the sooner foreign-language-speaking pupils engage with language shift, the better. At the same time, however, schools have always understood that the expansion of linguistic repertoires is an important facet of the educational process. Many obvious tensions arise here. For example, the same school that values and teaches French or Spanish may do little or nothing to recognize, adapt to, or build upon the Hausa, Turkish and Arabic that come in the door with new immigrant pupils. In the eyes of the linguist, all languages may be equal but, socially speaking, some are more equal than others. Schools are, as well, products and reflections of the larger society that surrounds them: one implication is that it will be easier to teach German in Nijmegen than in Nebraska – easier, and more immediately recognized as a useful and rational thing to do. Such matters return us to questions of social realities and attitudes. It is these, after all, and not any inherent linguistic features, that dictate the teaching of French and the ignoring of Bulgarian. And it is the interaction of attitudes with motivations that can make classroom language-learning contexts very different from those that obtain beyond the school gates. I attempt to describe the dynamics of these different settings because – among many other things – they illuminate the role of different *types* of attitudes and motivations.

I also discuss, in Chapter 10, something of the interesting relationship between language and power. It is perfectly obvious that those who have power can impose their language upon others, either directly or, more frequently, through the unofficial pressures associated with the attractions of the socially dominant. But, is it equally the case that improved recognition of hitherto unregarded minority languages actually 'empowers' their speakers? Will making room in the classroom for Hausa or Bulgarian materially affect immigrant children from west Africa and eastern Europe? I suggest here that, contrary to the popular equation, language is *not* power – not inevitably, at any rate – and that exercises in linguistic 'empowerment' are essentially compensatory in nature. This is not to deny that there may be positive benefits (in terms of children's 'self-esteem', perhaps) of attending more closely to maternal varieties, but it is generally a mistake – and sometimes an unrealistic elevation of expectations – to think of schools as empowering agents. None of this means, of course, that the teaching of foreign languages – particularly of the 'heritage' or 'allophone' variety – is either exceptional or inappropriate. I conclude the chapter, however, by reiterating that classroom practice and experience here can best be understood by reference to broader and more powerful social currents.

Such considerations lead naturally to discussions of multicultural and bilingual education practices. In Chapter 11, I begin by examining the nature of multiculturalism per se and, once again, I stress the importance of social perceptions. Multiculturalism as a social fact is not, of course, the issue: virtually all societies are internally diverse to some degree, which means that virtually all must come to grips on a *de facto* basis with different language and cultural groups in their midst. But multiculturalism as formal policy is another thing altogether, and it represents an important contemporary manifestation of very longstanding social issues of pluralism, assimilation, integration, accommodation, conformity – and many other reflections of the tensions that can exist between social coherence and unity, on the one hand, and heterogeneity and diversity, on the other. Advocates of officially sponsored multiculturalism argue that it is the only fair and just way for liberal democracies to recognize and react to cultural diversity. Opponents claim that it means a dilution of a necessary and highly desirable civic commonality. Any comprehensive coverage of these matters is obviously far beyond my scope here, but I do attempt to show some of the important bones of the arguments, as well as to comment upon historical tendencies and present-day trends. The discussion that follows – of multicultural adaptations at school – simply puts some specifically educational flesh on these bones. Again, much hinges here upon assessments of the school's potential as an agent for social change. I do suggest, however, that at the most general level, all good education has been, is now, and must be multicultural in nature: it would be a strange and, indeed, inconceivable educational policy that reflected only its immediate society.

Wishing to argue for some sort of multicultural 'middle ground', I end Chapter 11 by noting a distinction between weaker and stronger forms of multiculturalism. I draw no particular conclusions here, but I do point out that a recognition of the distinction is useful in itself, and may suggest further explorations.

The last two thematic chapters deal with bilingualism and bilingual education. In Chapter 12, I provide a very brief introduction to bilingualism. I am chiefly concerned here to give the reader some sense of the rather complicated nature of the phenomenon while, at the same time, trying to point out that actually *becoming* bilingual is an unremarkable and extremely common process. The fact that so many 'ordinary' people, in so many different social settings, are bilingual (or better) is an obvious testament to this. Difficulties in achieving some competence in another language are typically related to social circumstances – it is not lack of intelligence or aptitude that separates learners of French in Kansas from those in Quebec. Unsurprisingly, in this chapter, I also spend some time discussing the relationship between bilingualism and identity. Beyond the instrumental capacities of bilinguals whose limited repertoire extends only as far as social needs dictate, there are linguistic abilities that go much deeper. I suggest two broad possibilities here: those individuals who, from an early age, have a kinship attachment to more than one language community; and those who acquire another linguistic persona later on. Each circumstance can produce powerful and long-lasting effects upon identities.

Chapter 13 considers bilingual education. There are many varieties, and I draw extensively upon Colin Baker's typology here: he provides details along a spectrum ranging from no bilingual accommodation at all (the 'sink-or-swim' scenario that has affected so many immigrants in so many countries), to transitional programs that aim to move children into 'mainstream' classrooms as soon as linguistically possible, to several approaches that emphasize the retention and development of both languages. The 'strongest' forms of bilingual education are, in fact, *monolingual* immersion programs; for example, anglophone children learning in and through French. How is this different from a monolingual sink-or-swim approach in which (say) Spanish speakers find themselves in English-only classrooms? Why do we call the latter 'submersion' and not 'immersion'? While immersion programs operate in settings in which the children's maternal variety is dominant and therefore not at risk – and where their new language will thus become an addition to their repertoire – submersion occurs when the maternal variety is *not* that of the mainstream society, when it *is* at risk and when, therefore, there is the distinct possibility that the new language will eventually displace the original one altogether.

There is a large literature documenting (and debating) the educational outcomes associated with different bilingual-education scenarios, but some of the most important aspects of the topic are, again, those whose source is outside the classroom. That is why I conclude the chapter with a discussion of the politics of bilingual education. There are strong analogies here with the controversies surrounding multiculturalism and multicultural education; indeed, it is possible to see discussion of bilingual education as one sub-set of these. Should a liberal-democratic recognition of cultural diversity include – *actively* include – a specific language component? Or can worries about social cohesion and balkanization be legitimately extended to language matters? Surveys of public opinion in many countries have shown how confused attitudes can be. Many people in Australia, Canada, the United States and western Europe apparently believe in a sort of official tolerance of minority-group values and languages, and some wish to see tolerance replaced by more active and more positive legislated intervention. Others, however, are clearly worried by alterations to the social status quo, and these worries can range all the way from a more or less benign regret at change, to out-and-out racism. But the most interesting attitudes of all are those in which several strands of opinion seem intertwined, or in which a grudging acceptance of other languages and other cultures is accompanied by a desire for eventual assimilation and social 'unity'. All points of view here will naturally encompass educational facets, even in those settings in which groups arrange and underwrite language classes outside the publicly funded arena.

In Chapter 14, I provide a very brief summary statement. In fact, since I have given rather strong hints in the preceding section of this chapter, the closing chapter can be even briefer and more general than it would otherwise have had to be.

A Final Introductory Note

It is both a duty and a pleasure to acknowledge the help of a number of people: Brenda Berger, Susan Cameron, Angela Hagar, Rod Landry, Gerard MacDonald and Brenda McKenna, all members of the Angus MacDonald Library staff; Susan Hunston and Sarah Lawson, for assistance with the provision of material from the British Association of Applied Linguistics; Nik Coupland, Peter Garrett and Adam Jaworski, colleagues in Cardiff who helped with some detective work; John White, for information about Galton and religion; Peter Archer, for bringing me up to date on Irish advances in the study of linguistic and social disadvantage; Christopher Byrne, for some help with *tertium comparationis* and other classical matters; Édouard Langille, for one or two grammatical niceties; Gary Brooks, for the provision of a complete run of the *Journal of the History of the Behavioral Sciences*; and the particularly diligent publisher's reader, whose many careful comments led to a much improved manuscript.

Chapter 2

Discourse Analysis and its Discontents

Introduction

Midway through the last chapter, I noted that the current state of discourse analysis and its related sub-fields leaves something to be desired. Their rather rarefied undertakings – however engrossing they may be for the direct participants – are worrisome on at least two counts. First, their intrinsic assumptions and qualities are often dubious. Second, their increasing presence in several areas of language study – fortified, no doubt, by that perennial academic prejudice for the abstract over the applied – dilutes attentions and energies that would be better directed elsewhere. It is these concerns that fuel the brief treatment found in this chapter. It may not initially appear to be of a piece with other parts of the discussion, but a cautionary note or two about an approach that has steadily gained ground in recent years may perhaps be useful as a general underpinning for what follows.

Stubbs (1984) provided an early discussion of the applicability of discourse analysis to studies of language in education. Writing at a time when such analysis was a 'recent and open-ended field' (Stubbs, 1984: 204) – it is no longer so recent, of course, but it is probably even *more* open-ended – he notes that contemporary linguistics has neglected language use in specific areas (e.g. education, medicine, law and religion). It is not that these areas have been entirely neglected, but rather that linguistics has left them to other disciplines (notably sociology). Citing Milroy (1984), who refers specifically to forensic matters, Stubbs (1984: 236) claims that 'if socially responsible linguists do not do such analyses, then they will be done, but less well, by others'. I think it is entirely reasonable to argue that linguistic insights can complement those from other vantage points, but 'less well' is too dismissive of those others (see Edwards, 2003a, on the dangers of disciplinary tunnel vision).

Stubbs frames his argument as follows: 'What kind of understanding of language is relevant in teaching the mother tongue or foreign languages, or in teaching in general?' (Stubbs, 1984: 206). Teachers certainly need to understand language: it is a truism that underpins all educational effort. But how much, of what kind and under which auspices? More pointedly, how germane is the discipline of linguistics in these regards? A traditional point of rejection, based upon the perception (all too frequently accurate), is that linguistics per se is bound up with theoretical models, tricked out in specialist jargons and too uninterested in 'real language behavior' to be very relevant to the more immediate concerns of teachers. As Stubbs (p. 207) notes, many teachers 'have an image of themselves as practical and down-to-earth folks... taking a sensible standing [sic] against the impractical theorising of linguists, sociologists and psychologists of education, and all the rest'.[1] These outside intellectuals can thus be seen as rather 'sinister figures in the wings, faintly contemptuous, armed with the paraphernalia of expertise and tapping ominously their research findings' (here, Stubbs is quoting the words of Harold Rosen [1978], in the pages of the now-defunct *New Review*).

Teachers are surely right to have misgivings here. Indeed, beyond the points already noted, there is a further, most salient one that reflects a charge often (and often fairly) levelled against the social sciences: they do not provide practitioners with new insights so much as with old information, noxiously presented in pretentious bafflegab. Relatedly, although turning 'unconscious' knowledge into more explicit and articulated principle can be useful, 'good teachers may justifiably feel that it [discourse analysis] provides only a different slant on what they already do' (Stubbs, 1984: 238). From the other side, as it were, some linguists have denied that their discipline has anything substantial to offer to language teachers, anyway (Sampson, 1980). But both Stubbs and Sampson seem to be discussing an awareness and sensitivity that linguistics might (or might not) be able to enhance for teachers *of* language. Thus, Stubbs observes that discourse analysis could assist in the structuring of dialogues used in language-teaching material, going on to cite other possible applications, including heightening awareness of cross-cultural differences in discursive norms.

This is not quite the emphasis here, where we are more directly concerned with an expanded sensitivity *towards* language by teachers and others, and with the contributions that various disciplines might make towards (for example) eradicating inaccurate information about nonstandard dialects. Stubbs points to the analysis of teacher-pupil interactions in the classroom as another possible application of discourse-analytic study, cites several studies focusing upon miscommunication and misunderstanding, and comes closest to the present emphasis with a brief mention of work on aboriginal nonstandard English in Australia. On this matter, Chomsky (1977: 55–56) – quite dismissive of a sociolinguistics that he finds theoretically 'evident and banal', an undertaking with 'theoretical pretensions' but one whose very existence as a discipline is dubious – rather grudgingly concedes that work of this sort might be useful for combating educational misinformation and prejudice (see also Edwards, 1994a). So, there are possible openings here.

Discourse analysis, for instance, could conceivably be a diagnostic tool in highlighting cross-cultural or cross-subcultural differences; once made salient, these might suggest alterations in expectations, teaching methods and so on. Of course, surface variety is less important here than the social underpinnings that give rise to it. As Corson (2001) observes, variations in discourse 'norms' imply variations in cultural values. Two of the early and important ethnographic/discourse studies in this connection were those of Basso (1970) and Philips (1970, 1983). Both authors showed that the cultural norms of American Indians (the Apache of Arizona and the Sahaptin of Oregon, respectively) were sufficiently different from those of their white neighbors that reservation children often fell foul of their teachers. The most salient difficulty was a reluctance to speak in class. Traditionally, teachers were likely to categorize their Indian pupils as cold and unresponsive, sullen or shy; such classroom perceptions reflect and reinforce longheld stereotypes about Indian taciturnity. These generalizations are not all negative: after all, silence can be golden, and there is the myth of the 'noble savage', reserved and dignified, a model of *gravitas.* But in contemporary settings of cultures-in-contact, they can also lead to assessments of linguistic and cognitive deficiency.

There are at least three unfavorable consequences of teachers' perceptions of children's silence. First, since they will not have the type of feedback with which they are familiar, teachers may have only a partial or inaccurate sense of their pupils' abilities and academic shortcomings. Second, teachers may gradually adapt their classroom procedures so as to reduce unpleasant or uncomfortable situations; in so doing, however, they may lessen their role as a model of 'standard' norms and practice, a model by which nonstandard speakers typically develop useful 'bidialectal' skills. Third, teachers may draw very inaccurate conclusions about the cultures from which their pupils come (see also the observations of Wax & Wax, 1971).[2]

When touching upon conversational analysis in the classroom in the last chapter, I mentioned the recent work of Julé (2004). Her work with girls is particularly timely, given recent tendencies to swing the educational focus from girls to boys. For quite a long time, the literature was full of studies describing ways in which the presence of boys in the classroom was a hindrance to girls' education; much of it demonstrated, unsurprisingly, that patterns of male-female interaction outside the school gates were replicated within them. Now, however, interest in the education of boys seems to be growing: a recent popular treatment was titled *The War Against Boys* (Sommers, 2000). Some have argued that boys do not do well in a 'feminine' school environment, others feel that a more complicated male 'disengagement' with education is at work, while still others think that it is all something of a non-issue. There remains, however, considerable agreement that, whatever else may be the case, boys still tend to dominate in verbal interaction. Julé builds upon previous research, noting that male dominance is something with which teachers' behavior correlates, even though they may feel that they 'treat them all the same' (Corson, 1993: 144). Generally speaking, boys continue to 'receive a disproportionate share of teachers' time and attention' (Stanworth, 1981: 18), and girls may find themselves in a double bind. Spender (1980), for instance, has noted that the approval of girls' behavior by teachers (and others, of course) may depend precisely upon the very verbal restraint that allows the more forceful boys to maintain their dominant position. These sorts of gender-variant findings are quite general, cutting across class and ethnic lines.[3]

Julé's work illustrates these matters. Her analyses reveal that teachers typically dominate the 'linguistic space' in the classroom to an over-whelming degree and, of the small portion available to the pupils, the ratio of girls' to boys' verbal contributions is on the order of 1:10. There are, of course, limitations in any investigation, but Julé's findings with young Punjabi Sikh children in Canada mirror a great many others; hers, indeed, have a particular interest because they involve the joint influence of gender and ethnicity (a combination of influences that Corson [2001] explicitly points to as relatively neglected in the literature). While it is true that Punjabi Sikh culture is more open to gender equality than are some neighboring societies, the author notes that 'equity is not necessarily the lived experience' (p. 69). The results of Julé's small-scale study may thus highlight more clearly the silencing of girls at school, with implications for other cultural variants (or heterogeneities) in the classroom, or, indeed with *sub*cultural variants, as, for instance, with populations whose maternal dialects are nonstandard.

Discourse Difficulties

Language and ethnography

A couple of years ago, I was asked to act as a discussant on an academic panel convened in honor of Robert Kaplan, one of the leading lights in applied linguistics. As a friend and colleague, I was more than happy to do so, but I was ill-prepared for the flood of ill-advised psycholinguistico-educational verbiage. There is a field, for instance, called 'English for Academic Purposes' (EAP), which obviously cannot be any sort of independent enquiry; recent pieces by Ferris (2005) and Johns (2005) amply demonstrate that, when it is not restating the obvious, EAP exudes a pseudo-intellectualism that is likely to appeal only to those interested in 'critical pedagogy', or 'critical linguistics' or 'critical framing'. One can also indulge in 'contrastive rhetoric' or 'contrastive discourse analysis' (see below), two of whose proponents (Connor & Moreno, 2005) employ the Latin phrase *tertium comparationis* in their title and their text. Now, I have no Orwellian aversion to using the occasional *bon mot* or Latin tag, but putting such a generally unfamiliar phrase on the masthead is surely a rather transparent effort at impression-formation (as the social psychologists would say).[4]

Discourse analysis and the many 'critical' sub-areas with which it is often associated have become increasingly inward-looking. An excessive love of micro-theory has resulted in the sort of technical sub-specializations noted above (see also Wodak, 2006). The general area has also become a volatile one with much internal wrangling – an instance, perhaps, of the dictum that academic infighting is so vicious because the stakes are so low – and an increasing amount of jargon.

Consider first the ethnographic approach, whose emphasis upon the context within which social interactions occur can – as we have just seen – produce useful cross-cultural insights. It is a qualitative rather than quantitative exercise and often relies upon close and intimate contact for its data. 'Participant observation' in one form or another is the methodology of choice. The work of Dell Hymes (see Gumperz & Hymes, 1964) gave a specific linguistic focus to the enterprise: hence, the 'ethnography of communication'. Opposed to the reductionist and narrowly experimental tendencies in much social-scientific work, a phenomenological approach seemed a welcome and appropriate change. And it is true that there have been, from the beginning, some classic studies (e.g. Cazden, 1988; Heath, 1983). But, also from the beginning, the approach began to produce its own difficulties, particularly in its examination of increasingly narrower slices of reality. Holism, an emphasis upon so-called 'lived experience' (as opposed, one surmises, to some unlived variety), and a concern for procedural breadth and depth have tended to give way to a new reductionism.

Tusting and Maybin (2007: 576) have recently argued for a new term here – 'linguistic ethnography' – as part of an emerging interdisciplinary reconfiguration 'in the contexts of late modernity and globalisation'. The collection to which their paper is an introduction (Rampton *et al.*, 2007) and an earlier piece (Rampton *et al.*, 2004) flesh matters out here; the latter notes that:

> linguistic ethnography generally holds that, to a considerable degree, language and the social world are mutually shaping, and that close analysis of situated language use can provide both fundamental and distinctive insights into the mechanisms and dynamics of social and cultural production in everyday activity. (Rampton *et al.*, 2004: 2)

Rampton (2007: 585) goes on to say that linguistic ethnography is best characterized as a 'site of encounter' where various research perspectives can come together; the assumption is that 'the contexts for communication should be investigated rather than assumed'. These hardly seem original observations. And Wetherell (2007: 668) suggests that the contributions of linguistic ethnography to our understanding of identity would benefit if we dropped the latter term, replacing it with 'personal order':

> Personal order is derived from social order but is not isomorphic with it. A person... is a site, like institutions or social interaction, where flows of meaning-making practices or semiosis... become organised. Over time particular routines, repetitions, procedures and modes of practice build up to form personal style, psycho-biography and life history, and become a guide for how to go on in the present... In the case of personal order, the relevant practices could be described as "psycho-discursive"... those which among the sum of social practices constitute a psychology, formulate a mental life and have consequences for the formation and representation of the person.

I apologize for inflicting so much of this on the reader, but it is important to realize that this sort of wheel-spinning has come to attract more and more adherents. If one looks back over the publications record of those who now seem to specialize in pseudo-insights, one typically finds that they began their careers by writing, in English, about important things, in ways that reasonably intelligent people could understand. It is a great pity that they, and their fields of interest, have been seduced by false prophets.

An enterprise that might reasonably be expected to stress the 'macro' levels of social life (or, at least, to use more 'micro' optics to exemplify or complement wider concerns) has come more and more to devote itself to exceedingly fine-grained matters. Its relevance to larger settings – classrooms, for instance – has dramatically receded. This methodological narrowing has been heightened by divisions *within* the discipline, with the attendant proliferation of jargon, debates over terminology and, above all, a revived sense of the distinctions between 'pure' theory and grubby application. The predictable result is an increasingly incestuous field in which researchers speak only to one another: a replication, that is to say, of the disembodied and decontextualized sterility that the ethnographic thrust was meant to replace. In a criticism of the lack of attention paid to race and racism in discourse studies – an important criticism, given the stated aims of both discourse analysis and its more pointed relation, 'critical discourse analysis' (see below) – Yancy (1998: 3) has noted that the field too often reflects 'the words of white men engaged in conversation with themselves'. Luke (1995) and Rogers *et al.* (2005: 385) have made similar observations; the latter remark that, beyond inadequate attention to the languages and cultures of minority groups, discourse frameworks 'have continued to silence and oppress historically marginalized groups of people'. This, of course, is a much more serious charge, although its practical force is lessened by some of the other characteristics of the genre, characteristics that make it unlikely that it has any particular influence to either advance or retard the fortunes of the marginalized.

Examination of language in context, with a particular concern for the ways in which linguistic interactions illustrate and sustain positions of power and status, constitute the framework within which discourse analysis has arisen. This is, indeed, a framework of great potential interest and importance. Much of the work in the area, however, reflects very particular ideological assumptions about status relationships in various social settings, and about the constituents of those relationships. There is a strong post-structural and post-modern accent here (see Wardhaugh, 2006). Apart from left-leaning ideological tendencies, this means that the idea that there might be objective truth – unattainable as this may be in any complete way – is speedily and rather happily jettisoned in favor of a dynamic and often indeterminate subjectivity. What were once the parlor games of French intellectuals – whose personal lives, despite all their vaunted interest in 'decentering' and 'deconstruction', typically reveal a rather considerable centering on themselves – have taken on a bizarre totemic status in various academic fields.

Discourse analysis and its offspring

Discourse analysis is sometimes differentiated from conversational analysis; while the latter aims to assess how conversation 'works', the former may involve more structural analysis (see also below). It may also be applied to written samples, although some use the term 'text analysis' for this. As Stubbs (1983b) pointed out, early on, there is a good deal of overlap, not to say imprecision, in these terms. (Consider, by way of comparison, the common ground often trodden by the social psychology of language, sociolinguistics and the sociology of language.) Stubbs argued for discourse analysis as *the* avenue for studying classroom interaction, and cited an increasing dissatisfaction with traditional psychological work based upon experimental manipulation; later, Stubbs (1986) provided a discussion of language and education in which discourse analysis figured prominently (perhaps too prominently; see Viv Edwards, 1987). The thrust was given even more force by Potter and Wetherell (1987), who argued that discourse analysis should be at the center of the whole social-psychological enterprise: they point out that social life is, after all, largely a matter of discourse. Part of their argument, however, was also to dismiss some of the traditional emphases in the area (e.g. attitudes, particularly as elicited via questionnaires), and this clearly struck a chord. Antaki (1988), for example, observed that their work could 'rescue' social psychology from its current laboratory-orientated 'sterility' (see also Billig, 1988; Smith, 1988). Harré and Gillett (1994) and Harré and Stearns (1995) also discuss a new 'discursive' psychology, meant to largely replace existing experimental paradigms. In a review essay, Giles and Coupland (1989) offered a further assessment. While agreeing about the potentially significant role for discourse analysis within social psychology, they cautioned against elevating it too highly, or too independently, over other worthwhile approaches. And indeed, we should on principle be chary about new waves, and not be overly quick to discard existing methods and insights; eclectic perspectives, ones that stress methodological triangulation, are almost always preferable.

A parallel development to the one advocated above has been that which led from 'ethnomethodology' to 'conversation analysis', where the latter obviously converges and often overlaps with discourse analysis.

The trajectories are remarkably similar. Ethnomethodology (see Garfinkel, 1967) was also initially concerned with fuller and more realistic contextualization of interaction, advocating a more productive connection between fine-grained observation and the larger social canvas. But ethnomethodological inquiry was theoretically so broad in its remit that any disciplinary precision soon became quite unattainable.[5] As Lewis Coser (1975) put it in his presidential address to the American Sociological Association, ethnomethodology and allied undertakings are more like sects or cliques: closed systems in which members talk to other members, where insights exist that are denied to outsiders. In line with what I have already mentioned, we also expect to find here violent internecine struggles coupled with equally violent swings of focus: problems are not dealt with in the cumulative manner that is the hallmark of science; rather, old perspectives are simply replaced by newer fashions. Coser also remarks on the curious tendency (not limited to ethnomethodologists, of course) for those professionally interested in language and communication to be such poor communicators themselves. One of the most noticeable characteristics here is flatulent verbosity. Coser cites a hundred-word description (from Sudnow, 1972) that conveys the message that we should be careful when crossing the road. In a review of Garfinkel's 'seminal' text, Coleman (1968: 130) succinctly observes that ethnomethodology involves 'an extraordinarily high ratio of reading time to information transfer'. Just so.

The particular linguistic offspring of ethnomethodology is conversation analysis. Although it is notoriously difficult to draw boundaries among the various approaches here, conversation analysis does attend more to the intricacies and mechanics of talk itself – the sequencing of utterances, fluency and 'smoothness', the initiation and termination of conversational interchange, the rules and practices governing interruptions and interjections, the appropriateness of topics (and of the styles in which they are to be discussed) and the etiquettes of turn-taking – whereas discourse analysis is (theoretically) more likely to place such matters within the broader scope of power and status relationships. Given its emphases, conversation analysis could be of some use in understanding classroom dynamics. As Tony Edwards (1976: 180) put it, traditional classrooms are 'places contrived for the controlled transmission of knowledge. This is what gives them their peculiar identity as settings for talk'. (It should be noted here that some analysts, insisting on the study of 'natural' conversations, have seen classrooms as 'unnatural'. This raises questions, of course, about just what we are to construe as natural or artificial.) As well, in her study of language pathologies, Lesser

(2003) makes the reasonable claim that conversation analysis can prove diagnostically useful in some studies of aphasia; this can, of course, only occur with a base knowledge of the talk of 'ordinary' or 'normal' people (see also Čmejrková & Prevignano, 2003). While this may be a good example of the usefulness of conversational-analytic procedures, it also highlights potential shortcomings.

Conversation analysis has been applied in all sorts of settings, but it is clearly of greater potential use in situations that can draw upon reflective study: more applicable, then, in clinical speech analyses than in (say) emergency telephone calls to police or fire departments. (Speech analysts of various stripes very much enjoy getting to grips with dramatic 'real-world' exchanges.) Even scholarly insights into doctor-patient or lawyer-client intercourse are likely to allow for less contemplative analysis. To put it another way: the reams of conversational-analytic literature are not likely to come into play in the immediacy of important and/or highly emotional settings; they may allow (as Lesser implies, for example) some comparative insights when time permits. But consider this: when time permits, we are all pretty good at figuring out what conversations really *mean*. We have been learning all about this, all about reading (or listening) between the lines, from a very early age. We typically do not employ our more or less automatic skills here with the jargon of academic speech analysis, but this does not seem to have hindered us very much. Now, one could argue that a formalization of our inter-pretative exercises might be very useful – in-depth analyses, perhaps, presented back to us in ways that refine and improve our skills. This is *theoretically* so, but since conversation analysis, like its sister sub-disciplines, has increasingly become a rarefied parlor game for enthu-siasts, we ought not to bank upon revelation any time soon.

In a further iteration, 'critical discourse analysis' (CDA) has become a very popular format for the analysis of speech and language. Blommaert (2005) tells us that it is the most 'visible' of the current approaches to the study of language in society. There are, of course, others: anthropological linguistics, sociolinguistics, the sociology/social psychology of language and other more traditional avenues of enquiry. But since CDA is a field whose main arenas are those of 'political discourse, media, advertise-ment, ideology, racism [and] institutional discourse' (Blommaert, 2005: 21), it has clearly positioned itself to be timely and relevant. It is not ideologically neutral, of course. Concerned with real problems in the real world, more specifically with the illumination and redress of social inequality, it was 'perceived by many as liberating, because it was upfront about its own, explicitly left-wing, political commitment'

(Blommaert, 2005: 6). While making the obvious acknowledgement that no social-scientific undertaking can be entirely value-free, I have recently suggested some of the difficulties that may arise when advocacy is combined with scholarship (see Edwards, 2004a). Widdowson (2004: 173) has also touched upon this point: 'the proponents of CDA can be regarded as activists in that they are critical, but as discourse analysts they are academics... it seems reasonable to be critical of their work, as discourse analysis, where it appears not to conform to the conventions of rationality, logical consistency, empirical substantiation and so on'.

Seminal texts in CDA include those of Fairclough (1988, 1995), Wodak (1989) and van Dijk (1993), and they all stress the ideologically charged ramping up of discourse analysis, as suggested by Blommaert (above). As van Dijk (2001: 96) has put it, CDA is 'discourse analysis with attitude'. This politically sharpened approach, like its cognate disciplines, has its origins in the 'critical theory' of the Frankfurt School of the 1930s, whose leading lights (Theodor Adorno and Walter Benjamin among them) were committed to neo-Marxist criticism of capitalist privilege and social hegemony. It also draws upon 'systemic functional linguistics' (see Halliday, 1978, 1989), an approach that (again) stresses language as a creative social construction that both reflects and influences its social setting, as well as the related, but much more obscurely stated, views of Foucault (1969, 1971).

Much of the work in these areas alternates between the obvious and the impenetrable. This is occasionally acknowledged by 'insiders', some of whom have expanded on the matter. Thus, Verschueren (2001) and Blommaert (2005) note that much analysis restates the obvious, but from very particular points of view: 'one ideological frame is replaced by another – a capitalist framing of meanings is "criticised" by substituting it with an anti-capitalist one' (Blommaert, 2005: 32). Schegloff (1997) further discusses the imposition of analysts' own political leanings onto their data. In presenting his views, and those of Slembrouck (2001), Blommaert writes that 'stable patterns of power relations are sketched, often based on little more than social and political common sense, and then projected onto (and into) discourse... the analyst becomes the ultimate arbiter of meanings... the participant is pushed out of the analysis, so to speak' (Blommaert, 2005: 32–33).

Much of the content here has been discussed in clearer form from other points of view. You can read about the functionality of language, in its twin capacities of influencing and reflecting context, in the work of Bakhtin and his epigones, or you could turn to Herman (1961) on language choice, or Giles and his associates on speech accommodation theory (e.g. Giles & Coupland, 1991). The useful overview of CDA provided by Rogers *et al.* (2005) will demonstrate to all but the fiercest of fellow travellers some of the mundane truisms that the labors of 'critical' theorists have produced. Overall, it should come as no surprise to learn that criticisms of CDA focus upon its rather incestuous nature and its decontextualized approach to the micro-examination of written and spoken language – both deeply ironical, given the field's argument for social incisiveness and, indeed, social action. Rogers *et al.* (2005: 383) note that the analyses they conducted of the characteristics, contexts and results of almost four dozen CDA studies (specifically in educational settings) revealed that the work was essentially descriptive, focusing 'on the ways in which power is reproduced rather than on how it is changed, resisted, and transformed toward liberatory ends'; see also Luke (2004) on the 'deconstructive' rather than 'reconstructive' efforts here.

Meant to overturn a sterile empiricism largely practiced by and for members of the hegemonic 'mainstream', discourse analysis and its offshoots have increasingly become introverted and isolated enterprises. Like a game of chess (but more elaborate, in that there are infinite possibilities for redefinition and realignment of the rules), they are fascinating to their players, but increasingly divorced from social reality. I note that Paul Chilton (2004: x), in his recent book on political discourse, admits that 'I do not know if discourse analysts can have any serious impact on the genocides, oppressions and exploitations we are still witnessing', and one of his reviewers broadens the point by asking 'what effect discourse analysts could potentially have on world affairs' (Hodges, 2005: 247). The naïveté here is truly touching.[6] The attention that CDA gives to the larger context is also dubious in practice, even though it is theoretically intended to connect broader social theory with fine-grained attention to discourse. Rogers *et al.* (2005) note that this is an emphasis that distinguishes it from the more purely 'micro' approaches of, say, conversational analysis. Of course, how the latter could, itself, be worth the candle without some sense of the norms and imperatives of conversational settings is a question worth asking, even if, as Rogers *et al.* (2005: 378) point out, the idea of 'context' is limited: an emphasis upon the 'here and now of the interaction, not what came before or after it'. This is an emasculated notion of 'context', to be sure.

Putting aside worries about the lack of contextualization, the related matter of how particular speech and language samples are chosen from larger ongoing 'interactions' is important. Choices are frequently made without any compelling justification, raising questions of 'representativeness, selectivity, partiality, prejudice and voice' (Blommaert, 2005: 31;

see also Rogers *et al.*, 2005). One of the consequences would seem to be a potentially endless series of fact-gathering exercises, and observers have noted the difficulties in a field in which the explanations can be so much more detailed (and take up so much more space) than the phenomena under study. Hymes (1986), for example – some of whose work argues for and illustrates ethnographic approaches to the study of language diversity (see above, and Hymes, 1974) – has mounted some cogent criticism.

An excellent example of the matter is found in the work of Grimshaw (1989), who devotes more than 600 pages to an analysis of a committee's evalution of a doctoral dissertation. The actual transcript used here was less than 300 lines of text, representing about 10 minutes of conversation among four examiners! (This is clearly a great improvement on Borges's [1999] famous map of the world on a scale of 1:1, because here we have the potential for a map of the sociolinguistic world many times larger than the actual world itself.[7]) A reviewer pointed out that there is 'excessive description at the expense of analytical relevance... overly long and in too many places overwritten', and that some of the descriptions are 'impressionistic and ad hoc' (Firth, 1996: 1489), but also argues that Grimshaw has actually been too simplistic in places! In a companion collection, Grimshaw (1994: 453–454) admits that 'we have collectively produced neither a "comprehensive discourse analysis" [CDA] nor a "unified theory of sociolinguistic description"... we have, if anything, demonstrated that CDA is a chimera'. And Firth, while acknowledging – how could he not? – that Grimshaw's work shows 'how much can be extracted from a relatively short segment', ends his review by saying that 'for students of spoken interaction, such an experience confirms what is already known'. *Parturiunt montes; nascetur ridiculus mus.*

In its various guises and emphases, discourse analysis remains popular in many circles, but it is hard to see that it has created a break-through of any significance for its intended beneficiaries. It has done its practitioners some considerable good, at least within the inbred confines that they increasingly inhabit. I am well aware, of course, that most of the work, of most social scientists, most of the time, makes very little direct contribution towards the societies within which it operates. But we should surely be particularly careful when considering areas whose very existence is based upon the desire to produce applicable results, whose findings are generally gathered 'in the field', but whose sense of that field is restricted, and whose production of jargon and neologism increases at a geometric pace.

Notes

1. Stubbs himself illustrates one of the dangers here. It is hard to imagine saying to an overworked and underpaid teacher, particularly one who has immediate need to deal appropriately with heterogeneity in the classroom:

   > Both the overall macrostructure of narratives, descriptions, explanations, and the like, and also the micropropositional development of texts from sentence to sentence, are seen as cognitive schemas which play an important part in the comprehension and production of texts. (Stubbs, 1984: 226)

   Well, you might say that Stubbs is *not* talking directly to teachers here. But remember that his chapter – and the collection of which it is a part – is all about *application* in real-life settings. In his brief preface, the editor of the book says that it should be of interest to language teachers and 'educationists' (Trudgill, 1984). And consider, finally, that such high-flown phrasing tends to creep in wherever theoreticians meet practitioners.

2. Meaningful cultural variations may occur throughout the educational process, and in subtle ways. When I first came to work at St Francis Xavier University in northeastern Nova Scotia, I was struck by the passivity of my charges: compared with the urban students I had been familiar with, these seemed deferential and silent. To get any sort of classroom discussion going proved very difficult and, for some students, no technique of encouragement seemed to work. My expectations, like those of the white teachers on American Indian reservations, were low. And yet, I soon discovered that these students were as bright as any, that their written work was on a par with that of their urban counterparts (not that this is saying a great deal, of course), and that – with time, and particularly in seminar settings – they would indeed participate.

   I had simply been unaware of some of the cultural values of the Nova Scotian Scots: traditionally committed to educational 'improvement', having a very strong sense of place and community – it is not at all unusual for local people to know everything about their genealogical history, going back at least to the time of the Clearances – respectful to the 'dominie' and, until fairly recently, grounded in the Scots Gaelic language.

3. Coverage of the important gender issues in the classroom is hardly exhausted in my few paragraphs here. The most important dynamics, however, can be deduced from the broader literature on women's and men's language (see later chapters), for in linguistic (and other) reflections of social values and practices, the classroom is often a microcosm of the world outside the school gates. I should also bring readers' attention to Corson's (2001) excellent summary chapter, a section of a book whose overall purpose is broadly similar to that of this one.

   Rampton's (2006: 70) detailed ethnographic enquiry of urban working-class schoolchildren also highlights 'the broad contrast between boys talking and girls keeping silent'. He notes, however, that such a rough distinction masks some complexities: there are boys who generally keep quiet in the classroom, and there are girls who are vocal. The reasons for either participating or remaining silent vary greatly; the context – the topic of conversation, for example – must be taken into account; and so on.

4. There is something particularly ironic in using an unfamiliar Latin term in the American academic context. This, after all, is a setting in which facility with any language but English is uncommon, in which work in any language but English is essentially disregarded, and in which titles and references in any language but English must be given in translation. This seems to be true, even in circles where one might have expected a little flexibility. A few years ago, I published a piece about bilingualism (Edwards, 1999a), in a special journal issue devoted to the topic. My final sentence suggested that social-psychological investigations were a variety of historical study, that their findings were snapshots that should be retaken every now and then. My final phrase was *tempora mutantur, nos et mutamur in illis*, which I felt summed up the matter very nicely, and which I also felt was a reasonably familiar observation. In any event, it seemed to me that the interested reader for whom it was *not* familiar could very easily discover its meaning, and might even enjoy being nudged into a little detective work; I know that I do, when faced with something unfamiliar. (I have just done a Google search: it turned up almost 90,000 hits, of which the top two or three were quite satisfactory.)

I had, however, to engage in prolonged correspondence with the journal's publishers and copy-editors, who wanted me to add an English translation in parenthesis. After a certain amount of argy-bargy, I told them that that would defeat the purpose of the Latin version, and that I would rather drop the whole sentence. They then, to my great surprise, yielded the field, and the phrase appeared without English accompaniment. This was one of those small, unexpected victories that keep academic life so vibrant.

I note, incidentally, that Waxmann Verlag, in Münster, have been publishing a journal called *Tertium Comparationis: Journal for Comparative and Multicultural Education* since 1995. The words before the colon are of course redundant – but no doubt, it is hoped that they are redolent too.

5. Further phenomenological excursions became even less focused. Thus, Rose and Kaplan introduced us to the new field of 'ethno-inquiry'. The world, they point out, consists of both people and things, 'and it is the task of the ethno-inquirer to try to sort them out' (Kaplan, 1982: 15). For his part, Rose (1982: 19) reveals that 'wordly things are such critical matters that they may be given a name. They can be called mundanities'. For a critical statement on this nonsense, see Edwards (1983b). 'Ethno-inquiry' has apparently disappeared, I am glad to say, but it remains an example of the *bizarreries* that continue to arise.

6. Another recent reviewer of Chilton's book on political discourse is Hailong Tian (2006). Could anyone – well, anyone who isn't a discourse analyst by birth – read his review, with its painful accounts of Enoch Powell's famous 'rivers of blood' speech and Bill Clinton's 1999 announcement of air strikes against the Serbs, without shuddering at the lengthy but empty and jargon-ridden restatements of the obvious? And could anyone doubt that this is but a reflection of wider noisome practice within the field?

7. In his argument for a closer relationship between psychology and linguistics – more specifically, between social psychology and discourse studies – Robinson (1985: 136) makes the following observation: 'Unfortunately, the

implications for further work are infinite in more than one respect. Spatially and temporally there can be no end to studies that would be of practical use to individuals in their daily lives'. This is certainly true. Indeed, it is quite unremarkable, for who would argue that our investigations into the human condition are nearing their end? Still, Robinson's mention of infinity does bring to mind Borges's famous map.

At least Grimshaw's (1989) study – as mentioned in the text here – used real language excerpts. Some of the texts and other samples that are put under the discoursal microscope are made up by the investigator, thus heading us even more dramatically towards maps much larger than reality.

Chapter 3
Disadvantage: A Brief Overview

Introduction

If one is interested today in those educational difficulties that seem to follow group lines, one might turn to the literature on multicultural and multi-ethnic education, on diversity in the classroom, on minority-group issues, on cultural heterogeneity, on educational 'empowerment', on intergroup and intercultural schooling, and so on. Representative treatments can be found in Banks (1996), Manning and Baruth (2004) and Nieto (2004). Alternatively, if one is especially interested in linguistic matters, the burgeoning field of 'variationist sociolinguistics' could recommend itself: see Chambers *et al.* (2002); see also Chambers (1995), James Milroy (1992) and Lesley Milroy (1987). Part of its obvious remit is the study of dialect differentiation along class lines, and this continues a tradition particularly associated with the work of Labov on the 'social stratification' of language (see, for instance, Labov's [2006] study of English in New York City). Trudgill's 'triangle model' shows how dialect differences become less pronounced as one moves up the social-class hierarchy; as Coulmas (2005: 29) then observes, 'the speech of the disadvantaged or underclass is more pronouncedly regional than that of middle-class speakers' (see also Trudgill, 2000, 2002).

The more contemporary research directions rarely, however, get to the heart of difficulties faced by children at school, difficulties often exacerbated by linguistic practices and perceptions. At the 'macro' level, for example, the commendable concern with diversity in the classroom often jumps more or less immediately to what I shall style below as the 'difference' position. Given the validity of this position (as we shall see), this is entirely reasonable, but it does mean that some real-life problems are rather skipped over. At more 'micro' levels, we often find variationist linguists attending to fine-grained distinctions of syntax and pronunciation. It is perhaps telling that, in his chapter on class variation, Coulmas (2005) gives us only one paragraph on the 'Bernsteinian' era (see below). It is also telling that the title of this chapter is 'Standard and Dialect: Social Stratification as a Factor of Linguistic Choice', and that Coulmas goes on to discuss the fact that 'dialects can be chosen' (Coulmas, 2005: 18). This is certainly correct, and there is, in fact, a large literature on linguistic 'accommodation'; the work of Giles and his colleagues is noteworthy here (see Giles & Coupland, 1991; Robinson & Giles, 2001). Again, however, the idea of choosing appropriately from one's speech repertoire rather sidesteps the issues of importance for young, nonstandard-dialect-speaking children.

So, very few researchers write about 'deprived' or 'disadvantaged' children any more. There are some good reasons for terminological changes, but also some that are rather less compelling, and many new coinages will soon fade away, just like those they replaced. Here is a contemporary observation:

> From a cultural perspective, many of the problems that language minority [sic] students experience in mainstream programs can be attributed to the school's devaluation of the home and culture of the students rather than to their cultural differences. In culturally and linguistically sensitive programs, students are not labeled 'at risk' – a cultural-deficit approach. Culturally sensitive programs have moved beyond home-school discontinuity, cultural relativity, or cultural difference theory and have made room for more equitable, culturally sensitive schooling defined in cooperation with the community. (Ovando & Gourd, 1996: 315)

This is a representative quotation, inasmuch as the new 'cultural sensitivity' that it trumpets goes hand in hand with muddled thinking. It is certainly true that the home backgrounds of some minority-group children are devalued in the classroom, but the second half of the first sentence is confused: the home-school differences are precisely what fuel 'devaluation'. In the second sentence, it is incorrect to equate the 'at-risk' description with a 'deficit' perspective, since it is entirely possible to reject the latter while acknowledging the former. The third sentence is the oddest of the three. How can cultural sensitivity 'move beyond' home-school discontinuity, when that is the foundation-stone of the matter? How can it move beyond the cultural relativity that is the theoretical basis for a different-but-not-deficient approach to disadvantage? How can it consider itself an approach separate from the 'difference' perspective that is the socio-educational manifestation of cultural relativity? And what do the fine concluding words about equitability and community cooperation signify, other than earnest intention? (There is also the infelicitous repetition of the words 'culturally sensitive' in this final sentence.)

As we shall see in the following chapters, three broad explanations have been proposed for group-based educational difficulties. The first holds that some populations suffer substantive deficiencies because of genetic inferiority; the second, that such deficits may be caused by faulty environments; the third, that what the first two positions view as deficits are, in fact, differences attributable to variations in environment that are – in themselves – neither better nor worse than 'mainstream' varieties. The first two explanations are essentially untenable, however, and the 'difference' viewpoint is the most reasonable on the basis of the available evidence. The implication is that difficulties faced by certain groups (lower-class ones, for instance) are deficits only in a social sense, only when assumptions of the correctness of other values (middle-class ones, for instance) are taken into account. While suffering from social rather than cognitive deficits is not necessarily a lesser burden, of course, accuracy is important here, and desirable interventions can have little chance of meaningful effect if they are based upon faulty models.

'Disadvantage' was a term first employed by those espousing an environmental-deficit thesis (Deutsch, 1967). Thus, it became closely associated with so-called 'compensatory education', a thrust largely built upon the environmentalist belief that inadequate patterns of early socialization could be remedied in school and pre-school programs (Bereiter & Engelmann, 1966). More enlightened adherence to 'difference' models, in which environmental deficit and remedial education are obviously seen as flawed and inappropriate conceptions (indeed, 'compensation' is hardly the *mot juste* if existing patterns are not inherently deficient), meant that 'disadvantage' became viewed in a negative light. Hill-Burnett (1979) argued, for instance, that 'disadvantage' was merely a euphemism for deficit; Adler (1979) discussed a portmanteau 'deprived/disadvantaged' concept; de Valdés (1979) used 'disadvantaged' and 'deficient' interchangeably; and Moss (1973: 19), in a contribution to an Open University block on language and learning, argued that 'whether you prefer to use "disadvantaged", "deprived" or some other term qualified by "socially", "economically" or "culturally" is less important than the fact that there is no child who can fit into such a category'. The anti-labelling sentiment here may be admirable (although less than crystal clear), but the impatience with distinctions of terminology is not. Typically associated with a deficit model, 'disadvantage' has become a word to be avoided. This is largely due, however, to a postmodern hypersensitivity that, in the final analysis, does no one any good. The term remains useful, and it need not be lumbered with unfair connotations.[1]

We are right to delete such inaccuracies as 'sociocultural deprivation' and 'genetic deficiency', but it would be a shame if 'disadvantage' was jettisoned too. We can discuss certain children as being at a disadvantage in society without casting the slightest aspersion upon their own culture, language, socialization and so on. Disadvantage signifies inequalities that we know to exist, and to the extent to which one is excluded from full participation, one is disadvantaged. A related reason for the retention of the term 'disadvantage', as opposed to limp difference-theory phrases ('culturally different', for instance), is that it can act as a useful counterbalance to the sometimes too sanguine outlook of difference theorists. That is, just as terming a child environmentally deprived may invoke an unwarranted halo effect, so difference theorists have sometimes been wont to see their subjects as neither needing nor asking for outside help. Those who emphasize the strengths of 'working-class culture' (and it certainly has some: recall Orwell's (1937) observation that 'there is much in middle-class life that looks sickly and debilitating when you see it from a working-class angle'), for example, ought to remember that there is no virtue in poverty itself, and that poor children who achieve at school do so despite, and not because of, material and other inadequacies. As Rutter and Madge (1977: 2) once noted, 'behind the words... the human predicament is real enough'. Retention of the forthright 'disadvantage' might be salutary here.

While there are a great many short- and long-term factors that may prove disadvantageous to individuals in many areas of life, the psychological, educational and linguistic disadvantage under discussion here reflects relatively enduring *group* conditions. The characteristics and lifestyles of some communities – the working class, immigrant populations and ethnic minorities among them – may lead to poor school achievement and generally dampened chances of success in the larger society. The assumption is that the 'cultures of poverty', often marked by class, or race or ethnicity, do little to prepare a child for the more middle-class contexts and consequences of formal education. While initial school entry implies, for all children, a break from the only life they have hitherto known, children from certain groups may be at a relative disadvantage because of a more sharply marked discontinuity between home and school.

Disadvantage is a sociocultural phenomenon, then, whose workings do not rest upon genetic intellectual disability; they emerge, rather, because of variations in patterns of early socialization. It arises at points of contact between groups that are at once distinguishable and yet part of the same larger society, which is why it is generally most immediately noticeable in educational contexts: the classroom is the earliest and arguably the single most important point of contact between social groups and sub-groups. Since disadvantage always involves a comparison between socially unequal populations, an implication is that many values and attitudes considered disadvantageous are only so when judged against a standard imposed from outside the group itself.

To repeat: the most accurate perspective on disadvantage defines it in terms of environmental *difference*. It is true, of course, that some aspects of some social environments, particularly those of early life, may give rise to problems that are very intractable indeed (inadequate shelter and nutrition, for example, can clearly have devastating long-term effects). Nonetheless, apart from clarifying aetiological matters, and thereby removing inaccurate biological or environmental-deficit burdens from the backs of those whose social problems are quite sufficient unto the day, the thrust of the disadvantage-as-difference position is that it makes alteration (indeed, even 'compensation', if the nature of the problems to be tackled is clearly understood) at least theoretically possible.

'Difference' is essentially a matter of *discontinuity*. While some of the earlier discussions did not use the latter term (see Ogbu, 1982a, however), it is obvious that discontinuities, particularly those between the home and the school, are the heart of the matter. If people did not stray out of their immediate social settings – if inner-city children, say, never left their neighborhood, never went to school – then disadvantage as conceived here would not arise. It is contact, and the ramifications of contact, that produce social disadvantage, and it is social perceptions and norms that translate that disadvantage into deficits. Now, some of the treatments in the literature are more explicitly discussing the idea of disadvantage as discontinuity; Kellaghan (2001), for example, has brought it front and center in a new overview on definitional matters.[2] An interesting development here is the incorporation of Bourdieu's ideas of varieties of 'capital'. Economic capital is, of course, the most obvious type, since the relationship between poverty and disadvantage, while not without its nuances, is a strong one. As well, however, Kellaghan reminds us of the importance of cultural and social capital. Disadvantage may arise in situations in which the home does not adequately 'foster cognitive and scholastic development', or where aspects of 'conduct... identity... social behaviour, attitudes and motivations' (Kellaghan, 2001: 7) may lead to difficulties beyond the immediate environments that produce them.

Kellaghan's illustrations of social and cultural capital make it clear that we are still essentially talking about the 'values and attitudes' of the home, and the implications they have for current and future developments. And Bourdieu's insights are not particularly new in themselves. Kellaghan cites work (by Bourdieu and Passeron) on social reproduction that dates to 1977 (and, in fact, to 1970 in its original French version).[3] Nonetheless, doors may be opened here to new and interesting linkages, because analyzing family settings in sub-divided ways may prompt greater subtlety of explanation: some may be financially poor, for instance, but rich in other ways; not all those who grow up in apparently disadvantaged circumstances are, in fact, disadvantaged themselves; and so on. (The work of Garbarino *et al.* [1997] has reinforced, for example, the rather obvious fact that most people who grow up in what would generally be perceived as unfavorable conditions become fully functioning adults.) In turn, increased explanatory subtlety can prompt consideration of matters that were insufficiently regarded before. For example, Kellaghan refers to the need for closer attention to those 'working-class' values that were traditionally, and often cavalierly, downgraded. Such examinations are always useful, but (as I have implied above) one would not wish to see a romanticized view of such values obscuring the reality of a society largely run on, and responsive to, more middle-class ones. More interesting, perhaps, would be the examination of the more general proposition that some aspects of some cultures may be intrinsically less valuable than others. Relatedly, interesting cases might be made for the likelihood and/or the benefits of disadvantaged children becoming 'bicultural'. That is, desired and desirable competences along broadly socially approved lines might coexist with original ones: a psychological pattern of addition rather than replacement. And finally here, more nuanced perspectives could make considerations of how schools might adapt to what children 'bring with them' – a partial reversal, that is to say, of the traditional requirements for pupils to conform themselves to the school – much more likely. I shall return to these themes later on, particularly to the linguistic aspects of 'bicultural' arrangements and to educational adaptations to nonstandard dialects in the classroom.

A recent overview by Pérez Carreón *et al.* (2005) has pointed to some of the difficulties involved in bringing the 'cultural capital' of the home to bear successfully upon school and classroom practice, particularly among poor, immigrant, inner-city populations. As they note, while virtually everyone accepts that parental involvement can contribute to children's success at school, there is much less unanimity when one begins to consider just *how* that involvement can best be marshalled. And, although Pérez Carreón and his colleagues do not mention it, there is also a great deal of rather pious lip-service paid to bringing parents 'into the classroom', when it is clear that, in many instances, their presence is really not wanted. This is a subject for another day, but anyone who has spent time with teachers will recognize that, over-burdened as they often are, they may resent rather than welcome direct parental 'engagement'. This is not true for all teachers or in all circumstances, but once one gets beyond structured occasions, like designated parent-teacher meetings, one is in murkier territory.

Disadvantage and Poverty

As I have already mentioned in passing, there is an unsurprising correlation between socioeconomic status (SES) and school achievement. It is not a simple linear relationship, however, as the meta-analyses of White (1982) and Sirin (2005) have shown; see also the multi-country study of Marks (2006) on between- and within-school differences in achievement. Studies typically base their investigations on parental incomes, occupations and levels of education, on the one hand, and on children's measured attainments – overall grade averages, standardized educational assessments, single-subject test scores (verbal skills, mathe-matics achievement, and so on) – on the other.

One finding is that the relationship between SES and educational achievement is greater at the level of the school than at the level of individual students; the wider generality of this American relationship remains to be tested, since it seems to apply in the United States because of the association there between school funding and district tax bases. It also seems that collecting family SES data from children is much less informative than going directly to the parents, since the former often over-estimate home resources; the disparities are greatest for young children, for those from single-parent families and for those at the bottom of the achievement tables. This is important, of course, since such children are typically the ones for whom we would like the most accurate SES data. A third finding – particularly important in the context of this book – is that SES (in Sirin's American study, for instance) is a stronger predictor of achievement for white students than for others. For minority-group pupils, including African Americans, the general neigh-borhood SES is more indicative (see Dornbusch *et al.*, 1991; Gonzales *et al.*, 1996). The inference here is that lower-class minority groups often live in neighborhoods with 'higher educational risk factors' (Sirin, 2005: 441). Perhaps these tend to swamp individual family variations. A related point was made by Krieger and Fee (1994) who showed that simply comparing median family incomes across groups may give a misleading picture of their relative SES. Their mid-1990s investigations in the United States revealed that, although white family incomes were on average half again as large as those of black families, the overall wealth of the former (their 'capital assets', most notably home ownership) was about *ten times* greater.

Nonetheless, while the two overlap to a considerable extent, disadvantage is not simply a synonym for poverty. Within areas of high unemployment, poor housing and low income, one certainly expects to find a concentration of social or educational disadvantage. It is also true that ethnic and racial minorities are very often poor (although external and visible markers of class or ethnicity may mask a great deal of heterogeneity). On the other hand, it would be logically incorrect to equate comfortable physical surroundings with absence of socio-educational disadvantage. It is clear that there are many 'good' homes in working-class neighborhoods and many 'poor' ones in middle-class suburbia; see Wiseman (1968) for an early expression of this, and Garbarino *et al.* (1997).

Recent statistics from Toronto – a heavily multicultural city, with more than a quarter of a million schoolchildren from virtually every country on earth – reveal something of the interaction between ethnicity and material poverty (Wente, 2006). While children from the poorest neighborhoods are three times more likely to drop out of school than are those from the richest ones (33 versus 11%), achievement differences among ethnic groups are more striking. Romanian and Chinese children (with drop-out rates of about 11.5%) and Gujarati, Bengali and Tamil pupils (about 16%) are the most likely to finish school, while the least likely to stay the course are Somali, Caribbean, Portuguese and South American children (whose drop-out rates are on the order of 40%). These figures are, broadly speaking, typical of other countries in which these immigrant groups are represented. Writing about the American experience, Steinberg *et al.* (1996) consider that ethnicity is the most predictive of children's school success, more important than parental wealth, two-parent families and stay-at-home mothers. The Asian students who do so well in anglophone contexts benefit from homes in which educational achievement is highly valued, and in which family habits and values reflect and support this. Their disproportionate presence in university-level education is as marked as that of black and Hispanic children – in opposite directions, of course.

If so much importance rests upon family 'culture', obvious questions arise about many contemporary educational innovations and practices intended to close the various achievement gaps. It is much too simplistic, however, to say that Asian parents value education more than do West Indian or Hispanic ones. If we assume that virtually all parents in all ethnic populations would prefer success to failure, then the questions of importance force us back a step or two: *why* do some parents support and reinforce 'school learning' for their children more than some others do? What accounts for the considerable variability in minority-group school performance (see Ogbu, 1983, 1987)? It is not too difficult to draw distinctions here among (for example) *degrees* of prejudice and discrimination suffered by different immigrant minority groups, nor is it difficult to predict the operation of various circular reactions, both positive and negative. Because of historical factors, good luck and, above all, minimal prejudice, Group A may be able to put its children on the beginning rungs of educational success. When success is achieved, greater penetration of the middle-class mainstream occurs, more material markers of success accrue, and the value of formal education becomes apparent. Group B, on the other hand, may be more significantly hamstrung from the beginning, and prejudice may have a more enduringly corrosive effect. In socially unfavorable circumstances, where opportunities are few and where the basic requirements of life consume virtually all the family energy and resources, it is easy to see that the rewards of formal education will be both less apparent and much less frequently achieved. If you cannot afford to buy educational lottery tickets, you are unlikely to win any prizes.

In a notable treatment of poverty, Rainwater (1970) outlined five major perspectives, four of which result from the combination of two polarized dimensions, weakness-potency and virtue-badness. A classic historical view holds that the poor are as potentially strong as anyone else, but somehow lack virtue; from such a perspective, they are immoral (or sinful). If poor people are seen as bad but weak, on the other hand, what was sin can be considered illness: moral flaw and demonic possession are no longer favored explanations for aberrant behavior, and an important implication is that poverty-as-social-pathology might be remedied. Compensatory interventions, for example, now become theoretically possible. A third combination links virtue and impotence: the poor are basically like the rest of us, but their coping skills are undermined by a lack of resources. An implication of this model is that people could be helped to help themselves. Initial aid and guidance could set them on their feet. At a societal level, this perspective undergirds efforts to assist the poor in 'underdeveloped' areas. Rainwater's fourth logical possibility is that the poor are both strong and good. They have defiantly turned their backs on mainstream society, where people are increasingly alienated and 'depersonalized', where psychological conditions may become so unpleasant that people may actually wish to 'escape from freedom' (as Fromm [1941] famously put it). Individuals and groups have certainly acted on this desire, and some of the more egregious instances have shown what a high price can be exacted. Seeing poor people as powerful and virtuous has often arisen from a romanticized middle-class view.

Rainwater labelled these four models the *moralizing, medicalizing, normalizing* and *apotheosizing* approaches. They are all essentially descriptive: they represent views of poverty, rather than explanations of it. But there is a fifth and more instructive approach, a *naturalizing* perspective, and it is one that clearly relates to the 'difference-deficit' controversy touched on in the previous section. On the one hand (Rainwater himself observed), a 'biological determinism' argues for innate deficiencies of intelligence. The perceived utility of eugenics and, more generally, a concern to look after people who cannot adequately judge for themselves, are elements that have traditionally informed the 'benign totalitarianism' associated with such a deterministic position. The other broad theme emerging from a 'naturalizing' perspective on poverty is one that stresses cultural difference: a group's lifestyle, socialization patterns, habits, values and attitudes are seen as adequate in the immediate environment, understood to have developed in ways most appropriate for that environment. A strong adherence to such a point of view might imply that no intervention at all in the lives of the poor is indicated (recall those romanticized assessments of the strength and vigor of working-class life). However, the obvious facts of group contact, and the obvious advantages of moving *beyond* immediate environments, mean that the proponents of a 'difference' view can logically support interventions aimed at extending the range of opportunities open to the poor, without condemning what they already possess, or do.

In the next two chapters, I will flesh out this introductory overview, largely by presenting something of the history and development of scholarly conceptions of 'disadvantage' (see also Edwards, 1989). It is always useful to come to grips with the bases of important arguments; as well, an historical summary makes particular sense here because the broad themes have remained remarkably unaltered since they were first formally presented in the literature (Edwards, 1999a). The most important and the most controversial research arguments about disadvantage were made some time ago, and this is why some of the references in what follows may seem a little dated. Although the scholarly caravan may have moved on, however, from discussions of biological or environmental inferiority, it would be naïve to think that such perspectives have disappeared. Some variants remain very powerful indeed. More reason, then, to try and understand some of the underpinnings.

Notes

1. See my very short piece on the connotation of guilt-by-association that 'disadvantage' came to have (Edwards, 1981).

    Corson (2001) uses the term 'disadvantage' at various points in his useful treatment of language diversity at school (i.e. Corson, 2001: 54, 80, 126) – although you will search for it in vain in the index. A very recent treatment of the plight of one group of black people in America (Edelman *et al.*, 2006) is entitled *Reconnecting Disadvantaged Young Men* (recent statistics concerning black unemployment, poverty and incarceration are given in Smitherman, 2006). In his new book on 'urban language', Rampton (2006) also uses the term in several places.

    Given the general demise of the term 'disadvantage', it is interesting that Coulmas (2005: 27) notes that the evolving category of 'social class' is no longer adequately captured by traditional labels (upper class, middle class, lower class, and their sub-divisions) and that some would jettison the term 'class' – and talk instead of 'social mobility' and 'social deprivation'. *Plus ça change*, and all that.

2. The work of Kellaghan and his colleagues at the Educational Research Centre in Dublin has for long been central (see also Archer & Edwards, 1982; Edwards, 1974; Kellaghan, 1977). A new report by Archer and Weir (2004) provides a valuable survey, focusing particularly upon a number of factors central to any effective intervention in disadvantage: beyond some familiar elements (pre-school provisions, parental involvement, etc.), attention is paid to some of the newer insights I touch upon in this section – alterations to school organization that will more accurately reflect what children first 'bring with them', for example, or coordinated linkages among relevant community agencies.

3. The late philosopher was quite capable of unnecessary obscurity. Thus, Bourdieu (1989: 59) described his notion of 'habitus' (which simply means the whole environment – physical, social, psychological – of an individual, with all its combinations of various species of 'capital', with all its possibilities and limitations) as 'a system of dispositions common to all products of the same conditionings'. In the same book, Bourdieu (1989: 60) also pointed to

    > the singular habitus of the [group] members... united in a relation of homology, that is, of diversity within homogeneity reflecting the diversity within homogeneity characteristic of their social conditions of production. Each individual system of dispositions is a structural variant of the others, expressing the singularity of its own position within the [group] and its trajectory.

    Bourdieu is far from the worst offender with this sort of bafflegab. When not being obscure, he veers to the other extreme: 'my work consists in saying that people are located in a social space, that they aren't just anywhere' (p. 50). Who would have thought it? 'Orwell! thou shouldst be living at this hour'.

Bourdieu's work does, however, have the inestimable advantage of being sufficiently elastic to prop up all sorts of arguments, in all sorts of arenas. I note, for example, that Corson (2001), citing Labov, Bernstein and Bourdieu as the three pivotal theorists in debates about nonstandard language, draws particular links between the last two – we can now understand the 'codes' as illustrations of variation in 'cultural capital'.

Chapter 4
Disadvantage: The Genetic Case

Introduction

Disadvantaged children's characteristic ways of dealing with the world often appear inappropriate or, at least, ineffective, in social arenas where different values and behavior are found and encouraged. Could differences here imply real deficits? Could we say that some varieties of knowledge, skill and attitude are inherently better than others? With its assertion that the underpinnings of disadvantage are ones of difference, and not of either environmental or genetic deficiency, the previous overview has anticipated the answers to these questions. But meaningful assertions require evidence, which is why – in this chapter and the next – I shall go into some detail about deficit arguments and their flaws. (This discussion will also frame the subsequent and more specific treatment of the relationship between language and disadvantage.) I turn first to genetic matters.

An appropriate introduction here involves the realization that any meaningful argument about group variation – between black and white populations, for instance – must rest upon firm definitional footings. Over the last two or three generations, not only have political considerations made discussion of genetic differentiation disreputable, the scientific community has increasingly rejected the very idea of different human 'races' (see Aldhous, 2002; Ossorio & Duster, 2005). Schwartz's (2001) characterization of race as a 'biologically meaningless' concept may be taken as typical here. However, a recent special issue of *Nature Genetics* (2004) shows that the matter is hardly a settled one. Some contributors argue, like Schwartz, that human 'racial' categories are not discrete, and are essentially socially defined, but others claim that obvious markers (skin color, hair formation and so on) suggest a small number of basic classifications. Furthermore, developments in our knowledge of matters at the level of DNA – that is, at the level of the human genome – make the picture more interesting still; for some critical comments about what might be termed the sociology of this new genetic research, see Carter (2007) and Tutton (2007). On this most elemental dimension, human beings show very little genetic variation. Ossorio and

Duster (2005: 117) note that 'any two unrelated persons, chosen at random from across the globe, are 99.9% identical in their nucleotide sequences [i.e. their DNA]'. An intriguing elucidation of what this might mean has just become available: reports in *Nature* by the 'Chimpanzee' research group (2005) show that the human and the chimpanzee genome may overlap by as much as 99%. Now, since we are very different from chimps, the other 1% (representing many million points of difference between the two genome codes) obviously remains of incredible importance; this, in turn, suggests that, given the existence of three billion DNA 'building blocks', an 'inter-human' difference only a tenth as large could still mean considerable variability.

While the scientific effort continues, social interpretations continue to demonstrate confusion and uneasiness with 'racial' classifications. For a bureaucratic example here, consider that the forms for many American federal granting agencies continue to ask applicants to indicate their race. The five current categories are American Indian or Alaskan Native, Black or African American, Asian, Native Hawaiian or Other Pacific Islander, and White (there are, in addition, two 'ethnic' classifications: Hispanic or Latino, and – rationally enough, if not very elegantly – Not Hispanic or Latino). But, as Washington's Office of Management and Budget (2005) makes clear (and these words appear on many of the application forms themselves):

> This classification provides a minimum standard for maintaining, collecting, and presenting data on race and ethnicity for all Federal reporting purposes. The categories in this classification are social-political constructs and should not be interpreted as being scientific or anthropological in nature.

Laversuch (2005, 2007) provides a comprehensive historical account of the 'racial terminology' used in the American census to describe African Americans and others. Applicants requesting official largesse in other countries (Britain, for example) may also be required to provide ancestral information nowadays, but the appropriate check-boxes are not accompanied by any social-political qualifiers.

An illustrative, if rather Pythonesque, situation recently occurred in another part of America. One-fifth of the entry-level places at the *Universidade de Brasília* is reserved for black candidates and about 4000 hopeful students identified themselves as black in 2004. They were required to supply photographs, which a six-person commission (one student, two social scientists and three representatives of the country's black political organization – the *Movimento Negro Unificado*) then inspected. Their job was to decide if the applicant was really black, and more than 200 people were rejected. Some three dozen of these lodged complaints and were interviewed (by another committee). Did they have links to 'black culture'? Were they members of the *movimento*? Did they have any *mulatta* girlfriends?

This might all seem very odd, in a '*mestizo* republic where racial identity was, in the formal sense, immaterial', according to Fry (2005: 26), who should, of course, have used the Portuguese word *mestiço* here. Indeed, precisely because there is so much mixing and, consequently, such wide variation in skin color, Brazil is often thought of as a society in which the racism still prevalent elsewhere is much reduced. Many years ago, however, a colleague of mine from São Paulo told me that the fine gradations of color simply translated into fine gradations of prejudice. Recent visitors may be seduced by the immediacy of the *favelas* of Rio de Janeiro that contribute to its 'reputation as a socially liberated Mecca' (Greenberg, 2005); and the 'constant, thrilling collision of the different social classes' on Rio's streets may reinforce the Brazilian 'myth of racial democracy', but the extreme disparity between haves and have-nots 'runs along racial lines'. In his review of a Brazilian study by Telles (2004), Fry confirms the point: 'Telles's data', he says, show that 'the lighter you are the better'. Daniel's (2006) comparison of race and color matters in Brazil and the USA is also relevant here.

These rather more accurate perceptions of Brazilian society were confirmed, in late 2005, when a dramatic discovery was made in Rio de Janeiro. A residential renovation project uncovered a long-lost burial ground for African slaves: the *Cemitério dos Pretos Novos* (the Cemetery of New Blacks). Containing about 20,000 bodies interred between 1770 and 1830, this cemetery is much larger than the now well-known African Burial Ground that was revealed during construction in Manhattan in 1991, a site containing the remains of some 500 American slaves and free Blacks. The Brazilian discovery was widely publicized, and several important facts emerged. Brazil was the single biggest new-world market for slaves, taking about half of the ten million people who suffered the infamous 'middle passage'. The *cemitério* grew on the site of the main slave market that had been moved from the town center to the unhealthy coastal marshlands of the Gamboa district. The shameful treatment of slaves – both the living and the dead – has been described as Brazil's holocaust, and it would appear that the treatment of their descendants still leaves much to be desired. In Brazil today, where almost half of the 190 million citizens are black or of mixed racial background, a recent United Nations Development Program report has provided yet further confirmation here: 'the data merely corroborate what is already visible to any observer: the farther one goes up... the power hierarchy, the whiter Brazilian society becomes' (see Muello, 2005). A quirky but interesting paper by Edmonds (2007) discusses how perceptions of race and beauty reveal themselves in the flourishing Brazilian plastic-surgery business. To undergo expensive cosmetic intervention – to alter a 'negroid nose', for instance, or an 'ugly' Indian body – is surely to give very tangible proof of a socio-racial hierarchy.

In his famous and much-reprinted book on rich and poor, urban and rural, separate and mixed, Gilberto Freyre (1936) argued that hybridity and cultural miscegenation were the touchstones of Brazilian society and its greatest strength, a mixing characterized by a 'reciprocity between the cultures, and not a domination of one by the other' (Philippou, 2005: 252). This is surely an inaccurate, if socially desirable, assessment; further, it is possible that Freyre's advocacy of racial equality in a society unwilling to fully embrace it may have actually reinforced what Skidmore (1974) later called 'the whitening ideal' in Brazil. In any event – to return to the *universidade* – there is surely a poignancy in the existence of an affirmative-action policy that would be out of place and, indeed, unnecessary in a truly *mestiço* society; see also Campos de Souza and Nascimento (2008).

Finally, thinking about 'racial' mixing reminds me of an anecdote recounted by Ernst Mayr, the famous evolutionary biologist; it concerns a journalist who travels to Haiti and interviews the president:

> Most indiscreetly the American newspaperman asked the President what percentage of the people were white. And the President of Haiti said, "Oh, about 95 per cent." The American newspaperman looked a little puzzled and said, "Well, how do you define white?" And the President of Haiti said, "How do you define colored?" And the American newspaperman said, "Well, of course, anybody with Negro blood is colored." Said the President: "Well, that's exactly our definition, too: anybody with white blood is white." (Mayr, 1968: 104)

The Genetic Case for Disadvantage

Eugenics and the roots of assessment

Historically, biological determinism has been the most pervasive of 'scientific' accounts for group disadvantage. It has always been a central feature of racist discourse that some groups are inferior to others, a perception that has led to a wide variety of actions, ranging from general paternalism, to Rainwater's notion of 'benign' interventionism, to considerably less innocuous actions. Some have argued that it is anachronistic to consider Victorian eugenicists – like Francis Galton, who coined the term 'eugenics' (see his *Inquiries*, 1883) – as racist in the modern sense of the term; their principles were based upon the science of the day, and they ought not to be thought of as some scholarly lynch mob. Galton himself apparently began to think about eugenics in mid-century, focusing on the concept in his 1869 book on 'hereditary genius'. The word 'eugenics' suggests 'well born' (Galton's own synonym was 'good in stock') and he referred to the practice as the 'science of improving stock'. In all this, he and his colleagues were following a very ancient line: selective breeding and informed interference with procreation have been discussed (at least) in virtually all societies.[1]

The zeal with which Galton and others pursued these matters, an enthusiasm that also animated later assessors of intelligence – those who saw the measurement of IQ as a useful screening device to maintain racial 'standards', and so on – has quite an evangelical aura. Indeed, in his 1869 book, Galton wrote about a 'religious duty' to practice eugenics, and Karl Pearson (his 'statistical heir') wrote about the new Galtonian 'religion' in his adulatory biography. The religious connection has been most carefully explored by White (2005, 2006a, 2006b), and Higham (1955: 150) refers to Galton's eugenics as a sort of 'secular religion'. There is, as White has pointed out, a strong streak of puritanism in Galton and his epigones, a Calvinism that consigns everyone to a predetermined fate. In fact, he bluntly states that 'all the early psychologists of intelligence had puritan family roots' (White, 2005: 428); while, at the end of his piece, he acknowledges that the correlation could be coincidental, he clearly feels that it is not.

White (2006b) also considers some of the later luminaries of intelligence assessment. The testing ethos often had religious or quasi-religious underpinnings, in an age in which spiritual motivations were more openly articulated than in our own, where it has nevertheless developed into a highly technical branch of the larger social-scientific exercise. White's glance at Philip Vernon and Hans Eysenck in Britain, and at Arthur Jensen and Richard Herrnstein in America, supports the idea of a generational evolution away from the puritanism of the past. Perhaps, however, it is not too far-fetched to see in the work of such researchers some new secularized form of devotion – a zealous scientism, perhaps. In any event, if we take into even minimal account the tenor of the (Victorian) times and the early years of the 20th century, concerns for knowledge, for advancement and – above all – for human 'betterment', can be clearly seen as central factors in that muscular Christian zeal that maintained an empire and created the new transatlantic colossus.

Galton had strong Quaker roots, as did his biographer and acolyte, Pearson. In America, Henry Goddard (1912) – the author of the famous investigation into the feeble-minded Kallikak family – was a Quaker, and Lewis Terman had a puritan background. Cyril Burt, the educational researcher associated with the Butler Education Act of 1944, and the resulting 'eleven-plus' examination, was of Congregationalist stock. He was also a great admirer of Galton, and White (2006b) reminds us that Burt's father held him (Galton) to be, along with Milton and Darwin, the epitome of the 'ideal man'. (Indeed, as Crook [2007] notes in his work on social Darwinism, there are many interesting connections between the Darwinian inheritance and the eugenics movement.) It is quite clear that the younger Burt shared this view. He was, more directly, a member of the Eugenics Society that Galton had established in 1908. All of this has a particular poignancy because of the revelations that Burt falsified some of his statistical data; see Edwards (1989). Like other puritan denominations, the Congregationalist offshoot of Calvinism was strongly motivated and ambitious, but somewhat restricted in its notions of charity: 'like the Quakers [they tended] to look after their own poor, while being indifferent to poverty in general, seeing it as part of the providential plan' (White, 2005: 431–432). This surely has obvious links with a genetic determinism where intelligence is concerned. Another luminary, William McDougall – an early social psychologist and interpreter of the 'group mind' that was so much a preoccupation at the turn of the (20th) century, and a eugenicist – was from the Dissenting background, which broadly includes Congregationalists and Quakers. A central and common tenet was a devotion to knowledge and, more specifically, to the idea that the material success to which knowledge could lead was a mark of divine approbation.

There were many others of similar description. White notes that linkages between puritanism and intelligence testing are not apparent in all cases, and he admits that there is generally no 'conclusive' evidence that dissenting beliefs influenced educational research. Indeed, some of the observations made by Alfred Binet – whose name became synonymous with intelligence testing – suggest that he may be one of the exceptions. In 1909, he wrote that those who believed intelligence to be an inherited and unalterable quantity demonstrated both a 'brutal pessimism' and scientific inaccuracy; see also Clarke and Clarke (2006). Nonetheless, while there will obviously be exceptions, and while White's scholarly caution is commendable, I think the case for religious zeal underpinning eugenic and assessment interests is compelling. There is, after all, a logic here. A belief that most of human intellectual capacity is a fixed matter, a concern for the efficient classification of human wheat and chaff that 'objective' testing seems to offer, and a sense that the best should be encouraged and the worst restrained – these and related assumptions are ideological rather than scientific in nature, and the ideology in question is clearly religious in origin.

Some have argued that a marriage of Calvinistic conceits and 'scientific' determinism necessarily implies considerably less intervention than Victorian scholars were in fact committed to. If all is predestined, for instance, why bother with education? Thus, in a series of papers in *The New Republic*, Walter Lippmann levelled many criticisms at the eugenics and testing movement; the famous American columnist argued at one point that its influence meant that 'the task of education had given way to the doctrine of predestination and infant damnation' (Lippmann, 1922: 298); see also below. Apart from the fact that arguments about religious predestination are many and nuanced, all the early intelligence testers would have said that, whatever their limitations, people ought to exert themselves as best they could, and other more fortunate souls should feel obliged to assist. Besides, as White (2006b: 48) has noted, 'none of them held that high innate ability is enough on its own. For Galton, one also needs "the habits of self-discipline and industry"... Burt and Terman agreed with him'. So did they all, in fact. Even those espousing a strongly hereditarian position, then, could allow for some environmental fine-tuning. And as well, of course, there were also those divine injunctions relating to industry versus idleness, to making sure that the devil found no work for unemployed hands.

While the evaluators of intelligence naturally measured along a scale, they were always (as White notes) particularly interested in the extremes. Galton argued, for instance, that 'an average man is morally and intellectually an uninteresting being' (Pearson, 1924: 384). The greatest interest will clearly attach to the intelligent élite (who now represent the religious few, the 'elect') and to those at the opposite end of the IQ continuum (who can now stand in for the many, the damned). Naturally, the evaluators themselves were always in the first select group; as for the others, they were 'democracy's ballast, not always useless but always a potential liability' (Terman, 1922: 658).

I began here by noting that the equation of 'Galtonism' with racism has generally been seen as inaccurate. A reassessment by Brookes (2004), however, takes a rather harsh view of Galton, who reiterated his 'racist views' with disturbing frequency. As against the idea that these views were essentially popular ones at the time is the fact that eugenics was not at all a popularly-received notion when it first emerged. Rather, it steadily gained in acceptance as the fin-de-siècle approached, and the economic conditions, the unprecedented patterns of immigration and sincere concerns for mass social welfare all combined to bring it to its zenith during the first third of the 20th century. Making use of primary source material, Lowe's (1979: 297) terse but careful analysis reveals the twin thrusts of the eugenics movement at this time: the assessment of intelligence and 'backwardness' and the 'obsessive concern with racial degeneration' (see also Lowe, 1980). The appeal of the 'self-direction of human evolution' (the motto of a eugenics congress held in New York in 1921) seemed undeniable. It was a very widespread appeal: Adams (1990), McLaren (1990) and Dowbiggin (1997) discuss the eugenics movement in Germany, Brazil, France, Russia, Canada and elsewhere. Societies were established around the world, and the international conferences devoted to the topic were supported and attended by some of the most eminent scientific and political figures of the time. The New York meetings had been preceded by an initial gathering in London in 1912, and a third large assembly took place – also at the Natural History Museum in New York – in 1932. At this last one, the 'problem' of African Americans was at the top of the agenda.

Eugenics and selection in America

Strong connections were naturally forged between the popular and widespread early 20th-century view that some groups were inherently less capable than others, and the burgeoning intelligence-testing movement pioneered by Alfred Binet, Lewis Terman and others. Evaluations of ability in ways now seen as clearly ethnocentric and biased in favor of the social 'mainstream' came to have unfortunate implications in eugenic practice and theory, in the passage of sterilization laws, and in immigration control – the last two being particularly important in America. It surely comes as no surprise to learn that scientific investigations of the period discovered mental deficiency to be especially prevalent among the black population. (As White [2006b] remarks, the testing movement in Britain focused upon class; in America, on race.) Relatedly, many Italian, Polish and Jewish immigrants were classified as feeble-minded compared with their British and northern European counterparts. Thus, the eugenicist Henry Goddard administered versions of the Binet IQ test to immigrants at Ellis Island. The tests were in English. Nonetheless, the results suggested (to the testers) that Jews, Italians and Poles were of feeble intelligence (Slotkin, 2005). In one early administration, Goddard found that 25 out of 30 new Jewish immigrants were feeble-minded: 'we are now getting the poorest of each race', he argued (Portes & Rumbaut, 1996: 197). Goldstein (2006) has recently written about the perceived 'Jewish problem' here, with particularly interesting notes on relationships – real and attributed – between Jews and blacks. More particularly still, he describes the classificational difficulties that the white mainstream associated with the Jews themselves: they were obviously not black, but were they 'white'? It seems an odd question now, but Goldstein shows how caricatured representations of Jews often gave them 'black' lips and hair, and how the presence of Jewish merchants in black neighborhoods was seen to be at once opportunistic and in opposition to white sensibilities. At the same time, more middle-class Jews emulated mainstream values – even to the extent of mounting black-face minstrel shows. Still, if Jews were somehow not fully 'white', they were – anti-semitic cartoons aside – clearly not black. How, then, were they to be understood?

> Growing recognition by white Americans that the Jews defied easy placement into the categories of black and white did not mean that the color line ceased to play a significant role in framing the "Jewish Problem" during the 1920s and 1930s. In fact antisemites in the period between the two wars became preoccupied with understanding the relationship between Jewishness and whiteness. If they could no longer defuse the danger they saw in the Jews by likening them to African Americans, they aimed instead to study, clarify, and expose their role as an unstable element in white society. (Goldstein, 2006: 125–126)

Handlin's classic study of race and nationality in America (1957) remains a fine source on the assessment and the subsequent restriction of immigrants in the first decades of the 20th century. Particularly relevant for my purposes here is his discussion of the influential report of the Immigration Commission (1911) and the later analysis by Laughlin (1923); the latter was supervisor of the Eugenics Records Office (see below), and an associate of the Immigration Restriction League led by Madison Grant (1916) – whose book, *The Passing of the Great Race*, extolled the unique virtues of the 'Nordic pioneers'. In his submission, Laughlin pointed out that 'the foreign-born show an incidence of insanity in the state and federal hospitals 2.85 times higher than that shown by the whole population, which latter are descended largely from older American stock' (see also Portes & Rumbaut, 1996: 162). It is unsurprising to learn, then, that the National Origins Act of 1924 barred much immigration, particularly from Asia and south-eastern Europe. These influential documents fuelled and reinforced the distinction between the desirable 'old' immigration (pre-1880) from northern and western Europe, and the 'new' and inferior variety originating in southern and eastern Europe. Higham's treatments (1975 and, particularly, 1955) also provide insightful overviews here. And a new and very readable book by Bruinius (2006) discusses the eugenic movement, the sterilization campaigns and other aspects of America's 'quest for racial purity'. His analysis of the influence of Harry Laughlin, who was often called as an expert witness in congressional hearings and important court cases dealing with eugenic matters, is particularly interesting; see also Black (2003).

It is important to realize, by the way, that the zeal for better 'selection' was not directed at potential immigrants alone. Rafter's (1988) collection of documents relating to some notable cases of family 'degeneracy' presents the famous Jukes and Kallikaks, as well as the 'hereditary defectives' among the 'Hill Folk' of Massachusetts, the 'Smoky Pilgrims' of Kansas, and others. Deutsch (2009) recounts the story of the 'worst family in America' – the Ishmaels, late 19th-century Indianapolis slum-dwellers who came to symbolize the need for urban eugenics programs; see also the original report on the clan by McCulloch (1888). As part of an excellent treatment of the eugenic 'idea' throughout history, Carlson (2001) also discusses the Ishmaels. A more general treatment of 'the arts and sciences of human inequality' is that of Ewen and Ewen (2006): their survey takes the reader from physiognomy to craniometry, from eugenics to modern sexism and racism. Murdoch (2007) provides yet another 'popular' account of the rise of the American testing movement, from the ideas of Galton, through the testing insights of Binet, and on to the excesses that resulted. Winfield (2007) focuses particularly on the way in which eugenic ideas became reflected in educational theory and practice; she suggests that education, as an arm of the larger society, continues to unfairly impose sorting-out procedures on its charges. Perhaps, she notes, 'our "at-risk" students today were the "imbeciles" and "defectives" of yesterday' (Winfield, 2007: 159).

Winfield began her account, incidentally, by reminding readers that, in *Mein Kampf*, Hitler outlines the modelling of his racist plans on the provisions and thrust of American legislation of the 1920s (see also the earlier essay by Crook, 2002). Indeed, Hitler was particularly appreciative of Grant's work, writing to the author and referring to his book as a 'bible'. Many writers have pointed to the lessons that the Nazis learned about the implementation of 'eugenic' ideas from the American experience; Black (2003) and Bruinius (2006) provide quite thorough treatments here. Roberts (2008) discusses eugenics and its Nazi implications as part of his new monograph on historical views of human beings as animals. Baum (2006) charts the rise of the idea of a Caucasian 'race'; along the way, he presents useful information about the inevitable consequences: conceptions of racial superiority and inferiority, eugenic movements, restrictions on immigration, and so on.

While attention to the domestic population actually preceded that given to newcomers, comparison soon began to be made. In 1855, Edward Jarvis had found that the proportion of immigrants in lunatic asylums in Massachusetts was greater than that of the native population, the ratio being about 5:4. Jarvis's study is notable for two reasons: it was the first American work to consider the relationship between immigration and mental illness, and it demonstrated that poverty was the mediating variable. That is, since there were proportionally more poor immigrants than poor natives, and since asylum inmates tended to be paupers, then it was to be expected that one would find more institutionalized immigrants than their overall population numbers would suggest. This second feature of Jarvis's work is of great importance, for it refuted any simplistic correlation between being foreign and being mentally ill. And yet, for many years afterwards, xenophobia and racism, coupled with eugenic enthusiasms, neglected this all-important clarification in favor of a more brutal and more direct correlation between immigration and feeble-mindedness. Thus, other studies of 'settled' immigrants that found apparently higher rates of mental illness often attributed these to 'psychopathic tendencies in the constitution of those who emigrate' (Portes & Rumbaut, 1996: 163). Rare indeed was the enquiry that gave any consideration to traumas of upheaval and relocation, or to the fact that new-world experiences were often less than favorable.

Several recent overviews have illuminated the impact of eugenic thinking on American programs meant to screen – and, in some instances, to compulsorily sterilize – the 'feeble-minded'. Kline (2001) demonstrates the broader social conceptions of sexuality and morality at work here (conceptions that we have seen probed in recent debates over human cloning). Stern (2005) focuses on the eugenics movement in California, where more than one-quarter of all involuntary American sterilizations occurred, and one of her chapters discusses 'quarantine and eugenic gatekeeping' along the border with Mexico. Molina (2006) investigates the negative public-health attitudes towards immigrants in Los Angeles: the Chinese were 'interlopers in the land of sunshine' (p. 15), the Mexicans were 'a diseased, charity-seeking group' (p. 136), the Japanese were 'ignorant, uncultured and half civilized' (p. 57). They were all representative of the 'vast masses of peasantry, degraded below our utmost conceptions... [with] no history behind them... beaten men from beaten races, representing the worst failures in the struggle for existence' (Walker, 1896: 828; see also Black, 2003; Bruinius, 2006).

All of this work was expedited by the rapid development of a reliance upon testing that has hardly abated since. Giordano (2005) provides an admirable overview of the growth of educational testing, remarking upon the racialized assumptions and underpinnings of many tests for immigrant and black populations. The zeal for assessment, the prejudiced and ill-formed judgments that drove it and gave it its shape, and the unfortunate consequences for those many individuals whose potentials and achievements were never given a fair opportunity to reveal themselves – these coincided with at least some scholarly concern. The famous Edwin Boring, for example, was able to point out as early as 1923 that intelligence is what intelligence tests test. While Boring intended to warn against a sterile and static circularity, it is interesting to consider that the statement could *also* be taken as an endorsement of the validity of existing measures of intelligence. The journalist – and inventor of the word 'stereotype' – Walter Lippmann (1922) deserves some credit for taking on proponents of testing and subjecting their flawed and incomplete thinking to criticisms that sound quite modern: 'intelligence' tests are generally nothing of the kind, they can be adapted to suit many purposes, they are not (what we would now call) 'culture-fair', they often build upon unproven assumptions about the relative importance of heredity and environment, and so on (see Block & Dworkin, 1976; Giordano, 2005); Pastore (1978) provides a commentary on Lippmann's writings. For an excellent overview of the evolution of intelligence testing, from Galton to Jensen, see Wickett (1990); for an historical consideration going back to the Greeks, Spearman's (1937) dated but still very informative work is recommended.

Louis Marshall, one of the founders of the American Jewish Committee, also pointed to the flaws in test methodology and administration, as well as to the pseudo-science, hypocrisy and racism that underpinned the whole enterprise. But the popular tide was running fast against the critics. This was, after all, an age in which one president (Harding) was popularly (but probably inaccurately) thought to be a member of the Ku Klux Klan, while another (Wilson) had 'rationalized the vigilantism of the KKK as a necessary counter to Black Reconstruction' (Slotkin, 2005: 220). In fact, as a testament to his friendship with D.W. Griffith, whose 1915 film, *The Birth of a Nation*, extolled the KKK, Wilson provided a quotation used in the film: 'The white men were roused by a mere instinct of self-preservation... until at last there had sprung into existence a great Ku Klux Klan, a veritable empire of the South, to protect the Southern country' (the line is apparently taken from Wilson, 1902).

It is interesting to consider that the American zeal for intelligence testing, initially built upon the Binet-Simon tests imported from France, was not matched in France itself. As Schneider (1992) has pointed out, the anglophone practice – obsession might be a better word – of trying to reduce intelligence to a single (IQ) number was considered too much of a blunt instrument there. But in Britain and America (particularly the latter), the intelligence-testing movement of the early 20th century was part and parcel of the growth of psychology itself (Samelson, 1977; and sociology, too – see Carter, 2000). In his doctoral thesis, Terman (1906) had said that the discipline needed more intimate connections with 'real life', and the heightened recognition it received (among psychologists conducting and assessing military intelligence-testing, for example) was a welcome development for the fledgling (social) science. A consequence, as Samelson (1978) pointed out a little later, was that psychology very soon found itself in the rather embarrassing position of having to shake off this powerful early reinforcement of its scholarly status: 'in 1920, most psychologists believed in the existence of mental differences between [sic] races; by 1940, they were searching for the sources of "irrational prejudice"' (Samelson, 1978: 265).

The unrelenting drive for evaluation and selection through standardized testing procedures was greatly reinforced and stimulated by similar trends in the Army. As Chapman (1988) notes, the American Army versions of the French (Binet-Simon) intelligence test – prepared by Lewis Terman and Arthur Otis (his student) – were to be further revised after the war for use in schools. The famous military 'Alpha' and 'Beta' intelligence tests were aimed at 'men who read and write English' (the Alpha form) and for 'foreigners and illiterates' (Beta). They were meant to serve a dual purpose: on the one hand, the Army wanted to know something of the competence of all those flooding into the service; on the other, the information gained was to be of use to those supporting the work of the Immigration Restriction League (founded in 1894 and, as already noted, subsequently led by Madison Grant) in its advocacy of literacy requirements for immigrants. But, of course, the not-so-hidden agenda was to encourage the arrival of 'Nordic' immigrants, and discourage that of others, particularly southern Europeans. The Army tests were flawed in basic construction. For example, they tested American 'cultural' knowledge that would have been 'familiar to English-speaking middle-class urban whites, but [not]... to non-English speakers and to blacks and whites from rural districts' (Slotkin, 2005: 229). As well, they were administered to large groups, not individuals, in a bewilderingly different variety of settings, they were scored by unqualified enlisted men, and so on. And yet, poor performance on these deficient tests was still ascribed to innate deficiency, and not to inadequacies in culturally specific areas. Thus, the Army tests, themselves built upon earlier exercises aimed at pre-war immigrants, now also served post-war purposes of immigration restriction.

The results of testing 2 million soldiers, 'many of whom were foreign born and illiterate' (Portes & Rumbaut, 1996: 197), firmly reinforced the nativist tendencies flourishing in psychological, educational (and many other) circles. Brigham (1923: 194) argued that 'the representatives of the Alpine and Mediterranean races in our immigration are intellectually inferior to the representatives of the Nordic race', and Kirkpatrick (1926: 2) added that innate deficiencies meant that no amount of 'Americanisation' could turn immigrants into 'intelligent American citizens capable of appropriating and advancing a complex culture' (see also Gould, 1981).

It seems bizarre that people could be tested in a language other than their own, about a culture with which they were unfamiliar, and that their shortcomings would then be attributed to genetic inferiorities. But we must remember that the tests were designed and administered in a context in which nativist minds were already made up. What was wanted was some 'scientific' justification for positions already taken. There were many psycho-educational traps awaiting unwanted immigrants, and a telling example of how difficult these were to avoid is found in Sandiford and Kerr's (1926) study of Chinese and Japanese children in Vancouver. The investigators found that their measured intelligence scores were well *above* those of their white schoolmates, and admitted that the two groups were the most intelligent residents of British Columbia. The prevalent arguments that it was the weakest who left home and became immigrants seemed unsustainable in this case, and so the authors took the other tack: it is the clever, resourceful and courageous ones who emigrate. Now, if feeble-minded immigrants are a burden to their new communities, surely clever ones enhance them?

Unfortunately, no: 'the presence of so many clever, industrious and frugal aliens, capable... of competing successfully with the native whites... constitutes a political and economic problem of the greatest importance' (Sandiford & Kerr, 1926: 365). Could there be a clearer illustration of the heads-I-win-tails-you-lose equation?[2]

As conflicts generally do, the 1914–1918 war highlighted many existing tendencies. For example, the American black troops serving in France often found an acceptance from their French counterparts there, as well as from civilians, that they were denied at home. This could not be allowed to continue and so, in early August 1918, one Colonel Linard – a French liaison officer with the Americans – issued a statement entitled 'Secret Information Concerning the Black American Troops'. This was published the following year in *The Crisis*, a black civil-rights magazine founded in 1910 by William Du Bois (see Linard, 1919). The statement has sometimes been attributed to General John 'Black Jack' Pershing, the commander of the American Expeditionary Force. This is mistaken, but Linard's observations did have the blessing of Pershing and his staff. Directed towards French officers, the short statement pointed out that intimacy between the French and the black American troops must be prevented, the latter must not be commended too highly ('particularly in the presence of white Americans'), and the 'native population' must refrain from 'spoiling the Negroes'. Above all, Linard told his readers, 'the black man is regarded by the white American as an inferior being'. The racist attitudes animating the whole exercise were not so much kindled by black-white fraternization in France as much as by the unwelcomed consequences of acceptance once the black soldiers returned home. After all, 'an experience of "undue social mixing" in France would undo the lifelong lessons inculcated by Jim Crow' (Slotkin, 2005: 255).

It is interesting – but perhaps not very surprising – to note that the Germans were vigorously 'reinterpreted' during the war. Henry Osborn, a Columbia University professor, argued that 'Prussian ferocity' derived from their Mongol ancestry (they were Huns, after all). Previous assessments that had classified the Germans as true Teutons would, of course, position them too closely to those favored 'Nordic' immigrants. No, they were essentially Asiatics, 'wild Tartars... most ancient savages of the steppes' (Slotkin, 2005: 217). The next step is not difficult to predict: Germans were associated with 'Negroes'. Slotkin's book includes a poster showing a slavering ape holding a club in one hand (labelled 'Kultur') and a swooning white woman in the other. This 'black Hun' has just stepped onto the shores of America, and the image is captioned, 'Destroy This Mad Brute: Enlist'.

Professor Osborn was hardly the only Ivy League scholar to quickly succumb to war fever. Recalling his student days at Harvard during the First World War, John Dos Passos (1963: 77) recounts his astonishment at how the professors,

> most of them rational New Englanders brought up in the broad-minded pragmatism of William James or in the lyric idealism of Ralph Waldo Emerson, allowed their mental processes to be so transformed by their conviction of the rightness of the Allied cause and the wickedness of the German enemy, that many of them remained narrow bigots for the rest of their lives.

As I have noted, eugenic points of view became more and more widespread. They appealed to many – perhaps most – politicians and social commentators of various stripes. Among the latter can be counted H.G. Wells and George Bernard Shaw. And, writing to the Prime Minister in 1910, Winston Churchill (as home secretary) argued that sterilization would check the 'unnatural and increasingly rapid growth of the feeble-minded and insane classes', something that 'constitutes a national and race danger which it is impossible to exaggerate' (Ponting, 1994: 100). In a letter to a prominent eugenicist, in 1913, Theodore Roosevelt made a similar observation:

> I agree with you if you mean, as I suppose you do, that society has no business to permit degenerates to reproduce their kind. It is really extraordinary that our people refuse to apply to human beings such elementary knowledge as every successful farmer is obliged to apply to his own stock breeding... we have no business to permit the perpetuation of citizens of the wrong type. (Bruinius, 2006: 190–191)

Grant (1916: 45), whose book I have mentioned above, proclaimed that 'the laws of nature require the obliteration of the unfit, and human life is valuable only when it is of use to the community or race'. The fact that, as late as 1916, Grant was able to write the following paragraph is an interesting indication – not only of widespread prejudice, but also of what it was considered acceptable to put in writing:

> The native American has always found, and finds now, in the black men, willing followers who ask only to obey and to further the ideals and wishes of the master race, without trying to inject into the body politic their own views, whether racial, religious, or social. Negroes

are never socialists or labor unionists, and as long as the dominant imposes its will on the servient race, and as long as they remain in the same relation to the whites as in the past, the negroes will be a valuable element in the community, but once raised to social equality their influence will be destructive to themselves and to the whites. If the purity of the two races is to be maintained, they cannot continue to live side by side, and this is a problem from which there can be no escape. (Grant, 1916: 78–79; see also Brace [2005] for useful notes on Grant and other prominent figures)

Grant's book sold in the millions, and was widely translated – most notably into German. While scholars frequently attacked his ideas, Grant had many academic supporters, including the noted biologist, Charles Davenport. The two collaborated to found the Galton Society in 1918; earlier, Davenport had established the Eugenics Record Office, under-written by the Carnegie Institution, and published his own very popular book on heredity and eugenics (Davenport, 1911). In retrospect, the efforts of eugenicists like Davenport and Grant can be seen as the last scientific (or, rather, quasi-scientific) gasp of a once-respectable (or quasi-respectable) set of assumptions. Of course, their passing from the academic scene hardly signified anything like a full and final disap-pearance. If more culturally sensitive sociologies and anthropologies were gaining strength, if the scientific bases of most eugenic arguments were increasingly seen to be flawed or non-existent, and if the attention given to lay commentators (like Grant) was increasingly challenged by that accorded to real scientific authorities – well, we must not imagine that victories were either swift or complete.

In his decision in a famous Supreme Court case about involuntary sterilization, Justice Oliver Wendell Holmes wrote, in 1927:

We have seen more than once that the public welfare may call upon the best citizens for their lives. It would be strange if it could not call upon those who already sap the strength of the State for these lesser sacrifices, often not felt to be such by those concerned, in order to prevent our being swamped with incompetence. It is better for all the world, if instead of waiting to execute degenerate offspring for crime, or to let them starve for their imbecility, society can prevent those who are manifestly unfit from continuing their kind. The principle that sustains compulsory vaccination is broad enough to cover cutting the Fallopian tubes... three generations of imbeciles are enough. (Laughlin, 1930: 52)

Finally here, early 20th-century assessments of feeble-mindedness and general incompetence also implicated language: a study by Goodenough (1926: 393), for example, concluded that 'the use of a foreign language in the home is one of the chief factors in producing mental retardation'. Similarly, Smith (1939) concluded, on the basis of her work with children in Hawaii, that attempts to use two languages hindered development. In his classic *Languages in Contact*, Weinreich (1953) summarized a history of such misinformation, presenting a long list of disorders associated with bilingualism: moral depravity, stuttering, left-handedness, idleness and excessive materialism are among the more bizarre items on the list. And Flores (2005) has recently summarized the matter for the Mexican-American population, a large and important constituency both then and now.

Contemporary manifestations

The ultimate excesses of the biological view became evident during the Second World War and these, together with other genocides of the 20th century, have made assumptions of innate inferiority rather less acceptable. Or so it might seem. There continue, for example, to be supporters of eugenic interventions, some of them quite notable. In 1970, William Shockley, a Nobel Prize winner in physics and the founder of 'Silicon Valley', argued that such measures might be useful in countering the alleged decline in American intelligence. He was very much caught up in Jensenist assertions that intelligence could be accurately ascertained and that certain steps might follow; see below. At one point, Shockley suggested financial compensation for black Americans willing to undergo sterilization (see Shurkin, 2006).

Much more commonly, however, we find that public disapproval has done little more than to drive racist assumptions underground, to make their expression less overt. In some important work, Jones and his colleagues (Jones & Sigall, 1971; Sigall & Page, 1971) led people to think that their attitudes could be accurately measured by machine. When they were asked to *verbally* express the opinions that they now believed were also being electronically monitored, some depressingly familiar perceptions were revealed. Indeed, there was a partial re-emergence of prejudices that had been expressed openly in attitude studies of the 1920s and 1930s, prejudices that had become socially unacceptable since then. The general argument made by the researchers was that 'socially desirable' responses disappear or become attenuated in settings where there seems to be no point in deception (a recent overview is provided by Plant *et al.*, 2003).

Racist actions remain a grievous social problem in many contexts, and the studies just cited suggest that the attitudes from which they stem may linger behind politically correct masks; and Smedley and Smedley (2005) point out that while 'race' itself may be a 'biological fiction', racism is real. Within post-war educated circles, however, respectable (or pseudo-respectable) arguments for innate genetic deficiency largely languished until Arthur Jensen proposed that American blacks were indeed below the intelligence levels of normal whites. In his well-known paper in the *Harvard Educational Review*, Jensen (1969) proposed that compensatory education for black children had failed, largely because its proponents had ignored genetic social-class and racial differences. Programs of compensatory education were (and sometimes still are) built upon the assumption that group differences in achievement and intelligence test performance are traceable to environmental causes, and so a simple and immediate response to Jensen's paper was that it espoused a racist view of society.

Over the ensuing 40 years, there have been recurrent academic arguments about innate intellectual inferiority. The controversy ignited by 'Jensenism' was repeated a quarter of a century later, when Herrnstein and Murray (1994) published *The Bell Curve* (see also Herrnstein, 1971, 1973). Some of the heat – and there often is more heat than light in such highly charged arenas, even among supposedly disinterested scholars – can be gauged by looking at Gould's (1994) spirited rebuttal; see also his earlier monograph on the measurement of intelligence (Gould, 1981), its post-*Bell Curve* revision (1996), and the collections edited by Jacoby and Glauberman (1995) and Fraser (1995) – both with further contributions by Gould. Beyond stimuli provided by further scientific advance, as with the human genome projects (noted above), resurfacings of the genetic thesis at less enlightened levels are as predictable as the vehement responses they evoke. They can be expected, in fact, whenever scapegoats are needed, whenever political conservatism is regnant, whenever liberal forces argue for renewed financial and social attention to poverty and oppression.

Nonetheless, the accusations of racism *tout court* routinely levelled at genetic theorists are often over-simplifications. Besides being the first contemporary research-based argument for important group variation in inherited capabilities, Jensen's thesis also provides the clearest evidence here. In 1967, he argued that 'low-average IQ' could not be seen as 'evidence of poor genetic potential' (Jensen, 1967: 10); in 1968, he acknowledged that there was 'little information' about the possibilities of a genetic basis to disadvantage (Jensen, 1968: 22). It was only in the notorious 1969 paper that Jensen came down on the side of a 'genetic hypothesis' (Jensen, 1969: 82; see also Jensen, 1973), although he still considered environmental interactions to be important. Regardless of its correctness, this demonstration of an evolving position is not consistent with a racist perspective, where intellectual stasis is the norm. Jensen can certainly be accused, however, of making ill-considered and inflammatory statements:

> Is there a danger that current welfare policies, unaided by eugenic foresight, could lead to the genetic enslavement of a substantial segment of our population? (Jensen, 1969: 95)

As we have already seen, assessments of inherent intellectual inferiority have generally relied upon intelligence tests and the measurement of IQ differences, and Jensen's investigations were no exceptions. Of course, some tests are clearly biased in favor of certain groups – not all the iniquities of the early 20th-century evaluations of immigrants have gone unremarked – and so Jensen and others have typically tried to avoid measures of highly specific abilities, relying rather upon tests tapping more general mental capacity. Distinctions between specific and general abilities all derive from Spearman's early 20th-century categorizations of intelligence (see Spearman, 1927; Spearman & Wynn Jones, 1950). Since then, many different types and classifications of intelligence have been proposed; for comparisons of different social populations, however, the avoidance of group-specific measures remains the most essential feature.

A basic and insurmountable difficulty remains, however. All tests – no matter how 'culture-free' or 'culture-fair' or 'non-verbal' – are devised at some time, by someone, to measure something. Even if the object is to tap highly abstract, non-verbal intelligence (for example), sociocultural determinations of intelligence cannot be avoided. While tests can obviously be made less directly related to the knowledge and skills available more to one group than to another, even measures of apparently general factors involve assumptions about intelligence that derive from a given set of values. To return to the central actors in this contemporary version of the drama, the argument that black and white children share much that is culturally common, and hence should not be discriminated against by tests of so-called 'general' ability, simply does not come to terms with the degree and subtlety of group differences that may exist.

When it was found that some groups more materially disadvantaged than American blacks outperformed them on non-verbal intelligence tests, Jensen and others claimed this to be a demonstration of the weakness of an environmentalist position. A specific instance was recorded by Hans Eysenck: he observed that the test performance of Inuit children was superior to that of black youngsters, even though the former apparently live under much harsher environmental conditions than the latter; indeed, some Inuit test scores were at or above the norms established for white children. Eysenck (1975: 110) summarized the matter as follows:

> if social and sensory deprivation, or other environmental deprivation factors, are postulated to account for IQ deficits in white working-class or coloured populations, then the logic of the explanation requires absolutely that a severely deprived group, such as the Eskimos [sic], should show evidence of IQ deficit; the fact is that they do not.

In fact, however, all that is demonstrated is the complexity of environmental factors, the difficulty in adequately assessing them, and the danger in simply equating material poverty with educational and social disadvantage; see Taylor and Skanes (1977) for a thoughtful response to Eysenck's assertions. To equate observable and rather gross indices of material deprivation with intellectual disadvantage, when such variables may not in fact be directly relevant, does not make for a strong case. There may exist all sorts of differences in all sorts of groups, such that some will score better than others on any given test, and such differences may or may not be related to poverty of physical environment. It is at least a reasonable assumption, however, that score differences may be related to more specific, less visible variables that exist and operate in the social environment. (In fairness to Jensen, Eysenck and their epigones, it should be acknowledged that the environmentalist position that they attacked *did* often base its arguments largely upon material deprivation; this emphasis, however, was a weakness of the environmentalist stance on disadvantage, not of the explanatory value of the environment per se; see below.)

Attempts have been made to control for environment by matching socioeconomic-status levels across the groups that are to be compared (black and white schoolchildren, for instance), but these cannot be very useful in contexts in which such matching does not really imply environmental equality. In societies where racial prejudice exists, for example, it is obvious that gross similarities in socioeconomic status may only mask the effects of that prejudice; thus, it would be naïve to accept that matching the educational and income levels of blacks and whites in America implied the establishment of environmental equality between them. A generation ago, Walter Bodmer succinctly observed that:

> the question of a possible genetic basis for the race-IQ difference will be almost impossible to answer satisfactorily before the environmental differences between US blacks and whites have been substantially reduced. (Bodmer, 1972: 111)

Given the difficulties, there has been some interest in studies of identical twins. On the surface, they would seem to provide an ideal test-case: since they are genetically identical, any differences found must be attributable to environmental influences. And, since the measured IQs of identical twins raised apart are typically found to be strongly correlated, it might appear that a strong case has been established for the relatively greater importance of nature over nurture. As Donald Hebb (1968) once put it, however, separated twins should be put in maximally different environments to properly test nature-versus-nurture hypotheses: send one of the infants to live in luxury, the other to the slums. This is an ethically unconscionable practice, of course. In fact, in those relatively rare instances in which identical twins have had to be brought up in separate environments, the degree of separation is typically minimized as much as possible.

These are the pivotal points in the genetics 'case', but there are many other interesting ones that I have had to omit in this brief survey. Test 'wiseness' and test motivation, for instance, are not equally distributed across groups; relatedly, the social-psychological and situational factors surrounding the actual administration of tests (who are the testers; where does the testing take place?) have been shown to be very important. There are technical genetic questions about the measurement and influence of heritability within and across groups. And even the high correlations reported between the measured intelligences of identical twins reared apart have been questioned. Colman (1987: 77) provided an excellent overview of the central issues here and, in summarizing them, noted how surprised he was 'to discover how little support, even of the most indirect kind, could be mustered for the hereditarian thesis'.

Arguments have remained controversial over the last several decades, even as they have faded from important segments of the literature. I recall, for example, that when Jensen gave an invited address at the University of Southampton in early 1999, various security measures were still required. In a sense, all of this is quite ironic anyway: if we were to follow the genetics case to its logical conclusion, skipping over some of the difficulties I have identified here, we would find that it has virtually no practical applicability at all! It was the alleged failure of compensatory programs, remember, that first motivated Jensen's attention. On the basis of his investigations, he concluded that alterations in curricular approaches were indicated. Specifically, he recommended instructional adjustments to help those children whose general abilities were of what he termed the 'level 1' variety – whose innate skills, that is to say, were more 'associative' than 'conceptual' (i.e. the more elaborative abilities possessed by 'level 2' individuals). Even on the basis of the summary I have presented here, however, we can see that the isolation of such ability levels can be questioned on the grounds of insufficient sensitivity to environmental nuance and, hence, in terms of gross over-simplification. As well, given that the levels clearly imply marked differences in intellectual capability, variant teaching methods could only serve to pull groups further apart. That is, even if cross-group genetic differences in intelligence were a significant factor to be reckoned with, could we reasonably teach some children in ways that might well downplay the elaborative and transformational skills required for full social participation? Such an approach could surely only be defended for the education of severely sub-normal children whose genetic disabilities are pronounced and obvious.

These are not, of course, the children under discussion and, given that fact, any applicability of the genetic argument evaporates. Measured intelligence differences between black and white children have typically been on the order of 10 to 15 IQ points. If we were to accept that demonstrable group differences do in fact exist, and that these actually reflect something of underlying intelligence, the magnitude of the differences would still be insufficient to cause great problems in the normal classroom; and they would certainly be too minor to warrant differential curricular treatments for the children so clumsily 'levelled'. In a response to Jensen's 1969 paper, Jerome Kagan pointed out that:

> genetic factors are likely to be most predictive of proficiency in mental talents that are extremely difficult to learn... learning to read, write or add are easy skills, well within the competence of all children who do not have serious brain damage... ninety out of every 100 children, black, yellow or white, are capable of adequate mastery of the intellectual requirements of our schools. (Kagan, 1969: 277)

Simply put, the point is this: even allowing the scope of the claims made by the 'nature' proponents (which has obviously not been my intention here), they have no practical relevance. Stephen Wiseman summarized it nicely a generation ago:

> the fierce controversies over the precise proportion of influence exerted by nature as opposed to nurture are of importance to the geneticist and the psychologist, but for the teacher I suggest that they are largely irrelevant. (Wiseman, 1973: 87)

Nonetheless, research on group differences in intelligence is as perennial as the heated reaction it evokes. A very recent example is provided by the investigations of Richard Lynn and Paul Irwing, whose thesis is that men have larger brains and higher IQs than women; this is the reason that men win most of the Nobel prizes and other lofty academic distinctions. A brief report on the work, in the *Times Higher Education Supplement* (2 September 2005; see also Irwing & Lynn, 2005), was accompanied by a piece by Irwing (2005: 12), who argued that it was necessary to analyze and interpret controversial data: 'the consequences of scientists suppressing data because they do not fit in with their preferred ideological world view are disastrous'. This is, of course, the most basic of scientific arguments: researchers must go where the data take them. Jensen made the same argument and, in strictly scientific terms, it is irrefutable. But where the objects of study are human beings, and where the context is one of both historical and contemporary controversy, one must be alive to the possibility that – as Hudson (1973) bluntly observed – investigations may fuel racism and may undercut or bring into question enlightened social response (see also Cronbach, 1975). The potential problems here are exacerbated, of course, when (as we have seen with Jensen) the studies are described or summarized in ill-considered ways, ways that are bound to give offense.

Also in September 2005, a popular Québec television show, *Tout le monde en parle*, presented the views of a psychiatrist who claimed (as a Radio-Canada announcement summarized it) 'que les Noirs et les Autochtones avaient en moyenne un quotient intellectuel inférieure à celui des Blancs'. Radio-Canada (2005) argued that the show is meant to be provocative, and that the management 'estime avoir fait le bon choix en diffusant les propos controversés du Docteur Pierre Mailloux'. The show's host and programming director argued that 'offensive... and hateful discussions should be debated publicly... since they exist in the underground of society, it took only one question [i.e. to Mailloux] to see racism and xenophobia emerge candidly' (Peritz, 2005). The broadcasters certainly knew about Mailloux from previous incidents: he has a 'track record of incendiary remarks'. His comments drew immediate fire from the Broadcast Standards Council, as well as from other interested parties. But Mailloux remained unrepentant: 'de son côté, [il] ne regrette rien des propos qu'il a tenus en entrevue et a répété toute la journée qu'il n'accepte pas que la susceptibilité empéche de parler d'études scientifiques'.

One thing, at least, seems clear, in this alarming and apparently unending cycle: we must not allow hate speech to slip into public discourse under the banner of scientific investigation.

Notes

1. Buss (1976) makes the argument that, in addition to being the father of eugenics, Francis Galton also launched the study of 'individual differences', or 'differential psychology'. His 1883 publication, for example, gave some considerable attention to gender differences. While ever the courteous Victorian gentleman, Galton was – like many other men of the time – rather taken aback by feminist developments. He felt that women had weaker intellects and powers of discrimination, going on to write that:

   > coyness and caprice have in consequence become a heritage of the sex, together with a cohort of allied weaknesses and petty deceits, that men have come to think venial and even amiable in women, but which they would not tolerate among themselves. (Galton, 1883: 39)

   Among many other things, Galton was a committee member of an anti-suffrage society.
2. An earlier example – this time involving indigenous Americans – is found in Stetson's (1897) study of the intelligence of black and white schoolchildren in Washington. His finding that the former outperformed the latter, on the basis of their comprehension and recall of poetry, was unpalatable and unacceptable to him and to others. Revisions of the procedure were immediately suggested. Wiggan (2007) comments on the matter (although his citation for Stetson's paper is inaccurate).

   It is not my purpose here to further discuss the art and science of testing in general, but I should alert the reader to the existence of an important contemporary literature on language testing in particular. The recent books by Spolsky (1995), Shohamy (2001) and McNamara and Roever (2006) are recommended here because their critical overviews are grounded in the appropriate historical and social context.

Chapter 5

Disadvantage: The Environmental Case

Introduction

Jensen is not the only contemporary researcher whose investigations of 'race' and intelligence have proved controversial. In the UK, the views of the late Hans Eysenck were not dissimilar and, in Canada, the work of Philippe Rushton is relevant. In a 1995 book on 'race' and behavior (a book praised by Jensen and Eysenck), Rushton argued for the existence of three races (Orientals, Whites and Blacks) and claimed that the data show the first group to be better socially organized, to show greater sexual restraint and to be more intelligent than Europeans, who, in turn, score higher on such dimensions than Africans and their descendants. It is entirely possible that – as he himself would no doubt claim – Rushton is simply going where he thinks the data lead. He rather blotted his scientific copybook, however, by appearing on Geraldo Rivera's 'trash-television' show in 1989, by speaking at a conference of the American Renaissance organization (a white-separatist group) – which led to a citation on the web-site of Stormfront, a white-supremacist body – and by accepting the presidency of the Pioneer Fund, a research agency whose position on matters of race and eugenics has occasioned much debate. Horowitz (1995) touches upon the important issues, both popular and scientific, that bear upon Rushton's work and, indeed, upon all modern studies of 'race' and intelligence.

The most recent statement by Rushton is that 'black people have lower average IQ scores than white people... we have concluded that genetic factors have a role to play in this difference, as evidenced by the fact that black infants adopted and brought up by white middle-class parents show little improvement in their IQ scores by late adolescence' (Lynn & Rushton, 2006). It would seem that, despite the cautions expressed by Bodmer and other geneticists (see Chapter 4), and despite a great deal of supporting evidence from sociological and psychological investigations, Lynn and Rushton continue to believe that the negative effects of living in societies in which racial prejudice continues its baleful course are substantially countered when black children are raised in white homes. See Brace (2005) for some discussion of these contemporary researchers into 'race'; see also Tucker (1994, 2002) for investigation of the political and financial backing that 'racial research' has had in North America.[1]

Environmental Deficiency

If 'genetic', 'hereditarian' or 'nature' arguments have failed to regain much lost ground in recent times – despite the best efforts of a few psychologists – the idea that some environments lead to substantive intellectual deficiency remains powerful. As Harwood (1982) has observed, it has been the dominant thesis since the mid-20th century, and it is still widely, if inarticulately, believed that certain lifestyles can be emotionally and cognitively crippling. (Remember here that we are discussing an allegedly group-level phenomenon: no one would deny that, in many *individual* instances, early deficiencies – in nutrition, say, or in parent-child attachment – can have tangible, unfavorable and some-times permanent consequences.) A study by Edwards and McKinnon (1987; see also following chapters) clearly demonstrated the continuing power of the disadvantage-as-deficit perspective among teachers. Tea-chers constitute a particularly important population here because they are in the front line, so to say, of educational disadvantage, and because their attitudes and actions can have a significant effect upon their classroom charges. More subtly – and as I remark in Chapter 1 – there is the ever-present danger that, if teachers are not well informed about disadvantage *before* entering the classroom, they may easily be assimi-lated to the prevailing 'deficit' ethos of the existing educational establishment. After all, in finding one's instructional feet, what could be more natural than to adopt the postures and practices of those already in place?

In the environmental-deficit assessment of the major underpinnings of disadvantage, genetic determinants are rejected in favor of contextual factors. Disadvantaged children are seen to arrive at school unprepared for its demands and challenges; their difficulties there and, by extension, in later life, derive largely from the unsatisfactory nature of their early physical, social and psychological background. It is the environmental-deprivation approach to disadvantage that has obviously provided the greatest impetus for compensatory education programs. There are several variants of the environmental position, but all of them assume that deprivations of one sort or another lead to educational and social disadvantage: they differ in explaining just how disadvantage arises.

In an early argument, *sensory deprivation* was thought to be the chief culprit. It has long been known that animals reared in isolation from others, or in severely abnormal social conditions, develop in aberrant and inappropriate ways; if the early conditions are severe enough, recovery becomes impossible. Among human beings too, we know that sensory deprivation (or perceptual isolation) has dramatic consequences. Observations of prisoners in isolation cells and the victims of 'brain-washing' or 'thought reform' are relevant here. The effects can be easily replicated in laboratory conditions. In studies at McGill University during the 1950s, well-paid subjects were required to lie on a bed with no visual, somaesthetic or auditory stimulation: few could endure the monotony for more than a few days, and none for more than six. Hebb (1968: 252) described some of the effects: 'the subjects in isolation complained of being unable to think coherently... they began to have hallucinations... [their] very identity had begun to disintegrate'. Other evidence for the importance of early stimulation derives from studies of institutionalized children who – while receiving adequate physical care – lived in dull and unstimulating quarters, lacking attention and personal contact. In famous work by Skeels and Dye (1939), Spitz (1946) and Dennis (1960), apathy, poor motor and mental performance, developmental retardation and 'anaclitic depression' (whose symptoms include listlessness, withdrawal, susceptibility to illness and anorexia) were documented consequences.

Could, then, the environmental conditions leading to social and educational disadvantage have to do with inadequate stimulation and interpersonal contact? The work of Hunt (1964: 242) was representative here; he argued that the 'effects of cultural deprivation [are]... analogous to the experimentally-found effects of experiential deprivation in infancy' (see also Hunt, 1961, 1975). Any analogy, however, between sensory deprivation in experimental animals and institutionalized children, on the one hand, and the 'cultural deprivation' (i.e. disadvantage) of poor children, on the other, is very weak. Lower-class neighborhoods, for instance, are not at all similar to the orphanages and hospitals studied by those students of anaclitic depression. Comparisons between the 'sensory stimulation' available in lower- and middle-class homes may reveal some interesting differences, but there is little to suggest that the *amount* of stimulation is markedly different. (Indeed, we might suspect that, in many poor surroundings, there is too much stimulation, too little privacy and personal space, and so on.) Any attribution of sensory deprivation to lower-class children, on the basis of work with animals or orphans, has obviously not thought through the implications of the term: 'it has nothing to do with the educational quality [however that might be measured] of the stimuli available, but only with their variety, intensity and patterning' (Bereiter & Engelmann, 1966: 27).

A more thoughtful approach to the environmental underpinnings of disadvantage has held that inadequacies in early socialization practices lead to cognitive and emotional defects in children, defects that then create difficulties at school. A representative opinion was that of Deutsch (1967: 39): 'the lower-class child enters the school situation so poorly prepared to produce what the school demands that initial failures are almost inevitable'. The major thrust of the *sociocultural-deprivation* position was therefore to try and isolate factors in early home environments that might result in the inadequate development of cognitive skills; as noted above, it is easy to see how this environmentalist view of disadvantage directly led to intervention programs of 'enrichment' or compensatory education. Some of the factors seen to suggest remediation include low socioeconomic status, poor material living conditions, and incomplete or dysfunctional families. More psychologically interesting variables include low value placed upon formal education, absence of books at home and poor parent-child interactions (most notably, deficient patterns of mother-child communication). The home environment, in short, is viewed as one of noise, crowding and physical discomfort, one in which children have little opportunity to learn and develop, and where the usual (i.e. middle-class) parental role of tutor and guide is restricted and inadequate. Perceptual, conceptual and verbal deficits are seen as the inevitable consequences.

In this cultural-deprivation stance, the other major category of disadvantaging factors involves the children themselves. They are seen to be more 'activity-orientated', for example, than conceptually motivated. They are allegedly more concerned with the here-and-now, less likely to anticipate or think about the future, and therefore unwilling to delay gratification; the emphasis is upon immediate reward. There is a diminished regard for matters of 'conscience', increased aggression, lowered self-esteem, poor academic motivation and restricted language abilities.

What is wrong with this picture? First, we find that, although many researchers have trumpeted the need to attend closely to details of the disadvantaged lifestyle, gross markers of socioeconomic status have always remained central in discussions of disadvantage; that is, despite the more detailed information available, the main pivot is still the equation of material deprivation with educational disadvantage (see Archer & Edwards, 1982). A second problem involves the presumed characteristics of disadvantage themselves. We should be cautious, for example, in interpreting studies in which aspects of the home life of individuals are discussed: how was such information obtained; does it derive from self-report, or from interviews with parents, children or teachers? Data concerning personal background are clearly important, but it is difficult to obtain and measure them with accuracy; in an early criticism, Gordon (1965) noted that much of the information here was essentially speculation. As in many other areas of social enquiry, carefully designed longitudinal studies would be much preferable to the snapshot investigations that have been vastly more common. Relatedly, in attempting to determine characteristics of the disadvantaged child at school, reliance upon standardized tests and observations may be inadequate, for reasons already touched upon.

Perhaps the most important point here, however – one that relates, at least in part, to the assessment difficulties noted above – is that we do not fully understand the relationship between early environment and the characteristics of disadvantage, nor are we on firm ground when considering possible links between these characteristics and school success (or lack of it). Mere classification and description are not sufficient. How can we account, for example, for the success of many children who live in disadvantaged areas and whose homes are inadequate in material and other ways? Wiseman, whom I have already cited on this matter, points out that 'bad homes and neighbourhoods are more effective in preventing the emergence of brightness than they are in producing backwardness' (Wiseman, 1968: 268). And how do we reconcile the poor academic performance of some immigrant and minority groups with the success of others? Ogbu's discussion of the 'caste-like' status that some – but not all – groups possess is germane here. His central argument is that minority status need not be disadvantaging per se; if, however, a group is downgraded, ignored or oppressed, and if social mobility remains uncertain regardless of achievement, then the stage is set for disadvantaged status (see Ogbu, 1978, 1982a, 1982b). But Ogbu's more nuanced view remains, itself, insufficiently sensitive to intra-group variation, as d'Amato (1987) and Erickson (1987) have demonstrated. The upshot is that finely detailed knowledge of the constituents of educational disadvantage remains incomplete.

In itself, this is not so much a criticism of the environmentalist position in principle as it is the lack of the necessary detail, which that position really requires. An additional point, however, *does* involve a criticism of the environmental-deficit position per se. It is that behind the environmentalist view, as it were, is a profound and overwhelming middle-class bias. Virtually all 'deficits' could be seen as strengths if the immediate context of the disadvantaged child were kept in mind:

> instead of discussing the supposed short-term gratification pattern of the disadvantaged youth... it would be possible to discuss the long-term gratification pattern typical of the middle class, with *its* consequences (e.g. inability to enjoy the present moment, generation of guilt over immediate pleasures...). (Gordon, 1968: 70)

Middle-class hedonism and the impulses of the 'me' generation are perhaps more apparent now than when Gordon wrote, but they add to the thrust of his remarks rather than replacing them outright. It is entirely possible for a prosperous middle class to indulge itself in the present *and* to simultaneously castigate itself for doing so, but it remains the case that, in the perceived absence of a favorable future, a here-and-now hedonism makes good sense for those lower on the social hierarchy.

Thus, a 'poor' conscience, aggressive behavior and other frequently discussed traits can easily be seen as not only appropriate but eminently sensible in certain environments. The general point is not that certain characteristics do not exist, but rather that it is incorrect to view them as substantive deficits, which is the essence of the 'difference' position on disadvantage, to which I now turn.

Environmental Difference

The 'difference' view of disadvantage does not deny that children from the lower classes (for example) perform poorly in school, nor that such children may arrive with different attitudes and values than their middle-class schoolmates. For proponents of this view, however, such differences are just that – differences. Invoking the charge of middle-class bias, difference theorists claim that a sociocultural-deprivation approach unfairly translates difference into deficit. (Some of the most important support for the difference position comes from studies of lower-class language, an area to which I shall turn later.)

As a first point, consider the oddness of the term 'cultural deprivation'. Since it is clearly impossible to describe a group as being deprived of its own culture, the real suggestion here must be that the culture in which certain groups are seen to be deficient is that of the middle class. As already implied, invalid comparisons arise when the norms and standards of one group are applied to the lifestyle of another group, and a forceful rejection was expressed by Keddie (1973: 8):

[cultural deprivation] is a euphemism for saying that working-class and ethnic groups have cultures which are at least dissonant with, if not inferior to, the "mainstream" culture of the society at large.

In their studies of American Indian life, Wax and Wax (1971: 129–130) reported that official evaluations routinely emphasized presumed deficiencies: the home was described as having 'no books, no magazines, radio, television, newspapers – it's empty! . . . the Indian child has such a *meager* experience'.

The researchers aptly referred to this as a 'vacuum ideology', one in which the implied remedy is not so much upon replacing inappropriate skills, attitudes and values as it is upon filling a void. Their concluding paragraph is worth citing here, since it represents well the criticisms made of cultural deprivation (note that, for 'Indian child', we could also read 'black child', 'immigrant child', 'lower-class child', etc.):

> If the Indian child appears as "culturally deprived", it is not because he is lacking in experience or culture, but because the educational agencies are unwilling to recognize the alienness of his culture and the realities of his social world. It is not that the child is deprived of culture, it is that the culture which is associated with his parents is derogated because they are impoverished and powerless. (Wax & Wax, 1971: 138)

If we combine the perspectives of educationalists like Keddie and anthropologists like Wax and Wax, it is easy to understand Persell's (1981) view that cultural-deprivation theories can be just as racist as hereditarian ones. As part of his argument that deficit philosophies are exercises in 'blaming the victim', Ryan (1971) thus noted that it would be more accurate to see schools as 'culturally depriving' institutions than to see children as 'culturally deprived'. Consequently, Ryan (1971: 61) argued that 'the task to be accomplished is not to revise, amend and repair deficient children, but to alter and transform the atmosphere and operations of the schools to which we commit these children'.

The 'difference' view of disadvantage claims that, to the extent to which lower-class society does not resemble that of the middle class, its members will be on a less than equal footing. Since it is assumed that there are no substantial or important intergroup variations in basic cognitive ability, any differences simply reflect varying adaptations to environments, most particularly in terms of early socialization. Inherent in the difference position is a respect for social diversity: cultural and social pluralism is seen to represent an enriching aspect of the larger society, not something to be eradicated.

Some researchers have questioned the frequent assertion – one with which I concur – that schools are middle-class institutions. If they are not, might it be the case that the home-school discontinuity for disadvantaged children is not, after all, significantly more marked than for their non-disadvantaged counterparts? This interesting possibility was noted, for example, by several contributors to a discussion of poverty edited by Feagans and Farran (1982), and the particular emphasis was upon linguistic variance. Tough (1982: 14) noted, for example, that learning in many schools is a passive activity, and that teachers' talk dominates classroom dynamics; in that and other ways, she suggested, 'many schools operate in a way that is similar to the disadvantaged home' (i.e. where, it is alleged, patterns of communication are frequently more authoritarian than interactive; see following chapters). Snow (1982: 258) stated that it would be hard to make a strong case 'that classrooms are much more like middle-class than like lower-class homes'. And Farran (1982) remarked that schools are definitely not like middle-class homes: they are more rigidly didactic, they are bureaucratic, they emphasize rules and regulations, and so on.

However, while the classroom is obviously not a clone of the family sitting room, the notion that the former is not, after all, a middle-class setting confuses the procedures of schooling with its institutional ethos and its intentions. To claim, on the basis of procedures alone, that a home-school discontinuity does not apply particularly to lower-class children is to ignore possible discontinuities based upon the purposes behind such procedures: these soon become apparent, are more relevant than the procedures, and may well lead to more difficulties for the disadvantaged child.

Compensatory Intervention?

From a 'difference' perspective, the notion of compensatory education is clearly rejected, since it implies that there is something deficient to be improved or replaced. A difference position emphasizes above all, the need for schools to change, and to accommodate to the needs of the disadvantaged child: this need not mean a *replacement* of what the child brings to school, but rather an acceptance of the value of all backgrounds. Still, rejecting a 'replacement' policy does not rule out attempts to enhance, broaden or add to children's repertoires; such attempts characterize more recent language programs, for example (see below). Efforts directed towards the widening of existing abilities and attitudes are predicated, above all, upon the *realpolitik* awareness that – however enlightened educational policies might be – the world outside the school gates remains considerably less so. While waiting for the millennium, then, children should be equipped with tools to help them make their way in less-than-perfect societies.

It is entirely reasonable, in other words, to reject the notions of cultural deprivation and deficit while still admitting that differences may constitute *social* deficits. This can occur, for example, if teachers react negatively to disadvantaged children and expect less of them than of others. A 'self-fulfilling prophecy' can be created when a child, sensitive to differential treatment from the teacher, comes to fulfill lowered expectation (see Alvidrez & Weinstein, 1999; Archer & Edwards, 1982; Rist, 1970; Wigfield *et al.*, 1999). Classic demonstrations of this are found in the 'Pygmalion-in-the-classroom' studies of Rosenthal and Jacobson (1968); see also Fuchs (1973) and Rist (1970). These soon led to others, including Cooper (1979), Cooper and Good (1983), an expanded treatment by Rosenthal and Jacobson (1992) and, most recently, a critical overview by Jussim and Harber (2005). Two recent papers have emphasized something I mentioned as particularly important, in the opening chapter here: thus, Terrill and Mark (2000) and Ladd and Linderholm (2008) deal with the influence of early labelling and expectations among beginning and 'pre-service' teachers. The former study focuses upon black children and second-language learners, while the latter demonstrated (again) just how easy it is to affect teachers' judgments – in this case, by showing them a video of children who were allegedly pupils in good, average or bad schools. The authors built upon an earlier investigation by Pichert and Anderson (1977), and were able to show that the perceptions of teachers who believed that the children they had seen were from poor schools 'selected and recalled more negative behaviors compared to those participants who believed they were viewing a "typical" school' (p. 237).

For the purposes of their study, it was important that the video prepared by Ladd and Linderholm depicted actions that could be variously or ambiguously interpreted. 'Was the image of a child patting another on the back a form of encouragement or support', they write (Ladd & Linderholm, 2008: 234), 'or was it hitting or pushing?' This is reminiscent of the classic study by Condry and Condry (1976) in which judges were shown a film of an infant confronting various stimulus objects; half were told that the baby was a boy, the others that it was a girl. Allowing for some variation attributable to judges' experience with infants, the results showed that different emotions, and different *levels* of emotion, were reported, and that these differences rested upon the sex of the judge and, more importantly, on the sex attributed to the baby. For example, when the child was described to them as being a boy, judges were more likely to see its reaction to a jack-in-the-box as being more angry and less fearful. Condry and Condry termed this the 'eye of the beholder' effect; see also Condry *et al.* (1983), for a roughly analogous 'ear of the beholder' one.

Ladd and Linderholm provide two very telling illustrations. Sample comments from judges who believed that the children they were watching were from a poor school included the following:

> This particular classroom was in complete chaos... the teacher has no control over her classroom... the children seemed to be bored with the teacher when they were not doing group activities... the teacher seemed to be at her desk or in one spot while lecturing to the class.

And here are some from observers – watching exactly the same videotape, remember – who thought the children on the screen were pupils from a good school:

> They [the children] were helping each other out... the teacher was walking around the room aiding [lending?] her assistance when needed... there was not much of the teacher in front of the class... they [the children] seemed to work well on their own. Lots of independent, thoughtful work.

The net import of these and other findings is that teachers may treat children unfairly, on the basis of stereotyped and erroneous views of their likely capabilities.[2] To break this vicious circle, difference theorists (should) advocate the provision of appropriate psychological and linguistic information to teachers. But even the most sanguine difference theorist has to admit the continuing strength of prevailing norms. As Cole and Bruner (1972: 176) put it: 'the great power of the middle class has rendered differences into deficits because middle-class behavior is the yardstick of success'. Indeed, if difference is commonly translated into deficit, it may be little more than semantic quibbling to insist on any distinction between the two. This does not mean that the game is not worth the candle – far from it, since the deep-seated *unfairness* that partial or inaccurate perceptions lead to remains an important motivation for change – but it does suggest how difficult change can be.

Not surprisingly, difference positions also underpin calls for large-scale social change. To eradicate disadvantage is, in part, a matter of changing traditional social views of the poor; it is also, however, necessary that society itself be changed so that poverty itself can be more successfully attacked. Thus, unlike the environmentalists who focus upon school as an agent for the integration of the disadvantaged into society at large, difference proponents see the school as but one part (albeit a very important one) of a much larger and more radical alteration of society.

It has become clear enough, I hope, that the 'difference' perspective is the only one that has logic on its side. By way of conclusion, however, one or two cautionary points suggest themselves. The first, as noted, is that difference theorists have sometimes tended to gloss over real problems and to over-romanticize the poor (shades of Rainwater's 'apotheosis'; see also Robinson, 1976). While many of the characteristics of disadvantaged children are best seen as differences and not deficits, there is no doubt that such children frequently suffer from actual deficiencies, including poor housing, over-crowding, ill-health and inadequate nutrition. In doing justice to their basic cognitive (and linguistic) skills, we should not forget that these arise despite, not because of, poor physical backgrounds. There is no inherent virtue in poverty and squalor. Or, as Aldous Huxley once remarked (1939: 79), 'poverty and suffering ennoble only when they are voluntary. By involuntary poverty and suffering men are made worse'. The other point has to do with the attention focused upon the school as an agent of social change. While deficit theorists, with their programs of compensatory education, are clearly more emphatic here than are those supporting cultural difference, the latter have also invested considerable energy in informing teachers and attempting to lessen misperceptions about disadvantage generally. It is worth pointing out that schools have historically followed the dominant social mainstream rather than lead it. It is also worth remembering that part of the 'failure' of compensatory intervention that motivated Jensen and like-minded researchers can be placed at the feet of political rather than educational agendas. The appeal and the underpinnings of the well-known American Head Start program, for instance, 'lay more in political expedience than in practical efficacy' (Harwood, 1982: 51).

To end on a positive note, however, the 'failure' of compensatory programs may have been overstated. Zigler and Valentine's lengthy anthology (1979) suggested that, while Head Start did not raise IQ scores, it did provide pleasant school experiences (and related services, improved health care among them) for very large numbers of children. Zigler and Seitz (1980) went on to note that success could – should? – be assessed in terms of improved social competence, physical health, educational motivation and achievement, and not only in terms of formal cognitive skills (see also Kellaghan, 1977). Perhaps we ask too much of educational programs in terms of future pay-offs; perhaps some interventions that positively affect children's lives can be accepted as good in themselves, regardless of what they may or may not lead to 10 years on. After all, we do not provide swings and roundabouts for youngsters with the view that by so doing we increase social competence, now or in the future; they are seen as pleasant in and of themselves.

A Forensic Post-script

In this chapter, we have seen how important the assessment of intelligence has been historically: for immigrants, for the lower classes subject to eugenic ideologies, for disadvantaged children in the classroom. The importance, the poignancy and the tragedy have arisen, in large part, because assessments have been mis-assessments. These, in turn, have generally rested upon faulty or inadequate testing instruments. Now, in a new contemporary arena of the greatest moment – of life-and-death significance, in fact – we are able to see that inadequacies and mismeasurements persist. It is also relevant to our larger story that this arena has been, and continues to be, one in which various disadvantaged populations are heavily over-represented. This last section is something of a digression, to be sure, but it highlights a dramatic chapter in the long and often troubled story of intelligence testing and its consequences.

Following the mid-19th-century M'Naghten rules, a defence based upon insanity – while often a very contentious matter – has long been accepted principle in British and American criminal justice systems. Similar, and sometimes more liberal, provisions exist in other countries. In what might appear to be a logical extension, the Supreme Court of the United States recently reversed a 1989 ruling that mental retardation ought not to exempt a murderer from the death penalty: thus, in 2002, the Court found executing the mentally retarded to be unconstitutional (McKinzey, 2005; Mossman, 2005).[3] While arguing that diminished intellectual capacities meant that the execution of the mentally retarded would be 'cruel and unusual punishment', the Court opinion left it to state jurisdiction to develop 'appropriate ways' to apply the provisions.

If a diagnosis of mental retardation is made, McKinzey (2005: 3) observes, then a death sentence 'must be converted – but to what? ...and who qualifies for this life-saving diagnosis? ...how about those who developed MR [mental retardation] after the crime?'

Sticky as these sorts of matters are, they are essentially legal issues. More complicated are those having to do with assessment itself. After discussing another capital case – that of José Lopez – in some detail, McKinzey (2005: 10) concludes by observing that:

> Atkins hearings [see below] will take predictable courses. The defense experts will find ways of explaining away normal IQs and adaptive functioning, and produce scores in the MR range. The prosecution experts will deride the new test scores and argue the defendant is merely a malingering crook.

The possibilities for judicial battles in which each side has its own psychiatrists are obviously much enlarged. But more central still is the question of the efficacy and the validity of the tests used to determine 'legal' mental retardation. (The similarity to issues raised by the scope and application of the M'Naghten rules – issues of 'legal' insanity as opposed to psychiatric conceptions of competence – is striking here.) After all, an IQ-test score can now mean the difference between life and death; you can be legally 'too dumb to die' (Talbot, 2003). Raven (2005) points out that the samples on which the test norms are based may be questioned and, if some potential participants in the norming exercises chose not to take part, what effect might that have on the norms themselves? As the author of one of the standard tests used here, Raven (2005: 68) refers to the 'apparently extraordinary application of psychological tests... tests of general cognitive ability are being used to determine whether murderers will be executed or not'. He is appalled because of the enormous weight now placed upon measures whose validity and discriminative powers are not up to the task. Questions about the adequacy and appropriateness of the norming samples (and many other technicalities of test construction) are hardly unique to this forensic application, but deficiencies are rather more important for convicted killers than for student-placement exercises. Relatedly, there are more mundane, but still vitally important, issues here. Are the test-takers paying – are they, indeed, capable of paying – sufficiently close attention to evaluations being made of them; are they properly applying themselves when presented with standardized psychological tests like the Wechsler intelligence scales and Raven's progressive matrices?

It does indeed seem that fine-grained distinctions have been vital. When, in early August 2005, Daryl Atkins was found – after all – to be mentally competent,[3] it was reported that his several IQ-test results were 59, 67, 74 and 76. The resulting average score (69) would have seemed to exempt him, if only by a hair, from the ultimate penalty, since Virginia law defines mental retardation as involving an IQ of 70 or below by the age of 18. Unfortunately, although Atkins was 18 when he committed murder, the intelligence tests were administered after that age (Lindsey, 2005). One needs neither judicial nor psychiatric genius to see the Kafkaesque absurdity here.

Although McKinzey's (2005) concern that the Supreme Court ruling might lead to attempts on the part of competent murderers to appear intellectually deficient seems not to have been borne out, the ruling has certainly reopened a number of old cases. Many prisoners now on death row may be mentally retarded, and their cases must be reconsidered. More interestingly, contemporary and enlightened views suggest that the mentally retarded are still *individuals*, that reduced criminal culpability arises from *particular* deficiencies that *some* may have – and that categorical judgments are therefore unwarranted (Talbot, 2003). As Mossman (2005: 100) has put it, 'mental retardation is an artificial category imposed on a spectrum of human capability'. At a very simple level, this is demonstrated by the fact that the professional criteria for defining mental retardation have altered over the years: the American Association on Mental Retardation (AAMR) has altered its definition 10 times over the past century or so (Mossman, 2005). Relatedly, Talbot (2003) points out that a lowering of the IQ cut-off in 1973 meant that the proportion of the American population defined as mentally retarded immediately dropped from 16 to 3%. Furthermore, the characterization of mental retardation by the AAMR and the American Psychiatric Association (APA) is not the same; the former now stresses classification in terms of levels of support needed, while the latter uses a more traditional approach, grading degrees of general severity.

The concerns and caveats become – if possible – even more heightened when we discover that the Atkins decision was praised by the mental health community (including the APA, the AAMR, the American Academy of Psychiatry and the Law, the American Psychological Association and others). In fact, a representative of the APA's judicial committee particularly welcomed the decision, claiming that it would raise no problems because 'mental retardation can be identified using time-tested instruments and protocols with proven validity and reliability' (Mossmann, 2005: 99). Given what has already been discussed here, this suggests a rather remarkable optimism, but it is even *more* remarkable since, in various *amicus curiae* interventions, the APA has for some time acknowledged that legal decisions ought not to slavishly follow psychiatric categorizations (Mossman, 2005).[4]

It is relevant to conclude here by noting that Atkins is black, Lopez is Hispanic, and most of the death-row inmates interviewed by Talbot (2003) were one or the other. The use of intelligence-test results, however dubious their accuracy, might be seen generally as a good thing. If one were opposed to capital punishment per se, for instance, one might endorse *any* way of lessening its frequency, particularly given the huge American prison population, with its sizeable over-representation of black and other minority groups. But the fact remains that current legal applications may mean life-and-death distinctions being drawn on flawed or inadequate data. It is unconscionable that Prisoner A, with a measured IQ of 68, should escape the fate of Prisoner B, whose score is 72. Beyond the difficulties already cited, anyone with the slightest familiarity with psychological testing knows that such minor differences are often fleeting and, if stable, often meaningless. Finally, since different states are free to establish different 'cut-off' criteria, it is also possible that a test result that would spare a prisoner in one jurisdiction would condemn him to death in another. And timing may also be of the essence: 'judged against yesterday's norms one should die; yet, given today's norms, one may live' (Raven, 2005: 68).

As Raven and Stephenson (2001) have argued, competence and incompetence in modern society – and the criminal ramifications thereof – are heavily dependent upon the rewards and punishments of the social environment. This suggests that, where environments are 'disadvantaging' in one way or another, changes in early social contexts, coupled with more informed perceptions of those contexts, are likely to be more humane and more effective than later attempts to sort things out, especially if such attempts are cobbled together in ill-considered ways.

Notes

1. Tucker (2002: 197) notes that, in 1999, Rushton (1995) had 'tens of thousands' of copies of an abridged version of his *Race, Evolution and Behavior* sent to social scientists in several disciplines. This is not quite as bizarre as agreeing to appear on trash television, but it is still very odd behavior. It certainly did nothing to endear Rushton or his ideas to a wider academic audience; quite the contrary, in fact.
2. There is a large literature outlining the many variables that can evoke stereotyped and often inaccurate perceptions. Something as simple as a child's first name can produce predictable effects. Teachers (and others, of

course) may form judgments on the basis of (say) the popularity or strangeness of names, or of those that immediately suggest a particular ethnic or social group. Recent work by Anderson-Clark *et al.* (2008) and Fryer and Levitt (2004b), for instance, has demonstrated the negative perceptions of white teachers that can be elicited when contemporary African American names are the 'triggers'; see also Christenfeld and Larsen (2008).

3. Prior to the Supreme Court decision of 2002, provisions existed at the state level for exempting mentally retarded people from execution. At the time of the earlier (1989) ruling, only two states had such legislation, but the number had grown to 18 by 2002 (Mossman, 2005; Talbot, 2003). It is something of an irony that, after lengthy judicial procedures, the defendant in the landmark case discussed here (formally designated as Atkins *v* Virginia, 2002) was found *not* to be mentally retarded, after all.

4. In fact, a very recent publication (Cosgrove *et al.*, 2006) suggests the need for even further caution. The authors examined the financial links between pharmaceutical companies and members of the APA panels responsible for the fourth edition of the association's influential *Diagnostic and Statistical Manual of Mental Disorders* (American Psychiatric Association, 2000). They discovered that 95 of the 170 scientists had at least one such 'financial association'. The ties took the form of research funding and consultancy or speaking fees. Cosgrove and her colleagues note that the connections were strongest in diagnostic domains in which drug treatment is primary; in two of the panels (those dealing with mood disorders and schizophrenia), *every* member was financially linked with a drug company. The authors do not claim to have proved the existence of inappropriate influence, but they do argue for a full-disclosure policy, which seems a modest enough recommendation in the circumstances.

In newspaper interviews, representatives of the APA have denied any pharmaceutical industry influence on *DSM* revisions, have regretted the 'innuendo' of the Cosgrove study, but have also agreed that transparency would be the watchword in future editions of the manual (Carey, 2006).

Chapter 6
The Language Debate

Introduction

The argument that discourse analysis should become the central component in a reworked social psychology represents one facet of a recent growth of interest in more fine-grained studies of language in the classroom. Despite my critical comments (mainly in Chapter 2) about the value of micro-level enquiry, there is little doubt that the new emphases here have allied themselves with a rejection of 'deficit' principles and the disembodied and artificial speech analyses associated with them (see Atkinson, 1985; Edwards & Mercer, 1986; Mercer & Edwards, 1981; Robinson, 1985). In one interesting analysis, Mehan (1984) suggested that classroom language may be of sufficient specificity to constitute a 'cultural code' in itself, one that must be mastered for school success. On the basis of what I have already discussed here, we could add a corollary: disadvantage may be understood as arising in part from differential mastery of this subtle and unarticulated style that combines both knowledge *and* its appropriate display.

One important advantage of this perspective is that it involves teachers as well as pupils. Mehan describes a study in which differences in language styles between lower-status children and their teachers were assessed and, following this, the latter were assisted in making some adaptations to the *children's* language patterns. With teachers phrasing their questions in the children's maternal style, their passivity and 'non-verbality' decreased; and, with the establishment of an enhanced participation, children could be gradually introduced to more standard usage. This type of educational adaptability is a long way removed from programmed intervention based upon assumptions of linguistic deprivation. While making a general argument similar to Mehan's, Young (1983) noted that such alterations in teacher practice do not always come easy. They typically have to combat longstanding traditions based more upon the maintenance of classroom dominance and control than upon the optimization of learning.

Setting aside conceptions and assessments of intelligence, debates about whether or not some language varieties are inferior to others have provided the most interesting sub-plot within the larger story of disadvantage. Evaluations of language were at once the main pillar of the deprivation position and, at the same time, the arena in which the 'difference' attack on that position was (and is) the most thoroughgoing and the most successful. So, even though the preceding discussions mean that the outcome here can be anticipated before we start, the illustrative value is very great.

As in the previous chapters, much of my purpose here is to present something of the background to current positions. For that reason, I have cited many studies from the 1960s and 1970s, the times when matters still extremely relevant in the 'real world' – in the contemporary classroom, to name one important arena – were being thrashed out in the literature. Of particular importance in all this is the realization that, although the 'difference' point of view may have won the day in intellectual terms, 'deficit' views of one sort or another remain dominant beyond the groves of academe. For two recent overviews, see Ng (2007) and Wright and Bougie (2007).

The educational stage has always been the most important here, and so we might begin this chapter by introducing two of the star players, characters whose continuingly appealing roles have contributed to a play with a run far longer than that of *The Mousetrap*. In *Speed the Plough*, first performed at Covent Garden in 1800, Thomas Morton introduced the famous Mrs Grundy. Like Mrs Harris, Sairey Gamp's invisible friend in *Martin Chuzzlewit*, Mrs Grundy never actually appears herself. She is respectfully invoked by Farmer Ashfield's wife, however, as the epitome of polite acceptability, and her name has since become synonymous with narrow puritanism, 'morality' and linguistic purism of the most conventional sort. Dame Ashfield's concerns in matters of propriety – 'What will Mrs Grundy say? What will Mrs Grundy think?' – have evolved into apprehensions with which those readers who remember school grammar classes will no doubt be familiar. They may be less familiar with Miss Fidditch, one of those schoolteachers who would rather 'parse than eat'. In Martin Joos's (1967) famous little book on style, *The Five Clocks*, Miss Fidditch plays a central role, considering herself as the prophet of the great god, Webster. Mrs Grundy and Miss Fidditch have had many relatives in school systems around the world, and their influence continues.[1]

Trudgill (1979: 21) reproduced some press reaction to his book on language variation at school (Trudgill, 1975). The general feeling was that any defence of nonstandard varieties was a blow against 'good' grammar and a support for 'incomplete and lazy' language. A writer in *The*

Guardian – in the Education Section, no less – claimed that children speaking what he called 'an East London dialect offshoot' (whatever that animal might be) are 'lacking entire sounds and words in their vocal repertoire'. A *Sunday Telegraph* columnist argued that failing to 'correct' lower-class grammar was denying children the very 'right to knowledge'. Lippi-Green (1997) provides many examples of widespread negative attitudes towards Black English (and other nonstandard dialects) in the United States; as we shall see, such attitudes can be just as common among teachers as among 'laypersons', and just as strongly held by nonstandard-dialect speakers themselves as in the public at large.

Deficient Language

Since class and regional differences in accent and dialect have always been the source of comment, imitation and derision, it is not difficult to understand the appeal of a formal deficit view of certain speech styles. One of the first scholarly attempts (perhaps the first; see Dittmar, 1976) to investigate class differences in speech was that of Schatzman and Strauss (1955). Following a tornado in Arkansas, lower- and middle-class respondents were asked to describe the frightening event. The former group were found to transmit much less information about the occurrence than were the latter. There was little attempt to set the scene, as it were, for the interviewer, and the respondents were apparently able to do little more than reconstruct the event as it had appeared to them directly and personally in 'particularistic or concrete terms' (Schatzman & Strauss, 1955: 333). There was much digression, which, though perhaps meaningful for the speaker, was irrelevant and/or confusing for the listener. The lower-class interviewees seemed to assume that the interviewer shared much contextual information when, in fact, this was not so. Middle-class informants, by contrast, were generally able to reconstruct the event in a logical and meaningful way. Schatzman and Strauss acknowledged that the lower-class people were communicating across class lines (i.e. to a middle-class interviewer) and were probably more unfamiliar with the requirements of the task – important points, as we shall see. Nevertheless, the investigators felt able to conclude that this group of respondents had a reduced capacity for perceiving and communicating abstract thoughts; some, they argued, 'literally cannot tell a straight story or describe a simple incident coherently' (Schatzman & Strauss, 1955: 336; see also Strauss & Schatzman, 1960).

In a related study, Templin (1957) obtained speech samples from lower- and middle-class white American children (aged between three and seven). In terms of complexity of utterance, analysis revealed that class differences were minimal: although there was some tendency for lower-class children to use simpler sentences (i.e. fewer phrase and clausal constructions), it was not the case that they *never* used more complex expressions. One could not deduce, then, that lower-class children were unable to produce certain forms, only that they made less use of them than did their middle-class counterparts; similar conclusions can be drawn from a longitudinal study reported by Loban (1963). The general point here – again, something to which we shall return – revolves around the difficulty of inferring linguistic *competence* from linguistic *performance*. After all, even if a child used a subordinate clause only once in a hundred utterances, some basic capability could be inferred. (In fact, as Dittmar [1976: 49] pointed out, even if *no* sentential complexity at all is produced, one cannot be certain of underlying competences: perhaps some can easily understand clausal complexities but lack 'a disposition towards producing them'.) An important question remains, of course – why does *habitual* performance take the form it does? – but this is somewhat different from talking about basic linguistic abilities and disabilities.

Basil Bernstein and his followers

Most relevant here, however, is the work of the late Basil Bernstein in the 1950s. Influential in sociological and educational circles, his reports of working-class and middle-class language appeared to support a deficit position, even though he later claimed that this was not the case. In the introduction to his 1971 book, for instance, Bernstein acknowledges early weaknesses and ambiguities (but see Tony Edwards, 1974). Consider here what Rosen (1972: 3–4), one of Bernstein's fiercest but most careful critics, had to say:

> Bernstein protests that his work has been misunderstood, misused and vulgarized... And he is absolutely right. However, as he also tells us his papers are "obscure, lack precision and probably abound in ambiguities" (Bernstein, 1971, p. 19), that is scarcely to be wondered at.

A little earlier in his argument, Rosen cites an even more interesting admission, in which Bernstein (1971: 11) refers to his early papers as 'conceptually weak... horrifyingly coarse'. Ultimately, as Rosen (1972: 15) suggests,

> you cannot protest very convincingly against the harm done by the label "linguistic deprivation" when your own theory points to a

deficit, indeed when you have actually stated... that "the normal linguistic environment of the working class is one of linguistic deprivation".

There is a Jewish proverb, Rosen reminds us, about trying to dance at two weddings at the same time.

Bernstein's linguistic insights centered upon 'public' and 'formal' variants. The former, he said, is chiefly characterized by an emphasis upon 'the emotive rather than the logical implications' (Bernstein, 1958: 164) of language; and subsequent elaborations (Bernstein, 1959) reveal that public language is grammatically simple, and generally limited in expressive possibilities. Its users, like those lower-class respondents described by Schatzman and Strauss (whose work Bernstein acknowledged), apparently have few syntactic and lexical alternatives, and are restricted to concrete and non-symbolic modes of expression. Public language is essentially the only linguistic variant available to the lower class. On the other hand, middle-class speakers – while willing and able to use the public variety – also have access to 'formal' language. Bernstein described this as essentially the mirror image of its poorer counterpart. Where the latter is simple, semantically implicit and conceptually weak, formal language is grammatically complex, semantically explicit and rich in symbolic possibilities.

In his earlier papers, Bernstein (1958, 1959, 1960) referred to characteristics of lower-class children often cited by the environmental-deficit theorists: difficulty in delaying immediate gratification and of planning for the future, 'volatile' expressive behavior and so on. He related the linguistic variants to those of social milieu, noting that:

> one mode [of speech], associated with the middle-class, points to the possibilities within a complex conceptual hierarchy for the organization of experience, the other, associated with the lower working-class, progressively limits the type of stimuli to which the child learns to respond. (Bernstein, 1960: 276)

Before long, to complete what appears to be quite a well-rounded picture of deficiency, 'public' and 'formal' language variants were translated into the more well-known 'restricted' and 'elaborated' codes (see Bernstein, 1962a). Bernstein's early experimental data are found in four connected papers (1958, 1960, 1962a, 1962b), and the most salient findings revealed class differences in verbal performance between public-school boys, on the one hand, and working-class messenger boys, on the other. The inferior verbal abilities of the messengers were to be explained, Bernstein

(1960: 276) noted, by the fact that 'the normal linguistic environment of the working class is one of relative deprivation'.

Such an interpretation made it difficult, of course, to believe that Bernstein was not an adherent of the 'deficit' viewpoint – this despite later disclaimers, and despite the occasional reference to the strengths of public/restricted codes ('emotionally virile, pithy and powerful... a metaphoric range of considerable force and appropriateness': Bernstein, 1959: 322–323). Rosen (1972), Tony Edwards (1974) and Dittmar (1976) were among the earliest doubting apostles here. One of the most cutting assessments, however, was that of Jackson (1974: 65), who begins a review (one that runs to almost 20 pages) of the first two volumes of Bernstein's work on 'class, codes and control' by noting that 'it is never entirely pleasant to have to say that a major scientific reputation is founded on a myth' (the 'entirely' is a nice touch here). Jackson concludes with the swingeing assertion that Bernstein's work is essentially an 'artistic interpretation of the world', and quite unscientific.

> That a work of art [Jackson goes on to say]... should have to be presented to the world as pseudo-science, presumably in order to gain recognition, research grants and a chair, is a savage comment on what we are prepared to finance and respect, and on the scientific standards of institutional sociology. (Jackson, 1974: 81)

A generation on, Joseph (2004: 69) provides a powerful retrospective assessment: 'Bernstein was clearly saying – despite his later vehement but disingenuous denials – that only middle-class people have true personal identities and full cognition of their world. Working-class people have strong social identity, shared with others who speak only the restricted code'. Strong words. Some may find them a little too strong, perhaps, but it is worth reproducing here Joseph's fuller commentary:

> When these statements [about codes] were interpreted in the only reasonable way they could be – as meaning that the language of the working classes renders their speakers cognitively deficient and indistinct as individuals – and when objections were raised to this, Bernstein reacted with shock, and over subsequent decades altered his statements to make them sound less like negative judgements on the working classes. He responded robustly to anyone who criticised [such] statements... and while he deserves credit for shifting his stance... he never came to grips with the inescapable implications of the early work that made his name. Efforts to rehabilitate him in the

1990s have not resulted in his reformulated views on social difference, language and identity having wide influence. They are still seen as being based on a form of linguistic determinism that has gone out of fashion. (Joseph, 2003: 69–70)

My only reservation with Joseph's observation, which neatly summarizes *l'affaire* Bernstein, is that saying that deficit models have become unfashionable is to downplay the social-scientific evidence that did much more than simply edge them off the catwalk.

A study by Hawkins (1969) – referred to by Coulthard (1969: 45) as 'the most interesting and challenging empirical paper... on restricted and elaborated codes' – prompted some revealing comments by Bernstein himself. Hawkins had asked middle-class and working-class children to make up stories on the basis of a series of pictures and, on the basis of the responses, Hawkins created two versions; the middle-class narrative is as follows:

> Three boys are playing football and one boy kicks the ball – and it goes through the window – the ball breaks the window – and the boys are looking at it – and a man comes out – and shouts at them – because they've broken the window – so they run away – and then that lady looks out of her window – and she tells the boys off.

And here is the working-class sample:

> They're playing football – and he kicks it – and it goes through there – it breaks the window and they're looking at it – and he comes out – and shouts at them – because they've broken it – so they run away – and then she looks out – and she tells them off.

The first version takes little for granted, Bernstein (1972a: 167) tells us, the reader does not have to see the pictures in order to understand the story, and the little narrative is thus 'free of the context which generated it'. This is not so for the working-class version, where the meaning is implicit and where the reader must have access to the pictures before being able to understand the paragraph. Bernstein argued that the importance of Hawkins' work rested upon the demonstration of class differences in responses to the same stimuli. There are some difficulties, however.

First, the stories are hypothetical: Hawkins himself made them up, rather than presenting actual examples produced by the children themselves.[2] Second, Bernstein and Hawkins consider the working-class version as less than ideal because it seems to assume that the reader shares background information with the teller (i.e. has seen the same pictures); the reader will recall that this was a communicative obstacle remarked upon by Schatzman and Straus. In this case, however, as Stubbs (1983), Trudgill (1975) and Coulthard (1969) all pointed out, the experimenter was present when the children constructed their stories, and thus *did* see the pictures. One might quite reasonably argue, therefore, that the working-class version was *more* appropriate in a context in which both speaker and listener had the same information in front of them.

An equation of working-class language with inferior language is especially unfortunate – even within the confines of Bernstein's own theoretical space – when it is realized that (for example) working-class children *can* use elaborated code under some circumstances. This is easily demonstrated. In British investigations undertaken at the height of Bernstein's influence, Robinson (1965) found that the grammatical usages of working-class children writing formal letters were not markedly different from those of their middle-class counterparts. Rushton and Young (1975) reported that class differences were influenced by the context of the task (in their study, different essay topics: imaginative, opinionative or technical). The most interesting studies here, however, are American ones.

In a series of investigations with black children, Marwit and associates (Marwit, 1977; Marwit & Marwit, 1973, 1976; Marwit & Neumann, 1974; Marwit *et al.*, 1972) demonstrated that the understanding – and the use – of standard English develops over the course of the primary-school grades. This does not imply any abandonment of maternal speech patterns. It is, rather an illustration of early and growing awareness of the differences, both substantive and evaluative, between standard and nonstandard varieties, and of the differential appropriateness of these varieties in specific contexts (see also Day, 1982; Gay & Tweney, 1976). More recent research continues to confirm the connection: Tannen *et al.* (1997) found that older nonstandard-speaking children can easily shift to the standard when the context suggests it.

In this connection, Piestrup (1973) reported that, when white teachers stigmatized the use of nonstandard language in the classroom, the children's use of Black English actually increased, or became more emphasized. The opposite was true in classrooms where teachers did not 'punish' the use of nonstandard forms. Beyond the facilitation of standard-dialect use per se, it is easy to see that acceptance of nonstandard dialects at school will likely increase the general 'comfort' level of the students, and this can be expected to produce educational benefits of all kinds (see Nero, 2006; Rickford & Rickford, 1995; Siegel, 2006, 2007). All of this is surely a specific example of a very general rule: the best way to expedite the learning of something new is to start with what children bring with them, to build upon existing competence and practice. With particular regard to language, it is clear that since *all* varieties, standard or nonstandard, have symbolic as well as communicative functions, to denigrate or dismiss them is to threaten or belittle an important marker of group solidarity; this is an important matter to which I shall return.

The early work showing that lower-class children could, after all, use Bernstein's more 'elaborated' codes is, in fact, evidence for the common phenomenon of 'bidialectalism', which, indeed, typically involves varieties of higher and lower prestige. The more standard format can be expected in formal or extra-group interactions, the more nonstandard medium in contexts of familiarity and intimacy. Both have their uses, which explains why one generally does not drive out the other. There may be compelling social reasons, for instance, for the maintenance of low-prestige varieties. Speicher and McMahon (1992) report on the peer pressure among their black informants to use Black English, or risk being labeled an 'oreo' (a biscuit that is black on the outside, but white in the middle); among native North Americans the cognate term is 'apple', among Asian Americans it is 'banana' and so on. This is a specific example of a much broader phenomenon: the ostracism that can follow attempts to leave one's group and join another.

Thus, a generation ago, Carranza and Ryan (1975) noted that Mexican Americans who abandon Spanish for the socioeconomic rewards of English may be seen by their friends as *vendidos*: 'sell-outs'. The same labeling was applied to French speakers in Quebec who moved to English; they were *vendus*. Of course, if one could make a clean and complete break, if one could leave behind one life and move seamlessly into another, these epithets would lose some of their force, and would perhaps reflect only some difficult, but temporary, period of transition. But, it is extremely difficult to make such moves, particularly, of course, when many other things besides language have to be adjusted. Indeed, some things, like skin color, cannot be adjusted at all (Michael Jackson notwithstanding). So, the danger is of ending up in some psychosocial no-man's land, of becoming 'marginalized'. In that case, labels and the attitudes sustaining them would have real and ongoing force. Such considerations give many people pause.

It would, however, be both wrong and incomplete to think that only negative possibilities restrain individuals from attempting cultural or linguistic shift. We should remember that there are strong positive forces binding us to our groups, even if those groups are low in status. They may lack social prestige but they are *ours*. Their ways and traditions are familiar, their speech patterns are our maternal inheritances, and – as mentioned – every language and dialect has symbolic value for its speakers. The 'identity function' is carried as much by Cockney as it is by Oxfordese, as much by Quebec *joual* as Parisian French. Ryan's (1979) brief paper on the persistence of low-prestige dialects remains instructive here, and a recent paper by Abd-el-Jawad (2006) discusses the persistence of minority *languages*: where the ordinary communicative functions have been largely (or wholly) replaced by a 'larger' language, the smaller may yet persist because of the strong symbolic value it retains for group members. Relatedly, a language no longer widely spoken may remain the repository of a group's tradition, literature and so on.

We should conclude this section with a general consideration of the influence of Bernstein – or should it be the early Bernstein or, perhaps, Bernstein misinterpreted? He made a number of attempts to justify his position (in 1971 and 1972b, for example), and his final arguments in response to criticisms of the codes were made in 1987 (revised and enlarged in 1990). Here, Bernstein gave particular attention to the work of Labov (1969), Stubbs (1983a) and Gibson (1984), and even refers to a brief criticism of mine (Edwards, 1987). The critics are seen to have ignored salient features of the theory, and to have been unfairly selective. As part of this defence, Bernstein (1990: 101) attempts again to say what his codes are and what they are not: 'a code is a regulative principle, tacitly acquired, which selects and integrates relevant meanings, forms of realizations, and evoking contexts'. It seems to me that, apart from reinforcing earlier criticisms about the opacity of his prose, this use of words like 'tacitly', 'relevant' and 'forms' provides for almost infinite slippage.

Bernstein (1997: 47) discusses the context within which his code theory was formulated and presented, and even tries to argue that the difference/deficit debate was 'of little theoretical significance' and 'obscured more than it revealed'. He also offers here a critical analysis of Labov's seminal 1969 paper, but pays no attention to the grammatical aspects that (as we shall see) constitute the most important element in Labov's convincing argument against deficit hypotheses.

Beyond its baleful influence in educational settings, Bernstein's work has been taken up in some (fairly limited) scholarly quarters, particularly where Halliday's 'systemic' linguistics and questions about possible variations in language *functions* across social groups are under consideration. These are areas where Bernstein latterly claimed that the import of his work was really to be found (see, e.g. Bernstein, 1996). Support here has typically built upon the notion that the codes reflect linguistic *performance* and not basic *competence*. In pointing to the growing sense that educational failure was linguistic failure ('this notion is in the air, so to speak'), Halliday (1973b) was obliged to acknowledge that the source of the equation could be found in Bernstein's work. What a pity, Halliday implies, that the codes have become the culprit, given 'the care which Bernstein has taken to emphasize that neither is more highly valued than the other' (Halliday, 1973b: x). This is surely very disingenuous, since we have ample evidence that – by his own admission – Bernstein took very little care in this regard. Furthermore, if you will call one of your variants 'elaborated' and the other 'restricted'...

Apart from the sympathetic writings of Halliday (1973a, 1973b, 1975), relevant collections include those edited by Atkinson *et al.* (1995), Christie (1999) and Power *et al.* (2001). Foley (1991) also takes the line that Bernstein has been misinterpreted, this time in a context of comparison with the theories of Vygotsky and Halliday. Of most interest, however, is the very recent anthology of Ruqaiya Hasan's papers, as edited by Webster (2005). This collection is an excellent resource if you are interested in Bernstein and the 'social-semiotic mediation of mind', or perhaps the 'meta-dialogism' of his 'exotropic' theory.

An interesting defense of Bernstein and his work has been mounted by Robinson (1998), who suggests that many of the views for which Bernstein was most vilified were not, in fact, his views at all. Robinson also maintains that academic criticism of Bernstein was essentially non-constructive, not 'Popperian-based' and often personalized. However, while such criticism certainly arose in some quarters, it would be a great mistake to imagine that more measured treatments were absent (see Edwards, 1989; and the following chapter). Robinson (2001) adds that the activities of members of Bernstein's research team (of whom he was one) came to a rather abrupt halt, largely because of mounting academic censure. Their publications, he argues, were simply ignored in the political and educational corridors of power. Mentioning Labov's work particularly, Robinson (2001: 238) laments that the criticisms came unaccompanied with any 'constructive alternative curriculum... [and] simply left the disadvantaged children to suffer the same fate as their ancestors'. Now, while it is very useful if a critical perspective is so accompanied, there is no logical requirement; indeed, it is quite common to recognize the inadequacy of existing approaches without being able to come up with satisfactory solutions. But Robinson is, in any event, mistaken in his assertion that the current state of affairs leaves children in some retrograde state of suffering. Adopting a 'difference' perspective on disadvantage, for example, hardly precludes intervention, although it does rule out, quite rightly, attempts founded on flawed understanding of children's linguistic and cognitive capacities.

Finally here, Blommaert (2005: 13) has noted that Bernstein's sense that the linguistic resources to which children have access are differentially distributed across class lines remains valid, corroborated as it is by Bourdieu's notions of social reproduction, language and symbolic power (see Bourdieu, 1991; Bourdieu & Passeron, 1977). This is hardly an endorsement of Bernsteinian insights, however, since no 'difference' theorist would have any quarrel with such a common-sense idea. The difference-deficit argument has always hinged upon the meaning and the consequences of social-class variations in language.

Bernstein and compensatory education

In distancing himself from 'deficit' theories, Bernstein also dissociated himself from programs of educational intervention, of 'compensatory education'. Indeed, Bernstein (1972b: 137) pointed out that the latter term was particularly unfortunate, since it implies that 'something is lacking in the family, and so in the child... the children become little deficit systems'. The simple fact remains, however, that Bernstein's work fuelled some specific scholarly extensions and, perhaps more importantly, subtly reinforced powerful existing currents in and beyond the classroom. Thus, when Trudgill (1975) investigated both Bernstein's work and the criticisms of it – what did Bernstein *really* mean? would it make more sense to consider the 'codes' as *sociolinguistic* variants rather than *linguistic* phenomena? – he emphasized its effects in educational and instructional settings. One of the simplest and clearest statements here is that of Cheshire *et al.* (1989: 6): despite Bernstein's 'strenuous' denials, they note, 'his work was widely interpreted in Britain, in North America and in Europe as suggesting that the standard language could be equated with the elaborated code and working-class non-standard dialects with the restricted code'.

Apart from the summaries and expansions produced by Bernstein's colleagues in Britain, the most important and the most damaging consequences of his work occurred within the American educational community. Hess and Shipman's (1965, 1968a, 1968b) work on mother-child communication and maternal 'control' is representative here. The lower-class family was seen to have 'imperative-normative' communicative patterns, with little of the personal and rational elements typical of middle-class mother/child interactions. The authors summarize their findings as follows:

> The meaning of deprivation would thus seem to be a deprivation of meaning in the early cognitive relationships between mother and child. This environment produces a child who relates to authority rather than to rationale, who may often be compliant but is not reflective in his behavior, and for whom the consequences of an act are largely considered in terms of immediate punishment or reward rather than future effects and long-range goals. (Hess & Shipman, 1968b: 103)

The clever but vacuous phrase that begins the quotation soon recommended itself to many 'deficit' researchers. Indeed, the general import of the statement as a whole links perfectly with the broader environmental-deficit perspective already discussed. Hess and Shipman go on to argue that, since the early life of the lower-class child is mentally stunting, intervention aimed at nothing less than 'resocialization' is indicated.

The criticisms that can be made of this sort of work are by now familiar. It is always difficult to generalize from psychological probings of one sort or another – especially with social groups for whom they are strange and artificial occurrences – to what actually takes place in the home. Assumptions about links between different types of maternal behavior and children's cognitive development are difficult to confirm. Powerful assumptions of the 'normality' and 'correctness' of middle-class attitudes and lifestyles may infect even the most sensitive assessments of lower-class environments. And so on.

Somewhat more sophisticated work on class differences in the 'language of maternal control' was presented by Cook-Gumperz (1973). On the basis of tape-recorded interviews, working-class mothers were observed to employ 'imperative' modes of control, while the middle class utilized a broader and more personal mode. Nevertheless, considerable intra-class variation was also found. Related to the broad tendencies of class differences in control techniques was the use of elaborated code in the middle-class mothers' speech, and restricted code in that of their working-class counterparts. Similar work was reported by Robinson and Rackstraw (1972): in response to various questions, middle-class children were found to give more information, and to explain and amplify upon their answers more fully, than did working-class children; the answers of the latter often involved simple appeals to authority or custom.

I have already referred to the environmental-deficit position as the chief stimulant to interest in compensatory education (see Deutsch, 1967). It is now possible to be more specific, and to see language as the central pillar of many intervention programs, whose essential *raison d'être* was to combat the chimera of 'verbal deprivation'.

In one of the earliest and best-known programs, Bereiter and Engelmann (1966: 39) began from the premise that disadvantaged children are retarded in reasoning ability and language skills: their language is 'immature', they lack 'the most rudimentary forms of constructive dialogue'. In fact, Bereiter and Engelmann claimed, more than once, that the disadvantaged child attempts to get along without language wherever possible. 'Language', they said, 'is apparently dispensable enough in the life of the lower-class child for an occasional child to get along without it altogether' (p. 31); or, a little further on, 'language for the disadvantaged child seems to be an aspect of social behavior which is not of vital importance' (p. 42). On this bizarre and ludicrous basis, Bereiter and Engelmann – who clearly never bothered to observe lower-class children at play – put together a remedial program. (Labov's [1969: 33] reaction reflects the astonishment felt by linguists confronted with the blindness – or deafness – of the deficit theorists: 'the view of the Negro speech community which we obtain from our work in the ghetto is precisely the opposite... we see a child bathed in verbal stimulation from morning to night'.)

The most immediate problem for Bereiter and Engelmann was to break down what they termed the 'giant word' syndrome. The 'deprived child' cannot say 'I ain't got no juice' but, instead, 'Uai-ga-na-ju' (p. 34). The authors considered this phenomenon directly consistent with Bernstein's notion of restricted code, and the remedy consisted largely of intensive and highly specific drills in the use of 'correct' English. Detailed instructions are provided for teachers – Bereiter and Engelmann's book is, in fact, essentially an educational manual – one example of which will be more than sufficient:

(A) Present an object and give the appropriate identity statement. "This is a ball."
(B) Follow the statement with a *yes-no* question. "Is this a ball?"
(C) Answer the question. "Yes, this is a ball."
(D) Repeat the question and encourage the children to answer it. (p. 140)

Throughout the program, it is apparent that the authors' conception of the language of disadvantaged children is startlingly inaccurate. To anticipate later arguments a bit: Labov (1969) observed that the authors' belief that usages like 'they mine' is incorrect and illogical reveals a lack of awareness of Black English grammar, in which the deletion of the present-tense copula verb ('are', in this case) is a regularity. Labov also pointed to their unfortunate dismissal of 'In the tree' as an illogical answer to the teacher's question, 'Where is the squirrel?' Everyone uses such economical elliptical statements and, in fact, their use clearly shows that the listener has paid close attention to the grammatical context of the question.

Another well-known American project for disadvantaged black children was that of Klaus and Gray (1968; see also Gray & Klaus, 1970). Characterizing the children's home life as noisy, disorganized and inadequate for the 'proper' development of cognitive skills, the authors acknowledge their debt to Bernstein. They define the restricted code as:

> one in which most of the meaning must be carried by other aspects of the total situation: facial expression, intonation rather than words spoken, the circumstances. The child, thus, does not learn to use language effectively. (Klaus & Gray, 1968: 8)

(Indeed, the essence of this quotation is traceable to Bernstein's earliest paper on class and language.)

Overall, early (pre-1970) programs of compensatory education were generally built upon linguistic-deficit theory, and often displayed some acquaintance with Bernstein's work in particular. This is true not only for the individual programs just touched upon here, but also for the massive American Head Start project, an intervention designed to give poor children pre-school experience that would allow them to enter the regular school itself on a more equal footing. Springing from President Johnson's 'War on Poverty' in 1965, and fuelled by Coleman's (1966) report on equality of educational opportunity (see also Jencks, 1972), Head Start was soon dealing with hundreds of thousands of children.

As the deficit perspective waned, however, later educational interventions looked somewhat more enlightened – at least, the term 'compensatory education' was increasingly seen as inappropriate, undercut by the insights of the 'difference' position. In Britain, for example, the Plowden Report (1967) focused attention upon the problems of children in urban areas and recommended the identification of 'educational priority areas' on the basis of a number of visible criteria including large family size, receipt of state benefits and poor housing. Virtually *all* intervention initiatives – early programs or later ones – have interested themselves in language matters and, to that extent, have remained 'remedial' in nature. Indeed, as I have already hinted (and as we shall see in more detail later on), an adherence to a 'difference' perspective does not rule out concern for children's linguistic repertoires or educational intervention per se. It does rule out, however, interventions built upon false footings. Thus, Bridget Plowden herself cautioned against programs predicated upon the idea that all should think 'the same way as we do ourselves'; she went on:

> education for the deprived child [should be] *complementary* to his home... rather than *compensatory*, which really means that the home has no merit. (Plowden, 1970: 12)

This view may not be fully within the approved 'difference' camp on disadvantage, but the words here suggest a considerable advance from the hard-line deficit approach that was still common when they were written.[3]

Although I shall shortly turn to some detailed criticisms of the deficit view of language, we know already from the more general discussion of disadvantage that deficit perspectives are flawed. So, just as we have rejected labels like 'cultural deprivation', as inaccurate and, indeed, nonsensical, we can also reject the more specific notion of 'verbal deprivation'. By extension, the philosophical underpinnings of 'compensatory' education are equally shaky: if the language of disadvantaged children is not deficient, then there is nothing to compensate for. We may, for practical purposes, wish to increase or broaden children's linguistic repertoires, but this is another matter (see below), and any attempt to do so is not likely to succeed if it is founded on deep misunderstanding of existing linguistic capabilities.

The ignorance of the importance of cultural relativism, and the blind imposition of middle-class standards to which this ignorance leads, have always been the major issues in critical discussions of compensatory education and verbal deprivation. Investigations of lower-class beliefs, attitudes and values by middle-class interviewers, using instruments standardized (if at all) with middle-class populations, often taking place in middle-class settings (the university clinic, the social-scientific laboratory) are likely to produce dubious results.[4] Recall, for example, that Hess and Shipman's studies in the 1960s led them to advocate the 'resocialization' of the disadvantaged child – this to involve strong and prolonged intervention in the family and, in some cases, actual removal of the child – a proposal based upon a direct imputation of lower-class family inadequacy. Even at the time, there were those who protested:

> Do we have the right to impose middle-class standards on lower-class and black families?... Are we confident that the middle-class value system, including the current school system, is an appropriate standard of health? If middle-class behavior patterns are to provide the outcome criteria, is it not necessary to seek and explore short-comings in *these* patterns? (Sroufe, 1970: 143)

Such cautionary observations, unfortunately, were typically only half heard. The more extreme suggestions of deficit-theory interventionists (schemes for wholesale 'resocialization' of children, for instance) were by and large resisted – although, it has to be said, their plans were often rejected on economic and not philosophical grounds – but calls for sustained attention to *middle-class* lifestyles were rarely heeded. Assumptions of the correctness or appropriateness of such lifestyles run very deep indeed. (I don't mean to suggest, of course, that bourgeois lifestyles have not regularly commanded attention. History reveals little nuance, however – where social analysis has not inordinately praised the middle class, it has called for its obliteration.)

As I have implied, the argument against compensatory education and language deficit is not quite complete. It is true that undercutting the deficit position necessarily means bolstering the opposing point of view, but it is reasonable to supplement this sort of 'negative' support with more direct and more positive evidence for the accuracy of the 'difference' argument. Therefore, we should now consider some further language details.

Different Language

Introductory observations

While the 'strong' form of the famous Whorfian hypothesis – that language determines thought – is generally rejected, no one denies the influence of language upon our habitual ways of considering the world (nor, of course, that the environment has some formative influence upon language development). Where languages come to be suited to the immediate needs of their speakers, one implication is that all valid considerations of language usage must also be sensitive to cultural variation; another is that assessments of languages in terms of 'better' or 'worse' are untenable. No informed opinion could hold that French is 'better' than English, or that English is 'worse' than German, and the principle holds regardless of the languages under comparison. As Lenneberg (1967) observed, there are no 'primitive' languages, no varieties that are inherently more complete or more logical than others; 'logic' in languages is simply a synonym for 'grammar'. Lenneberg's observation is only one example of a broadly held linguistic conviction; the fact that it was made when the 'deficit' perspective on disadvantage was at its peak is an indication of how linguistically ill-informed were the theorists of 'verbal deprivation'. (When I equate logic with grammar, incidentally, I obviously prescind from arguments for an underlying deep 'logic' common to all languages.) Similar insights apply to dialects – 'just as there is no linguistic reason for arguing that Gaelic is superior to Chinese, so no English dialect can be claimed to be linguistically superior or inferior to any other' (Trudgill, 1975: 26), and this chapter will provide supporting evidence.

(There is, of course, ample evidence that – beyond the enlightened and data-driven assessments of scholars – languages and dialects are not all of equal, or potentially equal, value. Fishman has made the point, directly and indirectly, throughout his work (e.g. Fishman, 1980, 1987; García, 1991). And Mackey (1978: 7) pointed out, some time ago, that 'only before God and the linguist are all languages equal. Everyone knows that you can go further with some languages than you can with others'. We shall certainly see supporting evidence for this, here and in other chapters.)

By an early age, and certainly by the time they go to school, all children within the normal range of intelligence have acquired a fluent grasp of their maternal variety. Since, as we shall see, *all* dialects are fully fledged, rule-governed systems across which comparisons of 'better' or 'worse' cannot legitimately be made, then it follows that all children learn 'proper' or 'correct' language. While 'a fluent grasp' is not the same as a perfect one, some linguists maintain that children are on the road to this perfection, that they are learning a proper language properly. In considering this proposition, Trudgill (1975) notes that we all make slips of the tongue, or say things that we don't mean to; fatigue is often a factor here, of course. He also realizes that we sometimes use words without knowing their proper or accepted meaning. He adds that, if we intend to speak in a particular dialect but then use a word or phrase from another, this could be construed as a mistake; terms like 'style', 'register' and 'jargon' could be substituted for 'dialect' here. And finally, Trudgill accepts that we often make mistakes in speaking a language that is not our first. But he is adamant that:

apart from these cases, however, we have to say that all normal adult speakers know and therefore use their own dialect... perfectly. No grammatical form which occurs in any... dialect is an error: with the exception of those instances we have just listed, native speakers do not make mistakes. (Trudgill, 1975: 45)

This has proved a difficult concept to accept in some quarters. Mrs Grundy and the great host of lesser prescriptivists obviously reject it. And more broad-minded observers often concur with Amis's (1990: 307) statement that 'there is a right way of using words and constructing sentences, and plenty of wrong ways'. Teachers form an obvious group here; as Lippi-Green (1997: 131) and many others have pointed out, they have traditionally had strong views about what is correct and incorrect, and have been 'firm believers in a standard language ideology' that underpins those views.

Many of Amis's linguistic observations are humorous, but some are ill-informed. It is not quite the case, for example, that 'linguists and lexicographers' have given 'their followers leave to spatter their talk and prose with any old illiteracy or howler that took their fancy', while remaining, themselves, scrupulous adherents of 'correct' language – 'like a parson grimly preserving his own chastity while recommending adultery to his parishioners' (Amis, 1990: 308). This brings to mind the polished standard of those who defend nonstandard variants, the cut-glass accents of those who go to the barricades for others. Hardly heinous, of course, but interesting. It would be a mistake, incidentally, to think that the late Sir Kingsley was simply a well-known specimen of the 'appalled of Tunbridge Wells' species; he was always interested in matters linguistic and, apart from reviews like the one I cite here, he wrote an interesting book on modern English usage (Amis, 1997).

The acknowledgement that there are no 'inadequate' or 'debased' dialects took longer to ripen within linguistics than did the parallel argument about language per se. Outside the academic precincts, it remains an idea whose force is rather weak. Few scholars are naïve enough to think that dissemination of enlightened linguistic thinking will quickly change social perspectives on the Black English Vernacular (BEV), Cockney or Joual. But linguists have interested themselves in the language of disadvantage because the proponents of deficit-language theory and the advocates of compensatory education were once well ensconced within the hallowed groves.

Investigations of disadvantaged language are also of great interest precisely because they are a gauge of prejudice, and studies of BEV are particularly noteworthy here. Fasold (2006) points out that, while the equation of BEV with 'bad English' is obviously false, the world beyond the academy still finds it to be 'uncontroversially true'. The essence of the matter was stated by Spears:

> If black English vernacular has economically handicapped blacks, why haven't varieties of nonstandard white English economically handicapped the majority of white Americans who speak them... I believe this is simply another way of side-stepping the fundamental issue of institutional racism. (Spears, 1987: 55)

This is not entirely fair, since many white Americans *have* been held back in one way or another because of the way they speak. In terms of the degree and the scope of handicap, however, Spears is quite right. Even blunter was Foster (1997: 11): 'the reason that African American English has drawn such fire is not because it is inferior, but because it is spoken by Black people'. And James Baldwin wrote in the *New York Times* (1979) that 'it is not the black child's language that is in question, it is not his language that is despised. It is his experience'.

We must acknowledge at the outset, of course, that an excellent and obvious case can be made for acquiring greater facility with the standard forms endorsed at school and beyond. Drawing upon the strong linguistic evidence attesting to the validity of all dialects (see below), Trudgill (1975) has argued for a very liberal attitude towards nonstandard varieties at school; he feels that the best course of action involves changing the negative attitudes that unfairly stigmatize those varieties. This position is both logical and desirable. Until the millennium arrives, however, we should understand that problems are going to continue for certain groups of speakers; see Davies (1985). The German work of Ammon (1977, 1983) is relevant here, and Corson (1993, 2001) cites South American, Australian, Canadian, British and German research demonstrating the valued status of standard Spanish, English, Portuguese and German, and the low prestige of nonstandard forms.

Ammon *et al.* (1989), Hagen (1987), Tuveng and Wold (2005) and Wiggen (1978) make similar observations from European perspectives. Directly or indirectly, they all underscore the importance of *bidialectalism*; not, of course, a bidialectalism by *fiat*, but rather one that all the available data show will emerge naturally in tolerant conditions. In essence, this is an argument for a rather passive approach to the repertoire expansion that bidialectalism implies. Ammon has suggested that such an approach may not be the most expeditious in advancing the desired social mobility that standard-language usage can facilitate. However, his preferred 'solution' is a gradual disappearance of nonstandard varieties altogether, and he is thus more concerned with dialect transition than with dialect coexistence. The great problem here is that more active programs could easily have the effect of stigmatizing nonstandard varieties in the ears of their speakers: think of those ill-considered American 'deficit' interventions. Children generally do not respond well to approaches, however benevolently inspired, that essentially suggest to them that their maternal dialect is in some way flawed.

It is possible, of course, that even passively encouraging the addition of more standard forms to less standard ones – a typical scenario here would be standard-speaking teachers implicitly acting as models for their pupils, whose own varieties would be accepted in the classroom – might contribute to the eventual eradication of the latter. Perhaps, that is, bidialectalism cannot be maintained permanently (see Moses *et al.*, 1976, for an early discussion of this). This is an interesting question, and one that crosses the boundaries between language and dialect. Nonetheless, providing people with additional linguistic flexibility would seem an easy matter to justify – always providing, of course, that addition does not become replacement for those who value the former but do not want the latter. In terms of group identity maintenance, there are compelling reasons for the persistence of varieties lacking in social prestige. These can fuel a rejection of attempted language or dialect shift (at an individual level) or, more likely, a bilingualism or bidialectalism in which some variety of broader utility is added to the maternal medium of home and hearth.

It is quite true that suggesting the utility of dialect expansion can be very easily taken as an implicit argument that the existing variety is, in fact, flawed. It is a delicate undertaking, then, to effectively promote addition rather than replacement: teachers (and others) must obviously tread very carefully here. But it is an entirely worthwhile objective, and one whose importance is obvious to anyone who understands social stratification and its linguistic markers. It is also easier, perhaps, than it might first seem, for the sensitive teacher will in most cases be met by sensitive children, who are well on the way, themselves, to an understanding of the workings of that wider stratified society beyond the school gates.

Demonstrating difference

I am about to discuss here the important work of William Labov and his colleagues on BEV, but it is important to realize that, central as it is in the literature, it was not the earliest formal demonstration of the linguistic validity of that dialect. The work of Lorenzo Dow Turner (1949) has been unjustifiably neglected until relatively recently (see the 'biographical dedication' to Turner in Holloway & Vass, 1997; see also his entry in Stammerjohann, 1996), and it is not unfair to suggest that part of the reason for this neglect is that Turner was himself a black scholar. He is now, however, receiving some greater measure of attention, and his investigations of the Gullah dialect of South Carolina are increasingly recognized for the pioneering efforts, in both focus and scope, which they so obviously were. Whatever the ultimate assessment of the 'African-ness' of BEV may be, Turner's work on creolization will remain pivotal.

Labov was certainly, however, among the earliest scholars to system-atically refute the 'deficit' viewpoint, and his now-classic assault on 'verbal deprivation' appeared in 1969. He illustrates how interactions typically involving white middle-class interviewers and apprehensive black youngsters made 'defensive, monosyllabic' responses very pre-dictable and, conversely, how easy it was to dramatically increase the amount of speech produced by creating a more relaxed setting. The general suggestion, simply, is that 'verbal deprivation' is an artifact of inappropriate techniques. Labov also notes the important distinction between the comprehension of a statement and its reproduction. By means of a simple experiment, in which a child hears a statement and is asked to repeat it, he shows that a black child who hears 'I asked Alvin if he knows how to play basketball' might well repeat it as 'I ax Alvin do he know how to play basketball' or perhaps 'I axt Alvin does he know how to play basketball'. While such 'errors' are fuel for deficit theorists, it becomes clear that they simply reflect the regularities (in grammar and pronunciation) of the child's dialect, and are not substandard attempts to imitate the patterns of the more 'standard' variety. With regard to basic cognition and the grasp of *meaning*, it is clear that there is no deficiency: the child has understood the sentence and has then reproduced it in a familiar form (see also Marwit, 1977; Marwit *et al.*, 1972). The insight here was strengthened by Baratz (1969), whose study showed that white children make similar alterations between what is heard and what is replied: given the sentence 'Do Deborah like to play wif the girl...?', most repeated it as 'Does Deborah like to play with the girl...?'

Labov also questioned the basic idea that Bernstein's elaborated code was in fact the more desirable of the two, noting that the most desirable language is often the simplest, and that lower-class speech can be more direct and powerful than the hesitant and qualified style of the middle class: often 'turgid, redundant and empty' (Labov, 1969: 34). In general terms, then, Labov suggested that the 'non-verbality' of disadvantaged children is a myth (see also Keddie, 1973), that it is dangerous to infer underlying ability from particularities of language usage, and that arguments for the superiority of the middle-class elaborated code may be facile.

Labov also turned more directly to the central question here: the internal adequacy (i.e. the 'logic') of disadvantaged and nonstandard language. The arguments all revolve around the central point of rule-governed usage. To show that a dialect is not some inaccurate and deficient approximation of 'correct' language, it is necessary to demonstrate that it follows rules of its own. Two or three of Labov's examples here will make the point that such regularity is indeed a feature of Black English and, by extension, of all dialects (see also the similarly pioneering work of Shuy, 1970; Wolfram, 1969). References to 'Black English' and its rules should not, incidentally, be taken to mean that the variety is some linguistic monolith, spoken by all black people. The investigations of Labov and most other American linguists focus upon inner-city urban populations, and the linguistic features they report are not necessarily found in other communities (in rural black settings in Nova Scotia, to cite one context: see Edwards, 1999b). Similarly, in her study of Barbadians in New York, Callender (2005: 17) notes that the common use of BEV as a synonym for AAVE (African American Vernacular English) neglects other varieties: thus, 'black dialects of English that are not American have been largely unrecognized'. Hinton and Pollock (2000) draw particular attention to the neglect of regional variation in BEV, calling explicitly for more study of smaller and rural communities. Of course, the essential points made by linguistic researchers about dialect validity remain unaffected.

One frequently stigmatized feature of BEV is the deletion of the copula verb, in sentences like 'We goin' to the store'. In other instances, however, the verb appears: 'She was goin' with me', for instance. The regularity here depends upon tense (present or past) and it maps perfectly onto a more standard template. Thus, where standard English allows verbal *contraction* ('They are going' can legitimately become 'They're going'), so BEV allows *deletion*. And, where standard usage bars contraction (in past-tense usages, for example), so BEV disallows deletion. Different rules, to be sure, but equally 'logical'. It is worth pointing out here that present-tense copula deletion is hardly unique to BEV. In virtually all varieties of English it is common to hear constructions like 'This your car?' (as a policeman might ask a double-parked motorist). Such verbal ellipsis also occurs in 'headline' English ('Richard Burton dead') and on signs ('Exit at rear'). Beyond English, too, the practice is common. Even in Latin, Mount (2006) points out, it is quite normal to say 'Paris Hilton bella', with an implied but absent 'est' between the second and third words; his book is instructive and entertaining, even though his description of Ms Hilton is not universally shared.

BEV also changes the positive 'He know something' to the negative 'He don't know nothing'. That is, like many languages around the world, it customarily employs the double negative so frowned upon by Miss Fidditch, Mrs Grundy and their many relatives. Of course, speakers of standard English also use double-negative constructions; they are not deemed ungrammatical, because of the clue found in the stress. Thus, it is perfectly acceptable to say 'He does *not* know *nothing*' – meaning that he does, in fact, know *something*. And exactly the same sort of emphasis is employed by the black speaker who says 'He *don't* know *nothing*'. Emphasis is thus used by all speakers when a double negative is intended, but black speakers may use the *unstressed* double negative in contexts in which others may use the single negative.

Yet another regular feature of BEV is the omission of the possessive 's', giving rise to sentences like 'This Jane house'. Here, the important point is that no ambiguity is introduced; where it might be possible – does 'the man teacher' mean the instructor who has a male in the class, or the instructor himself? – matters are resolved with emphasis and contextual cues (Torrey, 1973).

There are also pronunciation differences, of course. Some of the more common variations found in BEV include 'th' becoming 'd' ('they' becomes 'dey'), or 'f' ('with' becomes 'wif') or 't' ('something' becomes 'someting'). It is instructive to recall that these forms are not unique to BEV ('th' becoming 'd' or 't', for example, is common in working-class Dublin English; 'wif' is common in parts of Cardiff; and so on). As with the more important grammatical features, it is the regularity with which these pronunciation variants occur that is germane here (see also Wolfram, 1973).

The implications of these findings are obvious. BEV is a valid variety. It is not *substandard*, although we may legitimately term it *nonstandard*, where that label is clearly understood to be a simple and non-pejorative description of social fact. Black children and other speakers of non-standard varieties are not verbally deficient. The aims and approaches of most programs of compensatory intervention are misguided. BEV made a useful test-case, not only because it diverges from standard forms more markedly than do many other dialects, but also because it was for so long considered to be substandard and illogical English (see the very useful overview by Smitherman-Donaldson, 1988). And this consideration, as my earlier reference to Foster (1997) makes clear, is inextricably intertwined with longstanding prejudice against black people. It is worth mentioning at this point that many features of BEV dialects are encountered well beyond the black community. Roy Wilkins, the executive director of the NAACP (and editor of *The Crisis*, the magazine founded in 1910 by William Du Bois), made the point in 1971: BEV, he said, is 'more regional than racial... more southern than Negro... [it] is basically the same slovenly English spoken by the south's under-educated poor white population' (Wilkins, 1971: 78). The point was confirmed by the black academics interviewed later by Speicher and McMahon (1992). Regrettably, it is also worth mentioning that, like Wilkins, they also tended see BEV as a restricted approximation to 'proper' English; only a few considered it 'a full linguistic system' (Speicher & McMahon, 1992: 391; see also Pederson, cited in the *Globe & Mail*, 1997). We shall see further evidence of this within-community disdain for the vernacular when we turn to the discussion of 'Ebonics'.

The demonstration that Black English is a fully formed medium makes a very strong case against linguistic deficiency theories in general. The studies undertaken by Labov and his American colleagues naturally spawned many others, and it is fair to say that, in all instances where investigations have been linguistically respectable, the falsity of the 'deficit' view of nonstandard speech has been exposed. Where a nonstandard variety differs widely from standard forms (as with some varieties of West Indian English, for instance), then it approaches the status of a separate language, in which case there is little difficulty in viewing the system as merely different.[5] If, on the other hand, a dialect is not hugely variant from the standard, then it follows that most of it *is* standard. The 'gears and axles of English grammatical machinery are available to speakers of all dialects', as Labov (1976: 64) put it. His two-volume overview (Labov, 1994) provides an admirable summary of work on language variation and change, including buttressing replications of some of the early studies that I have reported here.

The summary position, then, is this: any deficit view of linguistic behavior is incorrect: no language, or language variety, has been shown to be more accurate, logical or capable of expression than another. Further, it is wrong to claim that some variations constrain basic intellectual or cognitive functioning. Rather, different language groups and sub-groups develop speech patterns that differ in their modes of expression, vocabulary and pronunciation. (There is also the matter of different groups assigning different *functions* to language, something that

Bernstein latterly claimed his work demonstrated; see above. There are interesting questions to be asked here, but none deals with inherent linguistic deficiency.) There is, then, a certain logic to Houston's (1970) assertion that the language of disadvantaged children – a representation, like all varieties, of particular cultures and environments – should be left alone and not changed in any way. There remains, however, the question of *social* liability. In effect, the rejection of deficit interpretations of language is a sort of ground-clearing: what, if anything, ought to be done about disadvantaged speech remains an open matter.

The Views of Teachers

The classroom represents the single most important point of contact between social dialects; it is where nonstandard speakers first become conscious of their own speech patterns, and where the regulations and impositions of the larger society first make themselves felt. Consequently, it is appropriate here to touch briefly upon teachers' attitudes. At a general level, it is clear that, like others, many teachers have implicit 'deficit' opinions about disadvantage, believing that inadequate environments stunt cognitive capacity. Such opinions then contribute to what Rist (1970) famously referred to as a circular and self-fulfilling prophecy: teachers expect certain children to do poorly at school; they treat them in certain ways; the children respond in certain ways; and initial expectations are confirmed. Rosenthal and Jacobson (1968) had earlier demonstrated how easy it is to experimentally manipulate expectations, and Fuchs (1973) showed how such 'manipulations' occur naturally: new teachers are 'socialized' by the attitudes and assumptions of those already in the classroom. In such a manner, disadvantage is perpetuated; see also my remarks in the introduction, and in the previous chapter.

When we turn, more specifically, to consideration of nonstandard language, two interrelated features present themselves: teachers' attitudes towards nonstandard speech per se, and attitudes towards disadvantage that are evoked by nonstandard speech. General research in accent and dialect evaluation reveals that speech particularities typically act as triggers for wider social stereotypes, but it is clear that a circularity is established whereby the presence of such stereotypes colors subsequent assessments of accent and dialect variation; and so on. In any event, it is easy to demonstrate that teachers' views of disadvantaged speech are just as likely as those of less enlightened observers to employ such deficit adjectives as 'wrong', 'bad', 'careless', 'sloppy', 'slovenly' and 'vulgar' (Trudgill, 1975: 63). Teachers have all too frequently assumed that nonstandard dialects are equivalent to 'restricted' codes, and the research reported by Shafer and Shafer (1975) and Thomson (1977) reveals that these assumptions are made in many geographic settings: the phenomena under discussion here are not limited to Britain and America, nor, indeed, to anglophone contexts. Trudgill (1975) has argued that the influence of Bernstein was unfortunate since, at a time when more enlightened views about speech and language variants had begun to circulate, the notoriety of 'public' and 'restricted' codes reinforced longstanding prejudices, and seemed to grant them some intellectual respectability. Bernstein's views – so easily assimilated by those holding traditional attitudes towards 'correctness' – remained in circulation; they surfaced, for instance, in John Honey's notorious arguments, first made in a pamphlet published by the National Council for Educational Standards (1983a), about the 'language trap' allegedly created by the noxious and inaccurate theories of linguists (see Chapter 7).[6]

There is quite a large literature revealing teachers' negative perceptions of disadvantaged speech varieties. The conclusions drawn in a Québec study summarize things nicely: 'a lower-class youngster's style of speech may mark or caricature him and thus adversely affect his opportunities in various situations, including the school environment' (Frender *et al.*, 1970: 305). In similar work, Seligman *et al.* (1972: 141) found speech style to be 'an important cue to the teachers in their evaluations of students. Even when combined with other cues, its effect did not diminish'. Choy and Dodd (1976) found that teachers in Hawaii consistently favored standard-dialect speakers in primary school; they were described as higher achievers, more confident and less 'disruptive' in class. The authors were also able to show how absurdly wide-ranging such evaluations can be: nonstandard speakers were thought less likely, for example, to have happy marriages. Granger *et al.* (1977: 795) found a 'distinct social class and racial bias' in their studies of teachers' reactions to BEV, suggesting that 'the teachers were attending less to *what* a child said than to *how* he said it'. The extensive program of research summarized in Williams (1976; see also Chapter 8) found that a recurring factor in studies of teachers' evaluations was what he labelled 'ethnicity/ nonstandardness' – a composite description of a number of discrete semantic-differential scales. Disadvantaged children were generally seen as being more 'ethnic' or more 'nonstandard' than others, suggesting a strong connection in teachers' minds between cognitive ability and likely academic success, on the one hand, and membership in certain groups, on the other. It is also significant that Williams and his associates found that such perceptions (of black, white and Mexican American children living in Texas) were held by *both* black and white teachers. This suggests that simply employing more teachers from traditionally disadvantaged groups may not lighten the evaluative load borne by children at school. In fact, it is very likely that, whatever their personal backgrounds, teachers become socialized into middle-class ways.[7]

The overall implication here is clear. Like everyone else, teachers maintain stereotyped and often prejudicial views of certain language varieties and their speakers. In one sense, then, the data documenting their attitudes merely reflect a specific aspect of a general phenomenon. But teachers' views are, of course, rather special because of the position they occupy in the lives of disadvantaged children. Beyond the demonstration (in the early studies mentioned above, and in many others) that speech patterns can influence teachers' evaluations of children, there is also the suggestion that the attitudes behind such assessments may affect children's educational progress. This is what lends a special poignancy to the discussion – an extension of which will be found in Chapter 8.

Reading Matters

The discussion so far has argued for the linguistic validity of all dialects and, as a consequence, for their acceptance in the classroom and elsewhere. This says nothing, however, about the practical utility of expanding repertoires, about adding some facility in standard forms to nonstandard maternal varieties. There are, after all, social conventions that are not likely to change in the near future, and these have the great and very important power of translating difference into deficit – social deficit only, perhaps, and deficit based upon misinformation and prejudice, but deficit nonetheless. A social convention that is easier to defend, having its ground in practicality, involves the language of reading and writing. Here, a good case can obviously be made for a common standard. It is a fair objection that this may favor those whose oral fluency is in the standard dialect, but for all children – even standard-speaking children – formal learning is required to move from spoken language to print. The evidence suggests that the effort involved here is not, in fact, appreciably more for nonstandard-dialect speakers.

In this connection – and reminding us of points made earlier in this chapter – Torrey (1973: 68) noted that:

> the difference in phonology between Standard English and Black English is not directly relevant to reading. All children who learn to read English have to break a fairly complex code of sound-spelling

relationships. The fact that the correspondences are different for speakers of Afro-American does not in itself prove that they are more difficult than for standard speakers.

This seems plausible, but as Harber and Bryen (1976) soon added, the possibility of dialect interference in reading cannot be completely ruled out. (Trudgill [1979: 17] has noted that *accent* differences might be thought to be more troublesome in many cases than dialect variations, but also that teachers report that this is not generally so: 'English spelling is probably sufficiently distant from pronunciation not to favor one accent over any other: all speakers are at an equal disadvantage'.) This explains why there have been periodic attempts to provide reading materials in nonstandard dialects.

Baratz's view (1970) is representative of early thinking here. Proposing that black children be given books written in BEV, she argued that reading competence in one's own dialect is a necessary prerequisite for standard-dialect reading ability. To further facilitate the attainment of this end, Baratz also called for 'transition texts' as a halfway-stop between BEV and standard-English books (see also Baratz, 1972; Baratz & Shuy, 1969; Stewart, 1972). This perspective has been broadened since Baratz's observations. Thus, Rickford (2005) discusses the use of 'bridging' materials for black children, citing a large-scale study by Simpkins and Simpkins (1981; see also Simpkins *et al.*, 1977). About 80% of some 500 secondary-school students were given materials that

> began with narratives and exercises written in Ebonics [see below]. They then went through a transitional series of readers written in a variety intermediate between Ebonics and English [sic], and ended with a final series written entirely in Standard English. (Rickford, 2005: 31)

The other 20% constituted a control group that used traditional reading books. After four months, the researchers report that this control group showed only 1.6 months of 'reading gain'. By contrast, those exposed to the bridging readers showed 6.2 months of such advance. These are quite dramatic findings. Yet Rickford points out that the negative publicity that was to prove so important 15 years later in the Oakland Ebonics debate made its mark here, too – to such an extent that the publisher of the 'transitional' readers halted their production. And, as in that later controversy, within-group criticism was not far to seek. John McWhorter (1997a, 1997b), for example, a well-known black intellectual, argued in the wake of the Oakland brouhaha that schoolbooks in BEV had no effect upon the development of reading skills. (I shall pay closer attention to the Ebonics debate in a later chapter.) As Rickford notes, however, the studies to which McWhorter referred were of the quick-and-dirty variety, lacking any 'time depth' (see also the earlier observations on this point by Simons & Johnson, 1974). Rickford and Rickford (2005) thus call for renewed attention to bridging materials, and outline the requirements of future research in the area.

Whatever the findings of educational researchers are, or will be, there is considerable evidence from a number of settings showing that many parents do not want to see their nonstandard language variety in schoolbooks. Their attitudes may be regrettable (reflecting inaccurate assessments of linguistic inferiority), or they may be less than fully informed (neglecting, for instance, the possibility of a bidialectalism that extends to reading), or they may be 'practical', at least in some traditional 'time-on-task' perspective (that is, parents may see the use of such books as antithetical to their views of the school as an agent of social advancement, and likely to delay or impair standard-language abilities). One thing is certain, however: parental attitudes cannot be ignored. Another is that their views may be somewhat more subtle than I have just implied. Covington (1976) pointed out, for instance, that black parents in Washington who wanted tolerance of their children's BEV in the classroom were, at the same time, strongly opposed to textbooks written in that variety; similar opinions have been reported by Harber and Bryen (1976) and Venezky (1970).

Beyond the social-political objections, criticisms of such educational initiatives involving nonstandard textbooks have built upon Torrey's point of view (above), arguing that it may simply be unnecessary because – while we obviously do not know everything about potential cross-dialectal problems – it seems likely that any such interference would be minimal. Trudgill (1975) echoed Torrey in the British context and, in the American one, Labov (1976: 241) further reinforced the point:

> Some writers seem to believe that the major problem causing reading failure is structural interference between these two forms of English [BEV and standard]. Our research points in the opposite direction... The number of structures unique to BEV are [sic] small, and it seems unlikely that they could be responsible for the disastrous record of reading failure in the inner city schools.

Besides the work already cited, a few other experimental studies have also suggested that reading materials in BEV might be useful, although the findings here are rather inconsistent (see Somervill, 1974, 1975;

Somervill & Jacobs, 1972; Thurmond, 1977). Venezky (1970, 1981), a well-known reading specialist, summarized the matter by noting that, if it could reliably be shown that provision of nonstandard reading materials would assist in skill development, there could be no reasonable objection. In the absence of such a demonstration, however, the time and expense involved in the production of these materials seem inappropriate. This is quite apart from the social objections already touched upon, as well as from important questions that would inevitably arise about the number of varieties to be represented in print, the best methods of capturing nonstandard pronunciation on the page, the timing of the transition to standard-dialect texts, and so on.

A variant approach here has argued for the elimination of points of dialect interference from reading texts; some sort of 'neutral' text was apparently envisaged. This attracts the same general criticisms already noted, but it does alert us to an attitude that has been steadily growing – in too 'politically correct' a manner, however, some might say – since Baratz, Torrey and Labov first presented their research results. It is simply that the deletion of certain features that are strongly and specifically associated with given social groups might be useful: more 'culture-free' or 'culture-fair' books, in other words. Such a practice could lead to stories stripped of all color and style, could be pressed into the service of retroactive 'cleansing', could be bowdlerization – but it could also produce more broadly useful materials (see Vick, 1974). It has already been used extensively, particularly with regard to gender descriptions and stereotypes. Of course, this is not in the service of nonstandard textbooks.

The most reasonable approach, in fact, tends to be almost a non-approach. Texts continue to be written in more or less standard dialect, but children are allowed to recite and reproduce meanings in their own dialect (see Simons, 1974; Venezky, 1970), or accent ('there is no reason why a person cannot learn to read Standard English texts quite well in a nonstandard pronunciation': Labov, 1972: 289). This point of view builds upon the experimental evidence concerning sentence repetition (as noted above): that is, children are likely to repeat material, standard or nonstandard, in their maternal dialect. The assumption is that the nonstandard-dialect-speaking child's *decoding* abilities (i.e. extracting the meaning from print on the page) will lead to *encoding* what has been read (e.g. reading aloud) in a nonstandard format.

It is also consistent with a *difference* view of nonstandard speech and language, of course. As we have increasingly come to realize the validity and the completeness of nonstandard dialects, so it follows that there is less and less to 'do' for the disadvantaged child in terms of curriculum alteration. Rather, the required changes are more attitudinal in nature, resting upon more accurate psychological, social and linguistic understanding. Just as with oral language, much depends here upon the knowledge and the sensitivity of teachers; and, as with speech, it is assumed that all children can develop standard-dialect reading skills. Given increasing comprehension, there is every indication that children will also have increasing choice on the 'reproduction' side of the equation. There is an abundance of models (both printed and spoken) here, ranging from classroom teachers and the books they use, to the wider world beyond the school gates. It is, of course, expected that children will not be left entirely to their own devices: they are in school, after all. Teachers who are, themselves, well-informed can gradually make clear the contexts in which standard usage is most appropriate and where, therefore, its use is likely to be most beneficial. But, as with other important aspects of life, much can be left to the evolving discretion of those most directly involved.

Some may think that this 'approach' is much too *laissez-faire*, but we should bear in mind that any more formal or strict approach (even if stemming from the best of motives) is not likely to work and may, in fact, widen the gap that already too frequently exists between the disadvantaged child and the school. In this regard, Bullock (1975: 143) made a sensible recommendation:

> The teacher's aim should be to indicate to his [sic] pupils the value of awareness and flexibility, so that they can make their own decisions and modify these as their views alter.

A short postscript: beyond possible contributions to skills development, it may be that books written in nonstandard varieties have other values. For example, materials produced in the local vernacular of Ballyfermot, a working-class suburb of Dublin, were seen to 'legitimize' that variety (Murphy, 1975) and books in BEV have, it is argued, reinforced the self-esteem of their readers (Edwards, 1989).

Notes

1. Miss Fidditch and Mrs Grundy may be candidates for the Freudian couch. It is now 'pretty generally recognized by psycho-analysts', observed Flugel (1934: 205), 'that anal factors often play a part in our attitude towards linguistic correctness'. Anal repression may lead to 'disagreeable feelings' in both speaker and listener: the former, guilty of a lapse of linguistic correctness; the latter, forced to hear speech 'murdered' by clumsiness. 'The

scholarly schoolmaster who is "disgusted" by the "howlers" of... his pupils affords one striking example of this kind' (p. 206).

Flugel's main authority here is Ernest Jones, the pioneer of psychoanalysis in Britain, and Freud's biographer (see Jones, 1918).

2. Bernstein himself (1971, 1972a) analyzed constructed data (see also Rosen, 1972, for a criticism), and the practice was more common than might be imagined, especially among 'deficit' theorists. Nowadays, the enormous benefits arising from constructing the data that are to be interpreted have proved most appealing to discourse analysts.

3. Lady Plowden died in 2000, aged 90, and Corbett's obituary in *The Guardian* (3 October) made a point of mentioning that her life of voluntary service constituted one of the last examples of the 'great and the good' caste at work in British public life, in which leadership roles on national bodies and commissions were traditionally filled by members of that caste. So, perhaps a hint of Lady Bountiful – 'as we do ourselves' – was to be expected. The *Plowden Report*, and 'Plowdenism', were heavily criticised from all sides, but it is instructive to remember the arguments made for parental involvement, for sensitive pre-school provision, for greater and more comprehensive attention to the very real problems of poor children at home and at school. For a useful retrospective, see Halsey and Sylva (1987).

4. Cross-cultural sensitivity remains key, however. Seeing how well disadvantaged children do on essentially middle-class tasks can be very useful, for example – provided the aim is to get some measure of likely problems in classrooms where such tasks are commonly encountered, and not to assess basic 'deficiency'. Similarly, while it is not unreasonable to probe nonstandard-dialect-speaking children for their knowledge and use of standard forms, it is absurd to use the findings as indications of maternal-variety development (see Baratz, 1969; Edwards, 1977a, 1977b).

5. One doesn't have to go to the Caribbean, however. In 1983, BBC television broadcast a series called *Auf Wiedersehen, Pet*, about Geordie brickies who go to work in Germany. The English newspapers carried stories from viewers who were appreciative, but who asked for subtitles. (The show made a brief reappearance at Christmas 2004.)

6. The Council has been described as a 'right-wing pressure group' (Crowley, 1989).

7. It would also be naïve to assume that those who have achieved positions of social security will necessarily be sympathetic to those they have left behind. The person who has climbed the ladder of success may be more likely to step on the fingers of those following than to help them – for to bring others 'up' is to dilute the singularity of one's own attainments. A more elegant expression of the same idea is found in *Julius Caesar* (II.i.22–27), when Brutus observes

> That lowliness is young ambition's ladder,
> Whereto the climber-upward turns his face;
> But when he once attains the upmost round,
> He then unto the ladder turns his back,
> Looks in the clouds, scorning the base degrees
> By which he did ascend.

Chapter 7

The Persistence of Linguistic Deficit

Theoretical Extensions

Most socially stratified societies have had rather firm ideas about 'correct' and 'incorrect' language, and nowhere have these ideas been more explicit than in the classroom, traditionally a forceful supporter of 'proper' language. The most important corollary was the school's role – strongly articulated within its walls, and strongly if sometimes implicitly reinforced from without – in the eradication of 'substandard' varieties. In this, the school has always had considerable power: it is a highly visible institution, whose forms and formalities typically adhere to prevailing middle-class points of view; it provides the first sustained break from the home environment in which linguistic contact across groups has been minimal; it receives children at a young age and extends its influence over them for a long time. For children speaking a standard variety, the home-school link is close, and the classroom may essentially be a formalized version of the home. For disadvantaged children, however, there often exists a marked home-school discontinuity, arising from that contact which is itself central to the very idea of disadvantage.

As I noted earlier, there has been some question as to whether or not the school really is a middle-class setting; some have claimed that it is actually more continuous with a working-class environment than others (myself included) have asserted. If this were so, it might imply less substance to the charge that disadvantage as a product of social comparison is highlighted and sustained at school. In the collection edited by Feagans and Farran (1982), for instance, several authors took the line that schools do not reinforce middle-class home practices; they also pointed out that learning at school is passive, with teachers' talk dominating, that classrooms stress rigidity, bureaucracy and order, and that schools are, in general, not unlike working-class homes (where, readers will recall, parents are allegedly more authoritarian, more interested in order than in curiosity, more likely to direct than to consult, and so on). If it were true, however, that lower-class homes do stifle intellectual questing under authoritarian rigidity – a dubious and unnuanced contention – it is also true that schools impose order precisely so as to facilitate that same enterprise: an imposition of the minimal order, that is to say, required for educational development to occur. (I don't deny, of course, the existence of some modern incarnations of Dotheboys Hall nor, more realistically, do I deny that many classrooms are not in practice what they should be in theory.) In fact, where the home-school discontinuity fuelling disadvantage is not as serious as is often imagined, this is probably due more to the fact that the working-class family is unlike its stereotyped representation in the literature than to the assumption that schools are closer to that stereotype and more removed from middle-class values.

In accepting that some speech styles are simply wrong, schools have of course reflected extra-mural deficit views of disadvantage in general and of language in particular. These views, incidentally, have been remark-ably similar across social groups, for it is a commonplace – and, after a moment's thought, the psychology here is not difficult to comprehend – that those with socially stigmatized speech styles often come to accept 'mainstream' perceptions of their low status and deficiency. The school's role in linguistic disadvantage has been a circularly reinforcing one: children arrive speaking a variety that is considered deficient; teachers, acting from the best of (ill-founded) motives, aim to replace this with a standard variety; they may also make attributions, based upon their perceptions of speech, about the intelligence, educability and likely scholastic progress of their pupils. The vicious circle implicit in Rist's (1970) famous 'self-fulfilling prophecy' is completed when children, treated differently because of presumed deficiencies, do in fact come to perform less well than others.

There is little doubt that, in many jurisdictions, schools are more tolerant of language variation today than they once were; again, this is related to attitudes beyond the school gates – more liberal ones, in this case.[1] But 'tolerance' rarely rests upon whole-hearted acceptance. Contemporary assessments of 'social inclusion', of the evils of 'marginalization' and 'stigmatization', of the inequities marked by race and class – these, rather than more fundamental shifts in belief and understanding, may be the operative principles at work in many instances. I shall suggest below that there has, in fact, been little real movement beyond deficit perspectives.[2] Beyond the classroom, of course, it is clear to anyone with ears to hear (or eyes to read: in the letters-to-the-editor sections of the newspaper, for instance) that perceptions of 'poor' English have not disappeared. Linguistic evidence of the Labovian sort does not work very fast or very completely on popular stereotypes; and attitudes, by their psychological nature, can be doggedly resistant to unpalatable fact.

Indeed, even limited gains within education ought not to be taken for granted. A recent example of the volatility here is found in the rejections of bilingual education programs in some parts of America, the assertion being that bilingual education has gone too far in promoting and sustaining minority languages, that an undesirable balkanization must be resisted and so on. Flores (2005) discusses the links between such programs and linguistic disadvantage for the Hispanic children who constitute the great bulk of the bilingual education constituency in America. Bedore and Peña (2008), Commins and Miramontes (1989), Delgado-Gaitan (1992), Gifford and Valdés (2006) and Jiménez (2000, 2006) investigate further the continuing 'deficit' assumptions that are made about Hispanic children – and others whose maternal language is not English – by teachers and some researchers. Related events beyond the schoolroom include the occasional but recurring efforts to formally designate English as the official language of the United States, and of the success of such efforts at the state level. More than half of the 50 states now have official-English legislation. Several of these, it is true, have designated English as *co*-official with another language, as have some American territories; in one case – the Northern Marianas – trilingualism is official (Chamorro, Carolinian and English).

As well as acknowledging that reasoned academic argument may not always penetrate as far or as quickly as we would wish, it is clear that the 'limited-gain' argument I have cited above also applies within the hallowed groves themselves. The Feagans and Farran (1982) collection, already mentioned, brought together some well-known writers, all of whom were well aware of the latest research bearing upon linguistic difference-and-deficit matters; well aware, that is, that the best psycho-linguistic opinion of the time supported a 'difference' point of view. Yet, the editors noted in the preface that the deficit model became untenable not only because of 'new perspectives', but also because interventions based upon it did not work very well. The possibility is held out, in other words, that only *strategies* were misguided, not underlying assumptions. One of the chapter authors (Blank, 1982) considers that both difference and deficit approaches have difficulties, but fails to make clear that the difficulties are not of equal force: the linguistic objections to the fundamentals of the deficit position are overwhelming, while the sorts of 'difference' problems she discusses have to do with the assessment of appropriate ranges of skills for different social groups.[3]

Blank also suggests that deficit theorists have typically concerned themselves with semantic issues, difference theorists with syntax. Again, this inaccurately weakens the anti-deficit case, for it implies that the model might, after all, retain some validity. Tough (1982) argues here for a stereotypically 'deficit' view of speech patterns in working-class homes, an argument she had made earlier (Tough, 1977) and which she continued to make (Tough, 1985). Another contributor also muddied the picture by claiming that disadvantaged children *do* have deficits, which are not linguistic but are rather deficiencies of knowledge; these lead, then, to smaller vocabularies (Snow, 1982). While at first blush it would seem that matters of vocabulary *are* matters of language, it is apparent on reflection that the size and shape of a group's vocabulary are best understood as products of environmental exigency. And this brings us back to difference rather than deficit. After all, there are many human groups who lack the terminology of higher mathematics, who have no word for 'laser'; and what does this prove about any innate cognitive deficiency?

Overall, the argument that I made in the second edition of a book about language and disadvantage (Edwards, 1989, see also Edwards 2006) – and complementary suggestions made by Crowley (2003) in the second edition of *his* book on standard language – seem justified. Various types of 'deficit' models continue to have adherents, both within and without the educational world. There are 'important continuities with the thinking of the past, including the repetition of many of the same points of confusion and difficulty' (Crowley, 2003: 231). In similar fashion, Wolfram (1998a) recently acknowledged that 'entrenched myths about language inadequacy are like a jack-in-the-box that keeps springing back up'; he goes on to say that

> the exposure of one line of reasoning as objectively unjustified and illogical doesn't mean that linguistic equality will be attained. If the bottom-line belief is that one cultural group – and by extension its language – is inferior to another, then another line of reasoning will simply replace the old one. (Wolfram, 1998a: 105)

Perhaps there is something inherent in the nature of socially stratified societies that will always find a way to translate cultural difference into deficiency. But even if this rather gloomy assessment is correct – even if we can only hope to scotch the snake, not kill it – we should make whatever assaults we can on inaccurate and prejudiced interpretations.

The Honey affair

In Britain, some of the continuing controversy has been stimulated by the work of John Honey. It is worth considering here, not only because of the prominence it achieved, but also because it represents so well the continuing force of deficit perspectives. In an impressive collection devoted to the 'debate' over standard English, the editors note at the very beginning that the need for discussion 'became even more pressing after the publication of Honey's *Language is Power* (1997) with its peculiar mixture of half truths and ad hominem arguments' (Bex & Watts, 1999: 1). In fact, as we shall see very shortly, the most contentious aspects of Honey's book are reworkings and restatements of material he had introduced years before. Honey's writing would probably not have attracted much academic attention, were it not for the considerable coverage it received in the popular media. This coverage was largely favorable, because Honey was often seen as a champion of 'proper' English, daring to break academically imposed taboos, an unapologetic and provocative critic of the prevailing 'liberal orthodoxy' in education. 'You can't pull the wool over Professor Honey's ears', said the *Mail on Sunday*.[4] Furthermore, most of the journalistic accolades emerged from politically right-wing stances, and so most of the academic constituency – certainly that segment that had worked hard to eradicate narrow and essentially reactionary interpretations of language that translated differences into deficits – were put on their guard. Cameron (1995: 86) notes the 'respectful' media attention given to what was seen as Honey's 'daring' and 'iconoclastic' assault upon the prevailing orthodoxy; she then clarifies the difficulty that faced the academic community, and that prompted it to respond:

> To the extent that Marenbon or Honey can air their value judgements openly, whereas their opponents in linguistic science are more constrained by the norm of objectivity, the polemical advantage lies with the conservatives, and the linguists are likely to lose the argument. (Cameron, 1995: 100)

(The Marenbon to whom Cameron refers here produced a pamphlet [1987] in which he argued for the superiority of standard English, and that grammar 'prescribes by describing' [Marenbon, 1987: 20]: descriptive efforts create norms which should then be prescribed.)

Honey's various assaults on current linguistic ideas (1983a, 1989, 1997) make for interesting reading. In the first of these, a rather notorious pamphlet, he claimed that work supporting the position that all language varieties are equally valid systems – work, that is, supporting the 'difference' position – was without any firm basis. Furthermore, he considered it pernicious since, in the current climate of unease with the allegedly low standards of written and spoken English, such work acted to undermine attempts to raise these standards.[5] Disadvantaged speakers of nonstandard English thus fall into a 'language trap'; they need help in standard language in order to advance socially and economically, but the modern linguistic paradigm insists that schools should encourage the use of varieties of *non*standard English. The pivotal point, however (according to Honey) is that all dialects are *not* equally valid: there is something to the 'deficit' idea after all.

He argues, for example, that some varieties are superior to others in that they can express more rarefied concepts (he mentions higher mathematics, biochemistry and the philosophy of Wittgenstein). He is, of course, confusing words with concepts. Vocabulary is, in itself, only an indicator of relevant social ideas, beliefs, theories and so on: societies ignorant of higher mathematics will obviously not need terms to describe it. It is important to realize here that, as societies develop and change, so their languages alter. All dialects and languages are capable of expressing whatever the social environment demands; see also Crowley (1989), who enlarges his discussion of Honey by referring to other 'ideologists of the new right'.

Honey sees the scholarly acceptance of the different-but-not-deficient viewpoint as a reflection of Chomskyan influence, and of the contemporary fashion to avoid making moral judgments of societies and their languages. Chomsky is seen to bolster the difference argument by holding that all human beings share similar underlying linguistic capacities, that all languages are essentially similar at some deep level. Consequently, qualitative judgments are inappropriate across languages. I suppose this is true, but even if Chomskyan (and other, more recent) 'innatist' theories were completely transcended, the argument that all varieties are adequate for their users would still not necessarily be weakened – because one would have to claim that different groups of human beings differ markedly in their innate conceptual powers, a claim that has never been substantiated. In general, questions of variations in social development – possibly of inequalities in cognitive capacities, and certainly of marked differences in the operation of such capacities in particular environments – are large and vexed. I would simply argue that, whatever the verdict may be in terms of cognitive development in other areas, that of adequate language is a human universal (see also Edwards, 1985).

On the second point, it is true that cultural relativism has been a powerful influence in contemporary literature, and it is the case, as Honey implies, that this can lead to difficulties: an extreme relativism might seem to force us to embrace such repellent practices as Nazi war crimes, cannibalism and female circumcision. My argument, however, is simply that some aspects of relativism are more appropriate than others, that relativism itself is relative, and that it is possible to construct an intellectual position that allows us to legitimately criticize some features of societies while still permitting different-but-not-deficient analyses of others. I assume, for instance, that a society that condones cannibalism and believes in witchcraft is inferior, in these respects, to one that does not. I do not see that this constrains me to accept, as well, that language X is superior to language Y, even if Y-speakers eat their neighbors while X-speakers turn the other cheek.

Honey is particularly critical of Labov's work, claiming that it did not, after all, show the dialectal validity of Black English vernacular (BEV). But Honey pays only passing attention to the most important part of that work, the demonstration of the rule-governed nature of BEV; indeed, he attempts to undercut the very approach, noting that not all linguists agree on what the rules are. The lack of perfect knowledge and agreement, however, is a linguistic fact of life that is true for all varieties (including standard English), and it misses the essential point that linguists *do* agree that rules exist and are abided by.

When he turns to consider current educational practice, Honey errs again – this time in his supposition that acceptance of the difference position necessarily entails active school promotion of nonstandard varieties. Of course, it does not. The weight of the available evidence suggests that schools should accept nonstandard varieties as valid systems; two corollaries are that teachers ought not to try and stamp them out, and that children should not be penalized for using them. However, because of social realities, schools should continue to provide standard English models and to promote awareness of this dialect, within an atmosphere of tolerance and respect for all other varieties (see also Pennycook, 2001). It is important to remember here that a common standard can work to level the playing field just as easily as privileging one group over another: which role it fills, of course, depends upon how it is understood.

Overall, the importance of Honey's intervention is not in its handling and interpretation of linguistic evidence; Crowley (1999) provides some chapter-and-verse documentation of Honey's (1997) errors and rather cavalier presentation of evidence for his assertions. Rather, it lies in its very existence as an attempted defence of a linguistic status quo seen to be in danger. Honey is exercised over the increasing power of contemporary influences (including television) compared to traditional shapers of education and language (e.g. the Bible). He acknowledges that change is the inevitable order of the day, but clearly regrets it. In fact, his general thrust can be seen as a desire to defend traditional values. This may or may not be a laudable objective per se – a great deal depends, for example, on the assessed value of the old and the new – but one thing is sure: no reliable case of any sort can be built on inaccurate foundations.

Honey's work is best seen as an effort to breathe renewed life into a 'deficit' philosophy and, as such, it has stimulated some provocative and pointed reaction. One of the chief linguistic 'oracles' attacked in the 1983 pamphlet was David Crystal, whose response (Crystal, 1983) pointed to the highly emotional language in which Honey couched his attacks on the modern linguistic enterprise. 'A great industry has grown up', Honey had said (on p. 2), 'dedicated to disparaging standard English... based on fantasies, fabrications and unproven hypotheses'. This is a bit rich, as Crystal rightly notes, considering that Honey's own assertions of the unscientific, uncritical and misleading views supposedly promulgated by linguists verge on conspiracy-theory rhetoric, and that his own 'case' rests rather heavily upon secondary and often non-academic sources. The twin strands of Honey's argument are that these nefarious linguists hold all varieties to be equally good, and that any emphasis upon standard English must therefore be unjustifiable. Crystal neatly points out that the 'good-ness' that contemporary linguistics attributes to all languages and dialects is a linguistic and not a social matter – and that there is nothing contradictory in claiming that purely linguistic 'goodness' need not mean equivalence in a world where attitudes commonly translate difference into deficit. The real implication here is not any sort of 'language trap' to which disadvantaged children are condemned, but rather – as I have pointed out (Edwards, 1983a) – an enlightened and culturally sensitive policy of bidialectalism. Since Honey himself ends up with a recommendation for 'bilectalism', Crystal finds the whole argument to be a damp squib. Others have, too – see Graddol and Swann (1988) on the synonymy of 'bilectalism' and 'bidialectalism' – and with other arguments, as well: for instance, Honey (2000b) proposes that 'in any society (or subculture) in which educatedness is an admired attribute, prestige will attach to those linguistic forms which are perceived as characteristic of educatedness'. (Later, I shall have more to say about the *practical* difficulties associated with bidialectal policies at school, but the *theoretical* arguments for them are firmly based.)

Crystal's (1983) lengthy review of Honey's pamphlet appeared in a number of the newsletter of the British Association for Applied Linguis-tics, accompanying a second review (Hudson, 1983; see also Honey, 1983b, for a response to these two). Later on, Honey (1997) acknowledged how unusual such double treatment was in those pages, particularly since the work assessed was only 40 pages long. Such attention from the linguistic 'establishment' suggested to Honey a lashing-out at an argument that challenged widely-held but dubious views, a fierce reaction to a wounded professional *amour propre*. To others, however, Honey's pamphlet, whose style and argument (however unconvincing in an academic sense) led to wide coverage in both the broadsheet and the tabloid press, required a firm response. Thus, Hudson described the work as a 'prime example of demagoguery, telling the uninitiated what they want to hear'. Trudgill (1998: 460), in a trenchant review of Honey (1997), said that 'since he continues to masquerade as a linguist... and since the weight of uninformed journalistic opinion is on his side, we need to take every opportunity we can to make it plain that he is not speaking on our behalf'. In an American review, Kochman (1985: 161) calls Honey's pamphlet 'reactionary... elitist... intellectually dishonest... mean-spirited'.

Graddol and Swann (1988) present a very interesting analysis of the academic response to Honey's pamphlet. They argue that the rejoinders were not as disinterested as they might have been, and they identify three main 'response strategies'. In the first of these, Honey is seen as 'subversive', an outsider intent on smearing the scholarly community; consequently – even as they were responding to his work – some implied that it was both *infra dig* and useless to cross swords with such an opponent. Relatedly, there is a desire to deny Honey the 'oxygen of publicity'. The second strategy rests upon a sense of outrage and insult: much of the to-and-fro'ing in the popular and academic press reveals that many linguists felt under personal attack (I make reference to some of this exchange here; a fuller account is provided by Graddol and Swann [1988] in their appendix). A related feature here is that the self-defensive moves were often accompanied by reminders of the writer's own status in the respectable academic world, and of how tedious it was, then, to have to take time to respond to someone like Honey.

A third approach took Honey rather more seriously. Graddol and Swann point out that, whatever the underlying strategy, any academic response to Honey represents an intersection of 'professional' with 'lay' discourse, and points of contact here are traditionally fraught with danger, particularly where and when specific matters are underpinned by much broader ones. Thus, Graddol and Swann note that Honey's pamphlet was essentially a contribution to, and a reflection of, the 'new right' political order of the time. Consequently, when academics debated Honey in newspaper columns and letters, they were operating on the opposition's terrain of choice:

> the linguists wrote in order to protest at the misuse of misrepresenta-
> tion of their academic work, but the very fact that they appeared in

opposition to the right-wing correspondents would have confirmed the public impression that they represent the radical left. They are, it seems, in something of a trap. The more they protest at being characterised as politically motivated, the more they will appear to be so. (Graddol & Swann, 1988: 104)

I suggested above that the real motivation behind Honey's pamphlet could well have been nostalgic regret for a linguistic environment in which the influence of the Bible and the Book of Common Prayer has been eroded by vulgar modern villains – the author mentions the pernicious idioms of *Coronation Street*, of the commercialized media, of pop-celebrity culture. Crowley (1989: 271) also suggests that the 'reactionary nostalgic thought' of Honey and his 'fellow travellers' reveals a desire to return to 'Victorian values'; this strikes me as reasonably accurate, although possibly a little unfair to the Victorians.[6] It is not surprising, then, to find that Honey concludes his pamphlet by arguing that 'social justice' demands that disadvantaged children be provided with a 'ready facility in standard English, even at the expense of their development in their original non-standard variety [and] ... I am tempted to add, of their self-esteem' (Honey, 1983a: 31). After all, such a recommendation can rest perfectly well upon the assumption that pernicious elements in modern life have led to, or encouraged, or reinforced deficiencies in linguistic capability.

It is yet another of the internal curiosities to be found throughout Honey's little monograph that – as Crystal observes – his argument for promoting standard English, even if it means some wounding of the self-esteem, is made only a few paragraphs after Honey berates the bad old days when nonstandard forms were 'virtually outlawed', when insensitivity and 'straightforward suppression' were the order of the day. It also does Honey's case no good when he glibly asserts, *à propos* of self-esteem, that 'I am not excessively impressed by the argument that the teaching of standard English need cause all the consequences of shame, confusion, linguistic insecurity, alienation, etc.' (Honey, 1983a: 31). Honey presents no evidence for this assertion which, in the absence of any support, has a rather *de haut en bas* flavor.

After producing an intervening book on accent (1989) – in which, once again, a great deal of the source material was mined from the popular print and broadcast media (ironic, considering the laments made in his pamphlet) – Honey returned to the theme of language traps. This new production (1997) was subtitled *The Story of Standard English and its Enemies* – and no prizes will be awarded at this point for identifying those villains. The first two chapters, 'The language myth' and 'The dialect trap' remake Honey's pivotal points: modern linguistics holds, incorrectly, that all languages are 'equal'; and the force of Bernstein's valuable insights into more and less complex 'codes' was blunted by the arguments of 'the high priest of modern sociolinguistics... William Labov' (Honey, 1997: 23). Here and elsewhere, Honey laments the fact that his own work could not 'dent the authority' (p. 29) of what soon came to be the received linguistic wisdom. Taken together with the 'high priest' remark, the suggestion here is of an unscientific hierarchy, irrationally resistant to the truth. Thus, 'the Bernstein "deficit" model was rejected, and dismissed as unacceptable, simply because enough established figures in linguistics declared it to be so' (p. 29). Such a stance, of course, is not uncommon among those who feel their points of view have been neglected by the community they wish to contribute to, and to be recognized by. Still, a judicious application of Occam's razor might indicate more straightforward reasons for rejection.

Beyond the opening chapters, the whole book is essentially devoted to a refutation of Honey's critics: chapters treat those enemies of English who have attempted to rewrite the story of standard English, who have rejected prescriptivist models and approaches – rejected, that is to say, the widely-held belief 'that there is such a thing as correct English' (Honey, 1997: 144) – who have abdicated the noble duty of safeguarding the language, and whose *laissez-faire* linguistics have created an educationally 'lost generation'. At the end of the book, and particularly in the penultimate chapter ('The *Language Trap* debate'), Honey turns most explicitly on his various critics. He argues that, beyond their evident rejection of the content per se, linguistic scholars' reactions to his work were strongly motivated by their desire to stifle a 'dangerous insurgent' (see also Graddol & Swann, 1988). This seems fairly reasonable to me, actually, since Honey himself pulls no personal punches in his pamphlet, and elsewhere (Honey, 1983a, 1997, 1998). Among the heavyweights he has taken on are Trudgill, Crystal, Labov, Haugen, Lyons, Wolfram, Pinker, Harris, Aitchison and the Milroys, and it is surely not surprising that those placed in the spotlight would feel both personally and professionally aggrieved. (The old French witticism comes to mind here: *'cet animal est très méchant; quand on l'attaque, il se défend'.*)

Honey also points to the growing accusations of the polemical (right-wing) bias of his work, a damning thing in what is a generally left-leaning academy. There is probably some substance to this, at least in terms of more or less immediate reaction, but any such initial positioning would very soon become vitiated if substantive argument did not follow.

It seems that Honey is at pains to bring up his thesis, and its numerous critics, wherever possible. For example, in an extremely lengthy review of Mugglestone's (1995) interesting book on 'talking proper', Honey (2000b) finds the central argument about the relationship between speech and status undercut by the author's uncritical acceptance of the 'linguistic equality hypothesis'. Honey's point here seems to be an attempted dissociation of 'educatedness' and social éliteness. He criticizes Mugglestone's 'false correlation of accents with the social elite as such, rather than with people who were perceived as educated'. He acknowledges that 'to be a gentleman was one of the frequent accompaniments of educatedness', but rejects the notion that it was a 'defining characteristic'. (Crowley, 1999, provides a good discussion of Honey's difficulties with 'educatedness'.) Now, there is indeed a great deal to say and to understand about the relationships between speech style and social evaluation, and this is particularly so in the 19th-century setting closely examined by Mugglestone in her book (see also the earlier treatments of Brook [1963, 1970], Chapman [1994], McIntosh [1998], Mitchell [2001], Phillipps [1984] and Wright [2000] – discussions that range, indeed, well beyond the 19th century). It is disingenuous, however, to try and make a strong case for the dissociation just noted. It is entirely understandable that Honey would wish to do so, of course, for down that avenue lies the claim that there is, after all, some intrinsic superiority attaching to standard dialects – they are the educated ones, reflecting literacy and learning entirely foreign to 'barrow-boys or washerwomen'. But we have subtly stepped aside here from the basic matters of linguistic importance: linguistic adequacy and the fully fledged nature of all dialects.

Trudgill's (1998) review of Honey (1997) makes – very clearly, I should say – what are now familiar points. Two of the new ones are that the author is not a trained linguist, and that

> Honey is not a modest man... he genuinely believes he has succeeded, single handed, in demolishing the findings of generations of linguistic scholarship... he certainly gets plenty of publicity which... he shows every sign of enjoying. (Trudgill, 1998: 457–458)

When Honey (2000a) then made a rejoinder to Trudgill's review – don't worry, we are nearing the end of this circular comedy – he seemed to agree that his linguistic credentials were indeed rather slight and that, yes, he did enjoy his media limelight. Sour grapes on Trudgill's part, since Honey says that his celebrity 'may just possibly have been because my views were judged to be more widely credible' (p. 318). There are other possibilities, of course.

There are a number of interesting conclusions to be drawn from this episode, and I have hinted at most of them. But let me conclude here by re-emphasizing one or two of the most salient. Whatever the scholarly evidence may suggest, questions of the 'goodness' of language are typically political ones, resting upon social bedrock that is both wide and deep. The reported death of 'deficit' perspectives was an exaggeration. Second, the notion of the 'equality' of all language varieties should probably be abandoned. 'Equality' is obviously not the *mot juste* when some varieties have labyrinthine complexities of tense-marking, when others describe kinship relationships out to the furthest reaches of the family tree, and so on. (I choose these two examples, incidentally, since they refer to languages spoken by what the popular mind and press would describe as 'primitive groups' – those unfortunate societies having, as John Vincent suggested in *The Times* [23 February 1983], 'no social development'.)[7] Continued reference to the 'equality' of all varieties provides easy targets for deficit theorists. Although linguists and other scholars who make such reference are generally indulging in a bit of commonly shared shorthand, it would be more accurate to say that all varieties are sufficient unto the day, that all can bend and stretch as required, that the totality of a group's ideas and concepts can, at any point, be adequately depicted and discussed. More accurate, although admittedly less aphoristic, but less amenable to simple-minded socio-political manipulation.

Graddol and Swann (1988: 95–96) go a bit further, suggesting that, in the privacy of their studies, linguists reject the idea of 'complete linguistic equality', that they consider the notion to be a sort of 'working hypothesis' and admit that 'there are a number of naturally occurring language varieties which must be discreetly passed over to preserve the integrity of the doctrine'. And, with Hymes (1972), the authors also suggest a political imperative underpinning 'equality', an 'ideological confidence' in the notion.

I would say they are bending further backwards than necessary here. First, replacing the terse but inaccurate idea of 'equality' with what it is really meant to express deflates some of the necessity. This, in turn, allows us to see that the troublesome 'to-be-passed-over' varieties – Graddol and Swann mention children's speech, contact varieties and interlanguages – are not in fact troublesome at all. They too conform to fuller senses of 'equality'. There is also a very relevant point here; it is not often made, but it clearly bears upon all discussions of 'equality', and it undercuts all attempts to pervert or manipulate the idea. It is simply this. All human communities are speaking communities, and everything we know about cognitive capacity and social development makes it both easier and more logical to assume that they all have languages that serve their purposes. A bizarre opposite assertion would be that the languages of some groups are flawed, that (for example) a group might lack the linguistic capacity to fully discuss, up to the level of its *conceptual* knowledge, the trees and bushes in its environment.

To put it another way: given what is known about human cognitive development, the 'rule-governed' hypothesis that is (or ought to be) at the heart of all discussions of 'equality' makes much more intrinsic sense than some 'haphazard' one – and this, regardless of any specific empirical observation at all. For what group, wherever and however it may live, could maintain itself adequately with an incomplete or inconsistent communication system? These adjectives reflect exactly the sort of illegitimate cross-group comparison that, as we have seen, animates the very idea of 'disadvantage'.

Empirical Excursions

Accompanying the popular and theoretical persistence of 'deficit' perspectives are findings of an empirical nature. Many of these are, either directly or implicitly, related to Bernstein's influence – which, in its embrace of both researchers and teachers, has traveled far beyond the English-language sphere. Thus, for example, well after the initial assertions underpinning the 'difference' position, Gordon (1978) looked at the impact of Bernstein's writings upon a sample of primary-school teachers in Suffolk. They reported that deficit theory had been a part of their training courses, and that it expressed and reinforced ideas already widely current among teachers. A few of the teachers made critical remarks, but only those who had actually read papers by and about Bernstein were skeptical or critical. Those whose awareness was more informally derived were the most accepting of it. This is a fascinating and suggestive detail. When we consider that close and direct examination may lead to an awareness of the theoretical fragility of the 'codes', the fact that most teachers (like the rest of us) absorb new ideas rather less straightforwardly becomes a salient one indeed. One implication is, surely, that teachers ought to be given more opportunity for focused study, for opportunities to see that some emperors have a limited wardrobe.

Generally, Gordon's interviews revealed that Bernstein's formulations were attractive to teachers, confirming their existing views and assumptions about children's speech. Among the more interesting comments: 'Bernstein ...is saying something which most teachers take in through their fingers, as you might say it, every day of their lives'; and 'everyone knows that children from certain backgrounds do have a restricted code of speech... you can't mistake it when you meet it, can you?' (Gordon, 1978: 104, 106; see also Gordon, 1981). Mason (1986: 279) makes the explicit point that the deficit hypothesis is intertwined with Bernstein's theory, and has 'remained alive in the minds of many practicing schoolteachers'; she goes on to underline the distinction between concrete and abstract language as Bernstein's 'fundamental insight'. Such points of view take us back, indeed, to the pre-Bernsteinian assessments of Schatzman and Strauss (1955; see also Carrington & Williamson, 1987, for a reply to Mason). In two further examples, Jay *et al.* (1980) and Gullo (1981) treat social-class language differences from a Bernsteinian perspective; Gullo, in particular, apparently accepting the view that poor children's language is linked to the concrete present and is less used for abstract reasoning. Reports on the acceptance of Bernstein and 'deficit' among teachers outside the UK and North America can be found in Shafer and Shafer (1975), Thomson (1977) and Cheshire *et al.* (1989). Loman's (1974) interesting collection provides translations of work both 'for' and 'against' Bernstein; the editor's own two contributions attempt to provide an objective overview of the important issues; it is noteworthy that Loman refers particularly to Bernstein's often opaque prose. The idea that Bernstein was *not*, in fact, a deficit theorist has also been revisited: Atkinson's (1985) reintroduction to his work has thus prompted some re-examination (e.g. Davies, 1987; Tony Edwards, 1987a, 1987b).

Findings similar to Gordon's emerge from a later study undertaken in Nova Scotia, in which 96 teachers from 10 schools (seven primary and three secondary) were asked about educational disadvantage (Edwards & McKinnon, 1987). The schools served a rural population that was predominantly white and English-speaking, but there were also sizeable groups of French Acadian and black pupils. Teachers discussed disadvantage in general, indicated whether or not they had received any information about it during their training, and were then asked to judge the degree of importance of a number of home background and personal characteristics. They were also asked to consider language matters specifically. It was very clear that most teachers held an implicit 'deficit' point of view; here are two representative comments (Edwards & McKinnon, 1987: 337):

> Disadvantage suggests an informational and experiential inferiority... an inability to make full use of novel information and, conversely, to call upon past experiences in novel situations;
>
> [Disadvantaged children have] lack of experiences, poor language development... usually disorganized. They usually are not motivated by long-term rewards. Goals must be short-term. These students generally come from lower economic levels, but not always. A further characteristic of [disadvantaged] families I would say is disorganization and a low priority placed on learning.

Certainly, not all teachers phrased their feeling in such terms – which, indeed, show some familiarity with the literature or, at least, the jargon – but the general tenor of opinion is fairly reflected in these comments. There is some suggestion in these and other observations that teachers may have adapted new information to old attitudes; this is particularly evident in phrases like 'informational and experiential inferiority', which are redolent of the environmental-deficit literature. This, in turn, suggests a difficulty I have already touched upon. It is common to hear calls for teacher-training courses and in-service workshops to deal with the latest psychological and linguistic developments of interest. Teachers may not, however, get full or adequate presentations, and may simply assimilate what information they do get to existing frameworks, frameworks likely to reflect deficit perceptions.

Turning to language matters specifically, teachers pointed to poor grammar, vocabulary, articulation and reading as important aspects of disadvantage. Again, differences were generally seen as deficits. Some representative comments will again illustrate this (Edwards & McKinnon, 1987: 339):

> [Children often cannot] articulate their thoughts and feelings in such a way that they satisfy both themselves and their audience;
>
> The common element of experience among all disadvantaged children is infrequent interaction with adults in discovery activities where opinions and experiences can be shared;
>
> Both receptive and expressive skills seem to have low levels of value and priority when it comes to developing accuracy and fluency.

Again, we see beliefs that correspond strikingly with views expressed in the deficit literature. Children are seen to be unable to communicate adequately, they lack the experiences and interactions that are necessary for developing language skills and, indeed, it is suggested that their 'receptive and expressive' talents are not greatly valued anyway. This last point is particularly reminiscent of the linguistically misguided sentiments of deficit theorists of the 1960s.

Teachers are not malicious, they can hardly be said to be unsympathetic to language 'problems', and it is probably fair to say that there now exists greater tolerance for language variation than was once the case. Still, while teachers view language differences as springing from varied home backgrounds (true), they also often continue to see them as necessitating some sort of compensatory action (dubious). Several teachers in this study commented extensively on the 'poor' English learned at home, and the consequent need to teach children 'correct' English. This task, some felt, was analogous to teaching a new language altogether. The various programs and activities suggested as useful here were again echoes of the dreary recommendations of language-deficit theorists: language drills, speech therapy, and so on.

Where teachers were in contact with minority-group children, the speech patterns of these were singled out for attention. Many put black and Acadian children at the top of the lists of those having language difficulties. A fairly general view was expressed by one teacher as follows: 'Blacks have a slang language all their own. They will not use proper English when opportunity arises' (Edwards & McKinnon, 1987: 339). In the secondary school having the highest number of black pupils, 11 of the 22 teachers commented explicitly on the children's language problems.

Such findings are consistent with those reported elsewhere. In her discussion of the educational situation of Puerto Rican children in America, Walsh found teachers whose views seem to have 'effectively summarized all of the conclusions drawn from Bernstein's theories of restricted and elaborated codes' (Lippi-Green, 1997: 111):

> These poor kids come to school speaking a hodge podge. They are all mixed up and don't know any language well. As a result, they can't even think clearly. That's why they don't learn. It's our job to teach them language – to make up for their deficiency. And, since their parents don't really know any language either, why should we waste time on Spanish? It is "good" English which has to be the focus. (Walsh, 1991: 107)

Could we ask for a clearer or more succinct statement of the 'deficit' position? The very persistence of such views, more than two decades after the demonstrations by Labov and his colleagues is noteworthy in itself, of course – noteworthy and (as Lippi-Green, 1997: 111 observes) indicative of 'how seductive such rhetoric can be'. In any event, it is deeply disturbing to think that teachers still approach the children in their classrooms with this set of warped – and warping – assumptions.

The disadvantaged children reported on above were Spanish-English bilinguals, and this is important for at least two reasons. First, as with Edwards and McKinnon's (1987) French-speaking youngsters, we are reminded that linguistic 'deficits' are commonly alleged to exist both within and across language boundaries. The inner-city black children whose speech was the primary focus of both deficit and difference theorists were monolingual English speakers, so their 'problem' was at the level of dialect. In other contexts, however – with indigenous or immigrant ethnic-minority children – the problem is at the level of language itself: pupils arrive in the classroom without a knowledge of English (for instance). There are, of course, some interesting wheels-within-wheels here. For instance, many non-English-speaking minority-group children will be disadvantaged in some of the 'classic' ways outlined in earlier chapters. Because of this, it is very likely that the English they soon begin to acquire will not be some standard-like variety; on the contrary, it is generally a nonstandard dialect. The potential for jumping from a language frying-pan into a dialect fire is obvious.

Second, we note the impression that bilingual children can make on the linguistically naïve teacher: they (and their parents, too) are 'mixed up' and do not know either language very well. Such a misguided perception is perhaps more predictable when teachers who know only one language themselves and who live in an essentially monolingual environment are considering the competences of children who are at once materially disadvantaged and bilingual. But it is not limited to them.

The eminent linguist Leonard Bloomfield described a North American Indian in this way (Bloomfield, 1927: 437):

> White Thunder, a man around 40, speaks less English than Menomini, and that is a strong indictment, for his Menomini is atrocious. His vocabulary is small, his inflections are often barbarous, he constructs sentences of a few threadbare models. He may be said to speak no language tolerably.

This is an early illustration of what Hansegård (1968) later described (in studies of Finnish-Swedish bilinguals) as *halvspråkighet* ('half-language'). In contemporary usage, the term 'semilingualism' soon became enlarged: from a solely linguistic description, it went on to attain some prominence as a catchword with political and ideological overtones. Some categories of disadvantaged children, for example – including those in groups just touched upon here – were seen to be condemned to a life of linguistic half-light and shadow, because of deficient environments. At its base was the notion that linguistic capacity was of some finite or 'containerized' nature; and at its simplest, it implied that what you gain on the swings of one language you lose on the roundabouts of the other.

Using a 'fixed-container' metaphor for language acquisition and skills, however, is problematic. It is reminiscent of the old, and now discredited, craniometry axioms that linked brain size to intelligence and – even if we were to admit the likelihood of some finite-capacity model – all that we know of intellectual structures and functions suggests that the capacity (for languages, among other things) is large enough that few of us need worry about exceeding our limits. Early in his partnership with Watson, Sherlock Holmes explained his ignorance of many things by saying that the brain was like an attic, that one should fill it wisely according to one's needs. Near the beginning of *A Study in Scarlet*, he told his partner that 'it is a mistake to think that that little room has elastic walls and can distend to any extent'. There *are* limits, of course, but Holmes grievously underestimated them. He could easily have remedied his ignorance of literature and astronomy without displacing his knowledge of poisons or the many varieties of cigarette ash.

If there is any credibility at all to the idea of 'semilingualism', it must rest upon a rather rare complex of deprivations. It should certainly not be seen as any sort of looming danger attaching to linguistic duality, for which it represents only 'a half-baked theory of communicative competence' (Martin-Jones & Romaine, 1985; see also Baetens Beardsmore, 1986; Edelsky *et al.*, 1983). It is regrettable, to say the least, that the notion – and the underlying assumptions that it is built upon – should constitute yet another burden for linguistically disadvantaged children.

Notes

1. Schools are always better thought of as reflections of broader social currents than as leaders of enlightened opinion. As we shall see, problems typically arise very quickly when teachers are asked to pull against the tide flowing beyond the school gates.
2. Cheshire *et al.* (1989: 6) note that 'the legacy of Bernstein lives on' – and their collection demonstrates the persistence of deficit views among teachers in many European countries. Also, a recent number of *Language and Education* includes a piece by Myhill and Dunkin (2005) in which reference is made to the hypotheses of Bernstein and Tough. The reference is only a passing one, but it appears in a list of citations (to Alexander, to Barnes, even to Vygotsky) concerning classroom talk – and there is no indication at all that some insights may be more equal than others.

Wiggan (2007 – see also note 3) also comments on Bernstein's analyses without making any critical observations; consequently, they are simply presented as part of a very long, but very shallow, overview of studies in the area.

3. In his very recent overview of educational disadvantage, Wiggan (2007; see also note 2) also fails to come down strongly on the side of environmental difference. The author provides a reasonable coverage of both the genetic and environmental approaches to disadvantage, dividing the latter into matters of 'social class and cultural poverty, teacher expectancy, and student oppositional identity' (p. 321). He adds to these the unfair effects of standardized testing. He does not, however, make the deficiencies of the 'cultural poverty' assessment clear enough and, indeed, notes that 'it is conceivable that some aspects of all four [original] explanations affect student achievement' (p. 322). Much stronger and less equivocal summaries are needed if we are to fully embrace the different-but-not-deficient explanation for group disadvantage that I advocate in this book.

4. I have assembled these comments from the back-cover blurbs on Honey (1997).

5. Honey's pamphlet was published by the National Council for Educational Standards, described in a note in the *Times Higher Education Supplement* (2 January 1987: 6) as an 'influential group of right-wing lobbyists' (see also Graddol & Swann, 1988). Reactionary complaints about abysmal modern usage are, of course, as eternal as criticisms of the 'younger generation'. For my own review of Honey's pamphlet, see Edwards (1983a).

6. The second edition of Crowley's (2003) book extends the relevant exchange, in a brief discussion of Honey (1997); see also Crowley (1999). Holborow (1999) also presents the familiar criticisms of Honey's position; her espousal of a rather quaint Marxist perspective, however, means that she has little time for almost *any* contemporary linguist.

7. Bauer (1998: 82–83) touches upon American Indian languages whose verb constructions make distinctions between things that happened recently and those that occurred long ago, and between things that speakers know themselves and those that they have been told about:

> In these languages, I would require a different form of the verb *lose* to say in 1996 "England lost to Germany in the semi-finals" and to say in 1996 "The English lost the battle of Hastings in 1066". And both of these (which I only know because I have been told so) would require a different verb from "I lost my game of Scrabble this afternoon", which I know from my own experience.

Bauer goes on to mention that, in Maori, there are different pronouns for *we* when it refers (on the one hand) to 'you the listener and me the speaker' and (on the other hand) to 'me the speaker and someone else' (see also Evans, 1998, on Australian aboriginal languages).

These are just a couple of very simple examples; the interested reader can easily find dictionaries and grammars full of illustrations of the complexities of 'primitive' varieties.

Chapter 8

Evaluative Reactions to the Language of Disadvantage

Language Attitudes and the Minority-group Reaction

One of the most poignant aspects of the social evaluation of language is the widely reported tendency for nonstandard speakers to accept and agree with unfavorable stereotypes of their speech styles. Labov (1976) found, for instance, that those whose speech includes nonstandard or stigmatized forms are typically their own harshest critics. This is an example of what Lambert *et al.* (1960) called the 'minority-group reaction', in which the perceptions and stereotypes of the 'mainstream' are accepted by those outside it. The reaction is, of course, a particular linguistic manifestation of the much broader interplay between social dominance and subordination. It is important to note, however, that social relationships are dynamic, and that language matters often provide a useful perspective on change. The black respondents to whom Labov spoke in the 1970s are not the same as those interviewed by Ogbu (1999) a generation later (see below). As we shall see, their linguistic attitudes have become more complex: they continue to believe that 'white talk' is 'proper', and that Black English Vernacular (BEV) is not, but there is a pride in the use and the 'solidarity functions' of their vernacular that was not felt or, at least, not expressed, in earlier investigations.[1]

In 1960, Lambert *et al.* introduced the 'matched-guise' technique, a method of investigating reactions to speech variants. Judges evaluate a recorded speaker's personality, along any dimension of interest, after hearing him or her read the same passage in each of two or more languages, dialects or accents. The fact that the speaker is, for all 'guises', the same person is not revealed to the assessors (who typically do not guess this). Since any potentially confounding variables (pitch, tone of voice and so on) are, of course, constant across the 'guises', the ratings given are considered to more accurately reflect stereotypic reactions to the language variety per se than would be the case if separate speakers of each linguistic variant were used. (For a brief discussion of some of the criticisms that have been made of the 'matched-guise' technique, none of which are fatal, see Edwards, 1989.)

In this initial study, Lambert and his colleagues were interested in the reactions of French- and English-speaking Montreal students towards French and English voices. On most of the dimensions evaluated (ambition, intelligence, sense of humor, etc.), English-speaking judges reacted more favorably to English guises. Of greater interest, however, were the ratings given by the French-speaking raters, for not only did they, too, evaluate the English guises more positively than they did the French ones, they *also* gave less favorable responses to the *French* guises than did English-speaking judges. The researchers interpreted these findings as evidence of what they then termed a 'minority-group reaction'. That is, the French-speaking student judges, perceiving themselves as subordinate in some ways to the English-speaking population, apparently adopted (and even slightly magnified) the stereotyped values of this latter group. British matched-guise work lent some support here: Cheyne (1970) found that *both* Scottish and English judges tended to rate Scottish speakers as lower in status than their English counterparts.

d'Anglejan and Tucker (1973), in their study of French dialects, provided further confirmation of the 'minority-group' effect (not using matched guises). When French-Canadian students, teachers and factory workers (more than 200 in total) were asked their opinions of Quebec, European and Parisian French, they rejected the idea that Quebec French was inferior to the other two, or that Parisian French was the 'best' form of the language. Nevertheless, when presented with the taped voices of upper-class and lower-class French-Canadian speakers, and European French speakers, the respondents downgraded both Canadian styles in terms of qualities like ambition and intelligence; even in terms of likeability, the European speech style evoked more favorable responses. In 1975, Carranza and Ryan asked Mexican-American and Anglo-American students (of Spanish) to judge speakers of English and Spanish. Sixteen such speakers were presented, on tape, talking about simple domestic or school events. The personality characteristics to be evaluated broadly reflected either prestige (status) or what the researchers termed 'solidarity' (involving traits like friendliness, kindness, trustworthiness and so on). Over all judges, English was viewed more favorably when the speaker's topic was school-related, Spanish when it dealt with domestic matters. Further, English was reacted to more favorably on both status-related and 'solidarity' traits. One implication is that a low-prestige language variety may have more positive connotations in terms of qualities like integrity, social attractiveness and friendliness than it does when matters of intelligence, ambition, industriousness and competence are the issue; another is that this relationship seems to obtain both for members of the low-prestige group and for more middle-class speakers. In related work, Ryan and Carranza (1975) found similar results when considering the evaluations of standard English and Mexican-accented English made by Mexican-American, black and 'anglo' speakers: the former was assessed as higher in status than the latter. In a further refinement, Ryan *et al.* (1977) found that the *degree* of nonstandardness influenced judges' evaluations. Ratings of Spanish-English bilinguals, reading an English passage, showed that favorability of impressions decreased as degree of Spanish accentedness increased. Studies from the same period involving black American speakers are also suggestive. Tucker and Lambert (1969), for example, presented a number of different American English dialect varieties to three groups of university students – northern white, southern white and southern black – and found that all groups evaluated standard-English speakers most favorably.

The relevant literature here, largely from the 1960s and 1970s, when such work was at its apogee, is an extensive one and it confirms what has been well understood at a popular level for a long time. The speech patterns of regional speakers, of ethnic minority-group members, of lower- or working-class populations (categories that frequently overlap, of course) elicit negative evaluations, most importantly in terms of perceived status, prestige or 'educatedness', and this stereotypic pattern seems to hold whether or not the listeners are standard speakers themselves. Some of these early studies, undertaken before the more recent emergence of black or Hispanic 'pride', do reveal hints of linguistic and psychological developments to come. Flores and Hopper (1975), for instance, found slight preferences on the part of Mexican-American judges for the speech styles of *compañeros* who referred to themselves as 'Chicano'. But it would be naïve to assume that negative language stereotypes are generally waning in a broad societal sense. The feeling that one's own speech is not 'good' has historically been a very common phenomenon indeed, for reasons that are as clear as they are unfair. It is a particularly disturbing one, however, when we consider how easily the belief may be exacerbated by those who might be expected to know better: teachers, for instance. As Halliday (1968: 165) once observed:

> A speaker who is made ashamed of his own language habits suffers a
> basic injury as a human being; to make anyone, especially a child,

feel so ashamed is as indefensible as to make him feel ashamed of the colour of his skin.

Some have debated the depth of the injury here; no enlightened opinion, however, doubts the indefensibility, the unfairness, of the process.

The reliable theatrical tradition, in which a comic effect is produced through having a duchess speak with a Cockney accent, has its more mundane counterparts as well. Indeed, the perceived incongruity that produces comedy on the stage and in the cinema would not be effective without an audience fully alive to the powerful social connotations of linguistic variants. Given that people are aware of negative stereotypes of their own speech styles and, indeed, that they themselves have accepted them in many cases, we might ask why low-status speech varieties continue to exist. After all, it would seem that a realization of the potential limitations, in practical terms, of some varieties might lead to their eradication – or, at least, to the expansion of the linguistic repertoire, to the development of bidialectal capability. We know that this is not, in principle, a difficult accomplishment. It is very common among actors, for example; and, at less theatrical levels, the process of selecting from a linguistic pool of possibilities, according to perceptions of the setting, is even more common. It can hardly be alleged, either, that nonstandard speakers are without adequate models for repertoire expansion. Schoolteachers comprised the traditional set of standards here and, today, the pervasive influence of the public media means that virtually all nonstandard speakers have at least passive access to standard forms. Nevertheless, the levelling of local speech styles and, more pointedly here, the gradual disappearance of low-status variants that some had predicted as an inevitable consequence of the spread of the broadcast media, seems not to have occurred.

Language Attitudes and Group Solidarity

Among his other contributions, Fishman has always pointed to the salience of language attitudes (see, e.g. the collection of his papers edited by Hornberger & Pütz, 2006; and his own recent paean to 'positive ethnolinguistic consciousness': Fishman, 1996). Naturally enough, pride in one's culture often involves affection for the language of that culture. Linguistic pride and self-confidence can be resurgent when groups previously oppressed, discriminated against and thought to be inferior, rediscover a broader social strength and assertion, and this can be as true for cultural sub-groups and dialects as it is for larger populations and languages. Thus, Carranza and Ryan (1975) discussed the 'solidarity' function of language in contemporary American black and Chicano contexts. A language or dialect, though it may be lacking in general social prestige, may nevertheless function as a powerful bonding agent, providing a sense of identity. Indeed, it is a social and linguistic fact that *any* variety can be the voice of group identity, a central element in the revitalized 'consciousness' of nonstandard-dialect speakers.

But the solidarity function of language – the symbolic role of language, that is to say, in the articulation of group identity – is clearly not restricted to situations in which earlier self-denigration has now given way to admiration and allegiance. For we also observe a disinclination to alter speech styles on the parts of groups that seem not to have experienced any sudden upsurge in group pride, and who continue to adhere to the larger society's unfavorable stereotypes of their speech patterns: speakers of low-status dialects of urban British English are examples here. Can we put this down to a more generally liberal attitude towards speech variants per se? It is true that views are not as rigid as they once were. The linguistic variation to be found now in the mainstream media is an indication of this, and an even more interesting development is the aping of non-mainstream behavior, attitudes and speech style by certain middle-class constituencies (notably young people: see also the discussion of 'covert prestige', below). But prejudicial views obviously persist, even if their force has lessened in some quarters.

The solidarity function associated with a common language style, even if it is nonstandard and non-prestigious, is powerful and general. Group identity is a known quantity, and in that sense, is safe. Attempts to alter one's speech style, to jettison a low-status variant, or even to add another dialectal string to the bow, on the other hand, are risky undertakings. Failure may lead to a sense of marginality, a sense of not being a full (and fully accepted) member of *any* social group. As noted earlier, the Mexican American who abandoned Spanish for the socio-economic rewards of English risked being labeled a *vendido*, a 'sell-out', a linguistic quisling. The individual who wishes to add, and not to replace, may also fall between stools. The maintenance of Spanish (language and culture) may exist uneasily alongside the acquisition of English, particularly in a world in which bilingualism is often a way-station on the road to a new monolingualism, a world in which English increasingly threatens other variants (see Edwards, 1994a).

This sort of situation is not unrelated to that in which talking 'posh' is seen as affectation. Indeed, Bragg and Ellis (1976) reported the Cockney opinion that if a child were to speak 'posh', friends would label him (or her, of course) as 'a queer'. A generation earlier, Orwell (1941: 74) famously observed that 'nearly every Englishman of working-class origin considers it effeminate to pronounce foreign words correctly'. Kissau (2006: 415) reports that this attitude apparently persists: Canadian secondary-school boys report that the French classroom is a 'female domain', and not a place for males. One language teacher observed that 'there's still a lot of sexist thinking that a man doesn't learn languages. A man does math or engineering' (see also Carr & Pauwels, 2006, below).

Ogbu (1999) has described how black people in West Oakland (California) consider that 'proper' English is white English, and that BEV is poor slang or, less pejoratively, 'just plain talkin'. On further investigation, it is clear that BEV is seen as the ordinary vernacular, the 'low' variant in a diglossic situation. And Ogbu also finds that, although his respondents did not articulate the notion, they feel caught: the BEV that represents home, familiarity and group identity is threatened by the mastery of 'proper' English, a mastery that is seen as necessary for school and work success. They believe, in other words, in a sort of 'subtractive bidialectalism'. The 'dialect dilemma', the belief that the necessary acquisition of standard English will tend to erode the vernacular, is sometimes reinforced by a feeling (both within and without academia) that this process is part of the assimilatory intent of 'mainstream' school and society. Ogbu notes that, on the one hand, black professionals, advocates, educators and communities endorse the learning of standard English, but then turn around and condemn its acquisition on the grounds that it threatens 'Black English identity and racial solidarity' (Ogbu, 1999: 180).

But Ogbu argues that the belief may be just that – and does not reflect actual practice. After all, a more or less stable bidialectalism is the norm in many contexts, and it is certainly part of the repertoire of large numbers of black Americans. Is there, then, any real dilemma here? Well, it is possible, just as 'subtractive bilingualism' is possible – where the acquisition of a new language gradually ousts an existing one – but, in both cases, any 'subtraction' that occurs is a symptom of larger social forces that make resistance unlikely to succeed. In the case of black American culture and its current pervasiveness – well beyond the boundaries of the black community itself – I should think that a diglossic relationship between BEV and standard English is likely to endure for the foreseeable future. But if a 'dilemma' is perceived, it has at least a psychological existence. Ogbu's informants clearly feel that, when a black person 'is talking proper, he or she is *puttin' on* [italics added] or pretending to be white or to talk like white people' (Ogbu, 1999: 171–172). They told him that it is 'insane to pretend to be white', that speaking standard English is a pretence, a fake.

They don't actually speak of betrayal of the group here, but the implication is plain and quite similar to the *vendido* possibility noted above.

Ogbu's 'dialect dilemma' is the same phenomenon that Smitherman (2006) discusses under the heading of 'linguistic push-pull', a linguistic contradiction whereby black speakers simultaneously embrace BEV and dislike it. 'On the one hand', she says, 'Blacks have believed that the price of the ticket for Black education and survival and success in White America is eradication of Black Talk. On the other hand, Blacks also recognize that language is bound up with Black identity and culture' (Smitherman, 2006: 129). This 'push-pull' situation obviously affects many nonstandard-language speakers in many settings. The solution, a theoretically plausible bidialectalism by which you can eat your linguistic cake while still having it, is not always easy to maintain.

There is another very obvious factor that deters some nonstandard-dialect speakers from attempting to 'improve' their speech styles. If we consider, for instance, that negative reactions to BEV typically reflect broader social or racial attitudes, then it follows that, for a black person – or any other member of a 'visible minority' group – learning and using a standard dialect may not necessarily alter things very much. Indeed, there is some suggestion in the literature that black speakers who sound 'white' may elicit *more* negative attitudes. Some early studies by Giles and Bourhis (1975, 1976) demonstrated this among West Indians in Cardiff, and similar observations have been made in Canada and the USA (see Edwards, 1989).

It is not invariably the case that lower-class speakers consider their own language patterns to be inferior variants. At the beginning here, I mentioned how altered social circumstances – a reawakening of group 'pride' or 'consciousness', for instance – can lead to altered self-perceptions, including linguistic ones. This process is underlined by the increasingly common tendency to exaggerate or heighten, whether consciously or not, speech styles that were previously disapproved of. What was once an 'inferior' variety goes beyond mere equivalence with erstwhile 'better' forms, and comes to be seen as superior to them: more direct, more pithy, more animated. In this way, nonstandard speech comes to possess a new status for its speakers. In a study of black secondary-school students, Fordham reports (1999: 272) that BEV is now the 'norm against which all other speech practices are evaluated'; standard English is no longer privileged; indeed, 'it is "dissed" (disrespected) and is only "leased" by the students on a daily basis from nine to three'. There are attractions here, too, for some middle-class and more or less standard-dialect-speaking adolescents, a sort of 'street prestige' now associated with BEV in popular culture. The attractiveness of nonstandard dialect is not restricted to teenagers, however: there is also the socially broader phenomenon of *covert prestige*.

'Covert prestige' rests upon the related facts that the perceived directness and vibrancy of nonstandard speech are understood as 'macho' qualities and that masculinity itself is a favored quantity. The continued existence of nonstandard forms and the disinclination to abandon them will clearly be strengthened if their allure crosses group boundaries. Labov (1977, 2006) commented upon the covert-prestige phenomenon in New York, contrasting its effects with the 'hypercorrect' usage of nonstandard speakers who may (he suggested) feel linguistically insecure about 'stigmatized' features of their dialect, and who may attempt higher-status speech forms, particularly in formal contexts. In fact, in settings of the greatest formality, Labov reported that his lower-class respondents' use of prestige forms actually surpassed that of upper-middle-class speakers. Furthermore, when asked about their *customary* linguistic practices, the former tended to exaggerate their use of higher-status forms. The point of interest here, of course, is not the lack of accuracy of such self-reports but, rather, the psychological underpinnings that give rise to them.[2] Of course, the downgrading of personal speech styles that is revealed by hypercorrection rarely leads to wholesale abandonment of maternal nonstandard dialects, and it is here that the more latent prestige of the dialects can be seen as a sort of counterbalance.

Work in Britain has supplemented and confirmed these findings. In a summary, Trudgill (2000) notes that the masculinity of working-class speech may derive from the tough or rugged nature of working-class life; this rests upon evidence assembled much earlier. Trudgill (1972), for instance, had asked respondents in Norwich to indicate the pronunciations they usually gave to words commonly having more than one pronunciation (e.g. the word *tune* may be pronounced either *tyōōn* or *tōōn*, with the former being the more 'prestigious' variant). While Labov had found a general tendency for respondents in New York to over-report the use of higher-status pronunciations, Trudgill's results indicated that *males*, both working class and middle class, often claimed to use *nonstandard* forms even when they did not customarily do. (The trans-Atlantic variation, it has been argued, might be the result of a weaker assimilation of middle-class norms among members of the English working class, or to Trudgill's more subtle analyses of sex differences.) It seems clear that working-class, nonstandard forms have an attraction that cuts across class boundaries, and it is this attraction that provides the covert prestige associated with such forms. Since it is based upon associations between nonstandard speech and masculinity, covert prestige is essentially a male phenomenon. Thus, Labov (2006) notes that the positive masculine connotations of nonstandard speech, for men, do not seem to be balanced by similar positive values for women. Again, the work of Trudgill (1972) in Norwich bears this out. Unlike their male counterparts, the women in his studies there tended to claim more *standard* usage than they actually employed; see also the following section here.

A revealing anecdote indicates the cross-boundary attractiveness and, indeed, the utility of working-class usage. A few years ago, I was in the office of a middle-aged, upper-middle-class male American university professor. As the head of his department, he was being pressed by two or three colleagues (also male) on a current academic matter. He was clearly unable or unwilling to go along with their request. After a few minutes of polite and 'educated' give-and-take, my friend turned to the others, smiled broadly and exclaimed, 'Listen boys, you *know* there ain't no way I can do it'. His departmental colleagues immediately ceded the point. Falling into this nonstandard pattern was a signal of directness and firmness, of an egalitarian informality, of the truth. The essence here lies in the perceived contrast between no-nonsense usage, on the one hand, and inflated and often evasive language, on the other: straight shooting versus humbug – or, more frankly, bullshit. The latter has now become the object of increased scholarly scrutiny (see Frankfurt, 2005; and, for more 'popular' treatments, Penny, 2005, and Webb, 2005).

Gender Matters

The masculinity of nonstandard usage that Labov reported in the American context is, in some sense, the mirror image of the unfavorable connotations – the 'poshness', the 'effeminacy' – of higher-status speech styles. Working-class perceptions here, as reported by Bragg, Ellis and Orwell (see above), are reinforced by the covert prestige that influences middle-class speakers. Attitudinal dynamics underpinned by conceptions of the masculinity or femininity of speech styles are often particularly notable at school. They extend beyond dialects, too. Thus, as Carr and Pauwels (2006: 1) note in their opening sentence, 'from the moment when foreign language study becomes optional, classrooms across the English-dominant communities of the world are inhabited primarily by girls and staffed predominantly by women: boys for the most part disappear', and they go on to discuss the 'gendered shape' of language learning at school. They embed their findings in the broader educational context in which boys are gradually becoming the gender of concern – because they are more uninterested, disaffected and disadvantaged. Sommers (2000) provides a more polemical treatment of this broader context; see also Heining-Boynton and Haitema (2007) and Lindsay and Muijs (2006), as well as the discussions of boys' attitudes in the Ebonics section, below. Ewing (2006) and Younger and Warrington (2006) provide some cautionary notes, based on analyses in Russian, British and other European settings.

It would seem obvious that the masculine directness that is the basis of covert prestige would be less attractive to girls and women. Indeed, they are generally found to be more disposed towards standard, middle-class styles; a 'classic' study here is that of Fischer (1958). Thus, they have been seen by some to produce 'politer' and more 'correct' speech than do their male counterparts. A greater linguistic insecurity among women has often been considered central here, an insecurity that may rest upon a more pronounced status-consciousness, coupled with a traditional lack of social definition for women (as opposed to men, with occupational definitions to sustain them; see Labov, 2006; Trudgill 1972, 2000). Later analyses have, unsurprisingly, suggested that the picture is rather more complicated than that; beyond the well-known general work of Brown and Levinson (1987) – another so-called 'classic' – there are valuable and more recent summaries by Coates (1996, 2004), Crawford (1995) and Holmes (1995). Mills (2003) provides an interesting discussion that interweaves considerations of 'politeness' and 'nonstandardness' within the context of social power and its negotiation. Lakoff's (1975) important work on women's language has now been supplemented by discussions of men's language (Coates, 2003; Johnson & Meinhof, 1997); and Watts (2003) and Hickey and Stewart (2005) place the topic in broadest perspective, going beyond gender contexts per se. Salkie (2004: 29) has recently noted that 'politeness is what in the language field we call a Whelk (What every linguist knows)', and it is certainly the case that studies in politeness and its ramifications have increased dramatically in the last two decades. What is more important, however, as revealed in the approaches of several of the books just cited, is that studies of gender-and-language relationships – particularly those bearing upon differential usage of 'correct' or 'standard' speech – are now increasingly likely to treat both genders under the same roof. This is a welcome development from earlier work, in which the language of one gender was taken as a baseline from which to assess that of the other: need I specify which was deemed to set the general baseline?

A study by Edwards (1979a) tested some of the implications of language perceptions and prestige in a group of prepubertal children. Physiological sex differences relating to speech production are, of course, not very marked in such children, but earlier work had confirmed what common-sense knows: on the basis of speech samples alone, listeners can typically distinguish boys from girls with a high degree of accuracy; see Meditch (1975), Sachs (1975), Sachs *et al.* (1973) and Weinberg and Bennett, (1971). It is children's early adherence to social norms concerning male and female speech that allows such accuracy in sex-identification. In my study, voice samples of 20 working-class and 20 middle-class 10-year-olds were presented to 14 adult judges (Irish trainee teachers) whose task was, simply, to identify the gender of each speaker. As well, five other judges were asked to rate all the voices on four dimensions related to masculinity/femininity.

It was found, first of all, that – for *both* boys and girls – the voices of working-class children were perceived as rougher and more masculine than those of their middle-class counterparts; that is, the association between masculinity and working-class speech that I have already discussed was confirmed. As in previous work, there was a high overall degree of accuracy in sex-identification (about 84%, in fact), but the major finding of the study, one that further supports notions of covert prestige, was that the *errors* made were not randomly distributed. First of all, female judges were more accurate than their male counterparts in identifying children's gender. This accords with Meditch's (1975) results and, more importantly, with both scholarly and informal observations of females' greater sensitivity in interpersonal relationships in general, and in verbal interactions in particular. Secondly, beyond the differential accuracy of male and female judge-listeners, a significant interaction was found – in terms of errors made – between social class and gender. That is, among the working-class children, few boys were mistaken as girls, but errors made about girls were considerably greater. For the middle-class children, the pattern was reversed, and more errors were made with the boys than with the girls.

The explanation provided for these results can be briefly summarized here. It would appear as if the general masculinity of working-class speech caused girls to be misidentified as boys by the middle-class judges. Middle-class speech, relatively more feminine, allowed the operation of what we might term the 'boys sound like girls' principle. This reflects the fact that, at puberty, it is boys' speech that changes most markedly in assuming adult characteristics. Different social conventions operate for working-class and middle-class speech, young children are aware of these, and this awareness is exemplified, in their own speech patterns, by adherence to the appropriate norms. Differential accuracy in the identification of children's gender can then be seen as a consequence of these social processes.

Teachers' Views of 'Disadvantaged' Language

In an early Irish study (Edwards, 1974), 24 teachers of disadvantaged Dublin children provided information about their pupils via questionnaires and interviews. In addition, each teacher was given a list of 10 traits commonly associated with disadvantaged children in the literature, and was asked to rank these in order of importance as useful and accurate descriptions of disadvantage. On this ranking task, 'poor language ability' was ranked second in importance; only 'poor living conditions' were perceived to be of greater salience when considering the problems of the disadvantaged child. During the interviews, too, many teachers mentioned language difficulties of various kinds as an important aspect of their view of disadvantage. And the questionnaire data revealed that, overall, teachers reported 28% of the pupils (310 in total) as having difficulties associated with language; of these, about three-quarters were of the 'poor vocabulary' or 'poor self-expression' type.

In a subsequent investigation (Edwards, 1977b), speech samples were recorded from 20 working-class and 20 middle-class Dublin boys (with equal numbers taken from primary and fifth-level classes). All the children were, on the information of their teachers, average students. Adult middle-class judges were then asked to evaluate the children's intelligence, fluency, vocabulary, general voice quality (e.g. pronunciation and intonation) and communicative ability. On all measures, the more disadvantaged children were viewed less favorably than their middle-class counterparts. In interpreting the results, I reasoned that the lower ratings received on fluency and communication might well reflect 'poorer' performance, if the norms of the middle-class judges were taken into account; for the other measures, however – especially that of voice quality – we are presumably seeing more subjective impressions. These, in turn, reflect what we can, by now, understand to be pervasive social stereotypes that may have nothing to do with intrinsic voice elements.

Since these sorts of findings have been widely replicated across a range of contexts, it is as well to consider what they suggest. They indicate that teachers are, naturally enough, concerned about children's speech and language and – since they are obviously not isolated from broader social perspectives – they tend to see the speech of disadvantaged children as inaccurate, sloppy and likely to reflect lowered achievement potential. It would be wrong, of course, to assume that such views are set in stone, that teachers' expectations cannot be revised.[3] It is also important to remember that, while language is a central feature of personality (and perceptions of personality), it is not the only one. Teachers are constantly interacting with children, come to have access to a variety of information about them, and can therefore increasingly place speech in the context of other variables. A later investigation (Edwards, 1979b; see below) found, for instance, that teachers evaluating children (on the basis of speech samples alone) quite rightly had reservations about how well impressions would stand up once they had further information about the children. We should always bear in mind, then, that 'language studies' typically deal with only one aspect of children's behavior and, further, that the speech samples to be assessed are often presented in disembodied and somewhat artificial forms. Allowing, however, for the possibility of linguistic tunnel vision, the weight of evidence from many sources suggests the great importance of speech and language per se, as well as their intertwinings with other aspects of children's abilities, behavior and attitude. Whether alone or in combination, language matters are often pivotal elements in the perceptions and assessments made of children (and not only children, of course).

A relevant demonstration is found in the work of Seligman *et al.* (1972). In addition to considering reactions to voice alone, student teachers were also provided with photographs of the children, their drawings and written compositions. The researchers had, in fact, selected and combined such information (collected from third-grade boys in Montreal, and subjected to pre-test evaluation) so that the work of eight 'hypothetical' children could be presented to the teacher-judges. All possible combinations of 'good' and 'poor' voices, photographs and drawings/compositions were represented in these eight composites. Seligman and his colleagues found that all types of information influenced the ratings: boys who had better voices, who looked intelligent and who had produced good compositions and drawings were all judged to be more intelligent, better students and so on. Since speech style seemed always to be an important factor in the evaluations made, the study supports the contention that, even in the presence of other information, language acts as a central cue. The authors express the concern that animates all researchers: teachers may make serious judgments based upon information that may be irrelevant to considerations of children's ability and scholastic potential. (See also another early experiment – this one by Piché *et al.* [1977] – in which the contribution of speech factors to judges' assessments was rather more complicated. There were methodological differences between the two investigations, however, and the Piché study involved black children: an important variation.)

Evidence of the possible scope of the relationship between teacher ratings and speech style was provided in the Hawaiian study by Choy and Dodd (1976) already noted (in Chapter 6). When asked to rate primary-school children who spoke either standard or nonstandard varieties of English, teachers consistently favored the former. These children were seen to be more confident, better at school, less 'disruptive' in class and likely to achieve greater academic and social success. But the assessors were *also* willing to go well beyond school-related matters, to make predictions about more general social capabilities: judgments of how happy the children's marriages would likely be, for example. A useful summary discussion of this expansive evaluation is that of Ross and Nisbett (1991). They note that the tendency to account for behavior and its consequences in terms of internal traits of the 'actor' rather than external or 'situational' factors (they call it a 'dispositional' tendency) is so strong that 'people will make confident trait-based predictions on a small evidence base' (Ross & Nisbett, 1991: 124).

Williams and his colleagues conducted an important series of studies in the 1970s; collectively, these comprise one of the most comprehensive and sustained investigations of disadvantaged speech in the American context. The work builds from the familiar observation that many evaluations rest upon *stereotypes* elicited by the speech samples presented to judges. Whereas previous work had either focused upon the operation of the evaluation process per se (e.g. the Montreal studies of Lambert and his colleagues) or on the isolation of the features or characteristics of speech most important in that process (e.g. the work by Labov, Trudgill and others on speech-status markers), Williams was concerned with both (see Williams, 1970a). In a study of black and white primary-school children, Williams (1970b) asked Chicago teachers (white or black themselves) to rate the pupils on a number of semantic-differential scales: the dimensions included fluency, complexity of sentences, reticence and pronunciation, but there were also scales that asked for judgments about family socioeconomic status, degree of disadvantage and standardness or nonstandardness of speech. Factor analysis of the ratings suggested two important themes. One of these, labelled 'confidence/eagerness', reflected children's perceived confidence and social status. The other was also associated with social-status judgments, relating mainly to perceptions of ethnicity and the nonstandardness or standardness of speech: unsurprisingly, it was labelled 'ethnicity/nonstandardness'. The argument, then, is that teachers evaluated the speech samples (and the children) along two broad dimensions; one of these appears to relate to ethnicity and ethnic, nonstandard speech patterns, while the second reflects relatively personal attributes of children themselves. As to the specific speech cues eliciting the teachers' reactions, Williams identified a number of types: frequency of pausing, for example, was found to be negatively related to confidence ratings, and nonstandard grammatical variants (as found in BEV: see above) were associated with evaluations along the ethnicity/nonstandardness dimension.

In an expanded study, Williams _et al._ (1972) probed the evaluations made of low- and middle-status black, white and Mexican-American children by teachers in Texas. They confirmed the previously established two-factor model of teachers' judgments, and the findings that children of low socioeconomic status are considered more 'ethnic/nonstandard' and are viewed less favorably on variables underpinning the 'confidence/eagerness' dimension. Within the low-status category, white children were seen more positively, and as less 'ethnic/nonstandard' than were the black and Mexican-American pupils. Williams and his colleagues also found that the teachers' evaluations of the actual children representing each of the ethnic groups in the study correlated reasonably well with their more general semantic-differential evaluations of the three groups (when these were presented to them via simple written labels). This led the authors to suggest that, in rating the individual child, teachers may be fulfilling their own, more general expectations. They also note that black and white teachers' perceptions were remarkably similar. This important finding suggests that speech evaluations easily generalize across ethnic and class boundaries, and may reflect what many have seen as the rapid internalization of 'mainstream' social values by members of relatively non-prestigious groups who move into that mainstream – wholly, partially or, indeed, _in posse._

Further Refinements in the Study of 'Disadvantaged' Language

Social psychologists have generally investigated language perceptions directly (by finding, for instance, appropriate representatives of each of the speech varieties to be investigated) or indirectly (the classic indirect approach has been Lambert's 'matched-guise' technique; see above). In both the direct and the indirect approaches, speech samples are often 'pre-tested' by an appropriate group of judges, so as to ensure that they do indeed reflect the proper group. These sorts of studies have produced a sizeable body of evidence bearing on social perceptions, stereotypes and language attitudes. We can now predict with some confidence what sorts of reactions will be elicited when people hear varieties of Black English, Newfoundland English, Cockney, 'Received Pronunciation', Boston Brahmin English and many others.

Attitudes are dynamic and not static, of course. This suggests (among other things) that investigations must be repeated from time to time in order to pick up any changes. A recent example here is provided by Fabricius (2006: 119–120), who points out that 'Received Pronunciation' (RP: traditionally the highest-status variety in England) is sometimes stigmatized. Its speakers may be perceived as 'posh' or 'snobbish' (a longstanding view, as we have already seen) and their accents as reflective of an 'elitist discoursal stance'. Young people in particular, it is suggested, are now likely to repudiate 'attitudes that sustained accent prejudice'.

Accents and dialects change, too. Even the Queen's English has altered over the last half-century; it now shows some influences of 'Estuary English', a combination of London working-class speech and RP, first described by Rosewarne (1984, 1994). Analyzing the Queen's vowel sounds over four decades of her annual Christmas messages, Harrington *et al.* (2000: 927) found significant changes, evidence of a 'drift in the Queen's accent towards one that is characteristic of speakers who are younger and/or lower in the social hierarchy'. Her accent has moved closer to what the authors style 'standard southern British', although it remains 'clearly set apart' from it. Besides raising the intriguing notion that the Queen no longer speaks the Queen's English the way she once did, the import of these studies is a bit broader. It is one thing to describe the rise and appeal of the new estuarine accent among younger speakers, but it is another to show its effects upon existing speakers, especially RP speakers. The fact that the speech of the Queen herself is influenced by change suggests that, for more 'ordinary' individuals, the alterations are likely to be greater. As Harrington *et al.* (2000: 927) conclude, 'the extent of such... influences is probably more marked for most adult speakers, who are not in the position of having to defend a particular form of English' – to which we might add that they also live in rather closer proximity to those influences than does Elizabeth R.

As part of this little digression, it may be useful here to make a point about terminology. While common usage refers to language-attitude studies, most are actually studies of *belief*. If, for example, you assess responses to questions like 'How intelligent do you think this speaker is?' or 'How fluent is this speaker?', you may find out what the respondent believes. It would take further probing to add the affective or emotional dimension to the cognitive one reflected in belief, and such an addition is needed for a fuller attitudinal evaluation. The point becomes clearer if we consider more broadly based investigations. In many language studies, for instance, it is common to elicit responses to questions like 'How important is a knowledge of French for you (your children, this community, etc.)?' Clearly, one might feel that such knowledge was extremely important while, at the same time, heartily disliking the language, its speakers and the necessity to learn it (see also Goot, 1993, on the degree of 'passion' underpinning respondents' ratings).

If we concerned ourselves more directly with fully fleshed attitudes, rather than the beliefs commonly indicated by check-marks on scales, we might begin to find out more about the reasons behind judges' evaluations. Recent developments in 'perceptual dialectology' are relevant here. The term, particularly associated with the work of Preston and his associates, reflects a sort of marriage between the study of dialect variation and 'folk linguistics' (i.e. popular language attitudes, beliefs and stereotypes), so as to tap into the subjective 'real-world' perceptions that are often at variance with scholarly insight, and usually much more important. The data-collection methods used go well beyond structured interviews, questionnaires and the like: the intention is to allow respondents to more fully contextualize their points of view (Preston, 1989, 1999; see also Long & Preston, 2002; Niedzielski & Preston, 2000). For further comments on the desirability of broader evaluation exercises, see Edwards (1982), Palozzi (2006), and below.

Beyond predicting differential reactions to dialect varieties, we can also make predictions about those varieties produced by non-native speakers of English that show the influence of the first language. We understand, at a general level, how these reactions come about, via linguistic 'triggering', and how they reflect a set of stereotypical attitudes (or beliefs, at any rate) that listeners have of speakers. Investigators have not, however, gone very much beyond fairly gross explanations; that is, they have typically not related speech evaluations to particular speech attributes. Thus, although hundreds of experiments have revealed negative reactions towards BEV (for example), we have very little information relating specific linguistic attributes of that variety to such reactions. These could plausibly include pronunciation patterns, particular grammatical constructions, dialect-specific lexical items, or any combination of these and other factors.

In other words, the simultaneous consideration of both evaluation *and* the cues triggering it – advocated, and to some extent acted upon, by Williams and his colleagues – has not attracted a great deal of research interest. Social psychology *has* interested itself in *non*-linguistic features that may stimulate or influence evaluative reactions: matters of context, topic and salience, as well as degrees of emotionality, humor and abstraction, have figured in many studies. The closest approach, perhaps, to the investigation of linguistic elements is found in work on levels of formality/informality. It is also true that Giles and Ryan (1982: 210) made an argument for 'more detailed linguistic and acoustic descriptions of the stimulus voices as well as examining the relative evaluative salience of these particulars for different types of listeners', and Robinson (1985) also argued for improved collaboration between social psychology and linguistics. A related, although not so pointed, observation was made by Edwards (1982), in calling for fuller probing of the reasons behind judges' evaluative decisions. In general, though, social psychologists have done little in the way of isolating 'linguistic and acoustic' variables and relating them to evaluative judgments. This is hardly surprising, for such work is simply not their *métier*.

Recent linguistic research has dealt with features that characterize and differentiate language varieties, and some has focused on those very social-class and ethnic varieties that are of particular interest and concern here. Laver and Trudgill's (1979) chapter on 'social markers' remains a useful reference, alerting us to such phenomena as:

- the nasality habitually associated with some varieties of English (RP, for example);
- the wide dialectal variations in consonant pronunciation: thus, RP speakers pronounce *lock* and *loch* more or less identically, with a final /k/, but (some) Scottish pronunciations involve final /x/. To give another example, British English pronunciation of the post-vocalic /r/ in words like *cart* and *mar* is inversely related to social-class status, whereas in some varieties of American English (in New York, for instance) a positive correlation exists between /r/-pronunciation and status;
- grammatical variation (e.g. copula deletion in BEV: thus, standard English *they are going* becomes *they going*);
- lexical differences (e.g. some English speakers *brew* their tea, some *mash* it, some let it *steep*, some let it *set*, and so on).

If, however, linguists have been the ones to describe such variation, they have either been relatively uninterested in its relation to differences in social ratings or have simply assumed that the more obvious and salient linguistic markers are the relevant triggers. Like social psychologists, linguists too have generally stuck to their lasts. (There are some notable

exceptions: see, again, Laver and Trudgill [1979], as well as Graff *et al.*
[1983].)

We would benefit, therefore, from efforts to revive the double
emphasis of Williams and his colleagues, perhaps to bridge more the
work of psychology and linguistics. The effect would be to refine and
particularize our knowledge of how *specific* aspects of speech elicit
specific types of evaluative reactions. Recent useful forays in this direction
can be found in the collection edited by Milroy and Preston (1999). Of
course, even if we could isolate the most important speech cues, it is
unclear what immediate use this would have. Attempting to alter
specific speech characteristics, for example, would be difficult in itself
and – among speech communities of so-called 'visible minorities' –
probably of little 'stand-alone' benefit. On the other hand, a general
policy of addition to or expansion of a child's linguistic repertoire could
render such detailed information almost unnecessary. Nonetheless,
arguments have been made from within the American black community
that the acquisition of more standard features of English would at least
remove one potential stimulus to negative perception. As a black
educator said on an instructional video, 'At least they won't be able to
say that you didn't get that job "cause you speak poor English"' (see
Alvarez & Kolker, 1987).

In another useful development, Williams (1974, 1976) discussed what
he termed the 'latitude of attitude acceptance'. Not an entirely new
concept in the larger domain of social psychology, this is an acknowledgement that raters' evaluations may not be entirely adequately
expressed by making a single mark on some semantic-differential scale.
Having particular regard to language-evaluation studies, Williams
argued that determining judges' range of acceptance might be a useful
addition to that single mark. Beyond making a rating choice in the usual
way, judges could also indicate other generally acceptable rating
possibilities; likewise, ratings that would definitely be rejected could
also be revealed. An example might be:

This child sounds: passive <u>+ : **+** : + : : – : – : –</u> active

The three 'plus' signs towards the 'passive' end of the scale here could
indicate ratings generally acceptable to a judge: his or her 'latitude of
acceptance'. If one of these was circled or otherwise highlighted (I have
put it in **bold** here), that could be taken as the judge's single best
estimate. A position left blank (as in the mid-position, above) could
denote lack of decision or neutrality, with the three 'minus' signs

indicating possibilities definitely rejected; see also the reference made above to Goot (1993) on the assessment of evaluative 'intensity'.

Another Irish study (already briefly referred to above: Edwards, 1979b) did involve somewhat more detailed inquiry. In addition to testing the generality of the previous findings with regard to speech evaluations, two refinements were introduced. The first was the measurement of any sex-of-rater effects. Previous studies had dealt mainly with female teacher-raters – quite reasonably, since in North America most primary-school teachers are female. In the Irish context, however, the large numbers of male primary teachers prompted consideration of judges' gender as a possibly important variable. The second variant was to attempt to measure the judges' *confidence* in their ratings. The reasoning behind this was simply that respondents almost always comply with requests to fill in all the scales provided in evaluation studies, even though they may feel that some are less appropriate than others (indeed, raters often express doubts in this regard – typically at the conclusion of the experimental task). Judges' confidence, or the lack of it, could well be of some importance in the overall interpretation of results. Early on, Williams (1974) observed that respondents are willing to make judgments after very brief exposure to a stimulus voice and, as we have seen (in the Choy and Dodd study, for example) these judgments may be almost ludicrously wide ranging. The 'latitude of attitude' that judges were prepared to accept was seen by Williams to extend somewhat the investigator's understanding of the rating procedure and, in like manner, the assessment of judges' *confidence* in their ratings was here considered as an expression of how wide their implicit latitude of acceptance might be – if in fact it existed at all.

Two groups of twenty 10-year-old Dublin children (10 boys and 10 girls in each group) provided the speech samples here: one group comprised disadvantaged, lower-class children; the other was a middle-class sample. After a practice trial, the children were tape-recorded while reading a short passage, selected with the assistance of their teachers. Fourteen teachers-in-training (seven male, seven female) served as judges in the study, and they responded to 17 semantic-differential scales, which touched upon various aspects of the children's personality and background (e.g. fluency, intelligence, enthusiasm, likely school achievement, perceived degree of disadvantage). Accompanying each of these rating scales was a second seven-point scale on which the judges were asked to indicate the degree of confidence they had in the 'substantive' rating they had just made. Finally, all raters were interviewed at the conclusion of the study about their knowledge and opinions of disadvantage, language and the experiment itself.

The major results were as follows. First, on every scale, the disadvantaged children received less favorable ratings than did the middle-class children; the support for earlier work was clear. Factor analysis of the ratings showed all of them to be highly interrelated, and only one important factor emerged. We could recall here Williams's consistent finding of *two* important factors in teacher ratings: 'confidence/eagerness' and 'ethnicity/nonstandardness'. Since ethnicity was not a factor in the Irish context, it is therefore unsurprising that only one factor ('disadvantage-nondisadvantage') emerged here. This result suggests the validity of the idea that teachers' reactions derive from some overall elicited stereotype of disadvantaged children. One would not wish to deny that other scales and other speech situations might evoke other factors; in the school context, however, judgments of disadvantaged children – at least on scales relating to language and school ability – may well be rather unidimensional.

Turning to the 'confidence' scales, we see an analogous finding: non-disadvantaged children were judged with greater certainty than the disadvantaged. An interesting difference, however, occurred between the two sorts of ratings, with regard to the gender of the judges. Male teachers were found to give higher ratings on the substantive scales than were female judges; on the 'confidence' scales, however, the reverse was the case. Thus, it appeared that, overall, males made more positive ratings, but were less sure of them, while females were more confident about their somewhat less favorable substantive ratings. Apart from indicating that one is not dealing, in rating scales generally, with a simple response tendency for one gender to make higher or lower marks on a scale, there is an intriguing possibility here, and it is one that deserves further study (if only because scales remain so commonplace in social-psychological and sociolinguistic research). Perhaps males tend to over-commit themselves in their ratings, to make somewhat more polarized judgments – and then take the opportunity provided by the confidence scales to 'soften' their judgments, as it were. Females, having been more circumspect from the start, may not find this necessary.

Considering the confidence ratings as they related to each individual substantive scale, it was found that some of the latter tended to be rated with greater certainty than others. Since I have just pointed out that *all* the substantive scales were highly interrelated (in the factor analysis), it might seem that, if some smaller subset were required, it would not make much difference which scales were chosen. However, the results of the confidence judgments reveal that some scales have at least greater face validity than others. The generality here is this: judges were more confident when asked to rate aspects of personality that are more or less directly relatable to the speech sample itself (e.g. fluency, reading ability, pronunciation), and less comfortable when asked to assess such things as the happiness of the child and family socioeconomic status. It may be that a sort of halo effect is at work here: ratings about which judges are more confident are allowed to sway decisions that are requested under more dubious or far-fetched headings. Besides confirming, then, the now-familiar differences in judges' perceptions of disadvantaged children, the study also shows that – although willing to fill in all the scales provided – raters are clearly more comfortable with assessments that it seems more reasonable to make, given the stimulus sample provided. This variation in comfort level, and the commendable caution that must underpin it, are matters that researchers would do well to take to heart. Finally here, the differences attributable to judges' gender also suggest possibilities that may be important for those engaged in rating-scale research.

The most general implication of all these evaluation studies is clear. Listener-evaluators (teachers being a most important group here) are prone to stereotyped and often negative views of certain language varieties and their speakers. The importance of this derives from the evidence that *different* language varieties are not linguistically *deficient*. While the data about teachers' attitudes and evaluations simply reveal, in one context, a perceived relationship between certain language varieties and social deficit that occurs in other settings, teachers' views and behavior are of rather special significance in the lives of disadvantaged children. In a review of many sociolinguistic studies, Robinson (1972: 116) pointed out that speech may not always be an irrelevant or erroneous clue to a child's ability: 'if the self-fulfilling prophecy is fulfilled, then paradoxically the argument that certain language behaviours are associated with educational attainments has a reasonable (even if unnecessary) foundation'. This is a useful point, although it does not detract from the thrust of the studies reported here.

There are really two related issues in contention: one is the demonstration that speech style can influence perceptions and evaluations; the other is the manner in which the attitudes and beliefs that underlie such assessments may affect children's school progress. The latter is bound to be a more speculative aspect than the former, since it is so difficult to tease out, in natural settings, the influence of one variable among many. And, as Robinson implies, there is always the possibility that, because of pressure and prejudice, relationships found between speech and school success may actually have social validity. We may nevertheless consider, however, that attitudes towards the speech of disadvantaged children often contribute to an unfair and unnecessary handicap to their progress.

Notes

1. When considering phenomena like the 'minority-group reaction', we should remember that the lines of comparison are not simply drawn between majorities and minorities, but also among minority groups themselves. Preferences and prejudices here can reflect and reinforce actual or perceived positioning along social spectra. Disdained when they first arrived in America, the Irish were able to look down upon later arrivals once their own social security had begun to take form. Or, as in the Brazilian case discussed in Chapter 4, places on the social spectrum can reflect shades of skin color. Orwell wrote of some animals being more equal than others, and Allardt (1984: 203) rephrased the aphorism when he said that some minority groups are more minor than others.

   In America, the National Conference for Community and Justice (founded in 1927 as the National Conference of Christians and Jews, with a name change in 1998) has issued three reports – in 1994, 2000 and 2006 – on intergroup relations. The first of these revealed that more than 40% of black and Hispanic Americans felt that their Asian neighbors tended to be crafty and unscrupulous in business matters. About half of the black respondents, and more than two-thirds of the Asian Americans agreed that Hispanics had families larger than they could reasonably support. And some 30% of Asian and Hispanic Americans thought that blacks were quite content to live on welfare payments (Holmes, 1994; National Conference of Christians and Jews, 1994).

   The second report found some improvement in intergroup attitudes, and greater contact across groups. Still, only 30% were satisfied with the state of that contact, many reported instances of discrimination, and about 80% of the informants agreed that racial, ethnic and religious tensions remained serious matters (National Conference for Community and Justice, 2000).

   The latest report (National Conference for Community and Justice, 2006) reported some further improvement: now, some 42% reported satisfaction with the state of intergroup contact, with relationships with Hispanic Americans showing particular improvement. However, roughly the same percentage of respondents as in the 2000 report still thought that various tensions were still very much alive. Much more anti-Muslim discrimination was reported, and almost 40% of the respondents felt that it would be acceptable to have separation of the races, 'as long as they have equal opportunity'. And, in terms of the interrelationships among Asian, Hispanic and black Americans, these latest results not only showed important variations per se – black informants holding, for example, the most negative views of the state of intergroup contact – but they also revealed interesting between-group perceptual disparities. Thus, while black respondents reported that their closest relationships were with Hispanics, the latter were most positive about their relationships with whites – and whites, in turn, put Hispanics below black and Asian Americans in these terms!

Taken together, the findings of these three reports are interesting because they demonstrate the dynamic nature of intergroup contact, and the way in which it reflects broader social contexts. Thus, Hispanics are now much more numerous in America, and much more widespread, and ubiquity can often lessen antipathy. On the other hand, Muslim Americans are paying a social price for Islamic fundamentalism. Beyond this, two important points stand out. First, the general levels of 'life satisfaction' remain much lower among blacks than among either whites or Asians, and they continue to report the greatest levels of prejudicial discrimination. Second, it would seem that – despite the ruling in the landmark *Brown v Board of Education* case of 1954, that to be separate is to be inherently unequal (see Chapter 9) – a large minority of respondents still apparently fail to grasp the point.

2. When an American speaker says *kyōō'pon* instead of *kōō'pon*, we have another variety of hypercorrection; here it arises from the notion that, if higher-status speakers say *styōōd'nt* rather than *stōōd'nt*, then an analogous pronunciation must be 'correct' for *coupon*. The further interest here is that the more prestigious American pronunciation of *student* is itself a conscious adoption of British usage – and recent work by Boberg (1999) reveals some pitfalls.

   The American 'nativization' of foreign words spelled with < a > that have entered the lexicon (words like *macho* and *pasta*) has, Boberg suggests, a strong 'aesthetic' dimension. This favors a rendering of the sound as /a:/ (as in *father*) rather than as /æ/ (as in *fat*). And this 'aesthetic' sense derives from the idea that British usage – in which the /a:/ pronunciation is considered more typical – is prestigious usage. Ironies arise, Boberg shows, when the American /a:/-based pronunciation of such foreign imports, based upon perceptions of British elegance and 'correctness', in fact *diverges* from the /ae/ pronunciation given to such borrowings in standard British English; see also Edwards (1999a).

   Jones (2001) provides some background for this sort of work in a recent book on American anglophilia (see particularly her Chapter 4, 'Gee, I love your accent').

3. It remains the case, however, that teachers-in-training very rarely receive much information about the aetiology of disadvantage in general, or its linguistic aspects in particular – despite the fact that, as I have shown to many students over two decades, a reasonable grasp of the 'difference' position can be quickly acquired: this is not rocket science. See my introductory chapter for further details.

Chapter 9
Black English as Ebonics

Introduction

I have already discussed Black English and the very important role that the analysis of it has played in our understanding of the linguistic validity of *all* dialects. The importance here is of global significance, relevant wherever nonstandard dialects are derogated. Since Black English Vernacular (BEV) had for so long been a variety particularly lacking in prestige, it became clear that any demonstration of its linguistic validity as one English dialect among many would logically transfer to other less stigmatized nonstandard forms. The evidence presented by Labov and others for this linguistic validity and, therefore, for the communicative competence of the speakers of BEV, remains strong, even if the insights often remain regrettably unavailable to the public in general, and to teachers in particular.

In a recent discussion, Niedzielski (2005: 259–260) illustrates the continuing problems affecting black children. She cites work published in 1999 showing that 'while African-Americans make up approximately 12% of the US population, they make up an astounding 41% of the students in American schools labeled "educably mentally retarded"'. This attribution rests largely on language evaluations that continue to see more incorrectness, more impurity and more speech pathology in BEV; see also Adger *et al.* (1992). Another indication of bias is found in the hearing-assessment referrals made by teachers. Although black children are not statistically more likely than their white counterparts to have hearing problems – in fact, there is some evidence that, as a group, there is *less* hearing loss in the black community – they are much more likely to be referred to speech-and-hearing personnel. Data from a professional body of specialists reveal that black children are referred in proportions that are double their actual numbers in the population; see also American Speech-Language Hearing Association (1997).

Labov (1976) reminded us that speakers of nonstandard dialects typically understand standard forms with little or no difficulty. Relatedly, he noted that the 'gears and axles of English grammatical machinery are available to speakers of all dialects' (Labov, 1976: 64). Of course, nonstandard speakers may not regularly *use* the more standard variants: there are well-understood differences, in other words, between *competence* and *performance*. Indeed, the basic distinction here had been made clear at the very time that the 'deficit' position was at its strongest. As I have already pointed out, Trudgill (1975) observed that working-class children could use Bernstein's 'elaborated code' under certain circumstances; and, earlier still, Robinson (1965) had found that the *written* grammar of working-class children was not markedly different from that of middle-class pupils (see also Rushton & Young, 1975).

It is abundantly clear that the context in which language is displayed and recorded is of the greatest significance – something that Labov (1969) famously illustrated in his demonstrations that the vaunted 'non-verbality' of the black child could be made to disappear if interview and observation situations were made more appropriate. One implication here is that the use of BEV among black children varies (Edwards & Giles, 1984). Torrey (1983: 642) thus pointed out that:

> a teacher in a class of black children who hears BE forms frequently should not conclude that all or even most of the class members conform to the general description of BE... some individuals use only one or two BE forms, and others completely standard forms. Furthermore, some who use many BE forms in spontaneous speech are perfectly able to handle SE in reading and other language tests.

The black children so profoundly misunderstood by deficit theorists are, of course, possessors of a vibrant linguistic heritage and a rich oral culture. It is quite remarkable that such obvious markers of an historically longstanding tradition were invisible – or ignored – by 'deficit' proponents of remedial and compensatory education. Where Bereiter and Engelmann (1966) saw black children as lacking rudimentary forms of dialogue, unable to recognize single words and viewing language as something dispensable in social life (one wonders, still, how such blindness could have occurred), Labov (1969: 33) and his colleagues saw these same children living in a community 'bathed in verbal stimulation from morning to night'.

A study by Edwards (1999b) illuminates both the continuing difficulties in teacher's perceptions of nonstandard speech and something of the oral fluency of black children. Among a rural primary-school population in Nova Scotia, black children, white Acadian-French children and white children of English-speaking background were studied. Each child provided three speech samples: a set reading passage, a retold story (i.e. the experimenter tells the child a story, who then retells it – a technique used by Piaget, 1952, and somewhat more narrowly by Houston, 1973) and spontaneous speech on any topic of interest to the child. Adult judges then evaluated the children on standard personality dimensions. The main intent here was to see if perceived speaker favorability varied with type of speech sample evaluated.

It was found, first, that black children were generally evaluated less favorably than the other two groups; second, spontaneous speech tended, across the board, to elicit the highest ratings. Of greatest interest here, however, were the interactions found between group and speech type, and here it was found that the black children profited most, so to speak, from the spontaneous speech ratings. To put it another way: the differences in evaluations evoked by black children's reading/story-retelling and spontaneous speech productions were much more marked than those pertaining to the other two groups of children. The suggestion is that black children, whose culture is orally strong, will produce the best linguistic results ('best', that is, in the perceptions of white listeners) when the context allows them to show evidence of that cultural strength and richness. There are rather obvious implications here, both for further study and for interpreting and reacting to language behavior in more structured contexts (like classrooms).

Ebonics

In this section, I hope to show that the value – both intrinsic and generalizable – of attending to the sociology of BEV has not diminished.

The *Brown v. Board of Education* decision of 1954 is seen as a legal milestone in black education in America, the Supreme Court ruling unanimously that 'separate is inherently unequal'. Schools were told to desegregate 'with all deliberate speed' (see the latest treatment by Daugherity & Bolton, 2008). This overturned more than half a century of educational segregation underpinned by 'separate but equal' provisions that legitimated a most *unequal* state of affairs, and it held the promise of real educational equality. But this has generally not come to pass. Why not? Because other social obstacles to black progress have remained firmly in place, including the 'tremendous linguistic divisions between those who trace their ancestry to African slaves and those who do not' (Baugh, 2006: 91). There are threads, therefore, that connect *Brown* to the important cases in Michigan and California that I shall touch upon below; see also Ball and Alim (2006), Bartee and Brown (2007), Brown (2007) and Jackson (2005).

In the late 1970s, parents of more than a dozen black children at the Martin Luther King primary school in Ann Arbor, Michigan, alleged that the school was not properly educating their children. They were doing poorly at school and the parents' view was that teachers were unaware of the important sociocultural differences between these children and their white counterparts (80% of the school population), and that language barriers prevented school success. Indeed, the children had been (inaccurately, needless to say) labelled as educationally retarded and learning disabled, were relegated to speech classes for language deficiency, and were suspended, disciplined and held back. In July 1979, after a month-long trial in which several prominent linguists testified (none for the defendants), a federal court judge ruled that school authorities had failed to act to overcome language barriers, and ordered them to devise curricula to help the children (particularly with their reading development). That is, the schools were to adapt.

Contrary to some reports, the school was not required to teach BEV, nor were teachers required to learn it so as to communicate with their pupils – they already communicated well enough, and the essential problem was with the teaching of reading. (Work by McDermott and Gospodinoff [1981] and Lucas and Borders [1987] has since confirmed that dialect variation per se rarely leads to difficulties with classroom communication.) Of great interest, then – and of great significance for the present discussion – was the finding that BEV itself was not a point of interference. Rather, the barriers arose here because of the negative reactions to the dialect, coupled with inaccurate teacher expectations and (to put it bluntly) racist perceptions. The linguistic evidence in the case enabled the judge to find that BEV was a valid and distinct English dialect; at the same time, he supported the view that standard English (some form of standard American English, perhaps) was a necessary component of success in school and beyond. Indeed, the judge went so far as to say that BEV was not an acceptable method of communication in many contexts.

Naturally, the case received very wide publicity, and much of the press coverage was misinformed and distorted (see Venezky, 1981). As well, general opinion was divided on many aspects. Consequently, a symposium was planned to discuss the elements and implications of the King decision; this took place in February 1980. The conference itself became a media event with, among others, a BBC film crew and a team from the American National Public Radio organization in attendance. A book of proceedings soon appeared (Smitherman, 1981a), and this presents the fullest available account of the whole issue; see also Smitherman (1981b) and Zorn (1982).

As one of the linguists testifying at the trial, Labov (1982) also prepared some lengthy notes on the case, with observations on the educational treatment that the black children had received (and which had led to the trial). He wrote that, in invoking federal law directing educational authorities to act against language barriers found to impede pupil progress, the judge clearly did not believe that such law applied only in foreign-language situations. Although this may have been the original thinking in existing legal provisions (see Zorn, 1982; but also Bailey, 1981), the judge did *not* class BEV as a separate language. Labov went on to cite the trial as an illustration of linguists' involvement in contemporary, real-life issues; the abstract to his paper is worth quoting here:

> Though many linguists have shown a strong concern for social issues, there is an apparent contradiction between the principles of objectivity needed for scientific work and commitment to social action. The Black English trial in Ann Arbor showed one way in which this contradiction could be resolved. The first decade of research on Black English was marked by violent differences between creolists and dialectologists on the structure and origin of the dialect. The possibility of a joint point of view first appeared in the general reaction of linguists against the view that blacks were linguistically and genetically inferior. The entrance of black linguists into the field was a critical factor in the further development of the creole hypothesis and the recognition of the distinctive features of the tense and aspect system. At the trial, linguists were able to present effective testimony in the form of a unified view on the origins and structural characteristics of the Black English Vernacular and argue for its validity as an alternate to standard English. (Labov, 1982: 165)

Discussions and disagreements about the 'origins and structural characteristics' of BEV have continued. There are some very good treatments of its history and development; particularly recommended here are books by Lanehart (2001), Mufwene *et al.* (1998), Poplack (2000; see also Poplack & Tagliamonte, 2001) and Wolfram and Thomas (2002). Green's (2002) treatment is also of interest: although her book is essentially devoted to matters of lexicon, phonology and syntax, she does devote a final chapter to 'social' aspects of BEV. In fact, in about 30 pages or so, she touches upon all the key sociological questions: perceptions of BEV by researchers and the general public, the issue of bidialectalism involving BEV and standard English, and appropriate responses to BEV in the classroom. Of considerable interest here are debates about the 'African-ness' of BEV, on the one hand, and its status as one English dialect among many, on the other. These definitional matters are not only of narrow academic concern; they have figured in more public discussions too, notably the Oakland 'case' (see below), in which claims that 'Ebonics' was basically an African variety could have been important factors in the type of educational provisions to be made for black children at school (see Rickford, 2002; Smith, 2001).

As it turned out, the Ann Arbor case was a precursor to a still more widely discussed situation: the resolution of the Oakland, California, school board, in December 1996, declaring *Ebonics* to be the native *language* of its black students. There are several reliable overviews available in the literature; among the important monographs are those by Baugh (2000), Kretzschmar (1998), Pandey (2000) and Ramirez *et al.* (2005). My citations from the actual Oakland decisions are taken from the last of these sources. Among the best paper-length discussions are those of Barnes (2003), Baugh (2002), Deák (2007), Rickford (2002), Smitherman (1998) and Wolfram (1998). Recently, De Bose (2005) provided a language-planning approach to BEV, paying particular attention to its use at school.

And what is *Ebonics*? The term was coined by researchers taking part in a conference in St Louis devoted to the language of black children. Baugh (2004: 307) writes that the 'scholars at the 1973 meeting were all African Americans', but in the preface to his edited collection, Williams (1975) states that 'many' white researchers were also there. In any event, the term (constructed from 'ebony' + 'phonics') arose from the desire to define and describe black language from a black point of view. 'Ebonics' can be generally taken as synonymous with other terms – including Black English (BE), BEV and African American Vernacular English (AAVE) – although some have tried to draw distinctions (see Rickford, 2002). Speicher and McMahon (1992) observed that since BEV is not a dialect spoken solely by black people (see above) and since the term continues to be seen negatively in the media and elsewhere, the label 'Ebonics' may be preferable. They go on to say that 'it avoids direct reference to the race while maintaining an association with African-American culture and, therefore, a link to the African traditions that survived in the code' (Speicher & McMahon, 1992: 401). All reasonable enough, except that it is rather difficult to see 'Ebonics' as not making pretty obvious reference to black people!

In 1996, Oakland was one of a handful of cities in which a majority of the citizens were African Americans, and many of their children were doing very poorly at school (Baugh, 2004). Among the most contentious statements within the school board's famous resolution were the observations that 'validated scholarly studies... have also demonstrated that African Language Systems are genetically-based and not a dialect [sic] of English', and that black pupils were therefore entitled to financial support under the provisions of federal bilingual education programs for speakers of 'limited English proficiency'. Immediate criticism ensued, with the result that the Oakland board soon issued a 'clarification'. Because of 'misconceptions in the resulting press stories', the board now claimed that its intent had been misunderstood. Specifically, it denied that it meant to 'teach Ebonics in place of English', or to 'classify Ebonics (i.e. "Black English") speaking pupils as bilingual', or to condone 'the use of slang'. The first and last of these points are no doubt accurate, but the second is at least debatable. The statement of clarification also made a disingenuous effort to erase the bizarre usage, 'genetically-based', noting that

> the term "genetically based" is synonymous with genesis. In the clause, "African Language Systems are genetically based [no hyphen in this repetition] and not a dialect of English", the term "genetically based" is used according to the standard dictionary definition of "has origins in".

By itself, of course, this climb-down does not make the original phrasing any more clear, although the intent is obvious: Ebonics is an independent system, with a 'genesis' unrelated to English.

It soon became obvious that further changes would be necessary. Thus, in early 1997, an amended resolution was passed. The initial phrase now read: '... demonstrated that African Language Systems have origins in West and Niger-Congo languages and are not *merely* dialects of English' (my italics). Other sections were also altered, the board now wishing to make clear its intent to build upon existing language skills in order to 'move students from the language patterns they bring to school to English proficiency'. This is something mandated in federal bilingual education provisions, but, interestingly enough, the idea of 'moving' students implies a transitional thrust rejected by those proponents of bilingual education who feel that its essential remit should be to *maintain* original varieties while facilitating the growth of English skills. These proponents are concerned with separate languages, of course (particularly Spanish), and so, to the extent that the Oakland revisions allow Ebonics to be seen as an English dialect after all – if one with considerable African admixture – the reworked thrust remains in line with existing federal provisions of 'transitional' intent. The revisions rather muddy these waters, however. The intent in the original document was to instruct students 'in their primary language' (i.e. Ebonics), both to maintain that variety and to facilitate the acquisition of English. In the amended resolution, however, the main emphasis is upon mastering English while, at the same time, 'respecting and embracing the legitimacy and richness' of Ebonics.

Even in its revised form, then, the Oakland school board's declaration was not without ambiguities and infelicities: it was clearly not a document produced by professional linguists. It was perhaps an acknowledgement of this, coupled with the intense reaction to its activities, which finally led the board to delete references to Ebonics altogether (Baugh, 2004). The whole matter, however, remains instructive in a number of ways.[1] If we put aside matters of dialect-language distinction, and acknowledgements that both scholarly and official determinations have made it clear that Ebonics is a form of nonstandard English (and thus ineligible for support under the auspices of existing bilingual education legislation), we are still left with an intensely interesting and informative chapter in the sociology of language. Richard Riley, the American Secretary of Education, lost no time in making the official position clear. On Boxing Day, 1996, he stated that Ebonics was a nonstandard form of English and not a foreign language. 'Elevating Black English to the status of a language', he said, 'is not the way to raise standards of achievement in our schools' (*Globe & Mail*, 1996). Baugh (2000) and Richardson (1998) discuss Riley's reaction, and provide fuller details of other governmental and official responses.

Some of the most salient aspects of the whole affair have been briefly but usefully summarized by Wolfram (2005), who pointed to the public conceptions and misconceptions that it triggered. The school-board resolutions were seen variously to suggest, first, that Ebonics was a separate language *tout court*; second, that Ebonics was an *African* language; third – arising from the unfortunate term, 'genetically-based' – that African Americans were 'biologically predisposed' to Ebonics; fourth, that speakers of Ebonics were as eligible as (say) Hispanic Americans for federal bilingual education funding; fifth, that pupils were to be taught in Ebonics by suitably prepared teachers. And Baugh (2004: 316) provides a final important summary point: 'the Ebonics debate that began in Oakland was never fully resolved; in the wake of a hostile public reception, it was simply abandoned'. Among the chorus of voices, many were hostile (as we shall see below), and even the more enlightened ones were critical and cautious. An important issue was left hanging, while 'far too many African American students continue to attend underfunded and overcrowded schools' (Baugh (2004: 316). This, in combination with other social and political issues, ensures ongoing educational underachievement.

The language-dialect debate threw up some interesting discussions. It is clear that while classifying Ebonics as a separate language is not generally endorsed by linguists (see Baugh, 2002, 2004), this hardly implies a diminished concern for the speakers of Ebonics-as-dialect. Baugh (2006: 97) reminds us that a good case can be made for 'educational policies targeted to the needs of nonstandard-dialect speakers'. Relatedly, the term 'dialect' has no pejorative connotations in the eyes of scholars. Some of those who argued for Ebonics-as-language, however, accepted the broadly held popular belief that 'dialect' *does* mean a language form that is inferior, incomplete or inaccurate, and they have typically been motivated by well-intentioned concerns for the status of Black English. Hence the impulse behind the label of 'language', but also the inference that proponents of that label are not well-informed language scholars. Thus, as Steigerwald (2004: 12) points out, the claims of those who argue for Ebonics-as-language arise from 'the intersection of nationalist [sic] politics and sketchy linguistic science'. Of course, not being a linguist hardly means that one must forfeit one's opinion, but it is important to realize that arguing from conviction is not the same as arguing from evidence. The coexistence of the two perspectives can easily lead – as we know very well from many debates in many arenas of life – to misunderstanding and conflict, difficulties that can arise from lack of awareness or, more worryingly, from willful neglect or ignorance. Wolfram's (1998) report that he has often been asked if he 'believed' in Ebonics is telling in this connection.

One linguist, however, has proposed that Ebonics might be similar to Scots, which some see as a dialect of English, others as a language in its own right. Both varieties, Fasold (2006) suggests, are more or less equidistant from standard English. The question then becomes, as it does in other debates over language-versus-dialect status, a political one (see Edwards, 1985, 1994a), and actual degrees of difference, or invocations of mutual intelligibility, recede in definitional importance.[2] Linguistically speaking, Fasold's argument is not a strong one, but his intention is clear, and derives from his concern that 'dialect' has negative connotations, and that 'standard' can have unfairly positive ones. To most people, a linguistically unexceptionable statement like, 'Ebonics is a nonstandard dialect of English' means that BEV is an inferior variant. And, as Fasold (2006) goes on to clarify, while the term 'standard' involves distinctions that are non-pejorative to linguists, arising as they do from historical and social dynamics and having nothing to say of any intrinsic 'correctness', it generally conjures up exactly that sense of 'correctness' in the public eye. This is an entirely understandable reaction, of course, given that 'standards' typically signify minimum requirements, and 'specifications that must be met for acceptability' (Fasold, 2006: 194).[3]

Reactions to the Ebonics Debate – and to Black Underachievement

What about some specific examples of reactions to Ebonics? Wright (2005a) has assembled a bibliography of about 100 'scholarly references' and 55 newspaper articles (listed chronologically, from December 1996 to September 2003; Todd, 1997, also provides a sample of press reaction). A number of prominent black scholars rejected the Oakland approach, while at the same time endorsing the underlying motivation. Henry Louis Gates (cited by Rich, 1997), for instance, said that the original declaration was 'obviously stupid and ridiculous', but also that it was the 'sheer desperation of public schools in the inner city', the 'grave national crisis', that pushed the 'panicked Oakland board' to move as it did. Gates was also taken aback by the intensity of the reaction and the 'national fixation' on Ebonics. 'As an African American', he said, 'I'm desperate for solutions to illiteracy... I'd be open to any smart solution, but the Oakland school board didn't come up with one'. Yet it was the board's 'non-solution' that attracted all the attention, rather than the underlying problems (Rich, 1997).

Within a broader and ongoing spectrum of criticism of BEV and nonstandard varieties generally (see Lippi-Green, 1997) – both within and without the black community – it was clear that many black Americans were critical of the Oakland approach. Jesse Jackson initially decried the school board's declaration – to say that black students did not speak English was 'foolish and insulting... this is an unacceptable surrender, bordering on disgrace... it's teaching down to our children'; he later modified his views after meeting with board members and some prominent linguists (Todd, 1997: 15; see also McMillen, 1997). The reaction of one black journalist – Brent Staples of *The New York Times* – was such that it prompted a prominent linguist (Baugh, 2000) to accept a commission to write about the Ebonics controversy. Staples (1997) had joined the anti-Oakland brigade, claiming that the school board deserved the scorn that greeted its assertion that 'broken, inner-city English [is] a distinct "genetically based" language system'. He also made brief, but apparently approving, reference to a longer piece written four days

earlier by Heilbrunn (1997) in the *New Republic* – a dismissive paper that
Baugh (2000: 91) described as full of 'sweeping overgeneralizations' that
did great disservice to research across a range of scholarly disciplines,
demeaning it as 'Ebonology'.

The black critic with the highest profile was (and is) the popular
entertainer, Bill Cosby, who has been particularly outspoken about the
language and behavior of the black community. As reported by Freeman
(2006), Cosby said:

> Let me tell you something... your dirty laundry gets out of school at
> 2:30 every day: it's cursing and calling each other 'nigger' as they're
> walking up and down the street. They think they're hip. They can't
> read. They can't write. They're laughing and giggling, and they're
> going nowhere.

Smitherman (2006) points out that Cosby was a vociferous opponent of
Ebonics at the time of the Oakland trial, and he obviously remains so. In
a speech delivered in 2004, Cosby refers again to black youngsters

> standing on the corner... Everybody knows it's important to speak
> English except these knuckleheads. You can't land a plane with "why
> you ain't". You can't be a doctor with that kind of crap coming out of
> your mouth. (Cosby, 2004: 3)

Cosby's remarks were printed in *The Black Scholar*, in an issue almost
entirely dedicated to Black English; it is well worth consulting for a
contemporary overview of black scholarly opinion. Particularly interesting are the papers by Cole, who feels that Cosby has come out with harsh
but necessary truths, and by Kirkland *et al.*, who argue that Cosby is
linguistically ill-informed; see also the contributions by Black and
Woodford.

It is something of an irony, Smitherman (2006) reports, to find that
Cosby himself – beyond putting BEV into the mouths of some of his
cartoon characters – had in fact acknowledged the acceptability of code-
switching in his 2004 speech. 'You used to talk a certain way on the
corner', he said, 'and you got into the house and switched into English'
(Smitherman, 2006: 3). Odder still, she notes, is that in a much earlier
speech (to the Congressional Black Caucus in 1971), Cosby told his
audience that 'I think all you niggas need to... check yourselves out...
So I say good evening, niggas' (Dyson, 2005: 240). For a vehement but
informed denunciation, from a markedly left-wing position, of Cosby's
stance and the broader sociopolitical context of which it is a part, see
Cane (2004). McWhorter (2000, 2003) also provides further pointed

criticism from a linguistic perspective; and see Coates (2008) for a journalistic overview.

Beyond his intemperate language, Cosby is clearly upset by the poor educational achievements of black students, and ascribes much of this to attitude and language. This can be seen as a particular focus upon a much broader social issue; see Mincy (2006) for studies of the behavior and attitudes of urban inner-city black men. Among many aspects of the matter, it is clear that a sense of social 'marginalization', coupled with and fuelled by poverty and prejudice, can lead to an inability or an unwillingness to engage in important and potentially rewarding activities. Thus, for instance, a recent assessment of the poor academic performance of black children invokes the idea of *disidentification* with the school. The implication is that, to the extent that students do not 'identify' with the academic culture, they will perform poorly in the classroom. This seems an entirely reasonable supposition, and Osborne (1997), Steele (1992), Steele and Aronson (1995) and others have demonstrated that a lack of connection here is most pronounced among African American male teenagers.

'Disidentification' with the school is heightened when we consider that some students rather more pointedly develop what has been termed an 'oppositional identity' (Wiggan, 2007). This is obviously not something that applies solely to black students – an active and oppositional disdain for school is an historically and culturally widespread phenomenon (see also Ainsworth-Darnell & Downey, 1998; Farkas *et al.*, 2002; Goldsmith, 2004; Tyson, 2002). Stinson's (2006) overview is particularly useful here, as he considers various approaches to understanding the achievement gap that so often separates black and white students, boys especially. Of particular interest is the 'cool pose' often adopted by black male adolescents as a visible rejection of the life of the school. As Majors and Billson (1993) and Majors and Gordon (1994) have demonstrated, displays of 'ritualized masculinity' involving dress, posture, stance and stride, hairstyles, speech styles and other such 'statements' can all be important here. They signify a blatant and forceful rejection, to be sure, but they also act as markers of group solidarity. Whether they represent the most effective avenue of social progress is, of course, another matter entirely, and one that is much discussed both within and without the black community itself.

No one doubts that children uninterested in school are unlikely to do well there, or that a vicious circle can easily be generated. Almost two generations ago, Katz (1967) pointed to motivation as the central underlying factor: failure at school (particularly early failure) tends to sap motivation, decrease expectations, reinforce low self-esteem and so on. This is clearly true, but later research has added another possibility: low academic motivation may also stem from a view of education that sees it as unimportant and/or unattractive. (The two possibilities are obviously not mutually exclusive.) Graham *et al.* (1998) used a 'peer nomination' procedure to investigate this; that is, they asked students to tell them who among their classmates they admired and respected. Among white pupils, both boys and girls valued others who were doing well at school. The choices made by African American and Latino boys, on the other hand, suggested a devaluation of academic achievement; see also Taylor and Graham (2007). Similarly, Fryer and Levitt (2004a) have noted that studious black pupils had fewer friends than did poorer students, that working hard may attract accusations of 'acting white' and that – as a summary in *The Economist* (2008: 34) put it – it seems to be 'cool to be dumb... it would be hard to imagine a more crippling cultural norm'.

Graham *et al.* (1998: 606) go on to note that all participants in their study – boys and girls, white, black and Hispanic – associated 'academic disengagement and social deviance with being male, a low achiever, and an ethnic minority'. There seemed to be a general negative stereotype at work, one that viewed low-achieving minority-group boys as not trying hard at school, and not following school norms and rules. The researchers continue:

> We suspect that the African American and Latino boys in our research are well aware of how they are seen in the eyes of others and that this awareness may have influenced what appeared to be their relative indifference to those who display achievement behaviors that are valued by the larger society. Steele (1997) has written poignantly about how coping with negative stereotypes about their academic competence has led many African American students to academically disengage and discount the importance of school success. (Graham *et al.*, 1998: 618)

The more interesting questions are 'underneath', as it were: how and why does lack of interest arise in the first place, and how and why is it maintained when there is so much evidence of its negative life consequences? For the answers here, we have to look far beyond the school gates.

In all of this, of course – disidentification, oppositional identities, resistance to 'talking white' (see Chapter 8) or doing well in school – we must remember that we are not dealing with monolithic categories of students. Ainsworth-Darnell and Downey (1998) and Goldsmith (2004) suggest that, under some circumstances, black, Hispanic and other minority-group youngsters may be more favorably disposed towards school than are their white counterparts. Other researchers have shown that high educational aspirations may sometimes be expected as a reaction to social disadvantage, that success in the classroom can be seen as a powerful response to historical oppression and inequality; see Akom (2003), O'Connor (1997) and Perry *et al.* (2003). Sometimes, in other words, the disengagement that Ogbu and his associates have carefully documented over a number of years (see Fordham & Ogbu, 1986; Ogbu, 2003; and Chapter 8) is not quite so evident. A moment's reflection will reveal that both disengagement and its more positive opposite are entirely predictable responses to social disadvantage and prejudice, but it will also suggest that the latter requires more self-discipline and is likely, therefore, to be in shorter supply than the former. In any event, recent American social history shows quite clearly that minority-group difficulties are real and, some would say, on the increase.

While acknowledging the existence of broad social problems, it is still reasonable to think about what might usefully be done in specific areas. One could agree or disagree with Bill Cosby (1997), for example, when he says that 'legitimizing the street in the classroom is backwards. We should be working hard to legitimize the classroom – and English – in the street'. But the sentiments are not silly, and they are clearly widely held. Indeed, they can be understood in the light of earlier discussions about the way in which linguistic *difference* is translated into linguistic *deficit* through the power of social pressure. But these earlier arguments *also* pointed out that the difference-into-deficit transformation was based upon an invalid assessment of nonstandard dialect: it may be pervasive, but it is inaccurate and should therefore be contested wherever possible. It is clear that the black critics of Ebonics *do* generally see it as a deficient variety, a point of view that demonstrates their lack of linguistic awareness, and for which they may fairly be criticized. They cannot be criticized, however, for their genuine concern for black children, nor, obviously, can they be accused of rejecting BEV on racially prejudiced principles.

This accusation can, however, be levelled at many of the 'popular' reactions to the Ebonics debate, reactions that are merely specific manifestations of long-held stereotypes and prejudicial opinions. These were (and are) most easily seen in what passes for 'humor'; the Lord's Prayer rendered in Ebonics, or cartoons depicting the English language slain by the 'Ebonic plague', or showing a child at the blackboard – having written $7 \times 3 = 16$ – and then telling his teacher 'it's mathabonics'

(Baugh, 2000; Scott, 1998). Nowadays, the internet provides the quickest and most up-to-date point of entry into this vast and largely unpleasant world. I have just typed the words 'Ebonics humor' into a Google search, and near the top of the list of some 101,000 'hits' appears the following: 'Ebonics language lesson. Ever wanted to talk like a nigger? Then listen up'. The power of the public media was illustrated in a recent study of attitudes towards Ebonics (Barnes, 2003). Among a large sample of university students (roughly evenly divided between black and white, male and female), the author discovered that none was 'overwhelmingly in agreement about Ebonics as a communicative and teaching tool' (Barnes, 2003: 252). More specifically, she wrote that:

> it is clear that knowledge about the Oakland School Board resolution tended to negatively affect the viewpoints of many sample members. Awareness about the controversy reduced positive opinions about Ebonics and reinforced more negative views... This finding confirms the influential role played by the media in shaping public opinion. (Barnes, 2003: 258)

Barnes's results are not quite as straightforward as she presents them, but they demonstrate, at the least, considerable ambivalence about the status and possible role of Ebonics. It also seems likely that this ambivalence was, in many instances, pre-existing, but then became further reinforced by the popular press in all its forms. And, since that medium was generally negative – either downright prejudiced or, in the case of some black commentators and 'celebrities' of one sort or another, cautious and/or dismayed – it is also reasonable to suppose that ambivalence tended to be 'shaped' towards the unfavorable end of the attitudinal scale.

Notes

1. If nothing else, the Oakland affair has surely given the lie to Gertrude Stein's famous observation. 'What was the use', she said, 'of my having come from Oakland... there is no there there' (Stein, 1937: 289).
2. As Max Weinreich once observed: 'a language is a dialect that has an army and a navy'. And, as Fillmore (2005: 162) points out, 'deciding whether BBC newsreaders and Lynchburg, VA radio evangelists speak different dialects of the same language or different languages in the same language family is on the level of deciding whether Greenland is a small continent or a large island'.
3. I am reminded here of another connection between Ebonics and Scots. In the former, there exists a well-known game of verbal fencing called 'the dozens'; this typically involves an exchange of insults that continues until one of the players can make no comeback. (Some have argued that the term derives from the practice of selling deformed or mutilated slaves by the dozen – to be

sold in such a lot being an egregious insult to dignity and worth – while others suggest that it implies that the game of insults goes up to 12 exchanges.) As Smitherman (2006: 28) observes, the most important rule in the game is that the slanderous comments 'must not be literally true, because truth takes the game out of the realm of play into reality'.

In Scotland, the 15th-century practice of 'flyting' (i.e. quarrelling or disputing) also involved fierce and colorful insult; 'a stylized *tour de force* of mutually exchanged abuse, each contestant striving to outdo the other in brilliantly inventive invective... not to be taken as indicating personal animus' (Ousby, 2000: 282). There are parallels in other Celtic countries, in northern Europe generally, and in the Islamic world. In fact, such elaborate ritualized exchanges, often scurrilous in nature, occur widely, and particularly in oral cultures or those in which verbal dexterity per se has remained prestigious.

The classic Scottish example is *The Flyting of Dunbar and Kennedie*, which Scott found to be 'the most repellent poem he knew in any language' (Ousby, 2000: 282; Dunbar, 1508).

Chapter 10

'Foreign' Languages in the Classroom

Introduction

Once a privilege, access to education is now a right; indeed, most children are required to go to school until a determined age. Classrooms must often cater, then, for children from a variety of linguistic and cultural backgrounds, a circumstance that can give rise to educational pressures of various kinds. There are many different ways in which schools, and educational bureaucracies in general, can respond to issues raised by the heterogeneity of populations, but perhaps it is not unfair to see these as falling into two (very) broad categories. The first involves pupils adapting to the ideas and methods of the school; the second involves the school demonstrating, to a greater or lesser degree, a willingness to adapt itself to the pupils. The further back in time one goes, the more likely it is that one will encounter examples within the first of these categories. Conversely, present-day education in many parts of the world is likely to exhibit some adaptive tendencies – or, at least, it is now considered reasonable to discuss possibilities in this connection. In terms of responding to what is essentially a discontinuity between the milieus of home and school, both the maintenance of a relatively unaltered 'core' curriculum within a traditional milieu, and a policy of accommodation, can be understood to have positive and negative aspects.

The focus of this book is largely upon responses to children's varied language abilities, but these are often intertwined with considerations of message as well as medium. In terms of *what* is to be taught, for example, it is now common to read about the provision of group-specific information – history, culture, linguistic heritage, religion and so on – particularly where there are sufficient concentrations of indigenous or immigrant minority-group children. Questions of the degree to which content should be modified for specific student populations or, indeed, of the appropriateness of the exercise at all have become very heated in some settings. The value of learning about one's own group seems reasonable, but it may also be valuable to require all pupils to learn the same things. An educational program that is more 'adaptable' to local contexts may also be a program that prepares children badly for participation in the wider social milieu. Since many non-'mainstream' families see (accurately or not) their children's future directly related to success in the mainstream, approaches that focus too closely upon subcultural values may be at once well-meaning and dangerous. We do not, after all, wish to see education limiting children's chances. I shall return to these broader matters of multicultural education later on.

The issues of immediate interest in this chapter involve 'foreign' languages at school. I am not primarily concerned here with the 'traditional' teaching of languages (but see the following section) – French, German or Spanish as part of the regular secondary-school curriculum, for example – or with the large literature on the teaching and learning of modern languages. There have been many fads and fashions in teaching techniques and methods, in the use of technologies of various sorts, in the connections between language-as-subject and language-as-tool, and so on. The more relevant matters for my purposes have to do with the adaptations that schools make (or do not make) when dealing with linguistic heterogeneity: it is this that links the current focus with the preceding discussion of the educational treatment of nonstandard-dialect speakers.

Minority-group populations are commonly understood to be consti-tuents of a larger society who are outside some definable majority-group 'mainstream' in important ways. Two obvious and common points of differentiation are the relative size of the groups and the sociopolitical relationships that link them. (I realize of course that the idea of a 'mainstream' is itself dubious in some contexts, that a 'mainstream' in many societies is a dynamic and not a static entity, that there may be more than one 'mainstream' in a given setting, and so on.) There are different types of minorities, and the differences often reside in the varying ways in which groups come into contact: frontier populations (often exhibiting very interesting language variations from their more 'heartland' counterparts, for instance), migrant-worker concentrations (the *Gastarbeiter* in western Europe – whose immigrant status in several countries has now been exchanged for residential permanence), indi-genous groups now part of larger political units (the Welsh, the Bretons, the Catalans) and immigrant populations are all notable examples here. For present purposes, it is clear that indigenous minorities and immigrant groups are of the greatest interest. An allegiance to non-mainstream culture, or a mixed allegiance, means that immigrant populations and indigenous groups are to some extent separate, both in their own eyes and in the perceptions of others. In some cases, the separateness decreases over time, sometimes to such an extent that it is lost, but this is not inevitable. Some groups, or some group members, resist assimilation; for others, visible distinctiveness may mean a more enduring separateness, even if this is not desired. As with the earlier discussion of the discontinuities that may distinguish nonstandard, working-class speakers from some mainstream or middle-class population, the most germane matters here have to do with the points of contact between those who dominate and those who do not. It is the dynamics of these contact points that either produce or suppress linguistic accommodation, and this is true whether the accommodation is simply to ease minority-group speakers more efficiently into the dominant linguistic channel, or to contribute to some relatively enduring cultural pluralism.

Language, in all its forms, has always been the central feature of education. As we have already seen, concerns for language have generally coexisted with strong sentiments about what is correct and what is wrong, what is different and what is deficient. This prescriptivist tendency has both reflected and reinforced broader 'mainstream' opinion. We have also seen how certain groups of children whose language is not of the standard variety typically taught and encouraged at school – children of the working class, or of ethnic-minority origin or of both – have been seen as linguistically disadvantaged and in need of remedial or compensatory attention. The aim here has often been to *replace* an allegedly flawed maternal variety with a 'correct' one, although there is perhaps an increasing tendency to opt for a policy of repertoire *expansion*: to supplement the maternal variety, that is, with a more standard form. From a linguistic point of view, this is certainly a more enlightened approach, but putting it into effect is a delicate exercise that is rarely handled well, even when teachers are informed and sympathetic. Replacement remains the policy in too many settings, however, and even where more progressive views obtain, it regularly reappears whenever 'declining standards' are an issue, or whenever a previously disparaged dialect makes a bid for a place in the classroom.

When we move from dialect to language, we should first of all recall that linguistic prejudices and their important ramifications have often made a seemingly effortless leap from nonstandard to altogether separate varieties. In a previous chapter, for instance, I touched upon early 20th-century assessments of intelligence that regularly demonstrated the feeble-mindedness of non-English speakers, mentioned Goodenough's (1926: 393) observation that 'the use of a foreign language in the home is one of the chief factors in producing mental retardation', and alluded to Weinreich's (1953) compilation in which everything from idleness to moral depravity was seen to be a consequence of bilingualism. Flores (2005), whose work I have also cited previously, has provided a closer focus on these prejudices in her historical overview of Spanish-speaking schoolchildren in 20th-century America; see also Gifford and Valdés (2006) and Jiménez (2006). Early conceptions of an association among measured intelligence, the Spanish language and mental deficiency gave way to the idea that bilingualism was somehow an 'unnatural' state of affairs, and one that hindered educational progress. Focus then shifted, around mid-century, to the inadequacies of a 'culturally deprived' home and neighborhood, and then to the new spectre of 'semilingualism' – a twist on the problems of bilingualism, inasmuch as the price of bilingualism was now seen to be inadequacy in each language. As the century drew to a close, Spanish-speaking youngsters in America were seen to be 'at risk', their uneducated parents failing to instil in them any concern for, or interest in, formal schooling. *Plus ça change...*

Language Learning and Language Attitudes in the Classroom

If we move beyond stigmatized dialects and languages, we realize that, while schools have always concerned themselves with 'correctness', they have also recognized that competence in other languages is a mark of education. I noted in the previous section that my major focus here is not on the traditional concerns associated with language learning at school. Rather, the intent here – as in the earlier discussion of 'disadvantaged' dialect speakers – is to consider the linguistic and cultural ramifications of educational contact between groups of unequal social clout. How are the speakers of indigenous- and immigrant-minority languages dealt with at school, what value (if any) is placed upon their maternal varieties, to what extent should the school be open to alterations with these speakers in mind? These and other similar questions are central. But it seems useful to preface further comment with a brief discussion of broader aspects of language-at-school. After all, besides the historical value placed upon languages *per se*, besides the central position of Greek and Latin in the curriculum, besides the unremarked-upon addition of a modern European language to the repertoire of the well-rounded Victorian – besides all these, there have always existed contexts that have made the expansion of language repertoires simply necessary. The classroom is an obvious, if not always a very efficient, setting in which such learning can take place.

In situations of necessity it is clear that the efforts of the school are driven and reinforced by extra-educational forces. Conversely, where necessity is not a feature, schools must act more in isolation and, needless to say, their task is much more difficult. These simple facts account for many of the disparities observed in the success of language teaching and learning. One need not be a Solomon to see that there are more difficulties teaching German in Iowa than in Nijmegen. In the Iowas of the world – and there are many of them, especially in anglophone communities – the difficulty of creating an instrumental need for foreign languages means that language attitudes may become *more* important than in the Nijmegens (see below). Here, of course, schools have often done a poor job. Traditional classes, with their emphasis upon grammar and writing skills, have often made the learning of languages a passive, receptive matter for students. This is hardly likely to induce in pupils any sense that learning German is a different sort of exercise than learning trigonometry or ancient history. It does nothing to reduce the artificiality of a classroom in which teachers and pupils routinely but rather unnaturally use a language that is neither their maternal variety nor one that can be put to any immediate use. It is, additionally, neither an extension of the way first languages are acquired – where communication is stressed and where grammatical refinements come afterwards – nor a representation of normal, interactive conversation. Modern methods have attempted to remedy this. The chief development is to encourage a more 'natural' conversational interplay and there have been real strides made here. But, without going into the large literature on methods that is peripheral to my present purpose, it can be appreciated that school language learning will always either benefit from externally imposed necessity or suffer for the lack of it.

The perceived importance of attitude and motivation in language-learning exercises, and the enduring difficulties in encouraging and maintaining interest in classroom settings, have led to a specialist literature on language attitudes (or beliefs, of course: see above). I am not closely concerned here with the technicalities of this literature; good overviews can be found in Dörnyei and Schmidt (2001), Dörnyei (2005) and, especially, Dörnyei and Ushioda (2009). The latter comprises an excellent treatment, in 18 chapters, by all the important current researchers in the field. Beyond the introductory and concluding chapters, the two editors also provide substantive chapters themselves; additionally, there are noteworthy contributions by MacIntyre, Clément, Kormos, Segalowitz, Noels and many others. For recent treatments that embed discussions of attitude and motivation in the broader language literature, see Bhatia and Ritchie (2006) and Gass and Selinker (2008); the latter can be particularly recommended as a comprehensive introductory text. Throughout the literature, the generality is that favorable attitudes contribute to the ease and depth of second-language acquisition. This has become a widely accepted point: 'motivation appears to be the second strongest predictor of success, trailing only aptitude' (Gass & Selinker, 2008: 426). While there is much room for detailed consideration of the varied forms that motivation may take, the general point seems so obvious that it would hardly merit detailed attention. Some years ago, however, Macnamara (1973) appeared to take a contrary view, asserting that attitudes were of *little* importance in language learning. His argument remains a succinct and noteworthy one; it is instructive even where it errs.

Macnamara first noted that necessity may overpower attitudes: a child who moves from Birmingham to Berlin will learn German. This point, which applies also to adults, is clearly correct and most people can corroborate it from personal or indirect experience. At about the same time as Macnamara was writing, an illustrative confirmation was found in the report of a large-scale language-attitude survey in his own *pays natal* – the use of Irish was found to be more associated with ability than with attitudes (Committee on Irish Language Attitudes Research, 1975). This unsurprising relationship does not mean that attitudes are unimportant, but it does remind us that 'in certain contexts, attitudes are more likely to assume importance only after some minimal competence has been established' (Edwards, 1977c: 57). There is thus some reason to think that, in real-life contexts, attitudes may indeed be secondary in importance to ability. Macnamara's second point also has to do with language learning in the real world. He refers to the adoption of English by the Irish population, a language shift not accompanied by favorable attitudes. Indeed, most historical changes in language use owe much more to socioeconomic and political exigencies than they do to attitudes. However, Macnamara does acknowledge that attitudes of a sort – *instrumental attitudes* – may play a part in such broadly-based shifts. For example, while a mid-19th-century Irishman might have loathed English and what it represented, he may yet have come to grudgingly realize the usefulness of the language for himself and, more importantly, for his children. There would have been, therefore, no *integrative* motivation, no desire to learn English in order to facilitate cultural mobility, but a possibly reluctant instrumental one; for a discussion of these attitude variants that Macnamara draws upon, see Gardner and Lambert (1972).

Interestingly enough, Macnamara rejects the possibility of any really significant instrumental motivation in such cases – on a technicality, as it were; he claims that Gardner, Lambert and others had reserved this term to describe present learning for future purposes. However, whatever the views have been of what constitutes instrumental motivation, it is clearly incorrect to deny the term's aptness for the experience of the child transported to Germany, or of the Irishman's move to English. Just because the Irishman hated the English occupation did not mean that he could not appreciate the value of the language of his ascendancy masters. Just because the child cannot appreciate the future usefulness of German does not mean that he or she is unaware at some level of its present utility – and this is obviously an instrumental aspect. All of this led me to suggest a distinction between *positive* and *favorable* attitude (Edwards, 1983c). The two terms need not, after all, be synonymous: a positive position is one of certainty or assurance, but it need not be pleasant. 'I positively loathe it' is not an oxymoronic statement. To stay with the Irish example, we could say that the attitude of the mass of the 19th-century population towards the English language was positive and instrumental, but not favorable (and certainly not integrative).

The third strand to Macnamara's argument brings us back to the classroom. He contends that traditional language learning at school has been an unreal and artificial affair, an undertaking in which communication is subordinate to an appreciation of language as an academic subject. It is this lack of communicative purpose, and not children's attitudes, that he feels underlies their poor language competence. Although I would agree that a great failing in language classrooms has been the absence of any realistic usage, I do not think that this means that attitudes are of small importance. It is rather a matter of attitudes taking their proper position, which in many cases is secondary to language ability. In instances of societal language shift (from Irish to English, say) as well as in cases of individual necessity, the point is not that attitudes are unimportant, but that they are instrumental, if unfavorable. The argument that the classroom is an 'artificial' context may reflect a condemnation of traditional approaches, but it does not of itself indicate that attitudes are trivial. In fact, as noted earlier, attitudes are clearly of *considerable* importance (in language learning, and in other subject areas) precisely *because* of 'artificiality'. If a context is *not* perceived as pertinent to real life, or does *not* arise from necessity, then attitudes may make a real difference.

In fact, if we return again to the Irish situation, we can see that the notion of artificiality can extend beyond the classroom. With the establishment of the Irish state in 1922, and the subsequent revival emphasis upon schools as agents of Irish-language restoration, there arose a disjunction between official aims regarding Irish and actual, societal linguistic behavior. An ever-decreasing level of native competence has been accompanied by an increasing minimal competence in basic skills, produced entirely through education. It can therefore be argued that schools, and the attitudes towards Irish that they have encouraged, have been of the greatest importance in the maintenance of Irish (such as it is: see Edwards, 1977c; in preparation). It is worth pointing out here, by the way, that this brief treatment of the fortunes of Irish takes us back to the minority-group scenarios previously touched upon. Irish people in Ireland are obviously neither an indigenous nor an immigrant minority group; their original group language, however, has become a minority variety in its own home, as it were. This points to an interesting sub-division within the indigenous-minority category. If we consider, say, the Indian 'first nations' of Canada, it is obvious that both the speakers and their languages are of minority status; but if we look at areas like Ireland and Wales, it is equally clear that, while the autochthonous inhabitants are still in the majority in the land, their original varieties have become 'minoritized'. This is because their land and their languages have come into contact with powerful neighbors and rivals. It follows that language-revival efforts in such settings will have a special poignancy.[1]

With even a minimal sense of the interactions among attitude, motivation and perceived necessity, it becomes easy to understand the problems associated with teaching and learning foreign languages in the contemporary anglophone context – in Britain, in Australia and New Zealand and, above all, in North America. The difficulties arise because of contextual conditions having to do with power and dominance, and with the fact that, in a world made increasingly safe for anglophones, there is less and less reason (or so it seems to many, students included) for them to learn any other language. Swaffar (1999: 10–11) recently made some suggestions 'to help foreign language departments assume command of their destinies', and the usual suspects were pedantically rounded up: a redefinition of the discipline ('as a distinct and sequenced inquiry into the constituents and applications of meaningful communication'), more emphasis upon communication and less upon narrow grammatical accuracy, the establishment of standards, models and common curricula (for 'consistent pedagogical rhetoric') and so on. All very laudable, no doubt – but why do I think of Nero? It has always been difficult to sell languages in Kansas: wherever you go, for many hundreds of miles, English will take you to McDonalds, get you a burger and bring you safely home again – and a thorough reworking of pedagogical rhetoric doesn't amount to sale prices.

Broadly speaking, there are two paths through the woods, although occasionally they share the same ground. The first is for foreign-language teaching to satisfy itself with that shrinking pool of students intrinsically interested in languages and their cultures. These *are*, after all, the students nearest to one's own intellectual heart. The problem is that the 'natural' constituency here might prove too small to support a discipline at desired levels, and it is hard to nurture in any direct way. The other is to hope and work for a renewed instrumental interest, with whatever longer-term fallout that might lead to. To some extent, this is dependent upon a context that extends well beyond national borders, upon alterations in global linguistic circumstance that, while inevitable, are not always easy to predict. But one could argue, as well, that things might be done at home – in an increasingly multilingual Britain, for instance, or, in an America where the number of Hispanics has recently overtaken that of black Americans. This latter situation is an instructive one.

The study of Spanish in the United States is self-evidently important: it is a language with a lengthy cultural and literary tradition, with many interesting branches to the original trunk. At the same time, it remains a widely used variety around the world; with something like 300 million speakers, it runs fourth (behind Hindi, Chinese and English) in the usage sweepstakes. Academically, then, it is the ideal American second language, and so, with both a global and a national presence, it is no wonder that Spanish is indeed the linchpin of modern-language teaching in the United States.

The whole area, however, remains weak – weaker than one might first expect. Even though statistics assembled by the Modern Language Association (see Edwards, 2001) showed an overall increase of about 5% in foreign-language enrolments since 1995, only 1.2 million college students were represented here, fewer than 8% of the total. There were steep declines in some quarters: enrolments in German were reportedly down by 7.5% (90,000 students altogether), and those in French decreased by 3% (to about 200,000). But for Spanish, the figures were better. With enrolments up by about 8%, which translates to some 660,000 students, one can see that students of Spanish constituted 55% of *all* tertiary-level language students. Is Spanish learning in a healthy situation, then, or does it only seem so in comparison with weaker sisters? This may be an impossible question to answer. After all, how many students *ought* to be studying Spanish – or archaeology, or quantum mechanics, or sculpture? Still, one might expect that language study would be more immediately related to extra-educational factors – jobs, mobility, opportunity and so on – and, if that is so, then one might wonder why the strength of the American Hispanic community does not bolster the educational effort more.

In fact, despite America's multi-ethnic status in general, and its powerful Hispanic components more specifically, we come back to a context of anglophone dominance that obtains both within and without national borders. It is a context that makes some recent comments by Carlos Fuentes (1999) seem rather naïve – even though they are eminently understandable, reflective of the views of many and, indeed, attractive in their impulse. He asks why most Americans know only English and sees their monolingualism as a 'great paradox': the United States is at once the supreme and the most isolated world power. Why, Fuentes continued, does America 'want to be a monolingual country?' All 21st-century Americans ought to know more than one language, to better understand the world, to deal with cross-cultural problems, *y demás*. Obviously, monolingualism is not a paradox, and to say that Americans 'want' to be monolingual would seem to miss the point; it is simply that English serves across virtually all the important domains of their lives.

More subtly, though, it might be argued that Americans do indeed 'want' to be monolingual, or, to put it more aptly, they see no compelling reason to expand their repertoires. In such a climate, it is easy to see what the consequences are likely to be for language teaching and learning at school. Given some of the less rational ramifications of the 2001 attacks on New York City, it is also easy to see that not only do languages other than English appear unnecessary, their use can be seen as downright un-American, their speakers as unwilling to throw themselves whole-heartedly into that wonderful melting-pot, the continuing allegiance to other cultures a suspect commodity. And, of course, such broader perceptions feed back into the educational arena, and so we return yet again to the importance of the wider society beyond the school gates for what ultimately transpires within them; and, relatedly, to the important fact – occasionally overlooked or ignored – that schools are most efficient as reflections of that wider society and not as innovative vanguards of changing attitudes and behavior.

Language and 'Empowerment'

Again here, we can note the longstanding interests and many contributions of Fishman – for a recent expression, see Fishman (2006); see also Pütz *et al.* (2006). It is quite clear that power relationships – particularly, of course, those that are markedly unequal – are behind all substantive minority-majority interactions. Just as there are many examples of 'minority-group' populations that are numerically superior but socially and politically subordinate (the black populations of apartheid South Africa, for instance), so there are many examples of groups whose power far outstrips their demographic standing (think of the British Raj). Given a desire that the school should make some accommodation to linguistic heterogeneity, particularly where minority-group languages are involved and, more particularly still, where minority-group status overlaps with socioeconomic disadvantage, it is perhaps natural that some researchers would begin to focus upon the nexus of language and power. Since a disparagement of some varieties, whether nonstandard dialects or entirely separate languages, is clearly an important manifestation of broader negative stereotypes, it is understandable that some have thought to 'empower' the speakers of those varieties with a sort of linguistic affirmative action. Thus, Cummins (1986) argues that minority-group children can be 'empowered' if their maternal varieties are accorded some place in the classroom, and if their parents and communities are folded into the educational process. Such points are unexceptionable as they stand – as is Corson's (2001: 14) note that extended language repertoires are 'potentially empowering'. The rhetoric of empowerment, however, is often rather more pointed. Thus, Delgado-Gaitan and Trueba (1991: 138) define empowerment as the 'process of acquiring power... of transition from lack of control to the acquisition of control over one's life'. In a more cooperative tenor, Baker (2006: 417) refers to empowerment as 'movement... from coercive... to collaborative relationships, power sharing and power creating, where the identities of minorities are affirmed and voiced'. Cummins (1996: 15) also stresses that empowerment is 'the collaborative creation of power'.

One or two points should be added here. It is not clear, for example, that 'empowerment' is either particularly collaborative or something that disadvantaged groups and individuals can activate for themselves. On the contrary, it would be more accurate to see it as a compensatory device. That is, action on behalf of ethnocultural or sociocultural groups whose languages and cultures are seen to be disparaged, devalued or actually threatened, is seldom initiated before some sufficient rationale is perceived; in many settings, past and present, this perception has often seemed (to some, at least) a rather delayed reaction. Regardless, however, of whether or not intervention is seen to be too little or too late, considering empowerment within a compensatory framework surely has some telling implications. The very word 'empowerment' suggests an exchange between unequal partners. In its original senses, to empower meant to license or to authorize: it always bore an implication of inequality, since the one authorizing is clearly the one in control. This, however, can be a strictly limited sort of inequality, not one that necessarily conjures up broad images of strength on the one hand and frailty on the other. Authorizations and licenses can be for specific, and specifically restricted, commissions. Today, however, the sense has apparently expanded to include the relief of broad insufficiency through the intervention of general power.

Contemporary understandings and treatments of cultural and linguistic empowerment now typically assume that important psychosocial factors provide the most central rationale for intervention, and that such intervention is justified on the basis of longstanding oppression, prejudice, conquest, colonization and so on: historical or systemic *unfairness*, in a word. The sense is that what was stripped away or devalued ought now to be restored, and that it is eminently reasonable that those who have benefited most in previous contact settings should now be the ones to make some sort of restitution. But this sense is surely inseparable from another: that the individuals or groups currently disadvantaged are unable to resolve their linguistic and cultural dilemmas by themselves. All of which leads to the observation that empowerment inevitably involves the *bestowal* of something by the strong; and this, I suggest, is very different from the *taking* of power, so historically characteristic of those who *are* currently strong. I go further: the suggestion here is that empowerment, as it is commonly understood, logically implies, and actually reinforces, a continuation of group inequalities.

The school is the most obvious arena for exercises in empowerment aimed at ethnic-minority-group children (as well, of course, as those socially disadvantaged nonstandard-dialect speakers already discussed). Indeed, the school is often seen as *the* place in which to act on behalf of beleaguered, neglected or disparaged languages, as well as the cultures from which they derive (a broader matter that I shall turn to in the following chapter). It is an obvious place for some familiar reasons. First, school is a powerful institution that, while generally an arm of mainstream society, is nonetheless theoretically committed to the development of all who attend. In that sense, it is one of the most 'neutral' territories in which individuals are likely to find themselves: certainly a more enlightened setting than most beyond the playground. Second, school benefits from having a captive audience. Children in most societies must attend from an early age, and it is significant that going to school represents the first sustained 'break' from the home; they must then remain at school for a considerable period of time. Third, the educational context is a natural one in which cultural contact and its consequences might be discussed, understood, treated and so on.

A less familiar but hardly less important reason for school to be a common site of attempted empowerment is that it encapsulates that idea of empowerment-as-compensation noted above. School is at once a compensating mechanism *and* a continuingly strong arm of that society whose dominance creates the need for compensation in the first place. The potential conflicts here are not, of course, lost upon the participants. Internal contradictions can arise even where one may assume a general goodwill towards the 'others' within the school precincts. If, as is sometimes the case (and *was* often the case), school is a rather less generously minded institution, then it is easy to see that any 'compensation' on offer would be severely restricted, in line with the perceived requirements of the mainstream. Historical accounts of working-class education – where it existed at all – illustrate that the general aim was more to facilitate the continued production of workers than it was to assist in upward social mobility. Prior to the mid-19th century, at any rate, 'disadvantaged' pupils who were helped to rise by education were usually inadvertent beneficiaries of the workings of some Smithian invisible hand.

Even allowing for excellent intentions, dedicated teachers and adequate resources, there are strong grounds for thinking that reliance upon school as an empowering agent is naïve; and, as with naïveté in other settings, innocence coupled with ignorance can exacerbate matters. Since I shall return to broader matters of social pluralism, assimilation and the role of schools as agents of policy in the next chapters, I will simply leap to a summary point here: school cannot compensate for society. It is quite clear, incidentally, that proponents of linguistic and cultural empowerment are fully aware of this. Empowerment 'can be furthered by education, but also needs to be realized in legal, social, cultural and particularly economic and political events' (Baker, 2006: 418). This is clearly true (see also Delgado-Gaitan & Trueba, 1991, for similar sentiments), but such statements have become almost ritual ones among educational researchers. I think it is inappropriate to make such glancing reference to those extra-academic contexts when they are, in fact, the ones of the greatest importance, the ones whose determinations and values filter down to the school – not the other way around. Of course, I do not mean to say that schools are impotent in these matters, nor that they should inevitably wait to take their lead from society at large. I *do* mean to say, however, that it is wrong to suggest an importance and a centrality that they rarely have: wrong, and perhaps cruel, to imply that a measure of extra attention in the classroom will translate into anything meaningful outside it.

In line with earlier remarks about the expansion of the very notion of 'empowerment', it may be useful to consider a recent treatment that links that term with other educationally potent matters. In a short section of their well-known encyclopedia, Baker and Jones (1998) note that linguistic and cultural empowerment in the classroom is a catalyst for success and that, where parents can also be involved, the benefits may extend into the local community. More specifically, they suggest that such success may occur via the intermediate step of enhanced self-esteem; see also Wright and Bougie (2007). Since 'self-esteem' and its concomitants have become a sacred cow – and, like the real animal, often a barrier to movement – it is some relief that arguments have recently been made that too much emphasis on the alleged fragility of the young psyche, and too little on more traditional concerns for learning, is not a good thing for children in general, and particularly harmful for the disadvantaged.

Apart from the supposed linkage between empowerment and self-esteem, Baker and Jones discuss other related matters. They note, for example, that traditional testing procedures 'tend by their very nature to locate problems in the individual student... [and] may fail to locate the root of the problem in the social, economic or educational system'; improved assessment procedures, based upon 'advocacy', will focus upon the 'system'; and so on (Baker & Jones, 1998: 542). These matters, while not necessarily connected with considerations of 'self-esteem', nonetheless often accompany them in discussions of this sort. Educational 'empowerment' is thus seen to involve criticism of 'the system'. This is a reasonable corollary, it seems to me, but it is typically undercut (as it is in this case) by an immediate refocusing upon too narrow a context, a formulaic acknowledgement of the need to 'change the system' – but then a quick return to a decontextualized accent upon the school alone. The ritual nod usually takes the form of a statement that the school cannot go it alone; thus, Baker and Jones (1998: 542) make the observation, later repeated in Baker (2006: 418 – cited above), about the need for accompanying action in economic, social, political and other arenas. As I have implied, this rounding up of the usual suspects is perhaps worse than not mentioning them, for the implication is that, after all, they collectively constitute only some sort of minor extension to the *real* arena of action. Nothing, of course, could be more inverted.

Another difficulty – and, again, it is a regrettably typical one – revealed in the foregoing citations also involves 'the system'. While it is quite plausible to suggest that empowerment requires some examination of 'the system', it is not so reasonable to proceed on the assumption that the social context is to be blamed for problems illuminated through testing. This is, admittedly, a delicate matter, for it is a truism that a prejudiced or oppressive society extends a generally deadening hand over its disadvantaged and minority-group segments. But at the same time, it can be all too easy to inaccurately lay all problems at the social rather than the individual foot. The delicacy of the point here is sharpened when one considers that the attempt to lessen the burden of the disadvantaged individual in this way often proceeds from good intentions; once again, however, it is an example of empowerment-as-compensation. As such, it can be seen as condescending and demeaning, as actually reinforcing a debilitating scenario of victimization and passivity, as failing to accomplish any real playing-field leveling, as (at best) a delaying tactic rather than a solution – and, overall, as an example of attitudes and behavior increasingly rejected by those most directly affected.

Beyond these generalities, we should turn to some more specific educational programs aimed at speakers of foreign languages: bilingual education arrangements of various sorts, immersion education and so-called 'heritage-language' programs. Baker (2006) provides a very good summary of the varieties that exist under these headings, and I will deal with some of the important issues in the following chapters; here I shall only make a few remarks about 'heritage' languages at school.

Heritage Languages in the Classroom

There are several interesting matters that even a cursory glance at 'foreign' languages must touch upon. First, of course, are questions about the appropriate treatment of children's maternal varieties in the classroom: should educational accommodation be made and, if so, in what way? Second, there are political and ideological issues. Some of these have to do with the practicalities of instruction: how best to deal with dialect variations, for instance, but also considerations of costs, beneficiaries and so on. Others involve larger social concerns like cultural pluralism and assimilation. A common argument here, from those who favor the one-language approach that so often accompanies an assimilationist ideology, is that 'the government' ought not to use general tax revenues to support the languages and cultures of minority groups. Third, there are questions of provenance, definition and labelling. In

Canada, for example, language matters have arranged themselves in four categories: French, English, aboriginal varieties and the languages of the 'allophones' (essentially, the varieties brought by non-francophone and non-anglophone immigrants).

'Allophone' varieties in Canada are the ones specifically labelled as 'heritage' languages and, latterly, as 'international' languages. Obviously, neither adjective is specifically appropriate here; equally obviously, however, labels have significance, and name changes can reflect shifting sociopolitical underpinnings. Cummins (2005) lists some of the other language labels that have been applied: *ethnic, minority, ancestral, third, modern, non-official* and (in Quebec) *langues d'origine* and *langues patrimoniales*. Some of these terms have also been used in other contexts, too, and *community language* has proved particularly popular in Australia (Clyne, 2005), where it has the same connotations as heritage language does in Canada (i.e. immigrant varieties, but not indigenous ones).

The Canadian picture is broadly instructive here and, if we turn first to indigenous languages, it is a bleak one (as it so often is for autochthonous minority languages elsewhere). Prior to the coming of the Europeans in the 16th century, millions of North Americans spoke as many as 300 languages. In Canada today, just over 1 million people are of declared aboriginal origin: Indian, Métis or Inuit. Only about 17% have an aboriginal language as their mother tongue, and fewer still (11%) use one at home. Statistics are somewhat different for those who more formally identify themselves as Canadian Aboriginals. Drapeau (1998) reports, for instance, that about 33% of this group (which comprises some 625,000 people) can speak an aboriginal variety, and another 17% report some degree of understanding.

There are 53 aboriginal languages still extant in Canada, classified into 11 families and 'isolates' (languages for which scholars cannot find familial relationships). Accurate speaker estimates are rare (see Cook, 1998), but a simple comparison of overall population size and number of varieties will lead to obvious conclusions. Only 3 of the 53 have more than 5000 speakers (Inuktitut, Ojibwa and Cree: the last is the strongest, with some 60,000 speakers), and only these three are considered to have a good chance of survival. The 50 others range from 'moderately endangered' to 'verging on extinction'. Eight varieties have fewer than ten speakers each. The problems afflicting aboriginal-language maintenance, then, are easily understood, and indigenous cultures continue to be at the gravest risk, following conquest and much subsequent ill-treatment. Education through and about aboriginal languages has grown recently, but it is often restricted to the earliest school years. In any event, educational programs are always uncertain guarantees of 'ordinary' language continuity, particularly when other social pressures operate in the other direction.

A consideration of immigrant minority languages – the 'allophone' varieties to which, however inaccurately, the 'heritage' label has been attached – gives rise to an issue that can be added to those listed in the first paragraph of this section. It is one often heard in 'new-world' societies where immigrants (initially from Europe, in the main, but now often from Asia and Africa) constitute such a large presence.[2] Why not capitalize on all this cultural wealth, instead of railing against 'language problems' and the like? Why not further the scope of the Canadian social 'mosaic' in place of the American 'melting-pot'? All of this seems to make good sense because, even in a world made increasingly safe for anglophones, there are real and immediate benefits to multilingual competencies. Indeed, strong practical cases can often be made: being able to talk to customers in their own languages is a recurringly obvious example; and Americans and others have been reminded in recent years of how useful it might be to have more speakers of Arabic, Pashto and Farsi. Blanco (1983: 282) points to the strange mentality that 'allows the squandering of valuable linguistic resources, only to try to recapture or create them later'. Cummins (2005), too, advocates more inclusive recognition of heritage languages; like Blanco, he deplores the 'squandering' of resources, and he makes some useful and specific proposals for change; see also the collections edited by Fishman (1999, 2001).

Jaspaert and Kroon (1991) present some data on the educational treatment of both indigenous and immigrant languages in Europe, and Extra and Gorter (2001) provide a fine overview of the 'other' languages of Europe, one in which particular attention is paid to educational implications. In a related collection, Extra and Yağmur (2004) focus more specifically upon immigrant varieties in European cities: immigration is generally an urban phenomenon, after all. The contributors discuss situations in Sweden, Germany, The Netherlands, Belgium, France and Spain. As in the earlier volume, the emphasis here is upon the educational setting.

A very recent paper by Wallen and Kelly-Holmes (2006) discusses the 'new' immigration in Ireland, and its implications for languages at school. As everyone knows, Ireland has historically been a country of emigrants; now, because of European Union policies on mobility, and the strength of the Irish economy, it has received many thousands of immigrants (largely from eastern Europe) and refugees (from Congo, Somalia and other 'underdeveloped' regions). The current Irish Education Act notes that the 'language and cultural needs of students... should be catered for' (Ireland, 1998: 118), a declaration that would seem to bode well for the new immigrants. Of course, as Wallen and Kelly-Holmes (2006: 144) observe, the statement precedes the most recent waves of immigration, and was meant to apply to the language needs and wishes of Irish speakers in an educational system that has traditionally been bilingually minded, with room for both English (the language of everyday life) and Irish (officially the 'first language'). Nonetheless, there is a point of entry here that could be exploited for those wishing to argue for 'education rights in languages other than Irish and English'. Of course, even with the influx of Latvians and Lithuanians, of Brazilians and Congolese, the Irish scene is nowhere near as linguistically diverse as others. I mention the context here, however, because it reveals just how dynamic the politics of diversity can be: who would have guessed, even a dozen years ago, that questions of language-in-the-classroom would be important in the Irish context?

A new collection edited by Hornberger (2005) deals with heritage-language teaching in American and Australia. And a collection of papers assembled by Creese and Martin (2006a), treats 'complementary' schools in England. Sometimes referred to as 'community' or 'supplementary' schools, these are voluntary efforts that stress mother-tongue education, and they occur outside regular school hours. While no one would deny that particular religious or ethnolinguistic groups have a perfect right to make such arrangements for themselves, the most interesting question here – apart, of course, from pedagogical and linguistic effectiveness – is whether or not such groups should be obliged to do so. Creese and Martin (2006b: 1), for example, take the position that complementary schooling is a 'response to an historically monolingual ideology which ignores the complexity of multilingual England'. The implication is that a more enlightened system would and should have made provision for the children within the ordinary curriculum; see also Li Wei (2006) for some cogent discussion of the most important points.

The Canadian experience is again illustrative here, and it is the one that has generated the greatest and the most sustained interest. This is because the country has both indigenous and immigrant populations, because it also has – uniquely among 'receiving' countries of the new world – *two* ethnocultural 'mainstreams', and because its largest cities are probably the most multicultural in the world. Official statistics (see Department of Canadian Heritage, 2000: 5) reveal that, in 1996, 48% of the population in all Canadian metropolitan areas reported 'at least one ethnic origin other than British, French, Canadian or Aboriginal'. In the

Montreal/Ottawa region, the figure is about one-third, but in Vancouver it is 64% and in Toronto, 68%: thus, more than half of all Toronto schoolchildren come from homes in which neither French nor English is the mother tongue. (Burtonwood and Bruce [1999] report that ethnic-minority pupils now constitute the majority in inner London, too, as well as in other large English cities.) An added factor of interest, certainly not unique to Canada, arises when one considers that immigrant or 'allophone' populations are increasingly full citizens of their new countries; apart from the predictable crass opportunism that this creates among politicians, the development has important implications for the very notion of a 'mainstream'.

Canadian census figures present further details of a picture whose broad outline is already obvious: about 20% of the population (i.e. almost 6 million people) can speak a language other than French or English, and 10% speak such a variety most often at home. Immigration during the post-war years greatly increased the overall numbers here, but more interesting, perhaps, is the changing nature of the mixture of these 'allophone' languages. In 1971, German, Italian, Ukrainian, Dutch and Polish were the most numerous varieties; in 1991, Chinese speakers had dramatically increased (from 95,000 to over 500,000), and Punjabi also arrived in the 'top ten'; by 1996, Arabic and Tagalog had joined them.[3]

As Cummins (1998) points out, federal support for the teaching of 'heritage' or 'international' languages has not been very substantial. Wary of public opinion that has never been particularly well-disposed towards funding 'foreign' languages, it has usually taken the form of subventions to communities who – as with the 'complementary'-school arrangements in England – organize the teaching of their languages outside regular school hours. Saturday-morning schools are typical here. Direct educational initiatives are provincial matters in Canada, and the most extensive programs are therefore found in regions with the greatest numbers and concentrations of immigrant-language groups. In Ontario, for instance, well over 100,000 students learn more than 60 languages. However, the program requires both community involvement and minimum numbers of potential students and, again, classes take place outside the regular school curriculum. Similar programs exist elsewhere in the country (see also Edwards, 1993).

Notes

1. I am reminded here of a similar case, one that shows the dynamics at work at a more 'micro' level. About 15 miles from my university in Nova Scotia is a small Acadian village. Such have been the incursions of English upon

French, however, that it proved necessary for the villagers to establish a French-immersion school – this, for children whose surnames were Bouchard and Doiron, Landry and Pettipas.

2. As McBrien (2005) points out, refugees form an interesting sub-category here, one that is not always sufficiently distinguished from that of voluntary immigration. Many countries now have large refugee populations (see Cutts, 2000) and United Nations statistics reveal that children typically comprise more than half of such groups. There are specific educational implications for children who have often had rather more traumatic experiences than other immigrants. For a very recent investigation of refugee language issues, see Maloof *et al.* (2006).

3. The 10 most common languages in Canada now are Chinese (with about 800,000 speakers), Italian (700,000), German (650,000), Spanish (500,000), Portuguese and Polish (about 260,000 each), Punjabi (250,000), Arabic and Ukrainian (about 220,000 each) and Tagalog (190,000). The shift from the older European immigration patterns is clear. Marmen and Corbeil (1999) provide a succinct guide to many further details.

Chapter 11

Multiculturalism and Multicultural Education

Introduction

When we talk about any aspect of the 'social life of language', we are talking, in good part, about markers of broad social attitudes and values. It is true, of course, that in studies of Black English and other nonstandard dialects, there are linguistic and sociolinguistic facts to be ascertained and discussed, facts that demonstrate (for example) the rule-governed and valid nature of such variants. It is true that approaches taken to foreign languages in the classroom can (or should) rest upon clear conceptions of the mechanics of language contact. And it is true that provisions made for bilingual educational accommodations – something I shall turn to in the next chapters – may quite satisfactorily arise from pedagogical imperatives alone. But it is equally true that the very phenomenon of 'nonstandardness' suggests something of social stratification, of sociopolitical hierarchy, of prestige and stigma; that it is not so many years ago that speakers of foreign languages in anglophone contexts were routinely treated as if they were educationally retarded; and that bilingual education is always accompanied by heavy social baggage. All of this reflects the fact that, as well as being a carrier of communicative meanings, language is also the bearer of more symbolic and intangible meanings – meanings that, ultimately, have to do with questions of identity, of self-definition and definition by others, of 'groupness' and its boundaries. Considerations of languages in contact, then, are almost inevitably considerations of cultures in contact. Bilingualism and multilingualism implicate biculturalism and multi-culturalism.

Multiculturalism can be either a *de facto* description of an ethnically heterogeneous society or a matter of policy, or both. One may find societies that are multicultural on the ground, as it were, but officially monocultural, but it is rare to find formal policies of multiculturalism at governmental, educational and other such levels in contexts that lack any substantial or concentrated ethnic variety. Where official policies *do* exist, it is not always correct to read into them any great respect for diversity. They are sometimes rather grudging accommodations arising from the force of circumstance, politically opportunistic reflexes in settings where 'ethnics' are voting citizens or, indeed, attempts to block the activities of stronger minority groups by formulating minority-group policy in a blanket fashion. Apparently democratic responses that purport to consider the needs of all groups – large or small, strong or weak – can actually be a clever way of obviating or diluting meaningful actions for *any* of them. French governments, for instance, have used this sort of divide-and-conquer approach in dealings with minority groups in the *hexagone*: a continuation of the historically traditional centralization. In a recent variant, the primary player in *la francophonie* has appealed to other language communities to help it stand firm against the homogenizing evils of global anglicization. It is quite clear, however, that another aspect of French tradition is at work here. That is, while France continues to care very little for any language other than its own, it is desperate to enlist whatever help it can get for something that it does care a great deal about: its own linguistic loss of place in the world.

It is clear that any discussion of multiculturalism is one that may mean quite different things in different quarters. There have always been, of course, strong and disinterested sentiments supportive of cultural and linguistic pluralism. On the one hand, some groups may legitimately feel that their cultures are under threat from powerful neighbors. If a revitalized 'internal' monoculturalism is no longer seen as practical, an accommodation that allows some cultural duality can then be seen as an attractive option. Such a posture is likely to become more prominent in times like our own, when a pervasive global 'monoculture' casts its long shadow over all others. On the other hand, however, one need not be a member of a group whose language and culture is at (real or perceived) risk, to endorse some sort of pluralistic perspective. Just as educated people have always been interested in learning other languages, so an understanding of cultures other than one's own has always been a mark of enlightenment. Just as all well-rounded programs of education traditionally gave an honored place to languages modern and classical, so all such programs took learners beyond the confines of their own cultural immediacy. Although formal language learning in anglophone societies is obviously not what it once was, the cross-cultural components of education remain as central as ever, and this is so, even when they are not specifically identified as such. All education, by its very nature, transcends the time and place in which it finds itself. All good education is multicultural.

Unity and Diversity

At a societal level, interesting tensions very often exist between diversity and unity. Liberal democracies are obliged by their own deepest principles to consider the well-being of their populations, and not simply to ride rough-shod over all but 'mainstream' or majority-group interests. In many such societies, these principles are strengthened by the historically enlightened emphases I mentioned above. When translated from the educational arena per se to the broader social one, these may mean real concern, and not just pious lip-service, for the protection and maintenance of subcultures, particularly those seen to be at risk of assimilation. The concern takes greater force when the members of those groups are citizens (as I noted in the previous chapter). But tensions arise because, coexistent with what we might roughly call the 'liberal perspective' here, are fears of social fragmentation, of the dilution of a common civic polity. These *can* derive from nativist or racist sentiments, but it would be a great mistake to ascribe all such apprehensions to such unpleasant and unworthy reactions. In the Canadian context, for example, one frequently comes across the following sort of argument: since the Canadian identity itself remains a rather shaky commodity, due largely to the overwhelming presence of its all-intrusive southern neighbor, how can we ever expect a strong national ethos to take shape if our policies of multiculturalism and tolerance make a continuing virtue out of a balkanizing diversity? This is a rough paraphrase, but it is not an unfair characterization of the worry felt by some whose democratic credentials remain impeccable.

It is important to note that the tension between social diversity and social unity – at least, as this is reflected in official responses to ethnolinguistic heterogeneity – is both inevitable and dynamic. It is inevitable because the championing of individual rights that is the traditional liberal legacy has always had to at least consider rights that might inhere in *groups*. Indeed, some recent political philosophy has attempted to reconcile the two at some levels, as part of an effort to deal equitably with cultural and linguistic variation. And it is dynamic because social policy is not a science. It does not proceed in cumulative and self-correcting fashion, each advance building upon and making adjustments to previous insights; rather, it is subject to variations in social conditions and attitudes. The recent actions involving Islamist extremists and western targets provide the best contemporary examples. Thus, the strongly favorable Dutch stance on multiculturalism has been shaken by the 2004 assassination of Theo van Gogh, a provocative critic of religious orthodoxies, although fissures had already developed. For example, longer-established minority groups (particularly those from Surinam and the Dutch Antilles) have become increasingly differentiated from Muslim populations in the eyes of the 'mainstream'. Coenders *et al.* (2008) and Sniderman and Hagendoorn (2007) have provided useful overviews of changing Dutch positions, each attempting to put Dutch reactions in broader social context. The French attitude to their large immigrant populations was sharply focussed by the week of rioting and burning in the Muslim *banlieux* in 2005. The Madrid train bombing in 2004 and the London underground attack of 2005 have also led to policy re-examination, to say nothing of galvanizing all shades of public opinion.

An interesting recent development is the suggestion by the Minister for Higher Education that compulsory classes in 'core British values' be added to existing ones on citizenship. Supporters immediately noted that Bill Rammell's remarks (in May 2006) only built upon earlier suggestions in January – by Gordon Brown, then Chancellor – that the government should establish a 'British Day' and encourage citizens to put a union flag 'in every garden' (Helm, 2006a, 2006b). Reactions to these ideas were, at best, rather mixed (BBC, 2006), but there is no doubt that 'state-sponsored flag waving' strikes many as either American or (as one *Daily Mail* columnist put it) totalitarian in its impulse; see also Parekh (2006). Roger Scruton (2006) – a reactionary commentator, in a right-wing newspaper – did manage to put his finger on the essential fallacy in all this. Whatever one's views are of national 'values' (or of Professor Scruton, for that matter), it is clearly wrong to think that values are 'a kind of knowledge, to be put up on the blackboard... values are matters of practice, not of theory. They are not so much taught as imparted'.

In an apparent demonstration of Jungian synchronicity, I came across two analogous references within a week of reading Scruton's piece. Hugo Williams, the 'Freelance' columnist in the *Times Literary Supplement*, reported glumly on the recent announcement that Wellington College – the Berkshire public school established in the mid-19th century as a memorial to the Iron Duke himself – was about to provide 'happiness lessons' to its students. Reminding us that 'show, don't tell' is the motto for all successful creative writing, Williams's (2006) implication is that an indirect approach to something as important but as vague as 'happiness' is surely preferable to attempts to bludgeon it into children's heads. And Roger Schank, a cognitive scientist writing in the *Times Higher Education Supplement* (2006), argues that while the most important acquisitions for students are reasoning ability, communication skills and human-relations sensitivity, none should be taught as a subject. Indeed, we might want to go a bit further, and say that none *can* be taught as subjects in any meaningful way. (Schank's impressive educational credentials are, perhaps, a little sullied by his current occupation. He is 'Chief Learning Officer' at Trump University, an online real-estate college founded by 'The Donald' himself in 2005.)

All of this tends to a broad and venerable conclusion: the most important things cannot be taught, although they can obviously be learned. This does not lessen for a moment the importance of teachers, of course – they will always be needed to provide educational fuel, incentive and, often, inspiration – but it does remind us of the centrality of the recipients to the whole enterprise.

Another relevant development is the post-2001 American debate over border security and immigration, including the question of the twelve million 'illegal aliens' that was brought to the fore in early 2006. Among other things, this has reawakened interest in making English the official language of the country (*Agence France-Press*, 2006; see also Edwards, 1990). Proponents of 'Official English' in the USA have been directly or indirectly involved in legislative efforts at the state level: thirty states now proclaim English as official, with Ohio set to become the thirty-first. Success has eluded them at the federal level, however. The most recent attempt there occurred in February 2007; more than one third of the members of the House of Representatives agreed to 'declare English as the official language of the United States' (H.R. 997). Academic reaction has always been quick in these matters. For instance, in connection with an earlier (2006) legislative initiative – almost every sitting of Congress sees a proposal to make English official – members of the American Association for Applied Linguistics received an email message noting the organization's deep concern about moves to legally enshrine the status of English and to restrict the provision of services in other languages. They were urged to get in touch with their state representatives, and a template letter for this purpose was attached to the main message. Beyond the assertion that language matters are not an integral part of border security, four specific points were made: (1) the status of English does not need legislated protection; (2) respect for other languages in the United States is important for 'fostering national loyalty'; (3) for the 'unity of national purpose', it is preferable that citizens and residents have documents and services in their own languages; (4) attempts to heighten the importance of foreign-language learning 'for national security purposes' will be weakened if foreign languages are undercut at the federal level. Further details about 'Official English' and its ramifications can be found in Chapter 13 (see especially note 5 there).

Historical perspectives

Multicultural matters are important in many contexts, but they are obviously magnified in settings of greater ethnic diversity. They are particularly salient, then, among the immigrant and 'guest-worker' populations of western Europe, and are of even more longstanding prominence in the new-world 'receiving' countries, including Canada, the United States and Australia. All of these owe their contemporary existence to successive waves of immigrants and, although each began with dominant immigrant populations, their recent histories have been marked by great variation among incoming groups. As I noted in the last chapter, more than half of all the schoolchildren in Toronto (where the population of the greater metropolitan area is now almost five million) come from homes where neither French nor English is the mother tongue.

We have already seen that policies in late 19th- and early 20th-century America were strongly assimilationist, both linguistically and otherwise. The process began at Ellis Island, in New York harbor, where the names of immigrants were often changed. While it is a myth that brutal abbreviations and alterations were imposed by unfeeling and monolingual immigration officers, and while many changes resulted from the immigrants' own attempts to make their names more 'American' in one way or another, there is little doubt that the process was seen on all sides as both desirable and practical. After all, the languages of the new arrivals were often seen as exotic, unpronounceable and inferior to English. The famous melting-pot popularized by Israel Zangwill (1909) was at full boil. But Zangwill's democratic notion – that all the immigrants would be given this fiery baptism, and that all would emerge as newly minted Americans – was never the reality. Beyond the fact that some immigrant groups, as well as the indigenous peoples of the continent, were unwilling to undergo immersion, racial prejudice meant that many would be refused such immersion anyway. Slightly less obvious was the fact that some total amalgamation *à la* Zangwill was never on the cards: only *some* identities were to be melted down and re-cast. Assimilative forces were to be brought to bear upon certain categories of newcomers, whose task it was to accommodate themselves to an existing mainstream. That is why the term *anglo-conformity* is more apt – not only in the United States, but in Australia and in most parts of Canada – than some metaphor of a crucible in which *all* would be mixed, and from which would emerge, phoenix-like, a new culture in which the threads of all the earlier ones would be seamlessly and invisibly interwoven.

From the beginning, however, it was the tension surrounding diversity and unity that animated those thinkers who were neither so naïve as to think that the melting pot was a democratic cauldron with room for everyone, nor motivated by a crude nativism. An early proponent of an enduring multiculturalism was Horace Kallen (1915, 1924), who argued that there was no overarching American nationality but, rather, a collection of distinct groups who could perpetuate themselves indefinitely. Kallen's ideal was a harmonious diversity, a stable cultural pluralism. He made provision in his model for some assimilation through consensus, allowing for the *unum* in the national motto while emphasising the *pluribus*. (Part of the *unum*, incidentally, would be English as the common language.)

Most scholars, however, believed and hoped that the assimilation of immigrants would proceed in what was called 'straight-line' fashion, although a roaring and insensitive melting-pot was rarely what they had in mind. Thus, the prominent sociologist, Robert Park, considered that assimilation was not something to be forced upon immigrants; they should, rather, be helped towards full participation in national life. A natural progression was perceived, from competition and conflict to accommodation and incorporation (assimilation): the famous 'race-relations cycle'. Recent interpretations strongly suggest that Park and his fellow scholars were liberals (some were romantics) caught in a dilemma. Park himself felt that civilization subverts attractive and egalitarian 'small' cultures with their 'redemptive' solidarity and he was, in many ways, a champion of what he termed 'parochial culture' (see Lal, 1990). At the same time, he did not wish to repudiate larger society, whose attractions and advantages were clear. He and his colleagues were both progressive and pragmatic, but they also wished to incorporate earlier and 'smaller' group values in a broader society that was, itself, still developing. They struggled, as liberals often do, with the competing attractions of past and present, rural and urban, diversity and unity.

In most contexts, however, some sort of assimilationist model prevailed, either officially or – more powerfully, in democratic societies – unofficially; indeed it was really only in the 1960s that academic interest in the assimilation-pluralism equation revived. This was intertwined with what looked to some to be an ethnic-minority 'revival' or 'resurgence'. Many commentators suggested that this was surprising, that the recrudescence of ethnic consciousness was a reaction to 'straight-line' assimilation that had somehow crept up unseen. Speaking for many, an apologist for diversity noted that 'one of the most extraordinary events of our time has been the resurgence of tribalism in a supposedly secularized and technocratic world… ties of race, nationality and religion seem to have taken on new importance' (cited by Mann, 1979: 17–18).

In fact, however, it is debatable whether there was any ethnic 'resurgence'; it might be more apt to describe an ethnic *persistence* which became more visible in times which were at once tending more and more to some global 'monoculture' and, at the same time, more sympathetic to the plight of small-group identities.[1] In any event, the renewed visibility of what some called the 'new ethnicity' was celebrated in many quarters, not least by scholars professionally and personally committed to an enduring social diversity. More poetic than most, but not unrepresentative, Michael Novak observed that this phenomenon represented a 'true, real, multicultural cosmopolitanism… struggling to be born is a creature of multicultural beauty, dazzling, free, a higher and richer form of life. It was fashioned in the painful darkness of the melting pot and now, at the appointed time, it awakens' (cited in Gleason, 1979: 17; see also Novak, 1971).

Contemporary directions

A renewed grappling with the difficulties and attractions of cultural pluralism led many researchers to develop theories and models that depicted and supported a workable accommodation between unity and diversity. Sociological terms like *pluralistic integration, participationist pluralism, modified pluralism, liberal pluralism, multivariate assimilation* and *social accommodation* (among others) are indicative here. Some of the 'committed' were (and remain) critical of any sort of modified or attenuated multiculturalism, on the grounds that it can only be a detour on the road to the old and bad assimilation. Sociological models that attempt to capture some intermediate position between total assimilation and group segregation, however, are at least rough reflections of what most indigenous and immigrant populations aim for. Besides, even if some seamless assimilation is the ultimate social destiny, it is difficult to see how it might be avoided for significant segments of the population, short of draconian measures unlikely to be acceptable in democratic societies. (There are groups, usually having a strong religious core to their identity, whose voluntary segregation from 'mainstream' society can be quite enduring. I note, however, that recent reports suggest that, even among such stalwart populations as the Amish, the Mennonites and the Pennsylvania 'Dutch', the mainstream tends to erode group boundaries.)

The interest in examining or re-examining multiculturalism has continued more or less unabated, and a very important recent development has been the attention given to it by political philosophers. The importance here arises from the fact that, for the first time, efforts have been made to consider the matter from a general and disinterested point of view rather than from a *parti pris* stance. In 1992, for example, Charles Taylor wrote about the tensions underpinning multiculturalism as struggles for the 'recognition' of group identities. He argued that, in a world in which the old social hierarchies have collapsed – with their selective and inegalitarian bases for *honor* – and in which a democratic sense of individual *dignity* has arisen, the politics of equal recognition have assumed great importance. But demands for equality must coexist with demands for uniqueness; as Taylor puts it, the new 'politics of recognition' is closely tied to a 'politics of difference'. The demands of universal respect, on the one hand, and of particularity, on the other, suggest difficulties:

> The reproach the first makes to the second is just that it violates the principle of nondiscrimination. The reproach the second makes to the first is that it negates identity by forcing people into a homogeneous mold that is untrue to them. (Taylor, 1992: 43)

This is a rather neat exposition of one face of that unity-diversity tension that I have touched upon here.

Having due regard to the collectivist impulses that underpin multiculturalism (on the one hand), and to the traditional liberal-democratic view that argues for individual equality but remains as neutral as possible on the cultural 'content' of life (on the other), Taylor attempts to chart a middle course. He suggests an 'hospitable' variant of liberalism that should not claim *complete* neutrality. He also touches upon the extended demand that not only should all cultures be given some degree of support, but also that we ought to recognize their equal worth. But are all cultures really equally worthy? Taylor sensibly observes that while judgments of equal worth require investigation, we might reasonably start from a *presumption* of equality. His essay sets the stage for further and more detailed work that has only gained in importance (see, e.g. Kymlicka, 1995a, 1995b).

Appearing at the same time as Taylor's book were two other treatments of multiculturalism, the more polemical of them by a very eminent American historian. The title of Arthur Schlesinger's (1992) book – *The Disuniting of America* – provides a rather strong hint about his views of multiculturalism, and the work is essentially a panegyric to the assimilative power of America and a lament that that power seems to be on the wane. The theme appears early on: 'unless a common purpose binds [people of different ethnic origins] together, tribal hostilities will drive them apart' (Schlesinger, 1992: 10). While the author acknowledges the contributions of ethnicity, the fact that he refers to recent manifestations of it as an 'eruption' is suggestive; in fact, he argues throughout that its potency has preserved an unhealthy diversity. He points, rather curiously, to a 'separatist impulse' in the black community, to the challenge to social unity represented by the 'bilingualism movement' and to the growth of Hispanic influence. Ultimately, however, Schlesinger remains optimistic that assimilative forces will successfully deal with the new challenge of pluralism. In a tone that is all too evident in American treatments of subjects of global concern, he claims that now, more than ever, the United States should set an example of social cohesion. Not only do many find this staking out of the moral high ground distinctly unattractive, recent events and continuingly baleful social statistics make it an empty proposition. But Schlesinger, like many others, seems to believe that the American beacon shines on, undimmed, for all of us unfortunate enough not to already live comfortably within its light.

This American attitude, and reactions to it, has of course come very much to the fore with the events of 11 September 2001 and their aftermath. Thomas Friedman, the Pulitzer Prize-winning columnist for *The New York Times*, found many American intellectual stances distasteful (see Edwards, 2004b, for fuller details) and so he told his daughters one evening that, while they could bring home someone who was 'black, white or purple... you will never come in this house and not love your country and not thank God every day that you were born an American' (Friedman, 2002: 313). Some may be surprised to find such jingoism in the remarks of an educated person but, on the subject of patriotic pride, even otherwise sensitive Americans have long demonstrated the same sort of blindness. Recently, reading the essays of John Dos Passos, I found the author observing that 'we can't get away from the fact that most everybody in the world believes in his heart that life is more worth living for the average man in North America than anywhere else' (Dos Passos, 1964: 37 – but Dos Passos first published his observation in 1941). Allowing for variations in style, perhaps these sentiments have more to do with perceived dominance than with any particular state allegiance; a century ago, Cecil Rhodes reportedly said that to be an Englishman was to have won first prize in the lottery of life.

While Schlesinger's treatment is a rather crude and narrow one, he has, of course, touched upon many real problems that exist in democratic and multicultural societies. A strength of his book is the demonstration that issues of multiculturalism, racism, prejudice, language, the eurocentric canon, political correctness and perceived assaults on an anglocentric mainstream are all intermeshed. What underpins this interpenetration are still deeper matters of group voice, of social inclusion and exclusion, of unity and diversity. A weakness of the book, however, is Schlesinger's overly blunt defence of an American conservative status quo; while concessions are made to the civilizing value of cross-cultural sensitivity, the existing pattern is seen as essentially sound. It is entirely reasonable, of course, for Schlesinger to argue for quite specific positions. As well, I would not argue with the need for a defence against some sociopolitical assaults nor, indeed, would I want to hold on some *a priori* basis that existing patterns are unsound or untenable. My criticism is that some points are inaccurately or incompletely stated, and a work by an important scholar in a highly sensitive area is insufficiently nuanced.

One might think the same of the book by Robert Hughes since, in his introductory remarks, he acknowledges a debt to Schlesinger, 'whose own recent book... says much of what I say but said it earlier and better' (Hughes, 1993: xiii). Nonetheless, unlike the historian, the journalist Hughes excoriates both left and right in an attempt to defend a middle ground. This is his way of dealing with contemporary tensions and, on the surface at least, there is much to recommend it. In this sense, Hughes's argument is broadly reminiscent of Taylor's plea for a similar sort of position and, in fact, his book could be seen as a popularized version of Taylor's more scholarly discussion. We find Hughes to be supportive of a 'generous and tolerant' multiculturalism, but strongly opposed to what multiculturalism has become in a fragmented culture: a marker of pernicious separatist sentiments. Since the polyphonic message of multiculturalism is something that Americans, of all people, might most benefit from, Hughes finds it ironic (but sadly predictable) that multiculturalism in the United States is not so much about a proliferation of voices as it is a shouting contest. What he refers to as 'radical multiculturalism' is a guise for Europe-bashing; one might say that while lip-service is given to diversity, a genuine pluralism is far from the minds of most multiculturalists. Radical multiculturalism is also critical of much historical interpretation: Columbus the hero is now the blackest of villains (if one can still use that form of expression). Like Schlesinger before him, Hughes decries the corruption of knowledge in the service of some group's 'self-esteem' (neither author, however, is unaware of the social construction of knowledge).

Taken together, these three books touch upon virtually all of the continuingly important aspects of the multiculturalism debate. As I have already implied, it is clear that the varied aspects of this issue assume importance because, ultimately, they all have to do with clamors for equal 'voice', they all deal with the politics, the sociology and the linguistics of identity. And it is notable that (even in Schlesinger's monograph), concern is expressed in compromise, in mediation, in the 'middle ground'. The authors suggest that this territory has been quite inadequately mapped – and, more than a decade on, this remains the case.

Multiculturalism in Canada

Any introductory discussion of multiculturalism would be incomplete without some consideration of the Canadian case – for several reasons. First, Canada is unique among new-world 'receiving' societies in that it has had, from the beginning, *two* powerful cultural and linguistic mainstreams (if the noun can reasonably be pluralized). While Australia, the United States, Brazil and Argentina all have one clearly defined ethnolinguistic *fons et origo*, Canada is marked by a French-English duality. I am prescinding from some important matters, of course: the two components of Canada's ethnolinguistic duality are by and large geographically distinct; all features are in dynamic flux – consider the rapid and continuing rise of the Hispanic component in the United States; and my reference to dominant mainstreams does not apply to pre-European America. Second, Canada had the first official multiculturalism policy. The government position here formed the basis for national responses elsewhere, notably in Australia and Britain – but not in the United States, where there is no official federal multicultural policy. Many accommodations have been made in recent years, however, to the growing Hispanic presence; many services, both official and private, are available in Spanish. As well, a federally supported bilingual education program was instituted in 1968, and many have interpreted this (incorrectly, in my view) as a *de facto* endorsement of multiculturalism and multilingualism; see the more focused discussion in the next two chapters. Third, the Canadian multicultural policy has had to coexist from its beginning (in 1971) with another social-engineering initiative: official bilingualism.

Burnet was an early and incisive commentator on the Canadian multiculturalism policy, seeing it:

> as encouraging those members of ethnic groups who want to do so to maintain a proud sense of the contribution of their groups to

Canadian society. Interpreted in this way, it becomes something very North American: voluntary marginal differentiation among peoples who are equal participants in the society. (Burnet, 1975: 211)

She went on to note, however, that if the policy was construed as some wholesale maintenance of 'foreign' cultures in Canada, then it would not (and perhaps should not) endure.

The policy certainly attracted criticism from the beginning. At a theoretical level, the late John Porter (1972) observed that official multiculturalism might prove a regressive force by helping to maintain an ethnic stratification that places group interests above those of the individual. Another frequently voiced criticism has been that the entire multicultural thrust has been politically opportunistic, both in the larger sense of attempting some national reconciliation between the two 'charter' groups (i.e. the French and the English) and the others (the 'allophones'), and in the more specific desire to attract 'ethnic' voters. The difficulty (some said the absurdity) of attempting to support *multi*culturalism within a French-English *bi*lingualism was also quickly brought to the fore. A well-known Ukrainian-Canadian scholar (Lupul, 1982: 100) thus described a situation of 'political pragmatism' which

pleased no one... The failure to provide multiculturalism with a linguistic base especially displeased the Ukrainians; the loosening of the ties between language and culture angered the francophones who disliked any suggestion that the status of their culture was on a par with that of other ethnic groups.[2]

Much criticism of multiculturalism has indeed come from the francophone community. Rocher (1973), for example, pointed out that multiculturalism might undermine official bilingualism, might be incompatible with national unity, and could generally prove a regressive step for the French who have their own longstanding concerns with dominance and equality. The fear, above all, is that the francophones might be reduced to the status of the ethnic 'others', the 'allophones'. It could, of course, be argued that a multiculturalism policy must have a similar effect on the anglophone community, but this latter group is not in the same precarious position as the French. Indeed, a cynical view is that the (relatively) greater support for multiculturalism from the English sector existed because it was seen as a defusing of the French 'problem' in Canada. There is a dilemma here for francophones: a rejection of multiculturalism on the grounds just noted may have some substance but, equally, a non-interventionist policy on the part of the government could be seen as a tacit acknowledgement of ethnic 'melting', which would ultimately enlarge the anglophone proportions of the country.

A summary statement in a *Globe & Mail* [Toronto] leader in May 1985 remains insightful:

> Multiculturalism is a highly ambiguous concept. At one level, it affirms the legitimacy of all the world's cultures... At another, it encourages immigrants and their descendants to perpetuate original values and customs [the implication here is that not all of these are positive]. It is often said that only by nourishing their differences can immigrants hope for equality within Canada, a thesis hardly confirmed by experience.

We have returned, then, to the essential tension that applies in all multicultural contexts, well beyond the specifically Canadian setting.

Finally here, it is reasonable to ask what 'ordinary' people think about multicultural policies and applications. As part of a well-known overview of the contemporary scene, Raymond Breton (1986: 47–48) summarized a number of experimental findings and opinion polls as follows:

> the research results on popular attitudes do not indicate a strong and widespread demand for state intervention in the ethnocultural field, except for the symbolic affirmation of Canada as a multicultural rather then bicultural society. The demand for a federal policy of multiculturalism seems to have come primarily from ethnic organizational elites and their supporters, from government agencies and their officers, and from political authorities.

Recent developments have only reinforced Breton's comments. The Canadian population has a certain (unspecified, perhaps unspecifiable) level of tolerance for diversity, a certain fund of passive goodwill, a certain willingness to see the 'others' shape their lives as desired. It does not have any great sympathy for real changes in social institutions, for direct (especially financial) official involvement in ethnocultural affairs, for any substantial alteration to an anglo-conformity pattern. One could, of course, dismiss public opinion here as uninformed and narrowly self-concerned. The question of whether it would be wise or expedient to do so, and the even more interesting question of the degree of acuity revealed in public surveys might suggest, however, that such a blanket dismissal would be inappropriate. In any event, cross-national comparisons reveal that Canadian dynamics are similar to those in other countries with substantial immigrant communities.

Multiculturalism in Education

The impulse behind multicultural education is very largely a positive one. In a post-modern and politically correct environment it has, in many eyes, a motherhood quality, but one need not be an ideologue of any particular stripe to see in such education a progressive and liberalizing force. Indeed, we would be hard pressed to deny (in theory, at least) the utility and justice of an educational thrust that aims to alert children to the varied world around them, whether or not it exists in microcosm in their own classroom, to inculcate cross-cultural respect, and to form a bulwark against racism and intolerance. The problems arise from definition and interpretation, on the one hand, and from implementation, on the other.

What should a multicultural program look like at school? There are many possibilities, and probably no two programs could be identical, if only for the reason that local ethnic realities (which presumably should be reflected in such programs, at least to some extent) alter with context. However, there are two broad approaches. One, now almost entirely rejected at an intellectual level but still much in evidence, is a sort of ethnic show-and-tell in which cultural manifestations are paraded in a self-conscious and often trivial fashion. While the specifics of cultural variation do, of course, have a place in a more thoughtful program, little can be expected if they are presented essentially as varieties of the exotic. Children (and teachers) may look forward to these experiences, but largely as light relief from the *real* work of the school, taking their place with unexpected but welcome school assemblies and old-style lessons in religion and citizenship.

The second approach involves a broader and less superficial stance on multiculturalism. Programs here are often heavy with objectives and curricula and, while well-meaning, may be either leaden and insensitive or woolly and arbitrary. One representative writer discussed a multi-cultural curriculum focussing upon the 'subjective content of the teachers' and students' own consciousness'. He went on to write:

> As an action system, the classroom of teacher and students would examine the historical process which creates each individual. The shared solidarity, when related to common experience, would plant the seeds of collective change. (Connors, 1984: 110)

These are the sorts of vaporings that give academics a bad name. Going beyond the style, such as it is, there is an assumption here that schools possess a power for social change that history shows to be rare.

Schools acting in relative isolation from other social currents – and emphases upon multicultural awareness and its ramifications *are*, unfortunately, often seen as matters that can be neatly assigned to classrooms – have very limited potency. The realization of this is important for all those who wish schools to act as agents of change; thus, calls for schools to 'empower' minority students may be well-meaning, but they are usually naïve. Through example and practice, schools can legitimize cultural varieties and markers (including language), but educational legitimation is not empowerment. It may lead to it, or contribute to it, but (again) not when schools are asked to shoulder the load almost unassisted.

The vagueness of Connors's remarks reflects the insubstantial and intellectually empty nature of much of the writing on multicultural education. As I have mentioned already, few would deny the psychological and social benefits potentially associated with a heightened cultural awareness. In order for this to be realized, however, a minimum requirement is that any multicultural initiative be firmly embedded within an appropriate, valued and systematic context. This context already exists, in fact, in existing curricula, although there are immediately obvious difficulties that can quickly vitiate programs. The thoughtful removal of boundaries of convenience, for example, would seem paramount. Cross-cultural sensitivity might be said to rest upon cross- or multidisciplinary underpinnings: meaningful interconnections among social studies, history and geography, for example, would facilitate the emergence of multicultural themes. This is hardly a radical notion: can we conceive, in fact, of a meaningful history that is *not* multicultural? In fact, as I mentioned in the introduction, all education worthy of the name is multicultural.

Properly integrated programs, incidentally, would go some way towards alleviating the concerns of minority-group members themselves, many of whom have quite rightly been suspicious from the start. In Britain, the West Indian writer, Maureen Stone (1981: 77) argued a generation ago that schools should continue to stress 'core' knowledge. She rejected the vague 'affective' goals of much modern multicultural education:

> I want to suggest that MRE [multiracial education] is conceptually unsound... while at the same time creating for teachers, both radical and liberal, the illusion that they are doing something special for a particularly disadvantaged group.

Another black parent and educator made the related comment that 'Black parents don't want black studies or multicultural education for their children – that is for white children; black pupils need to be good at science, history, geography – at what society thinks of as things of worth' (Woodford, 1982). Even earlier, Coard (1971) had written about the insensitive and inappropriate educational practices that caused West Indian children in the UK to become 'educationally subnormal'; now, a re-publication of his work, together with a number of commentaries (Richardson, 2005), argues that schools continue to fail black children.[3]

The apprehensions here remain both potent and plausible, and we have seen specifically linguistic manifestations of them in the debates surrounding Ebonics. But, just as children can be bidialectal, having access to *both* nonstandard *and* more standard forms, so black children – all children – can and should be assisted to develop multicultural sensitivities that supplement more traditional educational offerings. But, to repeat, any promotion of such sensitivities must be an inextricable part of the whole educational enterprise. If it does not, it will be viewed as a possibly diverting but largely insubstantial adjunct to more obvious classroom concerns. Not only will this mean a failure to engage those 'mainstream' pupils who arguably stand in greatest need of enhanced cross-cultural awareness, it could also be interpreted as a lack of meaningful concern by those 'others' whose very presence reminds us of what a fully formed education ought to involve.

Although there is quite a large literature on multicultural education, most of it is quite unsatisfying, for a number of reasons (Banks & Banks, 1995, and Gay, 1994, can be recommended, however). First, some of the literature makes only brief remarks about the value of tolerance and diversity in the classroom, and then immediately focuses upon purely language issues (see Edwards, 1985). This is both distressing and understandable. It is distressing, because if multicultural education largely concerns itself with responses to language diversity, then it at once becomes a narrower (although certainly not worthless) undertaking, one that significantly overlaps with themes and approaches we have already touched upon here: in short, it loses any claim to independent existence. It is understandable because, compared with the intangible and unrealistic nature of much of the relevant literature, an emphasis upon language at least provides something solid to focus upon. Second, and particularly marked in the American context, much of the literature devotes itself to specific constituencies and issues: afrocentric education for black children, for instance, or programs designed for children of Hispanic background. This second tendency actually turns the idea of multicultural education on its head. A reasonable desire to pay closer attention to 'disadvantaged' ethnic populations can produce a curriculum that essentially replaces one existing unidimensional thrust with another. An ostensible concern for cultural pluralism writ large often turns out to be special pleading for some particular group. We see this most notably in programs that are actively committed to equity and social justice (see also below). Third, a great deal of the literature is couched in inflated but vacuous language. We have already had a brief exposure to this, but there are many examples. If you go, for instance, to the website of the National Association for Multicultural Education (an American organization based in Maryland), you will find a lengthy definition, parts of which read as follows:

> Multicultural education is a philosophical concept built on the ideals of freedom, justice, equality, equity, and human dignity... it challenges all forms of discrimination... it helps students develop a positive self-concept... it prepares all students to work actively toward structural equality in organizations and institutions by providing the knowledge, dispositions, and skills for the redistribution of power and income among diverse groups. Thus, school curriculum [sic] must directly address issues of racism, classism, linguicism, ablism [sic], ageism, heterosexism, religious intolerance, and xenophobia... students and their life histories and experiences should be placed at the center of the teaching and learning process... multicultural education demands a school staff that is culturally competent, and to the greatest extent possible racially, culturally, and linguistically diverse... multicultural education attempts to offer all students an equitable educational opportunity, while at the same time encouraging students to critique [sic] society in the interest of social justice. (National Association for Multicultural Education, 2003)

I apologize for such a lengthy extract, but it surely contains some interesting material. The most salient feature is the alternation between assertions that no educationalist could quarrel with and others that are rather more pointed. Freedom, justice, dignity, tolerance and even the slightly more dubious ritual nod in the direction of self-esteem – what teacher would gainsay these? Some of the other statements, however, make multicultural education sound more like a training ground for the politically correct shock troops of anti-discrimination and ethno-racial equality. Another point of interest here is the placement of children's 'life histories' and teachers' 'cultural competence' at the center of the educational exercise. What exactly is this meant to imply – that is, if it reflects anything more than some vague feel-good factor? Are we to understand, for instance, that in non-multicultural classrooms, children's experiences are *not* drawn upon by sensitive teachers, and that cultural *incompetence* is raging, even perhaps among those who teach history and social studies? Passing over the (presumably related) implication that the selection of teachers on racial, cultural and linguistic grounds is of a priority higher than the traditional search for skills in knowledge and pedagogy, I note that any (indirect) mention of knowledge – for pupils now, rather than for their teachers – occurs only at the very end of the Association's statement. It refers to 'educational opportunity', which we might charitably assume does in fact mean something to do with actual content learning, but the piece quickly returns to, and concludes with, the formation of junior social critics.

I do not want to be misunderstood here. I am, of course, interested in schools inculcating in their charges cross-cultural sensitivities, defences against intolerance and prejudice, critical capabilities that will alert them to social inequities outside the school gates, and so on. But I am deeply suspicious of attempts to formalize this, particularly when those attempts are phrased in language that reveals little real sensitivity itself, and when the classroom is apparently seen more as an indoctrination center than a place of learning.[4] Here, Olneck (2000: 318) describes multicultural education (a force, he says, that 'aims to resist and to displace Euro-American cultural domination'):

> Multicultural education integrates content and perspectives originating in the experiences of nondominant racial, ethnic and linguistic groups into the curriculum; it enables students to recognize the role of power in the construction of knowledge; it aims to cultivate democratic attitudes, values and behaviors among students; it utilizes culturally congruent pedagogy; and it reorders the schools' status and cultural systems to make them fair to those previously disempowered by Euro-American dominance.

It would seem that the production of junior cultural commissars leaves little time for arithmetic, literature and geography.

Setting aside the more bizarre expressions of multiculturalism-in-education, I believe that the many virtues of that enterprise have *always* been educational virtues, and that beneath them is a critical capacity for independent and disinterested analysis – a quality, again, that has always been the cornerstone of education. Here is a representative list of the essential components of effective multicultural education: 'the promotion of good reasoning, the development of concept of person [sic], the development of a concept and sense of self-worth, the development of a concept of society [?], and the understanding of such concepts as prejudice and stereotyping' (Wright & LaBar, 1984: 118). Putting aside the clumsy and unfocused expression here, in what possible way could these educational thrusts not relate to *all* good classroom practice? If the disinterested underpinning remains undeveloped, then it seems to me that educationalists and theorists can carry on as much as they like about equity, xenophobia, linguicism and all the rest: nothing substantial will happen, nothing will really transfer beyond the immediate confines of the classroom, because the necessary scaffolding will be absent.[5] If, on the contrary, teachers succeed in presenting information to students that both develops into knowledge and gradually hones the general critical faculties, then those matters of particular interest to 'multiculturalists' can be assumed to develop, too. A rising tide floats all boats.

An early critical investigation, one inappropriately neglected in a field always in need of careful scrutiny, is Bullivant's (1981) treatment of pluralism in education. While some of the particulars of his half-dozen contexts (Australia, Hawaii, Fiji, the UK, Canada and the USA) have now altered, his general observations remain important. This is simply because the animating tensions of multiculturalism-in-education are very much as they have always been. Bullivant's strongest contention is that multicultural education, a confused and confusing amalgam of methods and objectives, is just another form of dominant-group 'hegemony'. 'Multiculturalism', he suggests, 'may be a subtle way of appearing to give members of ethnocultural groups what they want in education while in reality giving them little that will enhance their life chances' (Bullivant, 1981: ix). We have already seen that there have been minority-group suspicions about multicultural education, as well as the argument that multiculturalism-as-policy represents a politically opportunistic response to 'ethnic' populations, particularly if they have voting power. Bullivant's second pivotal argument has to do with what he calls the 'pluralist dilemma': while a democratic concern for all citizens can theoretically be reflected in particularized educational approaches, these may contribute to 'weakening the cohesion of the nation-state [sic] by interfering with the enculturation imperative – the need to have enough of a common culture passed on to each generation of children' (Bullivant, 1981: 14). The tension here is between what Bullivant (citing an earlier author: see Butts *et al.*, 1977) calls 'civism' and 'pluralism', which is yet another restatement of the unity-diversity dynamic (see also Higham, 1974, 1975).

Bullivant's third major argument is that – very roughly speaking – schools should concern themselves with the 'civism' side of the coin, and leave the maintenance and/or development of 'pluralism' in private and voluntary hands. Activities under the latter heading can include ethnic-language retention, religious observances, and so on. This is a familiar position, and one of continuing concern inasmuch as it has animated scholarly philosophical interest. Kymlicka (1995a), for example, has argued that liberal democracies have to pay attention to those cultural features that Bullivant would leave to the groups themselves. This is not an abdication of the traditional liberal focus upon *individual* rights, he suggests, because such rights may be virtually meaningless without a maintained cultural context (see also Edwards, 2003b). Furthermore, Kymlicka and others have claimed that since traditional liberal 'neu-trality' in respect of the contents of daily life is a fiction – if only by default, all societies privilege particular languages, endorse certain educational endeavors, and so on – a refusal to countenance 'official' support at the group level for non-mainstream populations must logically be unfair. In his fourth argument, Bullivant cautions that it is naïve to think that, whether left in private hands or not, multicultural intervention can of itself help minority groups to cope with the 'political realities' of life. He notes, specifically, that many programs proceed on the flawed assumption that real 'empowerment' (Bullivant does not use the word itself) can originate or be substantially enhanced by classroom activities; see my earlier comments on this topic. He suggests going all the way back to Kallen's (1924) insightful view that any meaningful cultural pluralism grows out of political democracy and equity; it does not create it.

Strong and Weak Multiculturalism

It comes as no surprise that Bullivant concludes by agreeing with Glazer (1977: 24) that the work of education is 'centered on the common culture. Cultural pluralism describes a supplement... it does not, and should not, describe the whole'.[6] Clearly, Glazer believes that this 'supplemental' approach is something best left to unofficial agencies or communities. But, equally clearly, we can see that considerable change to 'the common culture' has occurred in the 30 years since Glazer wrote these words. If it has changed largely because of the growing and permanent presence of those who were not part of older mainstreams, then it is easy to see that the very notion of what constitutes multi-culturalism and multicultural education will alter. Glazer has returned to the topic several times – most notably in a 1997 book that proclaims *We Are All Multiculturalists Now*.[7] Glazer's new, if grudging, acceptance of the reality of multicultural education emerges from the particularities of the American context. As Kymlicka (1998) points out in an insightful review, the argument is that black students are the 'storm troops' of multiculturalism and that, had black people become more fully integrated into society, contemporary multicultural accommodations would not have occurred. This, Kymlicka thinks, is a correct but restricted view: it ignores the increasingly powerful presence of Hispanic Americans, for instance. As well, multicultural policies have been adopted in countries (most notably, Canada and Australia) without the American history of racial conflict. Glazer's sense is that multiculturalism is irrevocably part of the American educational system, and that the questions now have to do with what *forms* its presence will take.

Glazer's point of view is not the only one possible. In his short piece on 'boutique' multiculturalism, Stanley Fish (1998) argues that multiculturalism is impossible. On the one hand, the superficialities of weak ('boutique') multiculturalism hardly justify the noun at all. It is a sort of 'flirtation' or 'cosmetic relationship', one that stops well short of a thoroughgoing acceptance of difference. Fish refers to the scathing essay by Tom Wolfe (1970) on 'radical chic': Wolfe's description of the party for the Black Panthers held by Leonard Bernstein in his opulent Park Avenue apartment in 1970 remains, after almost 40 years, a delicious read. This weak stance may involve admiration, enjoyment or sympathy with the 'other', but it will not extend its appreciation to offences against 'the canons of civilized decency' (Fish, 1998: 69). There are many illustrations of what Fish means here, and he cites some obvious ones himself; thus, while 'boutique' multiculturalists may respect religious beliefs other their own, they will draw the line at (say) polygamy. Fish is essentially restating here the idea that toleration can mean very little if it covers only those things that are different but still generally 'acceptable'. This, of course, is a very interesting and murky area. Perhaps there may be broad acceptance at the extremes – there are probably very few among us, for instance, whose tolerance for the plurality of beliefs would embrace ritual cannibalism – but extreme behavior is rarely the issue.

(I mention cannibalism on purpose here. I am not thinking of Hannibal Lecter, but of a recent gruesome case in Germany. In December 2003, Armin Meiwes was put on trial for eating an apparently willing victim, one Bernd Brandes. The two had initially 'met' through the internet. Cannibalism is not a crime in Germany, and Meiwes was originally sentenced to about eight years for manslaughter; later, at a new trial in 2006, he was sentenced to life imprisonment for murder. How many, I wonder, would be willing to apply to cases like this some version of John Stuart Mill's 'harm principle' – the familiar notion, that is, that freedom should extend up to the point at which its exercise impinges upon the freedom of someone else. Does the fact that the victim in the Miewes case was a consenting partner in the bizarre act mean that this principle remained unviolated? Some might say that the barbarity of the deed implies mental illness, which, in turn, would invalidate any real freedom here. But, when we consider that Miewes was [and is] an apparently sane and rational man, the argument that he is mentally disturbed because he did something that must be evidence of psychological instability is begging the question. He was described by a neighbor, at his first trial, as 'friendly and sensitive' and – more to the point [perhaps] – a psychiatrist testified that Miewes was not mentally ill, although he did lack 'warm and tender feelings' for others, and seemed 'smug and self-assured'. That would describe a great many people, including virtually all rich and successful businessmen [for example]: they may be figurative cannibals, but few are literal ones. Food for thought...?)

On the other hand, Fish argues, there is a 'strong' multiculturalism, in which tolerance and 'deep respect' for different cultures trump both rationality and universalism. As many others have found out, however, a thoroughgoing tolerance meets its match when its object is intolerant. (At the political level, the corollary is this: should democratic regimes tolerate movements and attitudes whose *raison d'être* is the overthrow of democratic principle?) If one's tolerance *did* extend so far as to embrace an intolerant 'other', then, as Fish points out, it would no longer be tolerance. On the other hand, if the tolerant and liberal-minded find that there is, indeed, a sand-line beyond which they will not go (Fish mentions the Islamic *fatwa* on Salman Rushdie, but there are many other cultural practices – female circumcision, child slavery and so on – that are often cited), then they have given up respecting that other culture 'at the point where its distinctiveness is most obviously at stake' (Fish, 1998: 73). Fish continues:

> Typically, the strong multiculturalist will grab the second handle of this dilemma (usually in the name of some supracultural universal now seen to have been hiding up his sleeve from the beginning) and thereby reveal himself not to be a strong multiculturalist at all. Indeed, it turns out that strong multiculturalism is not a distinct position, but a somewhat deeper instance of the shallow category of boutique multiculturalism. (Fish, 1998: 73–74)

Suppose, however, that 'strong' multiculturalists really stuck to their guns and maintained a respect for some other culture no matter what it did or thought. Then they would have become 'really strong' multiculturalists. Such individuals, Fish suggests, those who would continue to respect a culture that was intolerant of another culture's distinctiveness, become in fact 'uniculturalists'. So, in the end, it doesn't matter. 'Boutique' multiculturalism is superficial and not really worthy of the name; 'strong' multiculturalism typically falters when the going gets rough; and 'really strong' multiculturalism, with its death-and-glory determination, turns into a monocultural stance. Hence the conclusion that Fish (1998: 75) arrives at: 'no one could possibly *be* multiculturalist in any interesting and coherent sense'.

I began this chapter by saying that multiculturalism was either a *de facto* state of social affairs or a matter of policy, and this most basic distinction extends into the classroom, too. There is a difference between teachers attempting to deal equitably and sensitively with cultural and linguistic heterogeneity, and explicit policies of multicultural education. The latter, I have suggested here, are generally problematic, their constituents prone to extremes. Either they are stated in vague generalities, often tricked out in the latest educational jargon, or they restate the obvious and thus reinforce my contention that all good education is multicultural in nature anyway. I want to conclude here by mentioning something that is either a contribution to the maintenance of the distinction – to the potential point at which a *de facto* multicultural reality produces social, political and educational policy – or, in fact, a restatement of that distinction. It is a dichotomy that I suggested to a Danish audience more than a decade ago: hard (or strong) versus soft (or weak) multiculturalism (Edwards, 1994b).

I modelled my argument on the debate surrounding Whorf's classic linguistic relativity hypothesis (Carroll, 1972; Edwards, 1989). Whorf himself had essentially argued that language determines thought: our own particular language influences the ways in which we see the world and, hence, our cognitive functioning. But this 'strong' hypothesis is rejected by linguists and psychologists, who cite such evidence as the possibility of translating from one language to another, and the fact that we are all capable of expanding and adjusting our language (our vocabulary, to give one specific example) if circumstances require. There is no good evidence, in short, to suggest a 'tight' connection between the particular language one speaks and one's basic thought processes. There *is* evidence, however, for the shaping influence of environment upon language. If, for instance, your community lives in a desert, and has done so for a long time, it is quite possible that your color vocabulary will not range over the nuances of green and red reflected in the language of speakers in more temperate climatic zones. If, however, your group suddenly finds oil under the sands, becomes very rich, and moves *en masse* to the Riviera, then you can be sure that lexical expansion will soon follow. So, while a 'strong' or 'tight' Whorfianism is unlikely, a 'weaker' variety makes perfect sense, for the reason just mentioned. It is plausible to accept that there is a circular and mutually reinforcing relationship between language and the environment (both physical and sociocultural) – and the upshot will be that language influences our customary or habitual ways of thinking. That is, there is a connection here, but it is a 'loose' one reflecting habitual ways of looking at the world, not cognitively inevitable ones.[8]

In like manner, I suggested that there is a 'soft' multiculturalism that acknowledges diversity, and may even make some formal accommodation to it at educational or social-policy levels, and a 'hard' version that underpins deeper and more permanent structural alterations. In practice, the first reflects an older social vision that – whether unarticulated or officially upheld – believes in some ultimate assimilation. It is an assimilation of choice, one might say, and not a forced or legislated one; nonetheless, assimilation is seen as a desirable end-point. Particular groups, or individuals within groups, may wish to maintain markers of ethnic distinctiveness, but most will acquiesce at some point to the social pressures and benefits associated with 'mainstream' life. This is the general pattern that has described the social trajectories of most new-world immigrants: the ethnic connection between a fourth-generation 'Polish-American' and her first-generation forebear is now largely a symbolic one. (Precisely because of its intangibility, symbolic ethnicity can be a very enduring matter, and it is not an inconsiderable or psychologically negligible quantity; for details, see Edwards, 1994a.) It is, in fact, essentially what Horace Kallen (1924) wrote about under the heading of 'cultural pluralism'. A typical linguistic manifestation here is this: first-generation monolingualism in the language spoken upon arrival at (say) Ellis Island; second-generation bilingualism in that language and English; third-generation monolingualism in English.

'Hard' multiculturalism, on the other hand, is a more clearly articulated policy that aims at an enduring diversity, an ongoing ethnocultural pluralism, a society with room for a broad array of languages and cultures. Harmonious intergroup relations are, of course, hoped for here; indeed, the argument is often made that it is precisely the recognition and cultivation of diversity that will lead to such relations. The belief is, as

Gerstle (2001: 349) put it, that 'cultural diversity and national pride [are] compatible... that ethnic diversity and a respect for ethnic and racial differences strengthened America'. Outright 'anti-multiculturalists', as well as proponents of 'softer' versions, make a counter-argument. Permanent ethnocultural heterogeneity is a recipe for social discord and (as in the Canadian case, for example), it will work against the gradual and desirable emergence of some overall national ethos.

There have been other similar distinctions. Higham (1982) wrote of 'hard' and 'soft' pluralism, Devine (1996) makes a 'strong' and 'weak' distinction, and Wood (1994: 48–49) – at about the same time I was discussing the matter in Odense – referred to 'hard' and 'soft' multiculturalism in America. Like Schlesinger, Wood is an historian, and the type of distinction he draws is a very pointed one, reminiscent of Schlesinger's (1992) earlier arguments:

> There is no doubt that our understanding of American history has been profoundly enriched by what might be called a soft multicultural approach... we used to call it pluralism, which assumed a process of assimilation. Celebrating the distinctiveness of one's group or ethnicity always has been part of the process of becoming American... what is new and alarming is the use of "identity politics" and what might be called hard multiculturalism to break up the nation into antagonistic and irreconcilable fragments.

The distinction here is overdrawn and unnecessarily conspiratorial. The real efforts of the 'hard' multiculturalists are not to break up the nation but, as I have implied above, to fundamentally alter its character. 'Hard' multiculturalists could point nowadays, for instance, to the powerful Hispanic population in the United States, and to the changes that this influential presence has brought to everyday life, as an example of a real sea-change in American society. 'Soft' multiculturalists look at the same picture, and bewail the passing of the status quo.

Notes

1. A point of comparison here: in formerly Communist societies, the emergence from under the dead hand of totalitarianism often signalled, unfortunately, a return to older ethnic rivalries. But this does not mean that democracy awoke the sleeping princess – she had always been there, waiting in the wings for a new chance to occupy the spotlight.
2. A much fuller story of Canadian multiculturalism from the important Ukrainian point of view, is found in Lupul's lengthy memoir (2005). Scholars from the Canadian Ukrainian community have, from the first, been keen observers of, and commentators on, the federal policy of multiculturalism.

3. Bernard Coard is far from an ordinary educational scholar. After his doctoral studies in England, he returned to his home in Grenada and joined a left-wing political party, which, under the leadership of Maurice Bishop, seized power in 1979. As the deputy Prime Minister, Coard then overthrew Bishop's government in 1983 – Bishop and some of his cabinet colleagues were unceremoniously shot to death. Shortly thereafter came the American invasion of the island. With some others (the 'Grenada Seventeen'), Coard was arrested, sentenced to death in 1986, and is currently serving a life sentence. He maintains his innocence, claiming that his conviction was at the hands of a kangaroo court (see Noel, 2005).

4. I am well aware that *all* education reflects some values and not others, that no classroom setting is free of the constraints and attitudes that characterize the society in which it takes its place. But two points suggest themselves here. First, is it any sort of advance to replace one set of constraints with another – as some of the more radical multicultural curricula, in an ironic rejection of the very principles of diversity that are supposed to animate them, would apparently like to see? Second, considerations of *degree* are relevant here. While it is logical to admit that no contexts are value-free, it is not illogical to suggest that some are more value-laden than others. Consider the following quotation from the eminent scholar of nationalism, Elie Kedourie (1961: 83–84), and replace the word 'nationalist' with 'multiculturalist':

> On nationalist theory... the purpose of education is not to transmit knowledge, traditional wisdom, and the ways devised by a society for attending to the common concerns; its purpose rather is wholly political.

This may seem a little too pointed to those with no experience of regimes that are other than liberal-democratic, and I would not want to suggest that modern theorists of multicultural education despise knowledge and wisdom. But I would argue that inappropriate pendulum positions become more likely with increasing adherence to particular ideologies and, further, that harmful consequences are likely to be exacerbated when those ideologies are, themselves, subject to the vagaries of often ephemeral cultural interpretation.

5. It is worth pointing out here that, like other important areas lying at the intersection of research and application, the entire 'multicultural enterprise' is most often associated with those who have pre-existing commitments to particular aspects of that application. Nothing wrong with that, of course – and, again, one can hardly argue for value-free investigation in any social-scientific topic – but on the ground, as it were, this does sometimes mean that disinterested scholarship is not always as front-and-center as one might like.

There are curious wheels-within-wheels here, too. I have on my desk a brochure advertising a journal of the World Communication Association. The *Journal of Intercultural Communication Research* is edited in Wisconsin and, among its 47 editorial-board members, only three (two from Japan, one from Canada) are at non-American universities. This is surely a little odd, given the journal's subject area.

6. This is a mistaken citation. Glazer's chapter occupies pages 85 to 109 in the anthology by Coleman *et al.* (1977), something noted correctly in Bullivant's reference list. Not only is page 24 not a part of Glazer's piece, the latter does

not include the comments cited by Bullivant! Nonetheless, the spirit of Glazer's opinion is accurately reflected in them.

7. Glazer was slightly anticipated here by the journalist and scholar, Louis Menand (1994); he pointed out that 'almost everyone today... is some kind of a multiculturalist'.

8. Even with 'strong' Whorfianism, it is, of course, legitimate to ask why those thought-determining languages developed differently at all. This would seem to bring us back to the environment again – and, indeed, Whorf himself noted the constant interplay of language patterns and cultural norms.

Chapter 12

Bilingualism: A Very Brief Overview

Introduction

There is a huge literature on what one might term the 'technicalities' of bilingualism and bilingual education: definitions (of course), the assessment and measurement of various degrees and dimensions of bilingualism, the relationship between language acquisition and other variables (age, gender, intelligence, motivation and attitude, socioeconomic status, minority-group membership, the sociocultural and sociopolitical context), the intricacies of borrowing, interference and switching across two or more languages, bilingual and multilingual literacy, the relationship between personal and societal bilingualism, types of bilingual education provisions, the effectiveness of programs of bilingual education. Obviously, it would be impossible for me to do more than provide the briefest of introductions here, but, in any event, a deep treatment of the nuts and bolts of bilingualism is not to my purpose. As will be seen, I am more concerned with the symbolic and group-identity aspects of bilingualism, particularly where 'smaller' languages come into contact with 'larger' ones.

Another reason for not providing much detail here is simply that this has been thoroughly done elsewhere, in topical surveys that are clear, up-to-date and easily accessible. Chief among these are the encyclopedia of Baker and Jones (1998) and Baker's smaller but still very comprehensive textbook (2006). The recent handbook by Bhatia and Ritchie (2004) is very useful, and several publishers (Pergamon, De Gruyter, Springer, Blackwell and Oxford University Press among them) have recently issued large reference volumes and encyclopedias on various aspects of the 'social life' of language; see also and Hamers and Blanc (2000), Li Wei (2000) and Romaine (1995).

Defining Bilingualism

Everyone is bilingual. That is, there is no one in the world (no adult, anyway) who does not know at least a few words in languages other than the maternal variety. If, as an English speaker, you can say *c'est la vie* or *gracias* or *guten Tag* or *tovarisch* – or even if you only understand them – you clearly have some 'command' of a foreign tongue. Of course, this sort of competence does not lead many to think of bilingualism. If, on the other hand, you are *conversationally* fluent in more than one language, then bilingualism may be an apt designation. And if, on the third hand, you are like the literary critic and essayist, George Steiner, who claims equal fluency in English, French and German, then bilingualism (actually *tri*lingualism in this case) seems apter still.

Giuseppe Mezzofanti, chief curator in the Vatican Library in the early 19th century, was reportedly fluent in 60 languages and had translating ability in twice that number. Georges Schmidt, head of the terminology section at the United Nations in the 1960s, knew 20 languages. George Steiner and all the other well-known polyglots – the Stoppards, Kunderas and Nabokovs of the world – typically have three or four languages (and so, of course, do many hundreds of millions of unremarked and unremarkable people). Even more common are bilinguals, with a paltry dual fluency. And then there is your cousin in Birmingham, who can just about understand what *c'est la vie* means. How are these fluencies related? Mezzofanti would seem to be more multilingual than Steiner, but the latter claims that his varieties are so equally deeply held that, even after rigorous self-examination – of which language emerges spontaneously in times of emergency or elevated emotion, which variety is dreamt in, which is associated with the earliest memories – no one of the three seems dominant. (Steiner and others have argued, in fact, that there may be important linguistic and cognitive differences between a person who has a clear and obvious first language, to which others have been added, and someone like himself, who is apparently maternally multilingual. Wierzbicka's [2005] perceptive paper on the different perspectives of mono- and multilingual people is relevant here.) And if there is some difficulty in comparing capabilities, given that both number and depth seem to be important, where might we place the Schmidts of the world? And your Birmingham cousin: ought she to count as bilingual at all? Beyond the informal interest that has always attached to polymathic capabilities, beyond the *Guinness Book of Records*, the assessment of linguistic competence has considerable scholarly importance.

As may be imagined, it is easy to find definitions of bilingualism that reflect widely divergent responses to the question of *degree*. In 1933, for example, Bloomfield observed that bilingualism resulted from the addition of a perfectly learned foreign language to one's own, undiminished native tongue. He did rather confuse the issue, however, by admitting that the definition of 'perfection' was a relative one. Weinreich (1953) simply defined bilingualism as the alternate use of two languages. In the same year, Haugen suggested that bilingualism began with the ability to produce complete and meaningful utterances in the second language; this suggests that your Birmingham cousin *is* bilingual. Generally speaking, earlier definitions tended to restrict bilingualism to equal mastery of two languages, while later ones have allowed much greater variation in competence. But since this relaxation proves in practice to be as unsatisfactory as an argument from perfection, most modern treatments acknowledge that any meaningful discussion must be attempted within a specific context, and for specific purposes.

Further complicating the matter of degree, this question of where bilingualism starts, is the fact that any line drawn must cross not just one general language dimension, but many more specific threads of ability. Consider, first, that there are four basic language skills: listening, speaking, reading and writing.[1] Consider further the possible subdivisions: speaking skill, for example, includes what may be quite divergent levels of expression in vocabulary, grammar and accent. Thus, there is a substantial number of elements here, all of which figure in the assessment of bilingualism. It does not follow that strength in one means strength in another; thus, Baker (1988: 2) noted that

> a pupil may be able to understand spoken English and Welsh, speak English fluently but Welsh only haltingly, read in Welsh with a reading age of six and in English with a reading age of eight, write poorly in English and not at all in Welsh. Is that pupil bilingual?

In general, given both the basic skills, and their subdivisions, there are at least 20 dimensions of language that might be assessed in order to determine bilingual proficiency. While in many cases it is quite clear which language is dominant (at least within some given domain), a rough reckoning may be quite inadequate if we wish, say, to compare groups of bilingual individuals, or if we wish to study the relationship between bilingualism and other personality traits.

Many tests have been used to measure bilingualism; these include rating scales and tests of fluency, flexibility and dominance. The first of these can involve interviews, language-usage measures and self-assessment procedures. In some ways, relying upon self-ratings has a lot to recommend it, but the strengths here rest upon the capacity of an individual to be able to self-report accurately, a roughly equivalent sense across individuals of what competence means, and a willingness to be truthful in response. None of these can be taken for granted. Indeed, some of the problems here can also affect the apparently more objective tests of fluency and flexibility. We might, for example, ask people to respond to instructions in two languages, measure their response times and, on this basis, try to ascertain dominance. Or we could present picture-naming or word-completion tasks, we could ask subjects to read aloud or we might present a word that occurs in both languages (*pipe*, for example, occurs in both French and English) and see how it is pronounced. We could simply test for extent of vocabulary, or see how many synonyms for a given word a person can come up with. *Und so weiter.*

As well, it can easily be appreciated that factors such as attitude, age, sex, intelligence, memory, linguistic distance between languages and the context of testing all have the potential to confuse and confound the picture. Furthermore, even if we were able to gauge with some accuracy, there would remain problems of adequate labelling. That is, measured individuals would hardly fall into one, or two, or four neat categories of ability, or degrees of bilingualism. I should also mention here the commonly held view that limits exist on linguistic capacities, that there is some finite available cranial space; indeed, this 'container' philosophy bedevilled the academic literature for quite some time. As I have already noted, the suggestion is – at its simplest – that what you gain on the swings of one language you lose on the roundabouts of the other. But all such metaphors are flawed in at least two ways: first, there is no evidence that a simplistic container model is appropriate at all; second, even if we were to acknowledge some finite absorption and retention potentials, all that we know of intellectual structure and function would suggest that they are quite large enough that we need not worry about exhausting our mental credit (think of Cardinal Mezzofanti). (Obviously, the linguistic aspects are but one part of a more general cognitive picture; the most recent neuropsychological research suggests the inadequacy of simple 'container' metaphors; see Fernyhough, 2006, for a cursory consideration of 'metaphors of mind'.)

There are some important dichotomies to attend to, as well. First, there is the distinction between *receptive* (or passive) bilingualism and *productive* (or active) competence. The difference here is between those who understand a language, either spoken or written, but cannot produce it themselves, and those who can do both. Second, there is a distinction between *additive* and *subtractive* bilingualism: with the former, the learning of another language means an expansion of the linguistic repertoire; with the latter, the new language may displace the existing one. Additive bilingualism generally occurs where both languages continue to be useful and valued; subtractive bilingualism, on the other hand, usually occurs in settings in which one language is valued more than the other, where one dominates the other, where one is on the ascendant and the other is waning.[2] A third important contrast is that between *primary* and *secondary* bilingualism, between a dual-language competence acquired naturally, through contextual demands, and one where systematic and formal instruction has occurred. Finally here, some writers have drawn yet another distinction: language *acquisition* is to refer to gradual or 'natural' linguistic development (in either first or subsequent varieties), while language *learning* is to be reserved for more studied and formal attainments (most typically, at school).

These are not watertight compartments, of course. For instance, one might pick up a fluently conversational grasp of a language in a relatively informal way, and later feel the need to add some reading and writing skills. Nonetheless, bilingual people in the *Gaeltacht* of Ireland or Scotland are obviously different from residents of Dublin, Glasgow or Edinburgh, who have more self-consciously set themselves to become bilingual, and lumping these two groups together under a single bilingual rubric might not lead to the most accurate descriptions.

Becoming Bilingual

The fact that a majority of the global population has at least some level of multilingual competence surely indicates that adding a second language is not a particularly remarkable feat. English and American monolinguals often complain that they have no aptitude for foreign-language learning. This is usually accompanied by expressions of envy for those multilingual Europeans, Asians and Africans, and sometimes (more subtly) by a linguistic smugness reflecting a deeply held conviction that, after all, those clever 'others' who don't already know English will have to accommodate themselves in a world made increasingly safe for anglophones. All such attitudes, of course, reveal more about social dominance and convention than they do about aptitude.

Second-language acquisition has been dichotomized as *simultaneous* or *successive*. The first describes exposure to more than one variety from the onset of speech or, at least, from a very young age (some commentators have suggested age three or four as a rather arbitrary cut-off), while the second refers to the addition of a new variety to an existing one at a later age. Simultaneous acquisition most commonly occurs under the 'one parent, one language' heading principle: mother speaks German to the child, father speaks English. There are some classic accounts of this in the literature (e.g. Leopold, 1939–1949; Ronjat, 1913). Given the continuing reservations about bilingualism in some parts of the popular (anglophone) mind, it should be noted that the literature strongly suggests that general linguistic and mental development is not adversely affected. Bringing up children bilingually is not a risky business. Where negative consequences *have* been observed, these are almost always due to social, personal, cultural or other factors, and not to bilingualism per se. With appropriate social conditions, then, bilingualism is just as 'natural' as monolingualism; statistically speaking, indeed, it is much more natural. With sufficient motivation and opportunity, all normally intelligent people can learn another variety, and those who claim they are 'no good' at foreign languages are usually lacking one or both of these. This is not to deny that there may exist individuals who have a greater innate or acquired aptitude: a 'good ear' may be helpful, as well as a good memory and a capacity for self-initiated application; beyond these, adaptability and genuine interest in other cultures are no doubt important. But these factors are all of general value and do not form a package specifically implicated in *language* learning – and in any event they are dwarfed by contextual pressures and demands.

There are many formal methods for teaching languages. Generally speaking, older approaches tended to stress the memorization of grammatical rules and lexicon in the service of literary study, and little attention was given to oral language. In more contemporary school settings this has changed, although even high-tech language laboratories sometimes merely individualize older approaches, rather than signalling a change of course towards more conversational competence. Still, while it remains difficult for the classroom to become a representation of the street, the tendency is for more and more conversation. Students are encouraged to speak before learning formal grammar, and the use of the maternal variety is often kept to a minimum; in short, second-language acquisition is meant to resemble first-language learning as much as possible.

A number of theoretical perspectives inform language-acquisition practices, and I shall merely touch upon them here. Social-psychological theories have paid particular attention to motivational features, and this makes a good deal of sense. If we agree that language is a social activity, and if we accept that almost everyone is cognitively capable of learning second (and subsequent) varieties, then it follows that the force of the situation and the attitudinal atmosphere are central. The distinction that I have already mentioned between *instrumental* and *integrative* motivations for second-language learning was first drawn in the 1960s. The former refers to a desire to learn for utilitarian purposes, the latter to language learning as part of a wish to know more about, to interact with, and perhaps ultimately to immerse oneself in another culture. Perhaps, however, a well-fleshed instrumental attitude must include at least some integrative motivation, and one can also imagine a development of the former into the latter. In any event, Gardner and Lambert (1972) presented a well-known framework for second-language learning that incorporates the distinction. A later model, described by Noels and Clément (1998), has aimed to embed individual motivations still more deeply in the social setting. Of special interest here is the tension seen to exist between an integrative motivation and fear of assimilation; the model thus has particular relevance for those language learners who are also minority-group members, and whose first language is threatened by the forces of those speaking the second. A further theoretical develop-ment is the formulation of Giles and his colleagues (see Giles & Coupland, 1991) in which language learning is seen as essentially an *intergroup* process. Much more consideration is therefore given to assimilative tendencies and apprehensions, to the preservation of ethnic-group boundaries and identities.

A recent 'general theory' of second-language learning has been proposed by Spolsky (1989a). It synthesizes earlier and more particular-ized efforts and it also touches upon first-language acquisition. Spolsky's approach has five pivotal features:

(a)   it attempts to bring all aspects of language learning under one roof;

(b)   it aims for precision and clarity, so that the broad coverage does not blur details of varying contexts, goals and outcomes;

(c)   it assumes that all aspects of learning are interactive; although they need not be operative in all contexts, they all interpenetrate. On the subject of motivation, for example, Spolsky wishes to detail types and strengths;

(d)   it argues that all language learning must be seen within a social setting;

(e)   it holds that some conditions for learning are "graded": the more intense or favourable they are, the more likely a linguistic consequence becomes. Others are "typicality" states: they occur usually but not inevitably.

Application and prediction form the acid test in all such theoretical models (for a recent overview, see Mitchell & Myles, 1998), and some might suggest that they have done little more than codify and formalize what has been known for a long time. Nonetheless, they all usefully emphasize the importance of the setting and, within it, the desires, needs, attitudes and motivations of ordinary people. And they all scotch the myth that some people, or some groups, have no 'head' for languages, and that second-language aptitude is a rare commodity usually best seen in non-anglophones.

This brings us to another important topic: the relationship between bilingualism and intelligence. It is one thing to say that all normal people have the basic capacity to expand their linguistic repertoires, and that doing so exacts no cognitive price. But what of the notion that bilingualism can *increase* intellectual scope? It is an historically common view that one's personality expands with extra languages, particularly among those already bilingual and, more particularly still, among the social élite for whom an additional language or two was always an integral part of civilized life.[3]

Generally speaking, early studies tended to associate bilingualism with lowered intelligence, and it is unsurprising that many of them were conducted in America at a time of great concern with the flood of immigrants from Europe (roughly, 1900–1920). As we have seen in earlier chapters, the history of the intelligence-testing movement itself is a fascinating and detailed one, as well as an example of the misuse of 'science' when allied with ignorance and prejudice. In addition, however, to the negative associations between bilingualism and intelligence that stemmed from social fears and prejudices, there have also been more disinterested studies that pointed to problems here. Virtually all were flawed, however, by inadequate controls in their experimental procedures. The problem of statistical inference has been even more important: if one observes a correlation between measured intelligence and bilingualism, then has the first caused the second, or vice versa, or is there a third factor (perhaps unknown or unmeasured) that influences both and thus accounts for their relationship? Correlation need not imply causation.

Later research tended to show essentially no relationship between intelligence and bilingualism, and this work was generally more carefully done than the earlier studies. Controlling for gender, age and social-class differences became common procedure, and the lack of such control was increasingly seen to have produced the negative associations found previously. What some have seen as a turning-point came in the early 1960s, when findings showing a *positive* relationship between intelligence and bilingualism began to appear. In Montreal, for instance, Peal and Lambert (1962) found that 10-year-old bilingual children outperformed their monolingual counterparts on both verbal and non-verbal intelligence tests. The authors concluded that the bilingual child had greater mental flexibility and superior concept-formation skills, although they also admitted that the directionality of the correlation between bilingual ability and measured intelligence could not be ascertained. Following Peal and Lambert's investigation, many others have supported a positive relationship between bilingualism and intelligence. Equally, there have been dissenting views, as well as cogent criticism of the 1962 study itself. The latter center upon the 'directionality' limitation just mentioned, but also upon the generalizability of the results: important here are Peal and Lambert's use of only 'balanced' bilinguals, as well as questions about the representativeness of the sample of children and the difficulty of equating home backgrounds simply by holding socioeconomic status constant.

Beyond the problems in defining bilingual ability per se, other formidable difficulties arise. Do perfectly balanced bilinguals – persons in whom the two languages exist at equal levels of fluency – constitute the 'best' contrast with monolinguals? And, even assuming that we could adequately assess degrees of language competence, the measurement of intelligence remains problematic. How do we ensure comparability between groups of bilinguals and monolinguals: controlling for age, gender and some other variables may not be difficult, but what about socioeconomic status? Most measures of this may not come to grips well enough with home differences of vital importance; see the earlier discussion of disadvantage. And, again, the correlational problem: if we discover a relationship between bilingualism and intelligence, can we be sure it is a causal one and, if so, in which direction does the causality flow? Does bilingualism heighten intelligence, or does brightness increase the likelihood of functional bilingualism?

These and other difficulties mean that strong conclusions about bilingualism and cognition are not warranted. Some feel that there is a link between the two, but that any cognitive advantages attaching to bilingualism are rather slight; others have been mainly concerned to show that there is not a cognitive *price* to be paid for bilingualism. As McLaughlin (1978: 206) noted: 'almost no general statements are warranted by research on the effects of bilingualism... in almost every case, the findings of research are either contradicted by other research or can be questioned on methodological grounds'. And Paulston (cited by Rotberg, 1984: 137) added that bilingual education research is characterized by 'disparate findings and inconclusive results... a study can be found to support virtually every possible opinion'. Research (and experience) has shown that bilingualism does not lead to decreased or weakened capacities. Most people in the world are bilingual or better, and – while some are well-educated and socioeconomically secure – the social circumstances of the majority are modest. It would seem illogical to believe, then, that bilingualism per se is likely to involve any significant increase in basic cognitive and intellectual skills. It would surely be perverse, however, to deny that bilingualism can represent *another* dimension of ability and, in that sense, represent a repertoire expansion. I see nothing controversial about this, just as I would see nothing controversial in the statement that a number of years' devotion to the study of great literature can lead to a heightened or, at least, altered sensitivity to the human condition.

Bilingualism and Identity

Being 'maternally' or 'simultaneously' bilingual from the earliest age, learning another language (whether in an 'additive' or a 'subtractive' context) through force of circumstance, expanding a linguistic repertoire as part of one's scholarly or intellectual life – these are all important matters, and there is a large and often finely-detailed literature devoted to them and their many ramifications. But there is another approach to bilingualism, one that considers it from a less communicative but more symbolic perspective, and one that links the personal aspects of language and languages with features that operate at more collective levels.

If it is the linguistic condition of most adult human beings and if – as we are now regularly informed by some of the stranger practitioners of the linguistic arts – monolingualism is an aberration, an affliction of the powerful and a disease to be cured, then one might reasonably ask why bilingualism should elicit any specific attention.[4] As something easily available to the poor and the illiterate, something that can be almost effortlessly acquired by the youngest and most inexperienced members of society, it might seem to have attracted rather more than its share of academic attention. Naturally, I don't mean to suggest that language per se is now a completely open book to us. The workings of this marvellous facility, which sets us apart in tremendous degree if not in basic principle from even those clever apes and dolphins, are not fully transparent in either development or use. Still, within the broader study of language, what happens once could perhaps easily be seen as (*mutatis mutandis*) happening again. Why should a second or subsequent language warrant more than an extending footnote to the broader linguistic enquiry? Why should bilingualism occupy its own niche in the larger linguistic, psycholinguistic and sociolinguistic enterprise?

It is true, of course, that second-language acquisition cannot, in principle, be a precise replica of first-language learning, for the simple reason of being second. Heraclitus told us a long time ago that you can't step into the same river twice. The point I wish to make here, however, is that the technicalities of the broad linguistic enterprise – vital and interesting as they are – cannot, themselves, fully explain the depth of interest in multilingual accommodations. To understand them more fully, we have to move beyond language itself, beyond psycholinguistics, beyond experimental studies and educational programs that illuminate and facilitate repertoire expansion. We have to go beyond instrumental matters altogether, and consider issues of psychology and sociology, of symbol and subjectivity. In a word, we must think about the relationship between language and identity, and how it may alter when more than one variety is involved.

Speaking a particular language means belonging to a particular speech community and this implies that part of the *social* context in which one's *individual* personality is embedded, and which supplies some of the raw materials for that personality, will be linguistic. Since disentangling the linguistic features from all others is hardly an easy task, it has always been difficult to make a compelling case that membership in a given speech community has – in isolation, as it were, from other socializing threads – concretely specifiable consequences for personality. But some intriguing questions present themselves nonetheless.

Much of interest rests upon the degree to which bilinguals possess either two (theoretically) separately identifiable systems of language – from each of which they can draw, as circumstances warrant – or some more intertwined linguistic and, perhaps, cognitive duality. There is a 'popular' (and sometimes scholarly) notion that bilingual individuals must have a sort of split mentality: two persons in one, as it were. Grosjean (1982) and others have certainly reported that bilinguals themselves sometimes feel that language choice draws out, and draws upon, different personalities. But, as Baker and Jones (1998) and Hamers and Blanc (2000) tell us, the evidence here is anecdotal at best. Indeed, we could go a bit further and point to the large logical and rational difficulties that some two-in-one arrangement would create. But, in a 'weaker' sense, as it were, there are certainly indications that language choice may implicate different *aspects* of the personality. Bilinguals responding to interviews and questionnaires are liable to give slightly different pictures of themselves, depending upon the language used.

They may make different responses to objective or projective probes. Responses may be more emotional through one variety (typically, but not inevitably, their maternal language). They may more strongly affirm their sense of ethnic identity in one language than in another. And so on: see the various studies usefully summarized by Hamers and Blanc (2000). The fact that different social settings and variations in language-emotion linkages lead to different patterns of self-presentation does not logically imply separate personalities, but it does suggest an enhanced repertoire of possibility.

People belong to many groups at once, and all groups – all, at least, that have boundaries possessing some degree of permanence – have characteristics that mark their identity. Where language issues are central, the most salient group is often the ethnocultural community: overlaps of importance may occur because of simultaneous membership in gender, socioeconomic, educational, occupational and many other categories, but the base here is an ethnic one. The interesting point, then, is the significance of a bilingualism that links an individual to more than one ethnocultural community. How does it feel, we might ask, to have a foot in more than one camp? Is it this that could lead to that psychological splitting that we have rejected on more purely cognitive grounds? Or is such duality the origin of the expanded acuity and awareness that some have claimed for bilinguals? The short answers to these sorts of questions are all positive, or potentially positive, in a world in which complicated patterns of social relations are made still more intricate by a very wide (theoretically infinite, in fact) range of linguistic capabilities.

Of course, a great deal of bilingualism has very little emotional significance, impinging only slightly upon feelings of identity or 'belonging'. The purely instrumental fluencies needed to conduct simple business transactions, for instance, do not represent a psychologically important excursion from one's ethnic base camp. This is probably a rather larger category than is often thought. For example, the breadth of fluencies among that broad swathe of humanity that we have already labelled as multilingual does not in itself imply emotional or psychological depth. It may, more simply, reflect the exigencies of a complicated public life, with language capabilities developed only to the instrumental extent needed.

In a typical example of multiple instrumental linguistic abilities, we find a Mumbai spice merchant whose maternal variety is a Kathiawari dialect of Gujerati. At work, he usually speaks Kacchi; in the market place he finds Marathi useful; at the railway station, Hindi is usual.

English is the medium when he flies with Air India to New Delhi, and he sometimes watches English-language films at the cinema. He reads a Gujerati newspaper written in a dialect somewhat more 'standard' than his own. Our merchant sometimes has dealings with a Bengali colleague who routinely speaks both 'high' and 'low' Bengali – a man whose 'primary' wife speaks a dialect strongly marked as a female variant, and whose 'secondary' wife normally speaks Urdu. His office manager speaks Dhaki and his servants variously use Bhojpuri, Awadhi, Maithili, Ahiri and Chatgaya. This Bengali businessman has a cousin in Orissa, an Oriya speaker married to a Tamil: they use English at home, but their children are more likely to speak Bengali; they employ a Hindustani nurse and a Nepali watchman. I have drawn upon Pandit (1979) and Pattanayak (1986) for these examples; see some further illustrations in D'Souza (2006).

There are many bilinguals, however, whose competence is more deep-seated and whose abilities go beyond instrumentality, and these are typically the people one has in mind when considering the relationship between bilingualism and identity. There are two broad divisions of relevance here: the first comprises those bilinguals with a kinship attachment to each group (we will detour here around a large literature, and accept either real or perceived attachments); the second is made up of people who have, in a more formal way, acquired another linguistic citizenship, as it were. The latter division involves a so-called 'élite bilingualism', best exemplified by socially well-placed persons whose formal instruction would traditionally have been seen as incomplete without the acquisition of another language or two. Typically, then, élite bilingualism involves prestigious languages, although the term could reasonably be extended to cover the competence of those whose maternal variety is of lesser-used status, as well as of those lucky, intelligent or industrious enough to have achieved upward mobility through education.[5] Élite bilingualism is often discussed in comparison with 'folk bilingualism', where the latter signifies a necessity-induced reper-toire expansion; indeed, the distinction seems apt, particularly when one considers that, historically, the élite variety often had as much to do with social-status marking as it did with a thirst for knowledge and cultural boundary crossing. In earlier times, not to have known Latin or Greek or French in addition to one's vernacular would have been unthinkable for educated people, but unthinkable, perhaps, in the same way that it would have been unthinkable not to have had servants. Among the members of this group, there were (and are) many driven by purer scholastic motives, of course. But acknowledging this also means acknowledging that élite bilingualism need not rule out the motives of necessity more usually associated with the folk variety. It is just that necessity itself becomes a little more rarefied, a little more intellectual in nature.

In any event, it is not difficult to see that the life's work of a sensitive scholar could arise from, or give rise to, an extended group allegiance or sense of belonging. Indeed, this scenario also theoretically applies to those whose excursions across boundaries are motivated by nothing more than interest. After all, given a threshold of intelligence and sensitivity, the difference between the scholar and the amateur lies in formality of focus. The general point here is that we can ally ourselves, by more or less conscious effort, with another group, and that a formally cultivated bilingualism can act as the bridge here.

What of the other broad category, those bilinguals who have some real or understood blood attachment to more than one language community? Setting aside the technicalities associated with the onset and timing of bilingual acquisition, it is surely the case that the deeper the linguistic and cultural burrowing into another community, the greater the impact upon identity. This, in turn, suggests that those whose bilingual competence is nurtured early will, other things being equal, have a firmer foot in the two (or more) camps. It will usually be the case, of course, that one camp will have psychological and emotional primacy. But there are some cases where home itself is difficult to establish, at least in any simple unidimensional sense – some cases, that is, where bilingual or multilingual capacities, linked to their several cultural bases, develop so early and so deeply that a primary allegiance is hard to discover. (Think of George Steiner again, arguing [1992: 128] that his sort of 'primary multilingualism' may be 'an integral state of affairs, a case radically on its own'.) There are generally two ways to consider the situations of those whose bilingualism begins at the parental knees. The first is simply that two or more base camps are home simultaneously; the second is that one primary home indeed exists, but it is constructed, in a manner unique to the individual, from materials taken from several sources.

As we move towards the bilingualism of more 'ordinary' individuals, we move more obviously towards the idea of a unitary identity – woven from several strands, to be sure, but inevitably influenced by one language and culture more than by others. But, if we move from the Steiners of the world, whose literary and linguistic power, and the ability to reflect in meaningful ways upon its multifaceted origin, is simply unavailable to most people, we must not imagine that we have moved away from enlarged identities per se. It is both the obligation and the fulfillment of intellectual life, after all, to express what those who are less articulate also feel. There is, of course, a great deal of circumstantial evidence supporting the contention that it is the identity components, the symbols of the tribe, that energize languages beyond their instrumental existences: obvious examples are the relationships between language and ethnicity, and language and nationalism.

At these most potent levels of 'groupness', there are clear distinctions between monolingual majority-group speakers in their own 'mainstream' settings, and minority-group members who are very often bilingual by necessity (to take two extreme cases). For the former, the instrumentality of language coincides with its symbolic force, its identity-bearing capacity: the language of shopping is also the language of culture and tradition. For most people in this situation, the language-identity linkage is not problematic; indeed, it is seldom considered at all. Minority-group speakers, however, rarely have the luxury of inattention. For them, aspects of language and culture are often more immediate, and the crux of the matter is often a split between the language or languages that circumstances force them to use, and their maternal, traditional or cultural variety. The upshot, then, is that bilingualism and multilingualism can throw matters of identity into sharper relief, because of perceived threats to one (or more) languages. The result is that – beyond the linguistic technicalities, beyond variations in patterns of acquisition and development – the most compelling issues surrounding bilingualism are social and psychological. Beyond utilitarian and unemotional instrumentality, the heart of bilingualism has to do with identity and belonging.

Notes

1. It is not inappropriate to add a fifth item to this list: signing. While many recent treatments of language and communication take the deaf community into account, its status as a minority group is still often ignored. There now exists, however, a significant 'deaf culture' – described as a 'healthy sociological community' by the Canadian Association of the Deaf, and its sister organizations around the world – one that rejects the earlier and still socially prevalent 'medicalization of deafness'. Members of this culture reject such labels as 'deficient' or 'disabled' and, following this logic, some also reject medical interventions aimed at reducing or eliminating deafness: attitudes towards cochlear implants are particularly polarized here.
2. A notorious example here draws upon the distinction between the experiences of anglophone Canadian pupils in all-French classrooms, and those of Spanish-speaking youngsters in English-medium classrooms in the United States. See further details in my discussion of 'immersion' and 'submersion'.

3. There have been those who demurred. In the 17th century, for instance, John Milton (1644/1958) and Samuel Butler argued that expanded repertoires do not, in themselves, imply intellectual breadth. In 1662, in his unfinished *Satire Upon the Imperfection and Abuse of Human Learning*, Butler pointed out that 'the more languages a man can speak/his talent has but sprung the greater leak'; see Butler (1850) and, for an early 19th-century reworking of the idea, prefaced by some lines from Butler's poem, Hazlitt (1901).

4. Wierzbicka (2005) is certainly *not* among the 'strange' crowd here, but she does illuminate in very interesting ways the restrictions associated with monolingualism. She is particularly critical of theorists who write about language, particularly about basic matters like language development and the relationship between language and thought. She takes Pinker (1994: 21) to task, for example, noting that 'his lack of cross-cultural and cross-linguistic awareness undermines the validity of [his] theorizing'.

    Elsewhere, Wierzbicka (2005: 9) says that Pinker 'never looks at any languages other than English... all 517 works cited in the references [to *The Language Instinct*] are in English'. Steiner (1992: 127) had earlier argued for the study of *languages* rather than *language*, noting that many contemporary linguists are hampered here because few of them have 'inhabited the husk of more than one speech'. He cited the great Russian linguist, Roman Osipovič Jackobson: 'Chomsky's epigones often know only one language – English – and they draw all their examples from it' (Mehta, 1971: 79).

5. It is important to realize that any distinction between 'élite' and 'folk' bilingualism cannot be mapped seamlessly onto some 'school versus street' division. Immigrants very often learn their new language at school, but this is generally a matter of mundane necessity with nothing élitist about it. It is not the classroom per se that accords élite status; see some further comments in Edwards (in press-a).

Chapter 13
Bilingual Education

Introduction

In bilingual education, teaching *through* two languages is a permanent or semi-permanent feature in the classroom. Although such duality can arise for non-instrumental reasons, as part of a general educational philosophy – one designed, for instance, for those destined to become 'élite' bilinguals – a more common scenario involves need-driven programs of bilingual education. It may be considered pedagogically important, for example, to provide at least early schooling through the medium of children's first language (see also below). As well, if pupils' maternal languages are of minority status, then the desire to sustain and encourage those varieties, while also providing access to a 'larger' medium, may also suggest bilingual education. The idea here is usually that the basic educational foundations can be most firmly laid when the children's ethnocultural identity is not jeopardized.

Bilingual education has a very long history indeed, but it is in the relatively well-understood circumstances of Greek-Latin bilingualism (or diglossia) that we see the clearest foreshadowing of circumstances that have remained pertinent ever since. Lewis (1977) provided a brief survey, up to the time of the Renaissance, which remains useful. A more recent treatment is that of Adams *et al.* (2002). Focusing on the Roman age, Adams (2003) has produced a magisterial, if technically rather specialized, account. (The term *diglossia*, incidentally, is used to describe a relatively enduring relationship between two languages or dialects – traditionally, 'high' and 'low' variants. Etymologically, of course, it is simply the Greek for 'bilingualism'.) Cicero, Quintilian and other Roman luminaries preferred Greek to Latin as the medium of schooling, pedagogy was generally modeled on Greek curricula, and formal instruction in Greek often preceded that in Latin. Since children from patrician homes were often cared for by Greek servants and tutors, they were frequently bilingual before first going to school, anyway. Still, concerns were sometimes expressed about children speaking Latin with Greek intonation and – a precedent for more contemporary worries – about the possibility of somehow over-burdening a child's time and 'limited' cognitive capacity. Haarhoff (1920: 226) cites a scholar's complaint that bilingual education may be all right for clever students, but schoolboys of average ability find it frustrating and exhausting. Many came to feel that the imposition of Greek condemned the young to boredom and drudgery.

Acting upon this point of view, however, took some considerable time to develop. While the spread and influence of Latin was a natural consequence of Roman imperial progress, Greek retained a hardy cultural prestige. The Greeks themselves generally had a low opinion of Latin, only learning it for instrumental reasons – an attitude that was reinforced by the obvious intellectual attractions their own language continued to hold for others. In fact, the Romans themselves accepted the social superiority of Greek for a long time after they had dominated the hellenistic world. Of course, Latin spread and ultimately produced many lively offspring through which it continues to live, but it is generally agreed that this happened without much formal planning. Lewis (1977: 179) notes that the Romans 'made no effort to set up Latin in rivalry to [Greek] or to Latinize their political and military gains'. They were content, as some (but not all) subsequent empires have been, to let their military, mercantile and administrative conquests carry Latin throughout the empire.

The Romans knew that, just as all roads led to the eternal city, so all commerce led to Latin. Indeed, in a clever piece of reverse psychology, they sometimes erected barriers to their language, so that its acquisition became 'a privilege to be sought, like citizenship. The inhabitants of Cumae [the home of the famous sibyl, near present-day Naples], for instance, had to request permission to use Latin in public affairs and in the pursuit of trade' (Lewis, 1977: 180). This *laissez-faire* approach to their own language, coupled with a continuing reverence for that of the Greeks whom they had more or less completely subjugated by about 150 BC, meant a bilingualism that endured for a longer time than some might have predicted. As Latin expanded its own literary and intellectual scope, however, as it began to attract learners for other than purely instrumental purposes – and as competent Greek teachers became harder to find – Latin-Greek bilingual education declined. By the end of the 5th century it was virtually gone.

In all contemporary examples of bilingual education, there are recurring questions, many of them discussed among Roman educators. When should bilingual education be introduced, and for how long should it continue? What instructional weight should be given to each language, and how best can formal dual-language education be integrated with pre-existing and 'non-bilingual' curricula? Should bilingual education be available to (or, indeed, required of) all students – or just the brighter ones? Should it be extended across a broad range of pupils, or designed principally for those whose mother tongue is a 'minority' one, or a variety that will not adequately serve in all areas of life?

Varieties of Bilingual Education

When a large number of possible student populations, in a large number of different sociocultural contexts, is combined with various educational policies and desired educational outcomes, it is not difficult to understand the emergence of many types of bilingual education. In fact, Mackey (1970) listed almost 100 categories and sub-categories; see also Fishman's approaches here, as summarized by García and Schiffman (2006). It is Baker's (2006) typology that I shall draw upon here, however: it is easy to understand and quite comprehensive.[1] He lists 10 broad possibilities, including, for the sake of completeness, three *non*-bilingual educational settings in which minority-group children have often found themselves. Before we turn to these, however, we should note that the most basic of 'programs' is no program at all: children are simply put into existing mainstream classrooms, and left to sink or swim.

Not swimming, but drowning

The American setting is broadly instructive here. We find, first of all, that many leaders railed against any departure from the traditional mainstream classroom, a situation in which children must adapt to the school, while the latter remains essentially unchanged. Presidents from Teddy Roosevelt to Ronald Reagan have argued for an American linguistic and cultural crucible in which 'dwellers in a polyglot boarding house' emerge as unhyphenated, English-speaking Americans, and against any educational provisions 'dedicated to preserving [immigrants'] native language and never getting them adequate in English'.[2]

It may seem odd at first blush, but it is also easy to find similar sentiments among American immigrants themselves: many members of *U.S. English*, an organization dedicated to making English the official language of the United States, are themselves immigrants. This is often noted as evidence that the organization ought not to be seen as a narrow, chauvinistic and linguistically intolerant body – but the psychology is surely interesting. I cannot delve deeper here, other than to point to one or two possibilities.[3] It may be, for instance, that immigrants who have successfully re-established themselves in a new society become more patriotic than the natives; after all, there is no true believer quite as zealous as the convert. They may, then, evolve into ardent proponents of the traditional American monolingualism. An observation by the right-wing commentator Norman Podhoretz (1985) is instructive here, too: he notes that his 'humiliating' lack of English, in old-style submersion classrooms, was a spur towards social mobility and success. His point may be entirely accurate, of course, but it is also the case that success in adverse conditions sometimes tends to the maintenance of those conditions, not to their eradication. On the one hand, there is often the feeling that, if I had to struggle, why should things be made easier for you? On the other, if I manage to progress *per ardua ad astra*, it may be very much to my benefit to have my achievements remain as singular as possible. There is a glory in having reached the peak by oneself, a glory that will be diluted once the top of the mountain is crowded. Consider, as analogy, the woman who, by dint of incredibly hard work and sacrifice, finally makes a place for herself in a prestigious law firm, previously an all-male bastion: is it inevitable that she will turn around and help some of her sisters up the ladder, or is it possible that she will pull the ladder up after her? (See also Chapter 6 – particularly note 7.)

In the contemporary American context, the single most interesting case of an immigrant rejecting the bilingual education enterprise is that of Richard Rodriguez. In an initial paper about his boyhood, he argues that

> supporters of bilingual education imply today that students like me miss a great deal by not being taught in their family's language. What they seem not to recognize is that, as a socially disadvantaged child, I regarded Spanish as a private language... what I needed to learn in school was that I had the right, and the obligation, to speak the public language. (Rodriguez, 1980a: 29; see also 1980b)

Rodriguez admits that he would have felt less apprehensive if teachers had spoken to him in Spanish when he first entered the classroom but, in retrospect, feels that this would simply have delayed learning the 'great lesson of school: that I had a public identity' (Rodriguez, 1980a: 30).

In a biographical memoir, Rodriguez (1982) described a life in transition – from the son of poor Mexican immigrants, to post-graduate study, to a successful career as a writer of elegant and thoughtful English. Learning English at school loosened his ties with parents and relatives who remained Spanish speaking; or, as Rodriguez puts it, a growth in 'public individuality' (via English) was associated with a diminished 'private individuality' (through Spanish). But he also sensed the 'deepest truth', that 'intimacy is not created by a particular language; it is created by intimates' (p.32). This insight, Rodriguez claimed, was lost on the 'bilingualists' (he refers to bilingual educators). They 'simplistically scorn the value and necessity of assimilation' (p.26), they are 'filled with decadent self-pity', they 'romanticize public separateness' (p.27). Well, it is easy to see why Rodriguez's account ruffled feathers. It is also possible to fault him for over-generalizing from a sample size of one. But his account remains a provocative one.

In a later book, Rodriguez (1993) continues his personal examination of life and culture in America. As in the earlier work, his 'findings' are not to everyone's taste. Sometimes, indeed, the expression is all, and the content is dubious: 'European vocabularies do not have a silence rich enough to describe the force within Indian contemplation' (Rodriguez, 1993: 23). But consider the following:

> There are influential educators today... who believe the purpose of American education is to instill in children a pride in their ancestral pasts. Such a curtailing of education seems to me condescending; seems to me the worst sort of missionary spirit... To argue for a common culture is not to propose an exclusionary culture or a static culture... Now the American university is dismantling the American canon in my name... Hispanics and Asians have become the convenient national excuse for the accomplishment of what America has always wanted done – the severing of memory, the dismantlement of national culture. The end of history. (pp.169–171)

Among those critical of Rodriguez's posture, Ortego y Gasca (1981) reminded him that, for many years, Mexican-American children were left to 'drift like flotsam' in schools that made no accommodation for their lack of English, with the well-documented result that Hispanic drop-out rates were getting on for three times the overall American average. Blanco (1983: 282) notes the irony that Rodriguez's early loss of Spanish fluency was only remedied later: 'in high school, he learned to read and write Spanish as an English speaker would. Rodriguez is a perfect example of the American mentality that allows the squandering of valuable linguistic resources, only to try to recapture or create them later'. Kaplan (1983) makes another useful point when he says that, while Rodriguez correctly draws attention to the political abuses and inadequacies of bilingual education, he misses its essential value. Of course, Kaplan (1983: 126) notes, the bilingual education story is degraded by many non-altruistic words and deeds, but there is such a thing as 'genuine bilingual education – the dream that every child may have the opportunity to "have" two languages or more'. So, in an area where there *has* been progress, where the demagogues have not had it all their own way, Rodriguez's writings are a cruel cut indeed. With his personal experience and his 'power with words', he might have helped the cause; instead, in books that have attracted popular-press accolades, he has done just the opposite.

Millions of immigrant cases demonstrate that old-style 'submersion' works – if, by 'works', we mean that it produces at least a minimal degree of fluency in the mainstream variety. It was not part of its intention, of course, to bolster the languages that those to be submersed first bring with them to school. Despite the rather blustery manner of success stories like Podhoretz (who was not an immigrant himself, by the way, although his first language was Brooklyn Yiddish), we strongly suspect that the psychological costs may have been high and, more to the point, unnecessary. Nunberg (1986) rightly points out that linguistic submersion was far from an 'ennobling' experience, and not an especially efficient one, either. Perhaps some sort of bilingual provision at school would have helped all those early immigrants to America, both in their linguistic progress and in their psychological identity. But this, of course, is to miss an important point, and one to which I shall return: for most of those who comment upon any form of language accommodation in official or semi-official settings – whether they approve of it or not – such accommodation is more political than pedagogical. Roosevelt, Reagan, Podhoretz and company have a vision (of America, in this case) of a linguistically efficient and socially united country, a 'nation' in which one language is seen to integrate, and where more than one is considered both unnecessary and potentially balkanizing.

To return to Baker and his typology: two of the three *monolingual* contexts that he lists are also 'submersion' in nature, but programs here differ from the *laissez-faire* version (or non-version) that I have just discussed. Programs of so-called 'structured immersion' (still, in fact, *sub*mersion, as Baker points out) enroll only minority-group children, sometimes making 'withdrawal' or 'pull-out' provisions, by which the pupils are given extra, or compensatory, or specially designed mainstream-language lessons. The aim is clearly one of cultural assimilation and monolingualism in the mainstream variety. The third monolingual setting is a 'segregationist' one, in which minority-group students are forced to learn in their maternal language. Baker's discussion here treats this as a manifestation of *apartheid* policies through which the powerless and the subordinate are kept in their subaltern positions.

Not drowning, but swimming?

Among the remaining (seven) educational contexts that Baker discusses, three are listed as 'weak' forms of bilingual education. There are, for instance, 'transitional' programs, in which minority-group speakers are allowed instruction in their maternal variety until they are proficient enough in the mainstream language to move into 'regular' classrooms. This is a gentler alternative to sink-or-swim submersion, but critics will point out that its aims are still essentially assimilative, and it is relatively unconcerned with the languages that the children first bring with them to school. In fact, it can be understood as a sort of compensatory provision, to be phased out as early as possible. Transitional programs have been the mainstay of bilingual education in the United States, since it was first federally mandated in 1968, but they are frequently found in some form or other in other settings – wherever, in fact, immigrant children come to school in liberal-democratic societies.

A second form is 'separatist' education, a less violent manifestation of *apartheid*. Although Baker states that the goal here is 'limited bilingualism' – which justifies his characterization of 'separatist' programs as weak bilingual ones – his brief discussion emphasizes first-language *mono*lingualism, and it would be more appropriate, therefore, to place such programs in the monolingual basket. Think of voluntarily self-segregating religious groups (the Mennonites, the Old Order Amish, and so on) in which the 'apartness' is desired, and in which an endorsement of German (say) over English is a buttress to sociocultural isolation. A good argument could be made here that language practices depend upon the strength and degree – the orthodoxy, perhaps – of religious self-isolation; that is, in those societies whose borders are more permeable than others, we might expect to see educational provisions that *do* allow for some 'limited bilingualism'. There is, of course, a very wide range of possibility here. I have just been reading about some sub-groups within the larger Anabaptist tradition: some reject virtually all modern technology, some use trucks and vans but not cars (although they may gladly accept lifts), some drive cars if they are black, some allow electricity (but only in emergencies), some use machines if they run off batteries rather than the mains, some will describe themselves on websites so long as others construct and maintain them, and so on. A bewildering variety, many of whose intricacies are baffling to the outsider, and one that may be reflected in many different educational thrusts.

The third format here is one with which many readers will be familiar: mainstream classrooms within which there is some foreign-language teaching: the three-times-a-week language lesson from Mme Chiasson or Herr Schmidt – or, if the school can't quite run to native-speaking teachers, perhaps Mrs Foyle and Mr Tanner do the honors, making sure always to stay a lesson or two ahead of the pupils. These are the familiar provisions made in many educational regimes for *majority*-group youngsters. Baker places this format in the 'weak' division of bilingual education, arguing that the aim is, again, a 'limited bilingualism'. Many readers will no doubt agree that something like 'severely limited' or perhaps 'crippled' bilingualism would be nearer the mark, considering that 8 or 10 years of school French may enable you to rhyme off the pluperfect subjunctive of some irregular verb, but won't allow you to order a *croque-monsieur* and a Kronenbourg at the Brasserie Lipp.

The four 'strong' varieties of bilingual education listed by Baker are united in their aim of encouraging bilingualism. In 'dual-language' programs (obviously not a uniquely distinctive description), both minority- and majority-group children are in the same classroom, and both languages are used. Well-known examples in the United States are the Spanish-English arrangements first introduced in the early 1960s in southern Florida. There are a great many variants under the dual-language rubric: the most important variables are the amount of time given to each language, and the timing of each (by subject, on alternate days, etc.). A second strong form is 'heritage-language maintenance' education, designed for minority-group speakers. Here, the native language is used in the classroom, while the mainstream variety is gradually developed. A third is the 'mainstream bilingual' provision, in which majority-group children learn in two (sometimes more) 'big' languages. As Baker notes, classic examples here are found in social contexts (like Singapore and Luxembourg) in which the general population is bi- or multilingual, and in various types of 'European' or 'International' schools catering for socially or educationally élite parents who want their children to become bilingual.

The final 'strong' form is 'immersion' education, in which majority-group children learn through a foreign language. The term was first applied to anglophone children in Montreal learning through French, but what was an educational experiment in the 1960s has spread throughout Canada, and beyond. Putting English-speaking children in French-only classrooms in Canada is not the same thing as placing Spanish-speaking children in English-only schools in America. Why? Most importantly, while Spanish is of minority status and, consequently, under ongoing threat in the American mainstream, the English of the Canadian students is not at any such risk. 'Immersion', then, suggests that one is dipped into a new linguistic pool, but comes to the surface again with original capacities still intact. ('Submersion', as already implied, means that something original is being drowned and lost.) Beyond a desirable emphasis upon the production and subsequent encouragement of an ongoing bilingualism (and, indeed, biculturalism), Canadian-style immersion programs profit from being voluntary, and from having committed and well-trained teachers who are themselves bilingual. These are not features of submersion education.

The Effectiveness of Bilingual Education

There was, and is, great interest in the effectiveness of programs of bilingual education. Is there a best model? Are some programs clearly more effective than others? The assessments by Crawford (1989, 1992a, 2000) and Dicker (2003) provide many useful details on (American) bilingual education. The authors are clearly in favor of 'strong' programs, and concerned to protect them against unfriendly legislation and the assaults by the U.S. English organization. The many statements and papers reproduced in Crawford's (1992b) collection will also be found very useful. The recent surveys by Petrovic (2005), San Miguel (2004) and Wiese and Garcia (2001) emphasize historical developments in the American context, and Ferguson (2006) provides an overview from a European perspective. For more global overviews, Baker (2006) and Baker and Jones (1998) are central sources, of course.

It is worth saying straight away that many questions about bilingual education aims and outcomes are understandable but naïve: there are so many categories, so many variations in the populations catered for, so many different social contexts, so many ways of attempting to measure effectiveness. Even committed commentators have sometimes wondered if 'prolonged reliance on the native tongue reduces students' incentives to learn English' (any other 'mainstream' language could, of course, be substituted here), or if bilingual learning 'confuses the mind and retards school achievement' (Crawford, 1989: 86). There is, too, an apparently counter-intuitive aspect here, at least for those who subscribe to the efficacy of the 'time-on-task' principle – that is, the idea that the best predictor of success in learning is the amount of time devoted to the subject. Most of the eminent opponents of bilingual education represented in Imhoff's (1990) anthology, for example, could not be brought to understand that circumstances can easily undercut this principle.

Others may find it confusing, too: I note that, in his recent account of raising his own three children bilingually, Caldas's (2006) comments about time-on-task suggest a confounding of immersion and submersion learning contexts. (In fact, research suggests that, contrary to simplistic time-on-task conceptions, positive transfer can occur; as Yeung *et al.* [2000: 1005] point out in a defence of early education in the mother tongue, 'skills in a second language may be developed on the basis of skills already acquired in [the] first'.)

The ambiguities surrounding the effects of bilingualism itself (as noted by McLaughlin, 1978; see also above) are, if anything, multiplied in the educational context. Thus, Wiley and Wright (2004) have recently pointed out that, among a multitude of evaluation studies, one can easily find some research support for almost any critical position on educational effectiveness; see also Paulston's observation, in Chapter 12. Baker (2006: 267) notes that

> all programs could be effective... depending on the subtle chemistry of interacting ingredients, environments and processes. Attempts to prove the superiority of a particular model are pointless and unproductive.

As I shall illustrate further, the whole area is highly politicized, and many agendas are driven by sociopolitical considerations and sympathies, not solely by pedagogical ones. Hakuta (1991: 210) has written about 'being very doubtful that evaluation research in bilingual education will ever emerge out of the stranglehold of political forces', and Tannen (1998) has suggested that discussions of many controversial matters have become so politically and socially polarized that resolution sometimes seems impossible.

In a related point, those engaged in research exercises are rarely neutral, even by the general standards of social science. Indeed, Baker (2006: 287) notes that experimenters' hypotheses often 'hide their expectations' – a rather more pointed criticism (see also Hakuta, 2002). For such reasons, those interested in assessments of bilingual education have increasingly turned to so-called 'meta-analyses', investigations that simultaneously consider the methods and findings of numerous individual studies, looking for strengths and weaknesses, plausible generalities and unlikely assertions. It is both interesting (at least) and worrying that the original studies, adequately conducted to be suitable input for these grander meta-analyses, form a laughably small percentage of the total. In one large-scale re-examination, only 8 out of 175 evaluation exercises were judged relatively unflawed; in another, 18 out of 600 reports were considered 'methodologically sound and deserving of further examination'; in a third, 7 out of about 150 reports 'met minimal criteria'; and so on (Lam, 1992: 184). And meta-analyses themselves are hardly immune from attack. Baker's discussion of this very contentious territory reveals how biblical (or byzantine) the possibilities for analysis and interpretation have become. Referring, for instance, to a 500-page report produced by a panel of experts on bilingual education, he notes that its findings were immediately seized upon 'by opponents and proponents of bilingual education as justification of their quite different positions' (Baker, 2006: 268). Bilingual education has, in truth, become a large growth industry, and in its machinations its 'customers' often seem quite forgotten.

Can *any* generalities be extracted from research findings, not just those arising from highly politicized American programs of bilingual education, but also from the many variants elsewhere? For 'mainstream' children learning in immersion classrooms – anglophone youngsters learning through French in Montreal, for example – the evidence suggests that their bilingualism will be much deeper and broader than that acquired by their counterparts in more traditional settings. At the same time, there is no reason to suspect that there is any retarding influence upon their English skills, or upon their grasp of subject matter presented in a language that is not their first. Understandably enough, there may be some temporary 'delays' in some areas, but these typically disappear (in comparisons with non-immersion children) quite quickly. There seems little question, in fact, that immersion programs are the best option for mainstream children wishing to become bilingual through schooling. Canadian parents have increasingly understood that, which is why – even at a time when bilingualism-as-federal-policy has come under increasing strain – interest in immersion has increased.

The picture is not perfect, however. It is not true, for example, that immersion graduates have a native-like comprehension of their second language. Indeed, the French produced by Canadian immersion students has been variously described as 'somewhat artificial' or 'Frenglish' or 'fossilized interlanguage' (see Edwards, 1994a). And, at a broader social level, immersion education has not proved to be the hoped-for catalyst to bring the two Canadian linguistic communities closer together. More specifically, Genesee (1981) notes that some of the expected behavioral differences between immersion students and those involved in more traditional second-language learning at school have proved rather slight. Despite their technical superiority, the former do little reading in their second variety and, like the latter, report instrumental rather than integrative reasons for learning it. Although more likely to use more French in personal encounters, immersion pupils tend to do no more than the others to seek out or initiate such encounters. (It is true, of course, that immersion students in many contexts will not have a great deal of opportunity to use their acquired fluency; this hardly applies in Montreal, however, the setting in which Genesee reports.) This only reinforces the observation that schools – even immersion schools – are unlikely in themselves to promote societal bilingualism; see Mackey (1981) and our earlier discussions.

If we turn now to minority-group children, more the focus in this book than are 'mainstream' pupils, it seems safe to say that early education in the mother tongue is beneficial; see also Hakuta (1991) for a useful tabular presentation of 'research conclusions', a list that he uses when speaking to groups about bilingual education. This is a bald statement, to be sure, and will require all sorts of qualification according to circumstance and context. But a moment's reflection will suggest that an own-language alternative to a brutal sink-or-swim scenario must have a lot to recommend it, if only in terms of an increase in psychological comfort and a decrease in the distress related to lack of understanding. These less tangible, less measurable elements are often left out of all those research studies and 'meta-analyses': they are naturally concerned with what can be mathematically assessed, but a tunnel vision can easily develop in which more qualitative aspects are increasingly ignored altogether. I don't mean to imply, of course, that 'quantitative' researchers are themselves unaware that important matters remain out of the reach of their statistical nets, only that neglect can produce the same effects as ignorance. An interesting social-science development here has been to try and refine those nets, and make them capable of catching things like self-esteem, happiness, security and so on. We are then confronted with the ludicrous spectacle of the 'operationalization' of such intangibles – with the inevitable result that whatever is measured in their name is but a simulacrum (in the true sense of the word: a copy without an original).

An emphasis upon results is necessarily an emphasis upon the future – if we do such-and-such *now*, what will the effect be *later*? While this is eminently reasonable, it does rather neglect things that may be desirable in themselves. I have already asked if we would remove swings and roundabouts from the playground if definitive studies revealed that they had no measurable effect on post-primary academic achievement.

Transition and maintenance

Many of the questions surrounding bilingual provisions for minority-group children deal essentially with programs that are either *transitional* or *maintenance* in nature. As we have already seen, supporters of both varieties hope to ease the earliest passage of children from home to school, and thereby defuse some educational difficulties. They all subscribe to the famous UNESCO (1953: 11) dictum that holds that 'it is axiomatic that the best medium for teaching a child is his mother tongue'.

We should note that there have been dissenting views. Gupta (1997) points out that, in some multilingual settings, it can be difficult to determine the mother tongue (recall the simultaneously trilingual George Steiner here). In contexts of dialect variation, it may be that the 'mother tongue' to be used in the classroom will be – perhaps has to be – a standard form quite unlike the nonstandard variants of the pupils and, in heterogeneous settings, mother tongue education may mean separate programs for different ethnic groups, a potentially divisive and undesirable situation. D'Souza's (2006) discussion of the very complex Indian situation is also instructive here. Apart from echoing Gupta's point about the very determination of a mother tongue – what is the mother tongue, she asks, for children who have no home, and who are forced to learn the language(s) of the streets? – D'Souza notes that the instructional medium must often be the dominant language in the state. Wee (2002: 285–286) has discussed the issue as it affects people in Singapore; he writes, for example, that 'it is entirely possible for some Chinese Singaporeans to agree that Mandarin... is their mother tongue, but at the same time to be unwilling to consider themselves native speakers of Mandarin'.

Even Phillipson (1992), whose career has been devoted to uncovering a linguistic 'imperialism' and 'linguicism' that serves the 'large' languages of the world at the expense of the 'small' ones, has felt obliged to record that *not* providing English-medium education to African-language-speaking children was interpreted locally as a colonialist desire to maintain groups in subordinate positions. (To ignore indigenous languages altogether can be equally insensitive, of course.) We have already seen here how parents themselves may reject maternal-language education for their children. Sometimes this is based on a more or less accurate assessment of the relative worth of competing varieties, and sometimes it reflects a regrettable ignorance of the possibilities inherent in some sort of bilingual program; in all decisions, however, we must acknowledge that the children's best interests are uppermost in the minds of their parents. Baker (2006) touches upon the matter, too, referring to research with indigenous populations in the American southwest. And an observation by Spolsky (1989b: 451) – also in a southwestern context – reminds us that many 'ordinary' people have issues to deal with that are rather more immediate than language choice:

A Navajo student of mine once put the problem quite starkly: if I have to choose, she said, between living in a hogan a mile from the nearest water where my son will grow up speaking Navajo, or moving to a house in the city with indoor plumbing where he will speak English with the neighbors, I'll pick English and a bathroom!

These sorts of issues complicate the linguistic picture in very real ways. Interestingly enough, they all have consequences for children and their communities at a group level, ones that involve, but also go beyond, purely pedagogical matters affecting individual youngsters.

To return to the distinction: there are, of course, ideological differences between those who support transitional bilingual education and those who argue for maintenance programs. The first group believes that the real aim – to be achieved as soon as is reasonable – is a transition from the bilingual classroom to the mainstream one. The second envisages programs that contribute to a more enduring bilingualism, ones whose objective is the expansion of the linguistic repertoire, not the replacement of one monolingualism by another. The transitional-maintenance dichotomy is not always clear, however, the result being a further sub-literature devoted to the *timing* of bilingual education provisions. Within transitional programs, Baker (2006) points out, there are 'early-exit' and 'late-exit' options: in the former, two years is the allotted time for bilingual education; in the latter, passage to the 'ordinary' classroom can be delayed for another three or four years. In some circumstances, however, a bilingual program that lasted until children were nearing or at the end of primary school might be styled 'maintenance'. Under the essentially compensatory provisions of federally funded bilingual education in the USA, the tendency has clearly been to effect a transition as soon as possible, but it is often found elsewhere, too: 'where there is a majority language and much immigration, then education is often expected to provide a linguistic and cultural transition' (Baker, 2006: 222).

Jim Cummins is one of the best-known specialists in bilingualism and bilingual education (and someone I have known for a very long time), and I well remember a conversation I had with him many years ago, a conversation that revealed some misapprehensions (on my part) fuelled by the transitional-maintenance distinction. Since the 1980s, my own writings had supported bilingual education provisions, but I argued for a transitional approach, on two related grounds. The available evidence seemed to suggest that transition to the mainstream was not always *necessary* for the gradual development of literacy in the mainstream language, not that transition itself need be harmful. So, given the exigencies of limited resources and funds – and, more importantly, the possibilities for that ethnic 'separateness' that Gupta (1997) has pointed to – I felt that an argument might be made, perhaps on the basis of a desirable social cohesion, for bringing all children under the one scholastic roof at some point. This went down rather badly with some of my academic colleagues, most of whom supported a continuing pluralism, in which bilingual education – *maintenance* bilingual education, that is – was seen to have an important linguistic and cultural part to play. Transitional programs were considered as cultural fifth columns. Then I discovered, through my discussions with Cummins, that what I was advocating as *transition* was, in fact, what most of my colleagues considered *maintenance*. That is, I had always rejected any facile 'early-exit' arrangements, always argued that minority-language-speaking children should be given all the appropriate help possible (see, e.g. Edwards, 1984, 1990). On the basis of practical matters having to do with resources, fairness across groups and so on, I didn't think that bilingual education could be justified for a more or less indefinite term. But neither did the others!

I felt a bit like M. Jourdain, Molière's *bourgeois gentilhomme*, who excitedly discovers that he has speaking prose all his life.

Bilingual Education in America: In Transit to Trouble

The American *Bilingual Education Act* (1968) was largely compensatory and transitional in tone and intent. As Venezky (1981: 201) noted, the goal was not 'cultural retention, encouragement of a pluralistic society, or improvement of native languages'. Now, if a transitional intent is the official mandate, but a maintenance-program preference animates many of those involved, most of the academic commentators, and some of the assessors, then we can see that, quite apart from the technical problems of evaluation, profound philosophical differences will also bedevil accurate assessments of program effectiveness. Although the emphasis in this section is upon the richly documented and very illustrative American setting, it is clear – with another reference to Baker's observation, above – that such ideological variation can be expected to confound dispassionate investigation well beyond American shores.

Amendments to, and reauthorizations of, the American bilingual thrust (in 1974, 1978, 1984, 1988 and 1994) have all occasioned further debate about what the overall purposes were, what they are and what they *should* be. The most pointed debates have been about how much time and energy should be devoted to the language that children first bring with them to school. The tendency over the last 40 years has been to increasingly restrict any 'maintenance' tendencies, and to support the maternal language 'only to the extent necessary for a child to achieve competence in English' (Baker, 2006: 193; see also Venezky, 1981, on the ever-narrowing focus). In fact, in later years, federal funding was increasingly given to programs in which maternal varieties were used very minimally, sometimes not at all (Wiese & Garcia, 2001). Reyes (2006) provides an example. During the 2000–2001 school year, about half of the eligible Hispanic children in New York City were in (transitional) bilingual education programs; the other half received English as a Second Language (ESL) instruction within the monolingual mainstream. By 2004–2005, participation in bilingual education had declined to about 30% and ESL-format enrolment had increased to about 66%.

We have already noted President Reagan's antipathy towards bilingual education, a stance that both reflected and reinforced broad governmental attitudes towards provisions for minority-language children. The most recent development – President Bush's 'No Child Left Behind' (NCLB) initiative of 2001 – replaces existing bilingual education legislation and buttresses still further the tendency towards English-medium schooling (see Evans & Hornberger, 2005; Throop, 2007; Wright, 2005b).[4] What was once called the Office of Bilingual Education and Minority Language Affairs changed its name, in 2002, to the Office of English Language Acquisition. Along with many others, Katz (2004) laments this monolingual orientation: not only does the new legislation roll back bilingual education initiatives, it also undercuts second-language acquisition for native English speakers, most of whose foreign-language instruction (such as it is) will not begin until secondary school. In a world in which – for all the power of English – multilingualism remains a powerful asset, this most recent emphasis has an isolating tendency for America and Americans. And, as part of this NCLB initiative, and as another reflection of the times, there is a very strong reliance upon standardized assessment devices: Crawford (2004) notes that the phrase should read 'No Child Left Untested'.

In fact, quite apart from the monolingual emphasis that has upset some observers of this new program, its general pedagogical implications are extremely disturbing. Schools are now required to annually test their pupils on reading and arithmetic ability; the results must then be made public and, more specifically, made public by *group* (black children, Hispanic children, ESL pupils, and so on). This is an important business: school funding can be dependent upon the scores achieved, schools can be subject to massive rearrangements, with teachers fired and new ones hired, private educational companies can be brought in to take over operations, and so on (see McNamara & Roever, 2006). There is no doubt that some successes have been achieved, in terms of improving children's assessed abilities, but it seems that those successes are largely with children who are 'border-line' cases. Those who are most seriously underskilled are not benefiting. There are, as well, some entirely expected outcomes.

The program rewards narrow 'teaching for the tests', and it 'privileges' the two areas singled out for assessment, reading and arithmetic. These are, of course, very important (arguably the *most* important) subjects, but less time is now given to other school subjects. In some cases, social studies and science have almost been eliminated, with virtually the entire school day given over to reading and maths. Schools have also been found to cheat in test administration and reporting. Given the initial motivation of the enabling legislation, however, the most obvious problem is that, while states must test, they are free to construct the tests themselves. In 2005, Mississippi children given Mississippi reading tests made the highest proficiency scores in the country; when, however, they were tested with the more rigorous National Assessment of Educational Progress instrument, they fell to the very bottom of the 50-state ledger! International observers have found it bizarre, to say the least, that laws requiring regular testing across America – with the results of that testing having the potential to effect massive alterations in schools in the very short term – are not accompanied by requirements for the use of uniform assessment instruments; that one of the consequences of the program has been to encourage a retrogressive drill-like emphasis upon what is to be tested; and that reading and arithmetic, important though they are, have been allowed in some instances to shoulder aside other classroom topics and practices. For an excellent and up-to-date journalistic account of NCLB matters – including some mentioned in this paragraph – see Wallis and Steptoe (2007).

Kozol (2007) provides a brief but succinct indictment of the way in which the NCLB provisions greatly reinforce the distressing trend towards the privatization of education in the USA, and the expectations of those in the 'education industry'. He cites the glee with which market analysts see 'the K-12 market [as] the Big Enchilada' (Kozol, 2007: 8).

Similarly, Larson's (2007) collection demonstrates the attractiveness of this 'industry' for the corporate vultures now hovering over the ramifications of the NCLB legislation. The broader issue of educational privatization is the subject of Weathers's (2007) working-paper. He writes from a 'critical discourse' perspective, which leads him to make statements about 'the colonization of democratic discourse' and 'the larger struggle over control of the symbolic space' (Weathers, 2007: 67, 89). I would argue that, while textual analysis of highly charged issues in the public arena is likely to confirm the debating and discourse strategies typically used when large amounts of money are at stake, microscopic examination of the 'symbolic space' is less important than forthright action in 'real space'.

A collection by Valenzuela *et al.* (2007) focuses on NCLB as it affects minority-group children. Particular attention is given not to test scores and other educational statistics, but rather to qualitative and ethnographic insights. Among the most cutting commentaries is that of McDermott and Hall (2007: 11), who, after invoking the horrors of *Hard Times* and Gradgrind's insistence on fact, go on to note:

> What a good idea, to leave no child left behind, and what a revolting development that its main effect has been to record just who is being left behind according to increasingly constrained versions of knowledge measured on high-stakes tests... NCLB eviscerates curriculum and teaching in classrooms.

The increased emphasis upon English proficiency, coupled with the intensive testing ethos of the new arrangements, certainly does mean more difficulties for children who are not native speakers of English (see Fine *et al.*, 2007). Not only are their particular situations given less attention, their inclusion in the school populations to be tested can result in lower overall 'scores' in what is termed the 'Adequate Yearly Progress' assessment. In terms of 'breaking out' ESL pupils, as they comprise one of the groups to be 'disaggregated' in the assessment reports, another problem is that the classification of these pupils, and the measurement of their language abilities, is not at all clear under the enabling legislation. Indeed, ESL children, unlike Hispanic or black youngsters, constitute a group that is by its nature in flux; see McNamara and Roever (2006). As Evans and Hornberger (2005) have written, the incentive for schools to do well on the annual testing exercises could – and should – theoretically mean that *more* attention will be paid to ESL children. It is in the collective interest, after all. But such a theoretical consequence is often swamped in the practical demands for more and more time to be given to the two key themes: literacy and mathematics. There is a number of good analyses of the issue, the rapid growth of which indicates the contentious nature of the NCLB legislation and its implementation. Particularly recommended are Abernathy (2007), Chrismer *et al.* (2006), Hess and Petrilli (2006), Poetter *et al.* (2006), Valenzuela *et al.* (2007) and Yell and Drasgow (2005). Grenoble and Whaley (2006) provide a brief but useful discussion of the new legislation in the context of *native* non-English-speaking youngsters and attempts to 'revitalise their flagging mother tongues'; see also Abedi (2004).

The transitional emphasis in America (and, indeed, in most other contexts) and the increasingly restricted scope of bilingual program initiatives have culminated in the legislated rejection of those initiatives in some quarters. In California, for example, a wealthy entrepreneur, Ron Unz, spearheaded a campaign that led to the passage of *Proposition 227* in 1998. The act stressed the need to teach children English 'as rapidly and as effectively as possible... children shall be taught English by being taught in English' (Baker, 2006: 196), and made bilingual education virtually illegal; for useful discussions of this important event in the life of bilingual programs in the USA, see Crawford (2004), García (2000) and Orellana *et al.* (1999). Since then, bilingual education in Arizona and Massachusetts has also been restricted. These were not particularly close contests: the winning majorities in the three states were 61, 63 and 68%, respectively. Dade County, Florida is famous as the home of the first American bilingual education program in contemporary times: the Coral Way school experiment started in 1963, well before federally funded programs were established. But even there, anti-bilingual legislation was enacted in 1980. While not specifically directed at schools, the law (passed with a 60% majority) compels official use of English only, and prohibits the financial encouragement of any other language or of 'any culture other than that of the United States' (Crawford, 1992a: 91; the text of the ordinance can be found in Crawford, 1992b: 131). A few years later, Floridians endorsed English as the official state language, by an overwhelming margin (84–16%).[5]

The most interesting examples here are the first and the last mentioned in the preceding paragraph. California and Florida are states with very large Hispanic populations, settings in which unofficial uses of Spanish have steadily expanded, but also settings in which anglophone reactions to it have predictably been the strongest. It is of some interest, too, that considerable numbers of Spanish-speaking voters in California have rejected bilingual education – naturally wishing to heighten their children's chances of success in English milieus, and apparently swayed by 'time-on-task' arguments in this regard. These have included Unz and Tuchman's (1998) assertion that all-English instruction was necessary for full participation in the 'American Dream'.[6]

The actual breakdown of the California results shows that about two-thirds of the white voters were in favor of the Unz proposal. The figure was 40% among Hispanic voters, and the levels of support in the Asian and African American communities were 57 and 48%, respectively. These are all interesting numbers, to be sure. A large minority of Spanish-speaking voters – the major beneficiaries of bilingual education – rejected it. African Americans, in the more or less immediate aftermath of the Oakland School Board controversies (see above) remained divided over the issue. 'Asians', who represent a number of language communities, and who could also theoretically benefit from bilingual education provisions, showed a little more sympathy for them than did their white counterparts, but their voting patterns also reflect their well-known educational and socioeconomic success, a success that is clearly not dependent upon any special educational programs.

Even allowing for some sort of 'backlash' on the part of English speakers, some commentators have found it strange that legislation that many have seen as springing from unpleasant nativist sentiment should have arisen in the two most powerful Hispanic enclaves. This is a complicated matter that I cannot delve further into here, but it should be remembered that strength of numbers – allied, in the Mexican-American case, with proximity to the homeland – does not seem to alter the basic dynamics of language shift in the United States (a point that applies equally well to the other large minority group that remains near its origins: the French-Canadians of New England). The rapidity of such shift may be affected by these factors, but its essential character, one that is shared by all the other immigrant groups in the country, is unaltered. Thus, Porcel (2006: 107) reminds us that, while Miami Cubans 'might have greater incentives and the best conditions for language maintenance among all U.S. Hispanics', they still show 'a clear pattern of transitional bilingualism'. (It is possible, of course, that the phenomenal growth of the Hispanic population in the United States, and its ever-widening geographical distribution, may yet create an entirely new situation in that country. This is the fear that motivates those agitating for English-only legislation at state and federal level.)

There are two other very salient facts about the Miami 'case'. First, while many other American cities have large immigrant populations, its anti-bilingual legislation of 1980 occurred when the Florida metropolis had the largest proportion of immigrants of any of them – more than one-third (Castro, 1992). And second, while Spanish was often heard in Los Angeles, Houston and elsewhere, it fell differently on Floridian ears: elsewhere it was

> the language spoken by the people who worked in the car wash and came to trim the trees and cleared the tables in restaurants. In Miami, Spanish was spoken by the people who ate in the restaurants, the people who owned the cars and the trees, which made, on the socio-auditory scale, a considerable difference... what was so unusual about Spanish in Miami was not that it was so often spoken, but that it was so often heard. (Didion, 1987: 63)

This is an important and perspicacious comment by the famous American writer, one that sounds an ominous note for all immigrants as they begin to ascend the socioeconomic ladder. They are not supposed to violate 'the norm of immigrant subordination' – and, when they do, reactionary consequences can be expected to follow (Castro, 1992: 181). In fact, the pattern is a remarkably robust one and involves more than a little conflict between the old-guard mainstream and the socially mobile newcomers. Those immigrants who were once on the receiving end of social prejudice themselves are just as likely to pass it on to newer waves of arrivals. Those escaping from the mid-19th-century famine were likely to read 'No Irish Need Apply' signs in Boston windows; but, a generation or two later, the politically savvy Irish were just as unpleasant to Slavs and Jews. It goes without saying that the Irish are not to be singled out here; almost all groups reveal similar unpleasant dynamics, and no one's hands are particularly clean when it comes to discrimination of this sort; see Morrison and Zabusky (1980) for a few indirect admissions of prejudicial attitudes and actions in this regard.

One of the most popular arguments of those opposed to bilingual education is that its implementation has created a substantial number of educators, administrators, researchers, consultants, evaluators and others. Their activities have reinforced those of teachers of foreign languages in the United States, a constituency that has generally been in a bad way for a long time. There is, then, a large group of educated people with strong vested interests in the continuation of well-funded bilingual education (and other language) programs, and the voices of such articulate defenders, it is claimed, are often 'privileged' over those of more ordinary citizens. Thus, Unz noted – correctly, so far as it goes – that his *Proposition-227* initiative was one of the most popular in California history; he also wrote that:

the number of academics, professors of education, who support bilingual education outnumbers those who oppose bilingual education by probably about a thousand to one... When I attended public forums... usually the audience was 95% against [the Unz proposition], sometimes it was 98%, sometimes 100%. And that's simply because the people who are most motivated to attend public forums dealing with bilingual education tend to be advocates of bilingual education, including a lot of bilingual teachers and bilingual administrators and bilingual academics. (Unz & Snow, 2002)

There are many intriguing threads that could be followed up here, not least of which are the likely correlations between typical academic political postures – left of center, broadly speaking – and support for such things as bilingualism, pluralism, the plight of the educationally disadvantaged and so on. It is worth noting, however, that Unz's observations are not his alone and that, indeed, they are corroborated by those views that are quite antithetical to his. Grinberg and Saavedra (2000) point out, for instance, that the empowering possibilities of bilingual education have been lost in a welter of bureaucracies and competing interests, all intertwined with the allocation of substantial amounts of money. Indeed, new 'fields of expertise' have emerged that have little to do with the legitimate beneficiaries of bilingual initiatives. Theoretical exercises and disembodied analyses of program effectiveness have become incestuous academic exercises. All of this means that, while educators and researchers may congratulate themselves on their activities, there now exists only 'the illusion that the needs of displaced and subjugated "others" have been addressed' (Grinberg & Saavedra, 2000: 433). Furthermore, if we put aside the contemporary polemics of Unz, and the jargon-ridden discussion of Grinberg and Saavedra, we find that clearer and more dispassionate expressions have existed for a long time. Only three years after the passage of the original enabling legislation for American bilingual education, Robert Roeming (1971: 78–79), a linguist, language teacher and editor of *The Modern Language Journal*, pointed to:

the interest of a professional group of second language teachers who may find it advantageous to perpetuate support for language study. This is not an unwarranted suspicion. It is supported by colleagues and laymen who find the funding of the Bilingual Education Act very providential at the point where the support of the National Defense Education Act was diminishing.

Varghese (2004, 2006) discusses the current situation of bilingual education teachers in America, noting that, whatever their motivations may be, the growing politicization and controversy have proved considerable hindrances to the recruitment and training of new members of the profession. Minaya-Rowe (2002) and – before the 1998 California legislation – Macías (1989) have also touched upon the matter. It is not difficult to see the creation of a vicious circle here. The increasing criticisms of bilingual education, its proponents and those who work in and around it lead to political outcomes like those in California and Florida. An educational arena becomes stigmatized, and its scope shrinks along both financial and social dimensions. There is room for fewer teachers, and fewer novices are attracted to what have become contentious classrooms, often in the public spotlight. The field thus shrinks further.

Education and Politics

I mention all this by way of introduction to a very abbreviated discussion of the politics of bilingual education. In my view, this is something that greatly overshadows the pedagogical aspects of the exercise; see Casanova (1991) and Petrovic (2005), who comments on the naïveté of those proponents of bilingual education who neglect issues of political power. As Baker (2006: 197) succinctly puts it: 'bilingual education is not simply about provision, practice and pedagogy but is unavoidably about *politics'*. This is because the treatment of people who are 'non-mainstream' in one way or another tells us more about views of their place in society, of desired (or unwanted) alterations in society itself, and of social hopes, fears and expectations, than it does about more pragmatic concerns with the maximization of classroom resources, the optimization of programs and assessments of educational best practice. The important matters, then, have to do with sociocultural definition, group boundaries – and identity. Under these rubrics, programs of bilingual education are seen (by their supporters) as potential agents of social change, as bulwarks of ethnolinguistic pluralism, as forces for group identities thought to be at risk.

Those who endorse these possibilities believe that cultural and linguistic diversity is a social good, that it reflects the appropriate liberal-democratic acknowledgement of the heterogeneity of populations in many societies, and is therefore to be encouraged wherever possible, that it represents a more finely-tuned attention to individual and collective human rights, and so on. As both legislative and public reaction has demonstrated, however, arguments for alterations to a more traditional mainstream status quo typically come up against strong opposition. From surveys and other forms of public-opinion assessment, it is clear that such alterations are viewed as both unnecessary and undesirable, especially where the prevailing monoculture is a powerful one. Such perceptions are often connected with more specific fears of social fragmentation and divisiveness. Sometimes these derive from the desire to protect the mainstream group (reasonable in some circumstances – ranging on racism in others); sometimes they are expressed out of sympathy for a minority population which, it is thought, might be better served by being brought into the mainstream as soon as possible. I need hardly add, I suppose, that expressions of sympathy for minorities are often simply more politically correct cloaks for nativist sentiments; or that a narrow concern with a particular minority group – and a lack of concern for others – is often presented under the guise of an endorsement of cultural pluralism per se.

The greatest concerns and the bitterest wrangling about bilingual education provisions are social in nature. The existence of those complexities already touched upon means that, even if purely pedagogical matters were the main focus, there would still be ample scope for debates over measurements and outcomes. But they would not be so vitriolic in nature if larger questions about social mobility, pluralism, ethnolinguistic diversity and assimilation – in short, about the face of society itself – were not intimately intertwined with cognitive and instructional ones. People can have fierce arguments about methods, but they only go to war over substance. Linguists and educators themselves have always acknowledged that bilingual education is not primarily a linguistic matter. Commenting on the early American bilingual education scene, for instance, Ferguson (1977: 43) stated that

> social, political, psychological, economic and other factors must surely outweigh the purely linguistic factors in any analysis of bilingual education efforts and in any actual policy planning for bilingual education.

The bluntest point of sociopolitical debate is, I suppose, between *any* educational provision for minority groups and none at all. Podhoretz and others may approve of the sink-or-swim approach that galvanized successful immigrants, but some will have other memories of submersion in foreign-language classrooms, and of punishments meted out for the use of their maternal variety. Indeed, among both indigenous and immigrant minority groups, egregious measures were often taken. In

Wales, for example, the 'Welsh Not' was a stick or sign hung around an offending child's neck. It would remain there until transferred to the next victim who lapsed into Welsh and, at the end of the day, the last stigmatized youngster might be beaten. In Scotland, a similar device (the *maide-crochaidhe*) was used and, in Ireland under the British, a 'tally-stick' – notched to indicate every time a child spoke Irish – acted as a record of misdemeanors (Edwards, 1989). Ngũgĩ wa Thiong'o (2004) has confirmed that Gĩkũyũ speakers in Kenya suffered in the same way, and Stoller (1977) wrote of such punishments for Spanish-speaking children in the USA. The practice may have been widespread, indeed, although some caution is needed in accepting *all* the accounts; see Edwards (in preparation).

Ngũgĩ wa Thiong'o is well known as a writer who abandoned writing in English as a sociopolitical statement. Many other 'colonial' writers have struggled with hard language choices, too. In the foreword to his famous novel, *Kanthapura*, Raja Rao discussed the problems of conveying one's 'spirit' in a foreign language. He admitted that English was not a completely alien language – intellectually it was in many ways the primary language for educated Indians (as Sanskrit and Persian were before) – but he argues that it was not the language of 'emotion'. He continues:

> We are all instinctively bilingual, many of us writing in our own language and in English. We cannot write like the English. We should not. We cannot write only as Indians. We have grown to look at the large world as part of us. Our method of expression therefore has to be a dialect which will some day prove to be as distinctive and colourful as the Irish or the American. (Rao, 1938: vii)

English has moved much further and deeper into the Indian consciousness since Rao expressed those sentiments (see Ashcroft *et al.*, 2006). The implicit question he raises, then, has even greater importance: to what extent can a population maintain a strong and independent psychosocial identity if its original language has been largely displaced – or, at least, displaced in important domains – by another? Many would argue that a 'full' or 'authentic' identity requires the maintenance of that first variety, but where does that leave the Indians, the Irish and others? And what of other groups who share languages, the Brazilians and the Portuguese, the Austrians and the Germans, even the Australians and the Canadians? Is it not possible for a population to take a 'foreign language' and make it their own – in style, in pronunciation, in idiom (see Edwards, 1985)?

Overall, the best evidence shows that bilingual education can be pedagogically useful and, in its ('late-exit') transitional format, can be easily justified. It can quite reasonably, then, be presented to the general public as a sensible and fair reaction to linguistic heterogeneity at school. Given appropriate resources and contexts, any return to 'submersion' approaches is unconscionable – and this conclusion logically permits answers to many of the questions posed in the last two paragraphs. The more active proponents of societal diversity and pluralism have objected, however, that transitional bilingual education formats, even in their more enlightened forms, actually expedite assimilation and should therefore be replaced with maintenance programs. They make a pedagogical argument, as well. It is claimed that maintenance bilingual education is necessary for the maximization of English proficiency – a point of view that still seems counter-intuitive to some, but one predicated on the assumption that a firm and continuing support of children's maternal competences is the best foundation for mastery of mainstream varieties. Here, I have already suggested that the matter is a bit more subtle: there is no compelling evidence for the necessity (on mainstream-language-proficiency grounds) of maintenance education; on the other hand, 'mainstreaming' may not be necessary for such proficiency. This allows us, then, to move on to considerations of maintenance education on other grounds: as a support for ethnolinguistic pluralism and a force against assimilation. We return, in a word, to broader sociopolitical themes, and this means that debates emerge more from ideological assumptions than from dispassionate considerations of 'data'. It would be incorrect, however, to conclude that there are in fact no 'data' of interest here.

First, there is no evidence to suggest that, in liberal-democratic societies, many markers of ethnic-group identity (including language) can be significantly maintained through formal intervention unless the group concerned is a voluntarily self-segregating one. (If a group has segregation forced upon it – a morally indefensible situation – then intervention is obviously in operation.) Some aspects of ethnicity, particularly symbolic and private ones, may remain for a long time, but they are not markers susceptible to formal efforts at sustenance (see Edwards, 1985). Macro-level language shift, on the other hand, is inevitable for most minority groups. Second, the idea that programs of bilingual education can significantly affect the larger social landscape presumes an altogether too powerful role for the school. When social pressures and historical developments have created a situation in which a community is seen to be at risk of language shift, we cannot expect schools to halt this. We can, of course, expect schools to reflect and reinforce larger trends existing outside their gates.

A third point here is that the use of bilingual-education initiatives as a form of social engineering can be seen as an inappropriate use of official power, one that reflects the assumption that diversity is not only to be approved of in a tolerant fashion, but also to be actively promoted to the level of official policy. This is hardly the place to go into further detail on this very interesting matter, but I should point out that a rich literature is now developing around the most appropriate responses that liberal democracies should make – are obliged to make – when faced with ethnocultural heterogeneity (see Edwards, 2003b, 2004a). Relatedly, it is obvious that the implementation of maintenance programs would benefit from a general public sentiment in favor of diversity and pluralism and – which would be sure to follow – from whole-hearted government support for ethnic-group interests. Once again, I can only touch (below) upon a large literature, this one dealing with the measurement of attitudes and beliefs about all aspects of 'non-mainstream' language and culture. Allowing for the fact that political correctness has cloaked negative attitudes that once were expressed more openly (see Edwards, 1990) – the implication being that there is as much intolerance in this area as there ever was – there are at the same time indications of some movement here. It seems, however, to be more towards a passive goodwill than anything else.

Canadian surveys, for example, have revealed some public sense that 'unofficial' languages and cultures can be strengths, but Berry *et al.* (1977: 43) famously reported that 'when money and effort are at stake... respondents switch to neutrality and even rejection of multiculturalism' (see also the similar findings reported by Breton *et al.*, 1980; Edwards & Chisholm, 1987; Edwards & Doucette, 1987). Palozzi's (2006) study of American attitudes towards English and other languages in the United States reveals the apparent ambiguities that so often occur in these surveys. Many of his respondents, for instance, endorsed the idea that it was 'un-American' for citizens not to speak English, while *also* agreeing that it was a good thing for immigrant children to know their parents' maternal languages. It would be easy enough to focus upon the first sort of response, and argue that Americans are mainly in favor of some 'English-only' arrangement, but a more complete assessment would suggest that a 'strict assimilationism' is in fact rejected, and a somewhat more liberal view of 'foreign' languages emerges. A useful analysis of the Australian scene (Goot, 1993: 226) points, as well, to the different understandings that are so often possible:

the most comprehensive survey of Australian attitudes to multi-culturalism has been variously interpreted as showing that multiculturalism enjoys a high level of support or very little support at all.

This sort of situation occurs because the sociopolitical stakes in survey outcomes are often quite large, because conceptions of multiculturalism and multilingualism are often vague and imprecise, because questions are not framed specifically enough (often on purpose) – and, quite simply, because 'many, even most, see multiculturalism as something of a mixed bag' (Goot, 1993: 251). Relatively frequent polling in Canada, Australia and other 'receiving' societies does not suggest any sea change in mainstream public opinion. Movement typically occurs only when attitudes become *less* favorable, which, of course, they predictably do whenever events cast the cultures and languages of minority groups in negative or threatening lights. A contemporary example is found in the current European and American antipathies occasioned by Islamist terrorism. One of the predictable, if unpleasant, consequences is a rise in narrow nativist sentiment – or worse (see Koopmans *et al.*, 2005, for a recent survey of the European scene). An example from recent history is the forced evacuation and internment of Japanese-Canadians and Japanese-Americans from their homes on the Pacific coast during the Second World War. And, of course, there are many well-known examples from the more remote past.

Notes

1. My Baker-based discussion here is a much simplified condensation of his own, and it omits many details, sub-categories, and the like; see also Hornberger (1991) for a bilingual program typology.

   A very recent book on bilingual education (García, 2009) provides a comprehensive overview of the issues. If the rather breathless blurbs on the back cover are to be believed, it has been written with an unusual combination of wisdom and heart, it will soon achieve classic status and, indeed, the author has 'unemployed a lot of researchers', since there will be no need for another book on the topic for a decade. But while García's book certainly presents a great deal of useful information, readers should be well aware that a strongly favorable stance is evident throughout. At the beginning, the author outlines her main thesis – 'that bilingual education is *the only way* to educate children in the twenty-first century' (García, 2009: 5; original italics) – and her conclusion discusses its 'transformative potential' (p. 387).

   Some may also find the fluency of the argument to be less than what might have been hoped for from a language specialist. It is one thing (perhaps...) for a blurb writer to use a non-existent verb ('unemploy'). But what is one to make of the author's use of 'languaging' and 'translanguaging' – terms that are at once ugly and wholly unnecessary? Should we be wary about taking advice from someone who writes that 'people language for many purposes' (García, 2009: 31) or that 'individuals and communities... usually language bilingually, that is, they *translanguage* when they communicate' (pp. 43–44)?

2. The first citation here is from a speech made by Roosevelt in early January, 1919 – just nine days before his death, in fact – but he had made many other similar remarks as early as 1907 (see also Davis, 1920). Ronald Reagan's observations can be found in his official papers (Reagan, 1982).

3. See, however, the interesting collection by Morrison and Zabusky (1980) in which about 140 immigrants tell their own stories. A few of them are famous (Alistair Cooke, Edward Teller, Lynn Redgrave), but the vast majority are ordinary working people. Their attitudes towards language vary considerably, of course, but most are strongly pragmatic.

4. In 2007, the *American Educational Research Journal* devoted a 175-page section (in volume 44, [3]) to the 'No Child Left Behind' program. Of particular interest for my purposes here are the papers by Hursh and Balfanz *et al.* The first places this new educational initiative within the context of those neo-liberal privatization and free-market emphases that seem so odd when applied to children in classrooms; the second focuses on the impact of NCLB upon the poorest of schools and the weakest of pupils.

5. The rise and the ambitions of the *U.S. English* movement constitute a natural opposition to bilingual education programs in America, although members of that organization have sometimes argued that they are not against 'foreign' languages per se. Fuller details of *U.S. English*, its successes and failures, and reactions to it from various quarters, constitute an interesting story in themselves. See Chapter 11 for some discussion of the machinations of U.S. English at the state level; see also Edwards (1990, in press-b).

6. Gloria Tuchman, a Mexican-American teacher, joined forces with Unz's 'English for the Children' movement.

Chapter 14
A Concluding Statement

Since I have provided short chapter overviews at the beginning of this book and since, more particularly, readers will find there rather obvious indications of my own assessments of many of the important themes, this last chapter can be a brief one.

The general underpinning for the work, and my motivation for undertaking it, rest upon my belief that teachers, students and researchers could profit from a broad-brush treatment of the important language issues having educational components or ramifications. To this end, I have provided what I hope is a useful combination of a fairly comprehensive and jargon-free survey with a rich and extensive set of citations for those who need or want them. Of course, I make references to recent research throughout the book, but perhaps it is also necessary to repeat that my reliance on many publications that some may see as venerable or, indeed, antique, is intentional. Many early insights have yet to be bettered, and have inappropriately fallen from general view. Many more modern ones have, I believe, strayed from the paths of the greatest immediacy and relevance for researchers and practitioners – unless, of course, the latter are themselves engaged in what is sometimes narrow work of very limited generalizability, sometimes work that smells strongly of the lamp. But it is not for such readers that this book has been written.

Many great writers, dramatists and other social commentators have observed, in one form or another, that the measure of a society is best discovered in the ways it treats its less fortunate members. This is certainly true when we consider those whose language brings them to the particular attention of the educational system. The attitudes and reactions toward language and dialect varieties derive, of course, from broader underlying ones, and this is why I devote the opening chapters to the manner in which we have understood social disadvantage and, indeed, created it. The word itself is now in bad odor in some quarters, but I argue that, if used appropriately, 'disadvantage' remains an accurate and useful description. It would seem perverse to deny the reality of social inequalities, or to ignore the stratifications that unfavorably position some groups of people. We do such groups no service by romanticizing their plight, or by suggesting that their disabilities are merely 'different abilities'. To make such a case is to reveal a posture that cannot be sustained outside the academic cloisters, and it usually accompanies ideological perspectives having little real connection to the lives of those who are apparently meant to be the beneficiaries of attention. In fact, there *are* many disadvantaging features and characteristics that are non-randomly distributed across society, and some have linguistic aspects.

Mealy-mouthed neologisms and periodic relabellings do little service, either to scholarship or to those being described. But it would be an even greater error to allow broad criticism here to undercut necessary refinements in our understanding of social disadvantage, linguistic and otherwise. In my opening chapters, then, I try to make it as clear as I can that disadvantage is real, but that it is neither the product of inherent genetic deficiency nor the result of crippling environmental deficits. (Of course, these can obviously accompany and reinforce it.) It is, rather, a phenomenon that can only occur in stratified societies, can only emerge when social comparisons become possible. It reflects the judgments of those in power upon those who are relatively powerless. As considered here, then, disadvantage is a social-psychological entity. It can thus be considered separately from the tangible or physical consequences of substantive genetic or environmental deficiencies.

But this means, in effect, that social disadvantage can be even *more* real, even more debilitating. This is because causes that are at once intangible and pervasive can long outlast those that we can more clearly identify and, if necessary, combat. We have learned a great deal over the years about the inaccuracy and the iniquity of most 'genetic' arguments, and intervention is always at least theoretically possible where environmental problems retard physical or mental growth. No, with social disadvantage, we are in the murky but potent realms of social perception, and the great lesson here is that *perception is reality*. When we think of social disadvantage, then, we can eliminate – as I try to do in the first few chapters – actual, substantive deficiencies as the main fuel of disadvantage, logically arriving at the position that such disadvantage represents social *difference*. Languages and dialects of low prestige occupy that status because they are not spoken by those who have the ability to assign terms like 'standard' and 'nonstandard'. There is nothing inherently wrong with any of them, however – one of the great truths of modern linguistics that should be much more widely disseminated – and we are right to utterly reject the term 'substandard'.

But it is much harder, and perhaps impossible, to root out those deeply felt beliefs, attitudes and prejudices that can undercut scholarly insight. Any survey taken along any High Street will quickly reveal that most people continue to have strong views about 'correct' and 'incorrect' speech and language. Stereotyped, inaccurate (as we believe) and often unarticulated views can make mincemeat of academic insight, and the upshot for the disadvantaged is that many features of their social lives – including language, the 'marker' that Bernard Shaw so famously remarked upon – become stigmatized. In this way, via stereotype and ignorance, difference is effortlessly translated into deficiency. But this does not mean – does not mean at all – that attempts to inform and educate about disadvantage in general, and about the intrinsic validity of languages and dialects in particular, are fruitless. We may hope that cumulative and unremitting efforts here will eventually have desirable results; and, even if we believed that favorable outcomes were unlikely, that in itself would be no reason not to persevere. Rabbi Tarfon put the case more generally, almost two thousand years ago: the fact that one is not always duty-bound, or able, to complete a task does not mean that one is therefore morally free to ignore it altogether.

Up to the end of Chapter 5, I have largely dealt with disadvantage in a general sense, but the next group of four chapters turns specifically to language issues. Much of the central theme can, of course, be anticipated. Disadvantage per se is properly understood as reflecting neither genetic nor environmental deficiency. Rather, its variant features, seen through the judgmental lenses focused upon it by the powerful middle class, are quickly altered from simple difference into socially debilitating defi-ciency. This is nowhere reflected more clearly than in language patterns and language attitudes. The elements of the basic controversy are very simple indeed, revolving around this question: can some languages or dialects be reasonably seen as better or worse than others; is there some logic, in other words, to a sort of linguistic hierarchy?

Roughly analogous to the genetic, environmental and 'difference' perspectives on disadvantage are the grammatical, aesthetic and 'differ-ence' approaches to language and dialect variation. Thanks to the concerted effort of linguists in the 1960s and 1970s, the idea that some varieties might be less 'logical' than others – that their grammatical machinery, their internal logic, so to say, was flawed – has been soundly rejected. All varieties are valid rule-bound systems of expressions and, indeed, a moment's reflection ought to make us realize how very odd and unlikely things would be were this *not* the case for all human groups. All varieties are, quite obviously, not equal at all points along the expressive continuum, but none has been found that is either inadequate for the current needs of its speakers or unable to make all necessary adaptations as those needs alter. There are no 'primitive' languages or dialects. As to grammar or 'logic', then, the case is clear. As to the second approach: it has been argued for a very long time, and often by very influential people, that some forms of language are better than others because of their greater intrinsic aesthetic appeal. Your language is ugly and guttural, full of stops and grunts, dominated by harsh consonantal sounds; my language is smooth and fluent, musical and mellifluous, with soft vowel glides and endings. But here again, despite very marked beliefs and preferences, experimental evidence shows quite clearly that aesthetic appreciation is in the ears of listeners. Dialect varieties that, within the larger speech community, are seen as harsh and unpleasant are not so perceived by outsiders.

The reason for this difference brings us exactly to the 'difference' position itself. For we now understand that aesthetic reactions to different varieties of language are intertwined with stereotypes of those who speak them. If outport Newfoundland English is understood, in the rest of Canada, as rustic, unsophisticated and hard on the ear, then it is because its users are seen as unsophisticated people living a hardscrabble life far from the centers of power and elegance. If those living on the island of Crete are the Newfoundlanders of Greece, then we may expect that Cretan Greek will be downgraded aesthetically by those speaking the Athenian variety. And, in fact, there is a generality here: the language of those living in and around the social and political centers of power is typically viewed as 'better' in all ways – including in aesthetic quality – than that of hinterland inhabitants. There is usually a broad consensus here, one accepted just as much by members of the latter group as by those living in the capital city.

If we move beyond aesthetics per se, and consider the many other evaluative dimensions along which languages and dialects have been judged, we find that the picture becomes somewhat more complicated. Those unsophisticated regional-dialect speakers whose forms are considered less grammatically correct and less easy on the ear will often fare better on other scales: friendliness, for instance, or integrity. That is to say, the *speakers* are seen to be friendlier, or more trustworthy, even though their voice qualities strike the listener as inelegant, and even though their grammar is taken to be but a crude approximation to what is 'proper'. To repeat: the assumption in all the work done in these matters is that speech – just like many other markers of personal or social status – acts as a trigger for social stereotypes. It can only operate, of course, among those who have some knowledge of those stereotypes. That is why judges who know no Greek are unable to make the aesthetic distinctions between Cretan and Athenian that are so blindingly obvious to those in the wider Greek speech community. That is why foreign visitors, sitting among an audience of native English speakers will not appreciate the humor when the stage duchess opens her mouth and talks with a Cockney accent.

So, as with disadvantage itself, our explorations in the social life of language reveal that differences among varieties are just that – differences. But, just as the alchemy of community ignorance and prejudice easily transmutes difference into deficiency, so stereotyping and other inaccuracies of social categorization have the power to turn linguistic variation into linguistic deficit. That being so, I felt it necessary in this context to devote some specific attention to teachers, on the one hand, and to speakers of Black English, on the other. The first is easy to justify. This entire book, after all, is about the play of language in the classroom, and teachers have at least a co-starring role in that drama. And speakers of Black English? The study of their particular dialects is especially rewarding precisely because those forms have so long been looked down upon along virtually all dimensions, and that, in turn, has occurred because their speakers have occupied the lower rungs of the social ladder. A corollary is that, if it were possible to show that the dialects of Black English were just as valid as any others, that would surely be a powerful support for the broader argument that *all* varieties are fully-fledged systems of communication. And that demonstration has, in fact, taken place, to the complete satisfaction of those who are disinterested and at least reasonably intelligent. The relatively recent controversies swirling around 'Ebonics' show only that not everyone yet possesses those qualities. They have also brought to light some of the further intricacies attaching to the 'difference' position. That is, if society at large has not yet fully grasped the scholarly demonstrations bearing upon the validity of different dialects – or, in many cases, continues to exhibit a wilful ignorance – what practices suggest themselves vis-à-vis nonstandard dialects at school?

In my last group of chapters, I move from nonstandard varieties to entirely separate languages. I attempt to outline something of the historical and contemporary ways in which schools have responded to foreign languages in their classrooms, and have tried to tease out some of the important features that are particularly to be looked for in multi-cultural and multilingual societies – increasingly common in many parts of the world. One of the most interesting aspects of this discussion involves, if not a paradox, then something of an irony. On the one hand, we see the traditional, and continuing, respect that education has always had for languages, the traditional emphasis upon helping students learn foreign varieties – in short, the age-old assertion that adding a second or third language to one's mother tongue is an essential feature of a properly rounded education. On the other hand, we see – particularly in the immigrant-receiving societies of the new world, particularly in urban contexts rich in linguistic heterogeneity – that not all foreign languages are accorded equal status. Sometimes this seems to be relatively easy to justify: in the United States, for instance, it is perhaps not unreasonable to give more attention to the teaching and learning of Spanish than to the acquisition of Malay. But, in other instances, it is clear that some assortment of those prejudices and stereotypes that I have just discussed is at work. If, for example, a school were to be confronted with a number of pupils of Malay background, perhaps a case could be made for some linguistic accommodation. This, at least, is the contention of those who claim that educational rigidity coupled with social, racial and other prejudices has neglected and failed to nourish many important linguistic resources. There is a 'human' side to this sort of argument, in that something of value to children and their parents is not given appropriate consideration; and there is a larger, societal side, too, inasmuch as all that neglect may come to have strikingly tangible consequences. When America intervenes in Iraq and Afghanistan, how many speakers of Arabic and Kurdish, of Pashto and Farsi, can it call upon?

But there are other points to be considered, too. How many languages can even the most sensitive school policy cater for? How are parental and community views to be properly taken into account? Before the passage of restrictive legislation in favor of French in Quebec, immigrants often had quite fixed ideas. The Italian community in Montreal, for example, wanted its children to attend English-language schools, arguing that the areas in which they lived would ensure that French would be acquired more informally in the streets, playgrounds and through social activities generally, and that Italian would be transmitted at the family hearth. There are also questions of social integration and solidarity to be borne in mind, and these are often particularly marked exactly in those jurisdictions having the greatest social and linguistic diversity. Although not always a popular message among many scholars who write about linguistic heterogeneity, the protection and maintenance of 'small' languages, and so on, a case can be – and is – regularly made that a common language unites and helps to reduce the likelihood of social balkanization, or worse.

I take no strong stand here, myself, but I would recommend that some of those committed scholar-activists at least pay more attention to such arguments. At a fairly benign level, we could cite the example of Canada. Here is a country whose history, formidable geography and patterns of settlement have combined to bedevil the emergence of a broad national sensibility. Matters are exacerbated, of course, because of the proximity to the American leviathan. Furthermore, the original British-French duality that once defined the country is increasingly overshadowed by the influx of immigrants from all parts of the world: Vancouver, Toronto and Montreal are now among the most multicultural of all cities. To consider these variables, and to consider also the reasonable desire to move towards a shared sense of 'Canadian-ness', must surely add some layers of nuance to all discussions of the value of an enduring multiculturalism and multilingualism. And, at an entirely less benign level, we see how recent violent events in Europe have brought about renewed concerns for social 'unity', for the integration of immigrants and for the continuity of important social values now seen to be under religious and other pressures. Sometimes, of course, these concerns take very unpleasant and xenophobic shapes – but when a tolerant community like The Netherlands, for long a beacon of multicultural flexibility, begins to reassess matters, it is surely reasonable to suggest some renewed attention to general questions having to do with the accommodation of linguistic and cultural diversity in liberal-democratic societies.

The final two substantive chapters in this book consider bilingualism and bilingual education, both of which now have a very large and varied literature. Some have found it interesting and perhaps a little perplexing that, as a capability available to everyone of normal intelligence, bilingualism remains less prevalent than its usefulness might suggest. As with other features of the social life of language, however, the picture becomes clearer when we take broader matters into account. I will return to only three of them at this point. First, given patterns of cultural and linguistic dominance and subordination, one should expect that bilingualism will be an unevenly distributed quantity. Except in circumstances where the languages in contact are of roughly equal socioeconomic clout, it is those whose varieties are less broadly useful, or less prestigious in important ways, who are most likely to expand their repertoires and to become bilingual (or better, of course). The speakers of the 'bigger' languages generally need to make fewer accommodations. There are, of course, exceptions – throughout history, the educated classes, scholars, and others living relatively privileged lives have always learned foreign languages; these have often, of course, been 'classical' varieties, and only rarely those spoken by the common people in their midst. Generally, however, just as all roads of commerce, education and culture lead to the Rome of the day, so there are accompanying linguistic pathways.

A second point to bear in mind when considering patterns of bilingualism has to do with identity. There are many motivations for learning new languages, and for most ordinary people these have to do with necessity, with mundane requirements for daily life, or with hopes for social advance and improvement. But, if language were solely an instrumental medium, then the acquisition of some new and more useful variety would very soon lead to the discarding of the original one. That this does not happen as quickly as mere practicality would suggest is an indication of continuing affections and, indeed, uses. The language of home and hearth can be retained even as another language takes over beyond the front gate. Furthermore, lingering linguistic threads can be detected even later in language-contact scenarios. When, for example, the original variety is no longer *spoken* even in the intimacy of the home, its symbolic value as a marker of group history and tradition can be maintained for a long time – just as long, in fact, as is desired. It may perhaps be said that, when a language has given up even this symbolic role, the group in question has indeed become seamlessly assimilated into another, although even at that point other markers of 'groupness' may yet be retained.

'Bilingualism' in these last circumstances has become rather attenuated, of course, and the developmental course that I have outlined above reveals a home truth: however long symbolic aspects of a language may remain, however enduring their influence – increasingly latent though it may be – over generations, these aspects rest upon the more ordinary, communicative ones. Symbolism can outlive instrumentality, but it grows out of it. The unavoidable corollary is that, when linguistic instrumentality fades, the important symbolic pillars of support – of social and psychological support – that even an unspoken language can continue to provide for the group cannot be expected to stand forever. They can, as I have just said, last for a very long time. Their power of endurance resides in their intimate and retiring disposition; their very intangibility means that they present no impediment to social mobility. Between the sixth-generation Polish American and her equally long-established Italian American neighbor, there may yet remain symbolic-language differences that can be highlighted according to need or desire – even though, for all obvious and visible intents and purposes, the neighbors are socially and culturally indistinguishable. But the symbolic attachments that my own family has to our Welsh past are now gone. Only the name remains as a reminder of distant origins, of another language, of values and customs long forgotten. Is this bad or sad? Well, it is certainly inevitable – has proved inevitable, in fact, for virtually every person on earth, if one takes a long enough view of things. Things change. Instability over time is the only constant in human life. And this, in fact, is the essence of the third point about bilingualism, however defined. The difficulties of maintaining a diglossic relationship among languages that continue to be spoken are replicated, if over a longer span of time, when one or more of them has retreated from the vernacular field.

Little remains to be said about bilingualism brought into the classroom, about formal programs of bilingual education. They can be expected to reflect, and sometimes contribute to, all the social influences and pressures that I have just described. The accommodations now made for children who come to school with a 'non-mainstream' language – either an immigrant variety or a 'small' indigenous one – are generally seen as a highly appropriate improvement over earlier sink-or-swim approaches. The philosophy of working with what children first bring with them, with the intent of improving educational outcomes and, at the same time, of reducing social and psychological pressures, seems unexceptionable. But these accommodations, this philosophy, are not above criticism and controversy. How many languages should a society cater for? How should choices be made among them? What impact will educational accommodations have upon the forging of a common citizenry? Won't multicultural and multilingual policies keep groups isolated, and encourage continuing social divisions? What about *e pluribus unum*? And, by the way, my ancestors had to struggle to find their place in the new world – no accommodations were made for them, and look what good citizens they became – why should newcomers have it any easier?

I am certainly not endorsing the impulses behind all of these questions (and many other similar ones); indeed, some reflect quite unpleasant social attitudes. But I am suggesting that they are part of the social fabric within which all language-and-education initiatives and programs must exist. Furthermore, I suggest that the pressures inherent in that larger fabric commonly have the effect of dwarfing purely pedagogical tendencies or desires. There are certainly instances, then, in which educational innovations of undeniable value have been shouted down, as it were, by unimaginative or bigoted forces. On the other hand, there are also examples of scholarly narrow-mindedness, of a tunnel vision that foolishly neglects wider issues and concerns, of enquiries that are too finely-tuned to only one context, of research enterprises that assume that the objects of study and the results of investigation can be treated in isolation.

Language diversity in the classroom is an important matter, and one that – as I hope to have shown here – deserves more attention. That attention should, however, be as comprehensive and as 'inclusive' as possible. For, broad as the topic is, and important as it is, it remains an element in a yet wider picture. It is impossible to understand, measure or implement language responses and language programs without knowing something of the lives of languages across the whole societal spectrum. It is impossible to understand the school by remaining within its gates. What should they know of schooling who only schooling know?

References

Abd-el-Jawad, Hassan (2006) Why do minority languages persist? The case of Circassian in Jordan. *International Journal of Bilingual Education and Bilingualism* 9, 51–74.

Abedi, Jamal (2004) The *No Child Left Behind* Act and English language learners: Assessment and accountability issues. *Educational Researcher* 33, 4–14.

Abernathy, Scott (2007) *No Child Left Behind and the Public Schools.* Ann Arbor, MI: University of Michigan Press.

Adams, J.N. (James Noel) (2003) *Bilingualism and the Latin Language.* Cambridge: Cambridge University Press.

Adams, J.N. (James Noel), Mark Janse and Simon Swain (eds) (2002) *Bilingualism in Ancient Society.* Oxford: Oxford University Press.

Adams, Mark (1990) *The Wellborn Science: Eugenics in Germany, France, Brazil and Russia.* Oxford: Oxford University Press.

Adger, Carolyn, Walt Wolfram, Jennifer Detwyler and Beth Harry (1992) Confronting dialect minority issues in special education. Paper to the Third National Research Symposium on Limited English Proficient Student Issues, Washington, August.

Adler, Sol (1979) *Poverty Children and their Language.* New York: Grune & Stratton.

Agence France-Presse (2006) Bush warm to 'national language legislation'. *Globe & Mail* [Toronto], 20 May.

Ainsworth-Darnell, James and Douglas Downey (1998) Assessing the oppositional culture explanation for racial/ethnic differences in school performance. *American Sociological Review* 63, 536–553.

Akom, Antwi (2003) Re-examining resistance as oppositional behavior: The Nation of Islam and the creation of a Black achievement ideology. *Sociology of Education* 76, 305–325.

Aldhous, Peter (2002) Geneticist fears 'race-neutral' studies will fail ethnic groups. *Nature* 418 (6896), 355–356.

Allardt, Erik (1984) What constitutes a language minority? *Journal of Multilingual and Multicultural Development* 5, 195–205.

Alvarez, Louis and Andrew Kolker (1987) *American Tongues* [video]. New York: Center for New American Media.

Alvidrez, Jennifer and Rhona Weinstein (1999) Early teacher perceptions and later student academic achievement. *Journal of Educational Psychology* 91, 731–746.

American Dialect Society (1943) *Needed Research in American English.* Chicago, IL: ADS.

American Dialect Society (1964) *Needed Research in American English (1963).* Tuscaloosa, AL: University of Alabama Press.

American Dialect Society (1984) *Needed Research in American English (1983)*. Tuscaloosa, AL: University of Alabama Press.

American Psychiatric Association (2000) *Diagnostic and Statistical Manual of Mental Disorders*. Washington, DC: A.P.A. (this is a revised and enlarged version of the fourth edition of the *DSM*, published in 1994).

American Speech-Language-Hearing Association (1997) *Omnibus Survey*. Rockville, MD: ASHA.

Amis, Kingsley (1990) Review of *The Oxford Guide to English Usage* (Edmund Weiner). In Kingsley Amis, *The Amis Collection*. London: Hutchinson (the review originally appeared in the *Observer*, 19 February 1984).

Amis, Kingsley (1997) *The King's English*. London: Harper Collins.

Ammon, Ulrich (1977) School problems of regional dialect speakers: Ideology and reality: Results and methods of empirical investigations in southern Germany. *Journal of Pragmatics* 1, 47–68.

Ammon, Ulrich (1983) Soziale Bewertung des Dialektsprechers. In W. Besch *et al.* (eds) *Handbuch der Dialektologie II*. Berlin: Walter de Gruyter.

Ammon, Ulrich, Klaus Mattheier and Peter Nelde (eds) (1989) *Dialekt und Schule in den europäischen Ländern (Sociolinguistica* 3). Tübingen: Max Niemeyer.

Anderson-Clark, Tracy, Raymond Green and Tracy Henley (2008) The relationship between first names and teacher expectations for achievement motivation. *Journal of Language and Social Psychology* 27, 94–99.

Andersson, Lars and Peter Trudgill (1990) *Bad Language*. Oxford: Blackwell.

Antaki, Charles (1988) Sounding board. *Times Higher Education Supplement*, 8 January.

Archer, Peter and John Edwards (1982) Predicting school achievement from data on pupils obtained from teachers: Toward a screening device for disadvantage. *Journal of Educational Psychology* 74, 761–770.

Archer, Peter and Susan Weir (2004) *Addressing Disadvantage: A Review of the International Literature and of Strategy in Ireland* (Report to the Educational Disadvantage Committee). Dublin: Educational Research Centre. The EDC is found within *An Roinn Oideachais agus Eolaíochta*. On WWW at http://www.education.ie.

Ashcroft, Bill, Gareth Griffiths and Helen Tiffin (eds) (2006) *The Post-Colonial Studies Reader*. London: Routledge.

Atkinson, Paul (1985) *Language, Structure and Reproduction: An Introduction to the Sociology of Basil Bernstein*. London: Methuen.

Atkinson, Paul, Brian Davies and Sara Delamont (eds) (1995) *Discourse and Reproduction: Essays in Honor of Basil Bernstein*. Cresskill, NJ: Hampton.

Baetens Beardsmore, Hugo (1986) *Bilingualism: Basic Principles*. Clevedon: Multilingual Matters.

Bailey, Richard (1981) Education and the law: The *King* case in Ann Arbor. In G. Smitherman (ed.) *Black English and the Education of Black Children and Youth: Proceedings of the National Invitational Symposium on the* King *Decision*. Detroit, MI: Center for Black Studies, Wayne State University.

Baker, Colin (1988) *Key Issues in Bilingualism and Bilingual Education*. Clevedon: Multilingual Matters.

Baker, Colin (2006) *Foundations of Bilingual Education and Bilingualism* (4th edn). Clevedon: Multilingual Matters.

Baker, Colin and Sylvia Jones (1998) *Encyclopedia of Bilingualism and Bilingual Education*. Clevedon: Multilingual Matters.

Baldwin, James (1979) If Black English isn't a language, then tell me, what is? *The New York Times*, 29 July.

Balfanz, Robert, Nettie Legters, Thomas West and Lisa Weber (2007) Are NCLB's measures, incentives, and improvement strategies the right ones for the nation's low-performing high schools? *American Educational Research Journal* 44, 559–593.

Ball, Arnetha and H. Samy Alim (2006) Preparation, pedagogy, policy and power: *Brown*, the *King* case, and the struggle for equal language rights. In A. Ball (ed.) *With More Deliberate Speed: Achieving Equity and Excellence in Education*. Oxford: Blackwell (*Yearbook of the National Society for the Study of Education* 105 (2)).

Banks, James (ed.) (1996) *Multicultural Education, Transformative Knowledge and Action: Historical and Contemporary Perspectives*. New York: Teachers College Press.

Banks, James and Cherry Banks (eds) (1995) *Handbook of Research on Multicultural Education*. New York: Macmillan.

Baratz, Joan (1969) A bi-dialectal task for determining language proficiency in economically disadvantaged Negro children. *Child Development* 40, 889–901.

Baratz, Joan (1970) Teaching reading in an urban Negro school system. In F. Williams (ed.) *Language and Poverty*. Chicago, IL: Markham.

Baratz, Joan (1972) Educational considerations for teaching Standard English to Negro children. In B. Spolsky (ed.) *The Language Education of Minority Children*. Rowley, MA: Newbury.

Baratz, Joan and Roger Shuy (eds) (1969) *Teaching Black Children to Read*. Washington, DC: Center for Applied Linguistics.

Barnes, Sandra (2003) The Ebonics enigma: An analysis of attitudes on an urban college campus. *Race, Ethnicity and Education* 6, 247–263.

Bartee, Susan and Christopher Brown (2007) *School Matters*. New York: Lang.

Basso, Keith (1970) To give up on words: Silence in Western Apache culture. *Southwestern Journal of Anthropology* 26, 213–230.

Bauer, Laurie and Peter Trudgill (eds) (1998) *Language Myths*. London: Penguin.

Bauer, Winifred (1998) Some languages have no grammar. In L. Bauer and P. Trudgill (eds) *Language Myths*. London: Penguin.

Baugh, John (2000) *Beyond Ebonics: Linguistic Pride and Racial Prejudice*. New York: Oxford University Press.

Baugh, John (2002) Linguistics, education, and the Ebonics firestorm. In J. Alatis, H. Hamilton and A-H. Tan (eds) *Linguistics, Language, and the Professions*. Washington: Georgetown University Press.

Baugh, John (2004) Ebonics and its controversy. In E. Finegan and J. Rickford (eds) *Language in the USA: Themes for the Twenty-first Century*. Cambridge: Cambridge University Press.

Baugh, John (2006) Linguistic considerations pertaining to *Brown v. Board*: Exposing racial fallacies in the new millennium. In A. Ball (ed.) *With More Deliberate Speed: Achieving Equity and Excellence in Education*. Oxford: Blackwell (*Yearbook of the National Society for the Study of Education* 105 (2)).

Baum, Bruce (2006) *The Rise and Fall of the Caucasian Race: A Political History of Racial Identity*. New York: New York University Press.

Bedore, Lisa and Elizabeth Peña (2008) Assessment of bilingual children for identification of language impairment: Current findings and implications for practice. *International Journal of Bilingual Education and Bilingualism* 11, 1–29.

Bereiter, Carl and Siegfried Engelmann (1966) *Teaching Disadvantaged Children in the Pre-school.* Englewood Cliffs, NJ: Prentice-Hall.

Bernstein, Basil (1958) Some sociological determinants of perception: An enquiry into subcultural differences. *British Journal of Sociology* 9, 159–174.

Bernstein, Basil (1959) A public language: Some sociological implications of a linguistic form. *British Journal of Sociology* 10, 311–326.

Bernstein, Basil (1960) Language and social class. *British Journal of Sociology* 11, 271–276.

Bernstein, Basil (1962a) Linguistic codes, hesitation phenomena and intelligence. *Language and Speech* 5, 31–46.

Bernstein, Basil (1962b) Social class, linguistic codes and grammatical elements. *Language and Speech* 5, 221–240.

Bernstein, Basil (1971) *Class, Codes and Control, Volume 1: Theoretical Studies Towards a Sociology of Language.* London: Routledge & Kegan Paul.

Bernstein, Basil (1972a) Social class, language and socialization. In P.P. Giglioli (ed.) *Language and Social Context.* Harmondsworth: Penguin.

Bernstein, Basil (1972b) A critique of the concept of compensatory education. In C. Cazden, V. John and D. Hymes (eds) *Functions of Language in the Classroom.* New York: Teachers College Press.

Bernstein, Basil (1987) Social class, codes and communication. In U. Ammon, N. Dittmar and K. Mattheier (eds) *Soziolinguistik: Ein Internationales Handbuch zur Wissenschaft von Sprache und Gesellschaft.* Berlin: Walter de Gruyter.

Bernstein, Basil (1990) *Class, Codes and Control, Volume 4: The Structuring of Pedagogic Discourse.* London: Routledge.

Bernstein, Basil (1996) *Class, Codes and Control, Volume 5: Pedagogy, Symbolic Control and Identity: Theory, Research, Critique.* London: Routledge.

Bernstein, Basil (1997) Sociolinguistics: A personal view. In C. Paulston and G.R. Tucker (eds) *The Early Days of Sociolinguistics: Memories and Reflections.* Dallas, TX: Summer Institute of Linguistics.

Berry, John, Rudy Kalin and Donald Taylor (1977) *Multiculturalism and Ethnic Attitudes in Canada.* Ottawa: Supply and Services Canada.

Bex, Tony and Richard Watts (1999) Introduction. In T. Bex and R. Watts (eds) *Standard English: Widening the Debate.* London: Routledge.

Beykont, Z. (ed.) (2002) *The Power of Culture: Teaching Across Language Difference.* Cambridge, MA: Harvard Educational Publishing.

Bhatia, Tej and William Ritchie (2004) *The Handbook of Bilingualism.* Oxford: Blackwell (paperback edition, 2006).

Billig, Michael (1988) Review of *Discourse and Social Psychology* (Jonathan Potter and Margaret Wetherell). *The Psychologist* 1, 23.

Binet, Alfred (1909) *Les idées modernes sur les enfants.* Paris: Flammarion.

Black, Edwin (2003) *War Against the Weak: Eugenics and America's Campaign to Create a Master Race.* New York: Four Walls Eight Windows.

Black, Ray (2004) Where did we go wrong? Bill Cosby and the anxiety of communal responsibility. *The Black Scholar* 34 (4), 16–19.

Blanco, George (1983) Review of *Hunger of Memory* (Richard Rodriguez). *Modern Language Journal* 67, 282–283.

Blank, Marion (1982) Moving beyond the difference-deficit debate. In L. Feagans and D. Farran (eds) *The Language of Children Reared in Poverty*. New York: Academic Press.

Block, Ned and Gerald Dworkin (eds) (1976) *The IQ Controversy: Critical Readings*. New York: Pantheon.

Blommaert, Jan (2005) *Discourse: A Critical Introduction*. Cambridge: Cambridge University Press.

Bloom, Benjamin (1969) The Jensen article. *Harvard Educational Review* 39, 419–421.

Bloom, Benjamin, Allison Davis and Robert Hess (1965) *Compensatory Education for Cultural Deprivation*. New York: Holt, Rinehart & Winston.

Bloomfield, Leonard (1927) Literate and illiterate speech. *American Speech* 2, 432–439.

Bloomfield, Leonard (1933) *Language*. New York: Holt.

Boberg, Charles (1999) The attitudinal component of variation in American English foreign < a > nativization. *Journal of Language and Social Psychology* 18, 49–61.

Bodmer, Walter (1972) Race and IQ: The genetic background. In K. Richardson, D. Spears and M. Richards (eds) *Race, Culture and Intelligence*. Harmondsworth: Penguin.

Borges, Jorge Luis (1999) *Collected Fictions* (A. Hurley, trans.). London: Penguin.

Boring, Edwin (1923) Intelligence as the tests test it. *The New Republic*, June (no. 35), 35–37.

De Bose, Charles (2005) *The Sociology of African American Language: A Language Planning Perspective*. New York: Palgrave Macmillan.

Bourdieu, Pierre (1989) *The Logic of Practice*. Cambridge: Polity (original: *Le sens pratique*. Paris: Minuit, 1980).

Bourdieu, Pierre and Jean-Claude Passeron (1977) *Reproduction in Education, Society and Culture*. London: Sage (original: *La reproduction: éléments pour une théorie du système d'enseignement*. Paris: Minuit, 1970).

Brace, Charles Loring (2005) *'Race' is a Four-Letter Word: The Genesis of the Concept*. Oxford: Oxford University Press.

Breton, Raymond (1986) Multiculturalism and Canadian nation-building. In A. Cairns and C. Williams (eds) *The Politics of Gender, Ethnicity and Language in Canada*. Toronto: University of Toronto Press.

Breton, Raymond, Jeffrey Reitz and Victor Valentine (1980) *Cultural Boundaries and the Cohesion of Canada*. Montreal: Institute for Research on Public Policy.

Brigham, Carl (1923) *A Study of American Intelligence*. Princeton, NJ: Princeton University Press.

British Broadcasting Corporation (BBC) (2006) Reaction to UK 'core values' idea. 15 May. On WWW at www.newsvote.bbc.co.uk.

Brook, G.L. (George Leslie) (1963) *English Dialects*. London: André Deutsch.

Brook, G.L. (George Leslie) (1970) *The Language of Dickens*. London: André Deutsch.

Brookes, Martin (2004) *Extreme Measures: The Dark Visions and Bright Ideas of Francis Galton*. London: Bloomsbury.

Brouwer, Niels and Fred Korthagen (2005) Can teacher education make a difference? *American Educational Research Journal* 42, 153–224.

Brown, Christopher (ed.) (2007) *Still not Equal: Expanding Educational Opportunity in Society*. New York: Lang.

Brown, Penelope and Stephen Levinson (1987) *Politeness: Some Universals in Language Use*. Cambridge: Cambridge University Press.

Bruinius, Harry (2006) *Better for All the World: The Secret History of Forced Sterilization and America's Quest for Racial Purity*. New York: Knopf.

Brumfit, Christopher (2001) *Individual Freedom in Language Teaching*. Oxford: Oxford University Press.

Bullock, Alan (1975) *A Language for Life* (Bullock Report). Department of Education and Science (London): HMSO.

Bullivant, Brian (1981) *The Pluralist Dilemma in Education*. Sydney: Allen & Unwin.

Burnet, Jean (1975) The policy of multiculturalism within a bilingual framework. In A. Wolfgang (ed.) *Education of Immigrant Students*. Toronto: Ontario Institute for Studies in Education.

Burtonwood, Neil and Robert Bruce (1999) Cultural sensitivity: American and British teacher trainees compared – a response to Thomas Deering. *Educational Research* 41, 94–99.

Buss, Allan (1976) Galton and sex differences: An historical note. *Journal of the History of the Behavioral Sciences* 12, 283–285.

Butler, Samuel (1850) *The Poetical Works of Samuel Butler: Volume 2*. London: Bell & Daldy.

Butts, R. Freeman, Donald Peckenpaugh and Howard Kirschenbaum (1977) *The School's Role as Moral Authority*. Washington, DC: Association for Supervision and Curriculum Development.

Caldas, Stephen (2006) *Raising Bilingual-Biliterate Children in Monoliterate Cultures*. Clevedon: Multilingual Matters.

Callender, Tricia (2005) A deeper level of diversity: Linguistic and cultural recognition for the 'new' black student in NYC: The Barbadian example. In Z. Zakharia and T. Arnstein (eds) *Languages, Communities and Education*. New York: Teachers College, Columbia University.

Cameron, Deborah (1995) *Verbal Hygiene*. London: Routledge.

Campos de Souza, Leone and Paulo Nascimento (2008) Brazilian national identity at a crossroads: The myth of racial democracy and the development of black identity. *International Journal of Politics, Culture and Society* 19, 129–143.

Cane, Don (2004) Bill Cosby rants against ghetto poor: The crisis of black leadership. *Workers Vanguard*, 17 September (no. 832). International Communist League. On WWW at www.icl-fi.org.

Carey, Benedict (2006) Study finds a link of drug makers to psychiatrists. *The New York Times*, 20 April.

Carlson, Elof Axel (2001) *The Unfit: A History of a Bad Idea*. Cold Spring Harbor, NY: Cold Spring Harbor Laboratory Press.

Carr, Jo and Anne Pauwels (2006) *Boys and Foreign Language Learning: Real Boys Don't Do Languages*. Basingstoke: Palgrave Macmillan.

Carranza, Miguel and Ellen Bouchard Ryan (1975) Evaluative reactions of bilingual Anglo and Mexican American adolescents toward speakers of English and Spanish. *International Journal of the Sociology of Language* 6, 83–104.

Carrington, Bruce and John Williamson (1987) The deficit hypothesis revisited. *Educational Studies* 13, 239–245.

Carroll, John (1972) *Language, Thought and Reality: Selected Writings of Benjamin Lee Whorf.* Cambridge, MA: MIT Press.

Carter, Robert (2000) *Realism and Racism: Concepts of Race in Sociological Research.* London: Routledge.

Carter, Robert (2007) Genes, genomes and genealogies: The return of scientific racism? *Ethnic and Racial Studies* 30, 546–556.

Casanova, Ursula (1991) Bilingual education: Politics or pedagogy? In Ofelia García (ed.) *Bilingual Education: Focusschrift in Honor of Joshua A. Fishman.* Amsterdam: John Benjamins.

Castro, Max (1992) On the curious question of language in Miami. In J. Crawford (ed.) *Language Loyalties: A Source Book on the Official English Controversy.* Chicago, IL: University of Chicago Press.

Cazden, Courtney (1988) *Classroom Discourse.* Portsmouth, NH: Heinemann.

Chambers, Jack (1995) *Sociolinguistic Theory.* Oxford: Blackwell.

Chambers, Jack, Peter Trudgill and Natalie Schilling-Estes (eds) (2002) *The Handbook of Language Variation and Change.* Oxford: Blackwell.

Chapman, Paul (1988) *Schools as Sorters: Lewis M. Terman, Applied Psychology, and the Intelligence Testing Movement, 1890–1930.* New York: New York University Press.

Chapman, Raymond (1994) *Forms of Speech in Victorian Fiction.* London: Longman.

Cheshire, Jenny, Viv Edwards, Henk Münstermann and Bert Weltens (1989) Dialect and education in Europe: A general perspective. In J. Cheshire, V. Edwards, H. Münstermann and B. Weltens (eds) *Dialect and Education: Some European Perspectives.* Clevedon: Multilingual Matters.

Cheyne, William (1970) Stereotyped reactions to speakers with Scottish and English regional accents. *British Journal of Social and Clinical Psychology* 9, 77–79.

Chilton, Paul (2003) *Analysing Political Discourse: Theory and Practice.* London: Routledge.

Chimpanzee Sequencing and Analysis Consortium (2005) Initial sequence of the chimpanzee genome and comparison with the human genome. *Nature* 437 (7055), 69–87.

Chomsky, Noam (1977) *Dialogues ave Mitsou Ronat.* Paris: Flammarion.

Choy, Stephen and David Dodd (1976) Standard-English-speaking and non-standard Hawaiian English-speaking children: Comprehension of both dialects and teachers' evaluations. *Journal of Educational Psychology* 68, 184–193.

Chrismer, Sara, Shannon Hodge and Debby Saintil (eds) (2006) *Assessing NCLB: Perspectives and Prescriptions.* Cambridge, MA: Harvard Education Press (*Harvard Educational Review* 76 (4)).

Christenfeld, Nicholas and Britta Larsen (2008) The name game. *The Psychologist* 21, 211–213.

Christie, Frances (ed.) (1999) *Pedagogy and the Shaping of Consciousness: Linguistic and Social Processes.* London: Cassell.

Clarke, Alan and Ann Clarke (2006) Born to be bright? *The Psychologist* 19, 409.

Clyne, Michael (2005) *Australia's Language Potential.* Sydney: University of New South Wales Press.

Čmejrková, Svetla and Carlo Prevignano (2003) On conversation analysis: An interview with Emanuel A. Schegloff. In C. Prevignano and P. Thibault (eds) *Discussing Conversation Analysis: The Work of Emanuel A. Schegloff.* Amsterdam: John Benjamins.

Coard, Bernard (1971) *How the West Indian Child is Made Educationally Subnormal in the British School System.* London: New Beacon Books.

Coates, Jennifer (1996) *Women Talk.* Oxford: Blackwell.

Coates, Jennifer (2003) *Men Talk.* Oxford: Blackwell.

Coates, Jennifer (2004) *Women, Men and Language.* London: Longman.

Coates, Ta-Nehisi (2008) 'This is how we lost to the white man'. *Atlantic,* May (301: 4), 52–62.

Cochran-Smith, Marilyn (1995) Color blindness and basket making are not the answers: Confronting the dilemmas of race, culture, and language diversity in teacher education. *American Educational Research Journal* 32, 493–522.

Coenders, Marcel, Marcel Lubbers, Peer Scheepers and Maykel Verkuyten (2008) More than two decades of changing ethnic attitudes in The Netherlands. *Journal of Social Issues* 64, 269–285.

Cole, Johnnetta (2004) On speaking truth to ourselves and doing right by our children. *The Black Scholar* 34 (4), 6–9.

Cole, Michael and Jerome Bruner (1972) Preliminaries to a theory of cultural differences. In I. Gordon (ed.) *Early Childhood Education.* Chicago, IL: University of Chicago Press.

Coleman, James (1966) *Equality of Educational Opportunity.* Washington, DC: United States Government Printing Office.

Coleman, James (1968) Review of *Studies in Ethnomethodology* (Harold Garfinkel). *American Sociological Review* 33, 126–130.

Colman, Andrew (1987) *Facts, Fallacies and Frauds in Psychology.* London: Hutchinson.

Commins, Nancy and Ofelia Miramontes (1989) Perceived and actual linguistic competence: A descriptive study of four low-achieving Hispanic bilingual students. *American Educational Research Journal* 26, 443–472.

Committee on Irish Language Attitudes Research (1975) *Report.* Dublin: Government Stationery Office.

Condry, John and Sandra Condry (1976) Sex differences: A study of the eye of the beholder. *Child Development* 47, 812–819.

Condry, Sandra, John Condry and Lee Pogatshnik (1983) Sex differences: A study of the ear of the beholder. *Sex Roles* 9, 697–704.

Connor, Ulla and Ana Moreno (2005) *Tertium Comparationis*: A vital component in contrastive rhetoric research. In P. Bruthiaux, D. Atkinson, W. Eggington, W. Grabe and V. Ramanathan (eds) *Directions in Applied Linguistics: Essays in Honor of Robert B. Kaplan.* Clevedon: Multilingual Matters.

Connors, Brian (1984) A multicultural curriculum as action for social justice. In S. Shapson and V. d'Oyley (eds) *Bilingual and Multicultural Education.* Clevedon: Multilingual Matters.

Cook, Eung-Do (1998) Aboriginal languages: History. In J. Edwards (ed.) *Language in Canada.* Cambridge: Cambridge University Press.

Cook-Gumperz, Jenny (1973) *Social Control and Socialization: A Study of Class Differences in the Language of Maternal Control.* London: Routledge & Kegan Paul.

Cooper, Harris (1979) Pygmalion grows up: A model for teacher expectation communication and performance influence. *Review of Educational Research* 49, 389–410.

Cooper, Harris and Thomas Good (1983) *Pygmalion Grows Up: Studies in the Expectation Communication Process.* New York: Longman.

Corbett, Anne (2000) Lady Plowden (obituary). *The Guardian,* 3 October.

Corson, David (1993) *Language, Minority Education and Gender.* Clevedon: Multilingual Matters.

Corson, David (2001) *Language Diversity and Education.* Mahwah, NJ: Lawrence Erlbaum.

Cosby, William (1997) Elements of igno-ebonics style. *The Wall Street Journal,* 10 January.

Cosby, William (2004) Dr Bill Cosby speaks at the 50th anniversary commemoration of the *Brown v. Topeka Board of Education* Supreme Court decision. *The Black Scholar* 34 (4), 2–5.

Coser, Lewis (1975) Presidential address: Two methods in search of a substance. *American Sociological Review* 40, 691–700.

Cosgrove, Lisa, Sheldon Krimsky, Manisha Vijayaraghavan and Lisa Schneider (2006) Financial ties between *DSM-IV* panel members and the pharmaceutical industry. *Psychotherapy and Psychosomatics* 75, 154–160.

Coulmas, Florian (2005) *Sociolinguistics: The Study of Speakers' Choices.* Cambridge: Cambridge University Press.

Coulthard, Michael (1969) A discussion of restricted and elaborated codes. *Educational Review* 22, 38–50.

Covington, Ann (1976) Black people and Black English: Attitudes and de-education in a biased macroculture. In D. Harrison and T. Trabasso (eds) *Black English: A Seminar.* Hillsdale, NJ: Lawrence Erlbaum.

Crawford, James (1989) *Bilingual Education: History, Politics, Theory and Practice.* Trenton, NJ: Crane.

Crawford, James (1992a) *Hold Your Tongue: Bilingualism and the Politics of 'English Only'.* Reading, MA: Addison-Wesley.

Crawford, James (ed.) (1992b) *Language Loyalties: A Source Book on the Official English Controversy.* Chicago, IL: University of Chicago Press.

Crawford, James (2000) *At War With Diversity: U.S. Language Policy in an Age of Anxiety.* Clevedon: Multilingual Matters.

Crawford, James (2004) *Educating English Learners: Language Diversity in the Classroom.* Los Angeles, CA: Bilingual Education Services (the 5th edition of *Bilingual Education: History, Politics, Theory and Practice*).

Crawford, Mary (1995) *Talking Difference: On Gender and Language.* London: Sage.

Creese, Angela and Peter Martin (eds) (2006a) *Interaction in Complementary School Contexts.* Clevedon: Multilingual Matters (*Language and Education* 20 (1)).

Creese, Angela and Peter Martin (2006b) Interaction in complementary school contexts: Developing identities of choice – an introduction. *Language and Education* 20, 1–4.

Cronbach, Lee (1975) Five decades of public controversy over mental testing. *American Psychologist* 30, 1–14.

Crook, Paul (2002) American eugenics and the Nazis. *The European Legacy* 7, 363–381.

Crook, Paul (2007) *Darwin's Coat-Tails: Essays on Social Darwinism.* New York: Peter Lang.

Crowley, Tony (1989) *The Politics of Discourse: The Standard Language Question in British Cultural Debates.* London: Macmillan.

Crowley, Tony (1999) Curiouser and curiouser: Falling standards in the Standard English debate. In T. Bex and R. Watts (eds) *Standard English: Widening the Debate.* London: Routledge.

Crowley, Tony (2003) *Standard English and the Politics of Language.* London: Palgrave Macmillan (2nd edn of Crowley, 1989).

Crystal, David (1983) Review of *The Language Trap* (John Honey). *British Association for Applied Linguistics Newsletter* 18, 42–50 (reprinted in *English in Education* (NATE), 1984 (18: 1), 54–65).

Cummins, Jim (1986) Empowering minority students: A framework for intervention. *Harvard Educational Review* 56, 18–36.

Cummins, Jim (1996) *Negotiating Identities: Education for Empowerment in a Diverse Society.* Sacramento, CA: California Association for Bilingual Education.

Cummins, Jim (1998) The teaching of international languages. In J. Edwards (ed.) *Language in Canada.* Cambridge: Cambridge University Press.

Cummins, Jim (2005) A proposal for action: Strategies for recognizing heritage language competence as a learning resource within the mainstream classroom. *Modern Language Journal* 89, 585–592 (this article is followed (pp. 592–616) by commentaries from Scott McGinnis, Terrence Wiley, Ofelia García, Nancy Hornberger, Janine Brutt-Griffler and Sinfree Makoni, and Kees de Bot and Durk Gorter).

Cutts, Mark (ed.) (2000) *The State of the World's Refugees, 2000: Fifty Years of Humanitarian Action.* New York: Oxford University Press and Geneva: Office of the United Nations High Commissioner for Refugees.

D'Amato, John (1987) The belly of the beast: On cultural differences, castelike status, and the politics of school. *Anthropology and Education Quarterly* 18, 357–360.

d'Anglejan, Alison and G. Richard Tucker (1973) Sociolinguistic correlates of speech style in Quebec. In R. Shuy and R. Fasold (eds) *Language Attitudes: Current Trends and Prospects.* Washington, DC: Georgetown University Press.

Daniel, G. Reginald (2006) *Race and Multiraciality in Brazil and the United States: Converging Paths?* University Park, PA: Pennsylvania State University Press.

Daugherity, Brian and Charles Bolton (eds) (2008) *With All Deliberate Speed: Implementing Brown v. Board of Education.* Fayetteville, AR: University of Arkansas Press.

Davenport, Charles (1911) *Heredity in Relation to Eugenics.* New York: Holt.

Davies, Alan (1985) Standard and dialect English: The unacknowledged idealisation of sociolinguistics. *Journal of Multilingual and Multicultural Development* 6, 183–192.

Davies, Alan (1987) Review of *Language, Structure and Reproduction* (Paul Atkinson). *Language Problems and Language Planning* 11, 370–372.

Davis, Philip (ed.) (1920) *Immigration and Americanization: Selected Readings.* Boston, MA: Ginn.

Day, Richard (1982) Children's attitudes towards language. In E. Bouchard Ryan and H. Giles (eds) *Attitudes Towards Language Variation: Social and Applied Contexts.* London: Edward Arnold.

Deák, Julia (2007) African-American language and American linguistic cultures: An analysis of language policies in education. *Working Papers in Educational Linguistics* (Graduate School of Education, University of Pennsylvania) 22 (1), 105–134.

Deering, Thomas (1997) Preparing to teach diverse student populations: A British and American perspective. *Educational Research* 39, 342–350.

Delgado-Gaitan, Concha (1992) School matters in the Mexican-American home: Socializing children to education. *American Educational Research Journal* 29, 495–513.

Delgado-Gaitan, Concha and Henry Trueba (1991) *Crossing Cultural Borders: Education for Immigrant Families in America.* London: Falmer.

Dennis, Wayne (1960) Causes of retardation among institutional children: Iran. *Journal of Genetic Psychology* 96, 47–59.

Department of Canadian Heritage (2000) *Annual Report on the Operation of the Canadian Multiculturalism Act.* Ottawa: Supply & Services Canada.

Derwing, Tracey (2003) What do ESL students say about their accents? *Canadian Modern Language Review* 59, 547–566.

Deutsch, Martin (1967) *The Disadvantaged Child.* New York: Basic Books.

Deutsch, Nathaniel (2009) *Inventing America's 'Worst' Family: Eugenics, Islam, and the Fall and Rise of the Tribe of Ishmael.* Berkeley, CA: University of California Press.

De Valdes, María (1979) Bilingual education program for Spanish-speaking children in the United States. *Canadian Modern Language Review* 35, 407–414.

Devine, Philip (1996) *Human Diversity and the Culture Wars.* Westport, CT: Praeger.

Dicker, Susan (2003) *Languages in America: A Pluralist View* (2nd edn). Clevedon: Multilingual Matters.

Didion, Joan (1987) *Miami.* New York: Simon & Schuster.

Dittmar, Norbert (1976) *Sociolinguistics: A Critical Survey of Theory and Application.* London: Edward Arnold.

Dornbusch, Sanford, Philip Ritter and Laurence Steinberg (1991) Community influences on the relation of family statuses to adolescent school performance: Differences between African American and non-Hispanic whites. *American Journal of Education* 38, 543–567.

Dörnyei, Zoltán (2005) *The Psychology of the Language Learner.* Mahwah, NJ: Lawrence Erlbaum.

Dörnyei, Zoltán and Richard Schmidt (eds) (2001) *Motivation and Second Language Acquisition.* Honolulu, HI: University of Hawaii Press.

Dörnyei, Zoltán and Ema Ushioda (eds) (2009) *Motivation, Language Identity and the L2 Self.* Bristol: Multilingual Matters.

Dos Passos, John (1963) Cogitations in a Roman theatre. *Modern Age* 8 (1), 77–83.

Dos Passos, John (1964) The use of the past. In *Occasions and Protests.* New York: Regnery (this essay was first published in *The Ground We Stand On.* New York: Harcourt, Brace & World, 1941).

Dowbiggin, Ian (1997) *Keeping America Sane: Psychiatry and Eugenics in the United States and Canada, 1880–1940.* Ithaca, NY: Cornell University Press.

Drapeau, Lynne (1998) Aboriginal languages: Current status. In J. Edwards (ed.) *Language in Canada.* Cambridge: Cambridge University Press.

D'Souza, Jean (2006) Language, education and the rights of the child. *World Englishes* 25, 155–166.

Dunbar, William (1508) *The Flyting of Dunbar and Kennedy* [sic]. Edinburgh: Chepman & Myllar.

Dyson, Michael (2005) *Is Bill Cosby Right: Or Has the Black Middle Class Lost Its Mind?* New York: Basic Civitas.

The Economist (2008) Nearer to overcoming. 10 May (387: 8579), 33–35.

Edelman, Peter, Harry Holzer and Paul Offner (2006) *Reconnecting Disadvantaged Young Men.* Washington, DC: Urban Institute.

Edelsky, Carole, Sarah Hudelson, Barbara Flores, Florence Barkin, Bess Altwerger and Kristina Jilbert (1983) Semilingualism and language deficit. *Applied Linguistics* 4, 1–22.

Edmonds, Alexander (2007) 'Triumphant miscegenation': Reflections on beauty and race in Brazil. *Journal of Intercultural Studies* 28, 83–97.

Edwards, Anthony (1974) Social class and linguistic inference. *Research in Education* 12, 71–80.

Edwards, Anthony (1976) *Language in Culture and Class.* London: Heinemann.

Edwards, Anthony (1987a) Review of *Language, Structure and Reproduction* (Paul Atkinson). *Journal of Language and Social Psychology* 6, 67–70.

Edwards, Anthony (1987b) Language codes and classroom practice. *Oxford Review of Education* 13, 237–247.

Edwards, Derek and Neil Mercer (1986) Context and continuity: Classroom discourse and the development of shared knowledge. In K. Durkin (ed.) *Language Development in the School Years.* London: Croom Helm.

Edwards, John (1974) Characteristics of disadvantaged children. *Irish Journal of Education* 8, 49–61.

Edwards, John (1977a) Reading, language and disadvantage. In V. Greaney (ed.) *Studies in Reading.* Dublin: Educational Company.

Edwards, John (1977b) The speech of disadvantaged Dublin children. *Language Problems and Language Planning* 1, 65–72.

Edwards, John (1977c) Review of *Report* (Committee on Irish Language Attitudes Research). *Language Problems and Language Planning* 1, 54–59.

Edwards, John (1979a) Social class differences and the identification of sex in children's speech. *Journal of Child Language* 6, 121–127.

Edwards, John (1979b) Judgements and confidence in reactions to disadvantaged speech. In H. Giles and R. St. Clair (eds) *Language and Social Psychology.* Oxford: Blackwell.

Edwards, John (1981) Disadvantage: Guilt by association. *Educational Psychology* 1, 101–103.

Edwards, John (1982) Language attitudes and their implications among English speakers. In E. Bouchard Ryan and H. Giles (eds) *Attitudes Toward Language Variation: Social and Applied Contexts.* London: Edward Arnold.

Edwards, John (1983a) Review article on *The Language Trap* (John Honey). *Journal of Language and Social Psychology* 2, 67–76.

Edwards, John (1983b) Ethno-inquiry: Renaissance or illusion? Unpublished paper, St Francis Xavier University (available upon request).

Edwards, John (1983c) Language attitudes in multilingual settings: A general assessment. *Journal of Multilingual and Multicultural Development* 4, 225–236.

Edwards, John (1984) Language, diversity and identity. In J. Edwards (ed.) *Linguistic Minorities, Policies and Pluralism.* London: Academic Press.

Edwards, John (1985) *Language, Society and Identity.* Oxford: Blackwell (in association with André Deutsch).

Edwards, John (1987) Elaborated and restricted codes. In U. Ammon, N. Dittmar and K. Mattheier (eds) *Soziolinguistik: Ein Internationales Handbuch zur Wissenschaft von Sprache und Gesellschaft.* Berlin: Walter de Gruyter.

Edwards, John (1989) *Language and Disadvantage* (2nd rev edn). London: Cole & Whurr (original, London: Edward Arnold, 1979).

Edwards, John (1990) Social purposes of bilingual education: *U.S. English,* the ELA, and other matters. In G. Imhoff (ed.) *Learning in Two Languages: From Conflict to Consensus in the Reorganization of Schools.* New Brunswick, NJ: Transaction.

Edwards, John (1993) Identity and language in the Canadian educational context. In M. Danesi, K. McLeod and S. Morris (eds) *Heritage Languages and Education: The Canadian Experience.* Toronto: Mosaic.

Edwards, John (1994a) *Multilingualism.* London: Routledge.

Edwards, John (1994b) Identity, soft multiculturalism, language and the mapping of the middle ground. Paper presented at *Multikulturelt Samfund og Etnisk Identitet* conference, Odense University, December.

Edwards, John (1999a) Refining our understanding of language attitudes. *Journal of Language and Social Psychology* 18, 101–110.

Edwards, John (1999b) Reactions to three types of speech sample from rural black and white children. In L. Falk and M. Harry (eds) *The English Language in Nova Scotia.* Lockeport, Nova Scotia: Roseway.

Edwards, John (2001) Languages and language learning in the face of world English. *Profession,* 109–120 (*Profession* is the Annual of the Modern Language Association).

Edwards, John (2003a) Language and the future. In H. Tonkin and T. Reagan (eds) *Language in the Twenty-First Century.* Amsterdam: John Benjamins.

Edwards, John (2003b) Contextualizing language rights. *Journal of Human Rights* 2, 551–571.

Edwards, John (2004a) Ecolinguistic ideologies: A critical perspective. In M. Pütz, J. Neff-van Aertselaer and T. van Dijk (eds) *Communicating Ideologies: Multidisciplinary Perspectives on Language, Discourse and Social Practice.* Frankfurt: Peter Lang.

Edwards, John (2004b) After the fall. *Discourse and Society* 15, 155–184.

Edwards, John (2006) Educational failure. In K. Brown (ed.) *Encyclopedia of Language and Linguistics.* Oxford: Elsevier.

Edwards, John (2008) English in Canada. In M. Matto and H. Momma (eds) *Blackwell Companion to the History of the English Language.* Oxford: Blackwell.

Edwards, John (in press-a) The treason of translation? Bilingualism, linguistic borders and identity. In H. Tonkin, M.E. Frank and M. Moen (eds) *The Translator as Mediator of Cultures.* Amsterdam: John Benjamins.

Edwards, John (in press-b) *Language and Identity.* Cambridge: Cambridge University Press.

Edwards, John (in preparation) *Irish: The Triumph of Failure?*

Edwards, John and Joan Chisholm (1987) Language, multiculturalism and identity: A Canadian study. *Journal of Multilingual and Multicultural Development* 8, 391–408.

Edwards, John and Lori Doucette (1987) Ethnic salience, identity and symbolic ethnicity. *Canadian Ethnic Studies* 19, 52–62.

Edwards, John and Howard Giles (1984) Applications of the social psychology of language: Sociolinguistics and education. In P. Trudgill (ed.) *Applied Sociolinguistics*. London: Academic Press.

Edwards, John and Margaret McKinnon (1987) The continuing appeal of disadvantage as deficit: A Canadian study in a rural context. *Canadian Journal of Education* 12, 330–349.

Edwards, Viv (1986) *Language in a Black Community*. Clevedon: Multilingual Matters.

Edwards, Viv (1987) Review of *Educational Linguistic* (Michael Stubbs). *Journal of Language and Social Psychology* 6, 141–144.

Elbow, Peter (2006) When the margins are at the center. In S. Nero (ed.) *Dialects, Englishes, Creoles and Education*. Mahwah, NJ: Lawrence Erlbaum.

Erickson, Frederick (1987) Transformation and school success: The politics and culture of educational achievement. *Anthropology and Education Quarterly* 18, 335–356.

Evans, Bruce and Nancy Hornberger (2005) *No Child Left Behind*: Repealing and unpeeling federal language education policy in the United States. *Language Policy* 4, 87–106.

Evans, Nicholas (1998) Aborigines speak a primitive language. In L. Bauer and P. Trudgill (eds) *Language Myths*. London: Penguin.

Ewen, Elizabeth and Stuart Ewen (2006) *Typecasting: On the Arts and Sciences of Human Inequality*. New York: Seven Stories.

Ewing, E. Thomas (2006) The repudiation of single-sex education: Boys' schools in the Soviet Union, 1943–1954. *American Educational Research Journal* 43, 621–650.

Extra, Guus and Durk Gorter (2001) *The Other Languages of Europe: Demographic, Sociolinguistic and Educational Perspectives*. Clevedon: Multilingual Matters.

Extra, Guus and Kutlay Yağmur (2004) *Urban Multilingualism in Europe: Immigrant Minority Languages at Home and School*. Clevedon: Multilingual Matters.

Eysenck, Hans (1975) *The Inequality of Man*. London: Fontana.

Fabricius, Anne (2006) The 'vivid sociolinguistic profiling' of Received Pronunciation: Responses to gendered dialect-in-discourse. *Journal of Sociolinguistics* 10, 111–122.

Fairclough, Norman (1988) *Language and Power*. London: Longman.

Fairclough, Norman (1995) *Critical Discourse Analysis*. London: Longman.

Farkas, George, Christy Lleras and Steve Maczuga (2002) Does oppositional culture exist in minority and poverty peer groups? *American Sociological Review* 67, 148–155.

Farran, Dale (1982) Intervention for poverty children – alternative approaches. In L. Feagans and D. Farran (eds) *The Language of Children Reared in Poverty*. New York: Academic Press.

Fasold, Ralph (1984) *The Sociolinguistics of Society*. Oxford: Blackwell.

Fasold, Ralph (2006) Ebonic [sic] need not be English. In H. Luria, D. Seymour and T. Smoke (eds) *Language and Linguistics in Context*. Mahwah, NJ: Lawrence Erlbaum.

Feagans, Lynne and Dale Farran (eds) (1982) *The Language of Children Reared in Poverty*. New York: Academic Press.

Ferguson, Charles (1977) Linguistic theory. In Center for Applied Linguistics (ed.) *Bilingual Education: Current Perspectives.* Arlington, VI: CAL.

Ferguson, Gibson (2006) *Language Planning and Education.* Edinburgh: Edinburgh University Press.

Ferneyhough, Charles (2006) Metaphors of mind. *The Psychologist* 19, 356–358.

Ferris, Dana (2005) Reflections of a 'blue collar linguist': Analysis of written discourse, classroom research, and EAP pedagogy. In P. Bruthiaux, D. Atkinson, W. Eggington, W. Grabe and V. Ramanathan (eds) *Directions in Applied Linguistics: Essays in Honor of Robert B. Kaplan.* Clevedon: Multilingual Matters.

Fillmore, Charles (2005) A linguist looks at the Ebonics debate. In J.D. Ramirez, T. Wiley, G. de Klerk, E. Lee and W. Wright (eds) *Ebonics: The Urban Education Debate* (2nd edn). Clevedon: Multilingual Matters.

Fine, Michelle, Reva Jaffe-Walter, Pedro Pedraza, Valerie Futch and Brett Stoudt (2007) Swimming: On oxygen, resistance, and possibility for immigrant youth under siege. *Anthropology and Education Quarterly* 38, 76–96.

Firth, Alan (1996) Review of *Collegial Discourse* and *What's Going On Here?* (Allen Grimshaw). *American Journal of Sociology* 101, 1487–1492.

Fischer, John (1958) Social influences on the choice of a linguistic variant. *Word* 14, 47–56.

Fish, Stanley (1998) Boutique multiculturalism. In A. Melzer, J. Weinberger and M.R. Zinman (eds) *Multiculturalism and American Democracy.* Lawrence, KS: University Press of Kansas.

Fishman, Joshua (1980) Ethnic community mother tongue schools in the USA. *International Migration Review* 14, 235–247.

Fishman, Joshua (1987) Language spread and language policy for endangered languages. In J. Alatis (ed.) *Georgetown University Round Table on Languages and Linguistics.* Washington, DC: Georgetown University Press.

Fishman, Joshua (1996) *In Praise of the Beloved Language.* Berlin: Mouton de Gruyter.

Fishman, Joshua (ed.) (1999) *Handbook of Language and Ethnic Identity.* Oxford: Oxford University Press.

Fishman, Joshua (ed.) (2001) *Can Threatened Languages be Saved?* Clevedon: Multilingual Matters.

Fishman, Joshua (2006) Sociolinguistics: More power(s) to you (On the explicit study of power in sociolinguistic research). In M. Pütz, J. Fishman and J. Neff-van Aertselaer (eds) *Along the Routes to Power.* Berlin: Mouton de Gruyter.

Flores, Barbara (2005) The intellectual presence of the deficit view of Spanish-speaking children in the educational literature during the 20th century. In P. Pedraza and M. Rivera (eds) *Latino Education: An Agenda for Community Action Research.* Mahwah, NJ: Lawrence Erlbaum.

Flores, N. and Robert Hopper (1975) Mexican Americans' evaluations of spoken Spanish and English. *Speech Monographs* 42, 91–98.

Flugel, J.C. (John Carl) (1934) *Men and their Motives: Psycho-Analytical Studies.* London: Kegan Paul, Trench, Trubner & Co.

Foley, Joseph (1991) Vygotsky, Bernstein and Halliday: Towards a unified theory of L1 and L2 learning. *Language, Culture and Curriculum* 4, 17–42.

Fordham, Signithia (1999) Dissin' 'the standard': Ebonics as guerrilla warfare at Capital High. *Anthropology & Education Quarterly* 30, 272–293.

Fordham, Signithia and John Ogbu (1986) Black students' school success: Coping with the 'burden of acting white'. *Urban Review* 18, 176–206.

Foster, Michele (1997) Ebonics: The children speak up. *Quarterly of the National Writing Project* 19 (1), 7–12.

Foucault, Michel (1969) *L'archéologie du savoir.* Paris: Gallimard.

Foucault, Michel (1971) *L'ordre du discours.* Paris: Gallimard.

Frankfurt, Harry (2005) *On Bullshit.* Princeton, NJ: Princeton University Press.

Fraser, Steven (ed.) (1995) *The Bell Curve Wars: Race, Intelligence, and the Future of America.* New York: Basic Books.

Freeman, Alan (2006) Young, drifting and black. *Globe & Mail* [Toronto], 1 April.

Frender, Robert, Bruce Brown and Wallace Lambert (1970) The role of speech characteristics in scholastic success. *Canadian Journal of Behavioural Science* 2, 299–306.

Freyre, Gilberto (1936) *Sobrados e mucambos: decadencia do patriarcado no Brasil.* São Paulo: Companhia Editora Nacional.

Friedman, Thomas (2002) *Longitudes and Attitudes: Exploring the World after September 11.* New York: Farrar, Straus & Giroux.

Fromm, Erich (1941) *Escape from Freedom.* New York: Holt, Rinehart & Winston.

Fry, Peter (2005) Over the rainbow. *Times Literary Supplement,* 28 January, 26.

Fryer, Roland and Steven Levitt (2004a) Understanding the black-white test score gap in the first two years of school. *Review of Economics and Statistics* 86, 447–464.

Fryer, Roland and Steven Levitt (2004b) The causes and consequences of distinctively black names. *Quarterly Journal of Economics* 119, 767–805.

Fuchs, Estelle (1973) How teachers learn to help children fail. In N. Keddie (ed.) *Tinker, Tailor... The Myth of Cultural Deprivation.* Harmondsworth: Penguin.

Fuentes, Carlos (1999) A cure for monolingualism. *Times Higher Education Supplement,* 17 December.

Gaine, Chris (2005) *We're All White, Thanks: The Persisting Myth about 'White' Schools.* Stoke-on-Trent: Trentham.

Galton, Francis (1869) *Hereditary Genius: An Inquiry into its Laws and Consequences.* London: Macmillan.

Galton, Francis (1883) *Inquiries into Human Faculty and its Development.* London: Macmillan.

Garbarino, James, Kathleen Kostelny and Frank Barry (1997) Value transmission in an ecological context: The high-risk neighborhood. In J. Grusec and L. Kuczynski (eds) *Parenting and Children's Internalization of Values.* New York: Wiley.

García, Eugene (ed.) (2000) *California's Proposition 227* (Special Issue of *Bilingual Research Journal* 24).

García, Ofelia (ed.) (1991) *Bilingual Education: Focusschrift in Honor of Joshua A. Fishman.* Amsterdam: John Benjamins.

García, Ofelia (2009) *Bilingual Education in the 21st Century.* Chichester: Wiley-Blackwell.

García, Ofelia and Harold Schiffman (2006) Fishmanian sociolinguistics (1949 to the present). In O. García, R. Peltz and H. Schiffman (eds) *Language Loyalty, Continuity and Change: Joshua A. Fishman's Contributions to International Socio-linguistics.* Clevedon: Multilingual Matters.

Gardner, Robert and Wallace Lambert (1972) *Attitudes and Motivation in Second-Language Learning*. Rowley, MA: Newbury House.

Garfinkel, Harold (1967) *Studies in Ethnomethodology*. New York: Prentice-Hall.

Garrett, Peter, Nikolas Coupland and Angie Williams (eds) (2003) *Investigating Language Attitudes*. Cardiff: University of Wales Press.

Gass, Susan and Larry Selinker (2008) *Second Language Acquisition*. London: Routledge.

Gay, Geneva (1994) *A Synthesis of Scholarship in Multicultural Education*. Napierville, IL: North Central Regional Educational Laboratory. On WWW at www.ncrel.org/sdrs/areas/issues/educatrs/leadrshp/le0gay.htm.

Gay, Judy and Ryan Tweney (1976) Comprehension and production of standard and black English by lower-class black children. *Developmental Psychology* 12, 262–268.

Genesee, Fred (1981) Bilingualism and biliteracy: A study of cross-cultural contact in a bilingual community. In J. Edwards (ed.) *The Social Psychology of Reading*. Silver Spring, MD: Institute of Modern Languages.

Gerstle, Gary (2001) *American Crucible: Race and Nation in the Twentieth Century*. Princeton, NJ: Princeton University Press.

Gibson, Rex (1984) *Structuralism and Education*. London: Methuen.

Gifford, Bernard and Guadalupe Valdés (2006) The linguistic isolation of Hispanic students in California's public schools. In A. Ball (ed.) *With More Deliberate Speed: Achieving Equity and Excellence in Education*. Oxford: Blackwell (*Yearbook of the National Society for the Study of Education* 105 (2)).

Giles, Howard and Richard Bourhis (1975) Linguistic assimilation: West Indians in Cardiff. *Language Sciences* 38, 9–12.

Giles, Howard and Richard Bourhis (1976) Black speakers with white speech: A real problem? In G. Nickel (ed.) *Proceedings of the Fourth International Congress on Applied Linguistics: Volume 1*. Stuttgart: Hochschul Verlag.

Giles, Howard and Ellen Bouchard Ryan (1982) Prolegomena for developing a social psychological theory of language attitudes. In E. Bouchard Ryan and H. Giles (eds) *Attitudes Towards Language Variation: Social and Applied Contexts*. London: Edward Arnold.

Giles, Howard and Nikolas Coupland (1989) Discourse: Realignment or revolution? *Journal of Language and Social Psychology* 8, 63–68.

Giles, Howard and Nikolas Coupland (1991) *Language: Contexts and Consequences*. Milton Keynes: Open University Press.

Giordano, Gerard (2005) *How Testing Came to Dominate American Schools: The History of Educational Assessment*. New York: Peter Lang.

Glazer, Nathan (1977) Public education and American pluralism. In J. Coleman et al. (eds) *Parents, Teachers and Children: Prospects for Choice in American Education*. San Francisco, CA: Institute for Contemporary Studies.

Glazer, Nathan (1997) *We Are All Multiculturalists Now*. Cambridge, MA: Harvard University Press.

Gleason, Philip (1979) Confusion compounded: The melting pot in the 1960s and 1970s. *Ethnicity* 6, 10–20.

Globe & Mail [Toronto] (1985) Mr Murta's mosaic. 15 May.

Globe & Mail [Toronto] (1996) United States. 26 December.

Globe & Mail [Toronto] (1997) Black English. 6 February.

Goddard, Henry (1912) *The Kallikak Family: A Study in the Heredity of Feeble-Mindedness.* New York: Macmillan.

Godley, Amanda, Brian Carpenter and Cynthia Werner (2007) 'I'll speak in proper slang': Language ideologies in a daily editing activity. *Reading Research Quarterly* 42, 100–131.

Goldsmith, Pat (2004) Schools' racial mix, students' optimism, and the Black-White and Latino-White achievement gaps. *Sociology of Education* 77, 121–147.

Goldstein, Eric (2006) *The Price of Whiteness: Jews, Race and American Identity.* Princeton, NJ: Princeton University Press.

Gonzales, Nancy, Ana Cauce, Ruth Freedman and Craig Mason (1996) Family, peer and neighborhood influences on academic achievement among African American adolescents. *American Journal of Community Psychology* 24, 365–387.

Goodenough, Florence (1926) Racial differences in the intelligence of school children. *Journal of Experimental Psychology* 9, 388–397.

Goot, Murray (1993) Multiculturalists, monoculturalists and the many in between: Attitudes to cultural diversity and their correlates. *Australian and New Zealand Journal of Sociology* 29, 226–253.

Gordon, Edmund (1965) Characteristics of socially disadvantaged children. *Review of Educational Research* 35, 377–388.

Gordon, John (1968) The disadvantaged pupil. *Irish Journal of Education* 2, 69–105.

Gordon, John (1978) The reception of Bernstein's sociolinguistic theory among primary school teachers. *University of East Anglia Papers in Linguistics* 1.

Gordon, John (1981) *Verbal Deficit: A Critique.* London: Croom Helm.

Gould, Stephen Jay (1981) *The Mismeasure of Man.* New York: Norton (revised and expanded edition, 1996).

Gould, Stephen Jay (1994) Curveball. *The New Yorker*, 28 November, 139–149 (reprinted in the 1996 edition of *The Mismeasure of Man*, and in Fraser's *Bell Curve Wars*).

Graddol, David and Joan Swann (1988) Trapping linguists: An analysis of linguists' responses to John Honey's pamphlet 'The Language Trap'. *Language and Education* 2, 95–111.

Graff, David, William Labov and Wendell Harris (1983) Testing listeners' reactions to phonological markers of ethnic identity. In D. Sankoff (ed.) *Diversity and Diachrony.* Amsterdam: Benjamins.

Grafton, Anthony (1997) *The Footnote.* Cambridge, MA: Harvard University Press.

Graham, Sandra, April Taylor and Cynthia Hudley (1998) Exploring achievement values among ethnic minority early adolescents. *Journal of Educational Psychology* 90, 606–620.

Granger, Robert, Marilyn Mathews, Lorene Quay and R. Verner (1977) Teacher judgements of the communication effectiveness of children using different speech patterns. *Journal of Educational Psychology* 69, 793–796.

Grant, Madison (1916) *The Passing of the Great Race.* New York: Scribner.

Gray, Susan and Rupert Klaus (1970) The early training project: A seventh-year report. *Child Development* 41, 909–924.

Green, Lisa (2002) *African American English: A Linguistic Introduction.* Cambridge: Cambridge University Press.

Greenberg, Michael (2005) Freelance. *The Times Literary Supplement*, 9 September.

Grenoble, Lenore and Lindsay Whaley (2006) *Saving Languages: An Introduction to Language Revitalization.* Cambridge: Cambridge University Press.

Grimshaw, Allen (1989) *Collegial Discourse: Professional Conversation Among Peers.* Norwood, NJ: Ablex.

Grimshaw, Allen (ed.) (1994) *What's Going On Here? Complementary Studies of Professional Talk.* Norwood, NJ: Ablex.

Grinberg, Jaime and Elizabeth Saavedra (2000) The constitution of bilingual/ESL education as a disciplinary practice: Genealogical explorations. *Review of Educational Research* 70, 419–441.

Grosjean, François (1982) *Life With Two Languages.* Cambridge, MA: Harvard University Press.

Gullo, Dominic (1981) Social class differences in preschool children's comprehension of wh-questions. *Child Development* 52, 736–740.

Gumperz, John and Dell Hymes (eds) (1964) *The Ethnography of Communication* (*American Anthropologist* 66 (6), Part 2).

Gupta, Anthea Fraser (1997) When mother-tongue education is *not* preferred. *Journal of Multilingual and Multicultural Development* 18, 496–506.

Guskey, Thomas (ed.) (2006a) *Benjamin S. Bloom: Portraits of an Educator.* Lanham, MD: Rowman & Littlefield.

Guskey, Thomas (2006b) Compensatory education for cultural deprivation. In T. Guskey (ed.) *Benjamin S. Bloom: Portraits of an Educator.* Lanham, MD: Rowman & Littlefield.

Haarhoff, Theodore (1920) *Schools of Gaul.* Oxford: Clarendon.

Hagen, Anton (1987) Dialect speaking and school education in western Europe. *Sociolinguistica* 1, 61–79.

Hailong Tian (2006) Review of *Analysing Political Discourse* (Paul Chilton). *Language in Society* 35, 303–306.

Hakuta, Kenji (1991) What bilingual education has taught the experimental psychologist. In O. García (ed.) *Bilingual Education: Focusschrift in Honor of Joshua A. Fishman.* Amsterdam: John Benjamins.

Hakuta, Kenji (2002) Comment. *International Journal of the Sociology of Language* 155/156, 131–136.

Halliday, Michael (1968) The users and uses of language. In J. Fishman (ed.) *Readings in the Sociology of Language.* The Hague: Mouton.

Halliday, Michael (1973a) *Explorations in the Functions of Language.* London: Edward Arnold.

Halliday, Michael (1973b) Foreword. In B. Bernstein (ed.) *Class, Codes and Control, Volume 2: Applied Studies Towards a Sociology of Language.* London: Routledge & Kegan Paul.

Halliday, Michael (1975) *Learning How to Mean: Explorations in the Development of Language.* London: Edward Arnold.

Halliday, Michael (1978) *Language as Social Semiotic: The Social Interpretation of Language and Meaning.* London: Edward Arnold.

Halliday, Michael (1989) *Spoken and Written Language.* Oxford: Oxford University Press.

Halsey, A.H. (Albert Henry) and Kathy Sylva (1987) *Plowden Twenty Years On* (Special Issue of *Oxford Review of Education* 13: 1).

Hamers, Josiane and Michel Blanc (2000) *Bilinguality and Bilingualism* (2nd edn). Cambridge: Cambridge University Press.

Handlin, Oscar (1957) *Race and Nationality in American Life.* Boston, MA: Little, Brown.

Hansegård, Nils (1968) *Tvåspråkighet eller halvspråkighet?* Stockholm: Aldus & Bonnier.

Harber, Jean and Diane Bryen (1976) Black English and the task of reading. *Review of Educational Research* 46, 387–405.

Harré, Rom and Grant Gillett (1994) *The Discursive Mind.* London: Sage.

Harré, Rom and Peter Stearns (1995) *Discursive Psychology in Practice.* London: Sage.

Harrington, Jonathan, Sallyanne Palethorpe and Catherine Watson (2000) Does the Queen speak the Queen's English? *Nature* 408 (6815), 27–28.

Harwood, Jonathan (1982) American academic opinion and social change: Recent developments in the nature-nurture controversy. *Oxford Review of Education* 8, 41–67.

Haugen, Einar (1953) *The Norwegian Language in America.* Philadelphia, PA: University of Pennsylvania Press.

Hawkins, Peter (1969) Social class, the nominal group and reference. *Language and Speech* 12, 125–135.

Hazlitt, William (1901) *Table-Talk: Essays on Men and Manners.* London: Grant Richards.

Heath, Shirley Brice (1983) *Ways With Words.* Cambridge: Cambridge University Press.

Hebb, Donald (1968) *A Textbook of Psychology.* Philadelphia, PA: Saunders.

Heilbrunn, Jacob (1997) Speech therapy. *The New Republic* 20 January (216: 3), 17–19.

Heining-Boynton, Audrey and Thomas Haitema (2007) A ten-year chronicle of student attitudes toward foreign language in the elementary school. *Modern Language Journal* 91, 149–168.

Helm, Toby (2006a) Fly the flag in every garden. *Daily Telegraph*, 14 January.

Helm, Toby (2006b) School lessons in British values. *Daily Telegraph*, 16 May.

Hélot, Christine and Andrea Young (2005) The notion of diversity in language education: Policy and practice at primary level in France. *Language, Culture and Curriculum* 18, 242–257.

Herman, Simon (1961) Explorations in the social psychology of language choice. *Human Relations* 14, 149–164.

Herrnstein, Richard (1971) I.Q. *Atlantic Monthly*, September (228: 7), 43–64.

Herrnstein, Richard (1973) *I.Q. in the Meritocracy.* Boston, MA: Little, Brown.

Herrnstein, Richard and Charles Murray (1994) *The Bell Curve: Intelligence and Class Structure in American Life.* New York: Free Press.

Hess, Frederick and Michael Petrilli (2006) *'No Child Left Behind' Primer.* Frankfurt: Lang.

Hess, Robert and Virginia Shipman (1965) Early experience and the socialization of cognitive modes in children. *Child Development* 36, 869–886.

Hess, Robert and Virginia Shipman (1968a) Maternal attitudes towards the school and the role of the pupil: Some social class comparisons. In A.H. Passow (ed.) *Developing Programs for the Educationally Disadvantaged.* New York: Teachers College Press.

Hess, Robert and Virginia Shipman (1968b) Maternal influences upon early learning: The cognitive environments of urban pre-school children. In R. Hess and R. Bear (eds) *Early Education.* Chicago, IL: Aldine.

Hickey, Leo and Miranda Stewart (eds) (2005) *Politeness in Europe*. Clevedon: Multilingual Matters.

Higham, John (1955) *Strangers in the Land*. New Brunswick, NJ: Rutgers University Press.

Higham, John (1974) Integration versus pluralism: Another American dilemma. *The Center Magazine* 7, 67–73.

Higham, John (1975) *Send These to Me*. New York: Atheneum.

Higham, John (1982) Current trends in the study of ethnicity in the United States. *Journal of American Ethnic History* 2, 5–15.

Hill-Burnett, Jacquetta (1979) Anthropology in relation to education. *American Behavioral Scientist* 23, 237–274.

Hinton, Linette and Karen Pollock (2000) Regional variation in the phonological characteristics of African American Vernacular English. *World Englishes* 19, 59–71.

Hodges, Adam (2005) Review of *Analysing Political Discourse* (Paul Chilton). *Critical Inquiry in Language Studies* 2, 244–247.

Holborow, Marnie (1999) *The Politics of English: A Marxist View of Language*. London: Sage.

Holloway, Joseph and Winifred Vass (1997) *The African Heritage of American English*. Bloomington, IN: Indiana University Press.

Holmes, Janet (1995) *Women, Men and Politeness*. London: Longman.

Holmes, Steven (1994) Survey finds minorities resent one another almost as much as they do whites. *New York Times*, 3 March.

Honey, John (1983a) *The Language Trap*. Kenton, Middlesex: National Council for Educational Standards.

Honey, John (1983b) The way linguists argue: A reply to Crystal and Hudson. *British Association for Applied Linguistics Newsletter* 19, 37–46.

Honey, John (1989) *Does Accent Matter? The Pygmalion Factor*. London: Faber & Faber.

Honey, John (1997) *Language is Power: The Story of Standard English and its Enemies*. London: Faber & Faber.

Honey, John (1998) The straw hippopotamus. *English Today* 14 (3), 41–44.

Honey, John (2000a) A response to Peter Trudgill's review of *Language is Power*. *Journal of Sociolinguistics* 4, 316–319.

Honey, John (2000b) The establishment of the English RP accent: A flawed interpretation? (a review of Lynda Mugglestone's *Talking Proper*). *Bulletin – The International Association of University Professors of English*. On WWW at www.phon.ucl.ac.uk/home/estuary/honey-muggles.htm.

Hornberger, Nancy (1991) Extending enrichment bilingual education: Revisiting typologies and redirecting policy. In O. García (ed.) *Bilingual Education: Focusschrift in Honor of Joshua A. Fishman*. Amsterdam: John Benjamins.

Hornberger, Nancy (ed.) (2005) *Heritage/Community Language Education* (Special Issue of *International Journal of Bilingual Education and Bilingualism* 8, 2/3).

Hornberger, Nancy and Martin Pütz (eds) (2006) *Language Loyalty, Language Planning and Language Revitalization: Recent Writings and Reflections from Joshua A. Fishman*. Clevedon: Multilingual Matters.

Horowitz, Irving (1995) The Rushton file: Racial comparisons and media passions. *Society* 32 (2), 7–17.

Houston, Susan (1970) A reexamination of some assumptions about the language of the disadvantaged child. *Child Development* 41, 947–963.

Houston, Susan (1973) Syntactic complexity and informational transmission in first-graders: A cross-cultural study. *Journal of Psycholinguistic Research* 2, 99–114.

Hudson, Liam (1973) *The Cult of the Fact*. New York: Harper & Row.

Hudson, Richard (1983) Review of *The Language Trap* (John Honey). *British Association for Applied Linguistics Newsletter* 18, 50–54.

Hughes, Robert (1993) *Culture of Complaint: The Fraying of America*. Oxford: Oxford University Press.

Hunt, James (1961) *Intelligence and Experience*. New York: Ronald Press.

Hunt, James (1964) The psychological basis for using preschool enrichment as an antidote for cultural deprivation. *Merrill-Palmer Quarterly* 10, 209–248.

Hunt, James (1975) Reflections on a decade of early education. *Journal of Abnormal Child Psychology* 3, 275–330.

Hursh, David (2007) Assessing *No Child Left Behind* and the rise of neoliberal education policies. *American Educational Research Journal* 44, 493–518.

Huxley, Aldous (1939) *After Many a Summer*. London: Chatto & Windus (the quotation is from the 1972 Penguin paperback edition).

Hymes, Dell (1972) Review of *Noam Chomsky* (John Lyons). *Language* 48, 416–427.

Hymes, Dell (1974) *Foundations in Sociolinguistics: An Ethnographic Approach*. Philadelphia, PA: University of Pennsylvania Press.

Hymes, Dell (1986) Discourse: Scope without depth. *International Journal of the Sociology of Language* 57, 49–89.

[US] Immigration Commission (1911) *Reports of the Immigration Commission*. Washington: Government Printing Office (in 41 volumes).

Imhoff, Gary (ed.) (1990) *Learning in Two Languages: From Conflict to Consensus in the Reorganization of Schools*. New Brunswick, NJ: Transaction.

Ireland (1998) *The Education Act*. Dublin: Government Stationery Office.

Irwing, Paul (2005) We must study the real world, not our world view. *Times Higher Education Supplement*, 2 September.

Irwing, Paul and Richard Lynn (2005) Sex differences in means and variability on the progressive matrices in university students: A meta-analysis. *British Journal of Psychology* 96, 505–524.

Jackson, John (2005) *Science for Segregation: Race, Law and the Case against* Brown v. Board of Education. New York: New York University Press.

Jackson, L. (1974) The myth of elaborated and restricted code. *Higher Education Review* 6: 2, 65–81.

Jacoby, Russell and Naomi Glauberman (eds) (1995) *The Bell Curve Debate: History, Documents, Opinions*. New York: Times Books.

Jarvis, Edward (1855) *Insanity and Idiocy in Massachusetts: Report of the Commission on Lunacy*. Boston, MA: White.

Jaspaert, Koen and Sjaak Kroon (eds) (1991) *Ethnic Minority Languages and Education*. Amsterdam: Swets & Zeitlinger.

Jay, Susan, Donald Routh and John Brantley (1980) Social class differences in children's comprehension of adult language. *Journal of Psycholinguistic Research* 9, 205–217.

Jencks, Christopher (1972) *Inequality: A Reassessment of the Effect of Family and Schooling in America*. New York: Basic Books (Jencks is the main author here, although seven collaborators are listed on cover and title page).

Jensen, Arthur (1967) The culturally disadvantaged: Psychological and educational aspects. *Educational Research* 10, 4–20.

Jensen, Arthur (1968) Social class, race, and genetics: Implications for education. *American Educational Research Journal* 5, 1–42.

Jensen, Arthur (1969) How much can we boost IQ and scholastic achievement? *Harvard Educational Review* 39, 1–123.

Jensen, Arthur (1973) *Educability and Group Differences.* New York: Harper & Row.

Jiménez, Robert (2000) Literacy and the identity development of Latina/o students. *American Educational Research Journal* 37, 971–1000.

Jiménez, R. (2006) A response to 'The linguistic isolation of Hispanic students in California's public schools'. In A. Ball (ed.) *With More Deliberate Speed: Achieving Equity and Excellence in Education.* Oxford: Blackwell (*Yearbook of the National Society for the Study of Education* 105 (2)).

Johns, Ann (2005) English for academic purposes: Issues in undergraduate writing and reading. In P. Bruthiaux, D. Atkinson, W. Eggington, W. Grabe and V. Ramanathan (eds) *Directions in Applied Linguistics: Essays in Honor of Robert B. Kaplan.* Clevedon: Multilingual Matters.

Johnson, Sally and Ulrike Meinhof (eds) (1997) *Language and Masculinity.* Oxford: Blackwell.

Jones, Ernest (1918) *Papers on Psycho-Analysis.* London: Baillière, Tindall & Cox (revised and enlarged edition).

Jones, Edward and Harold Sigall (1971) The bogus pipeline: A new paradigm for measuring affect and attitude. *Psychological Bulletin* 76, 349–364.

Jones, Katharine (2001) *Accent on Privilege: English Identities and Anglophilia in the U.S.* Philadelphia, PA: Temple University Press.

Joos, Martin (1967) *The Five Clocks.* New York: Harcourt, Brace & World.

Joseph, John (2004) *Language and Identity: National, Ethnic, Religious.* London: Palgrave Macmillan.

Julé, Allyson (2004) *Gender, Participation and Silence in the Classroom.* New York: Palgrave Macmillan.

Jussim, Lee and Kent Harber (2005) Teacher expectations and self-fulfilling prophecies. *Personality and Social Psychology Review* 9, 131–155.

Kagan, Jerome (1969) Inadequate evidence and illogical conclusions. *Harvard Educational Review* 39, 274–277.

Kallen, Horace (1915) Democracy versus the melting pot: A study of American nationality. *The Nation* (18 and 25 February), 190–194 and 217–220.

Kallen, Horace (1924) *Culture and Democracy in the United States.* New York: Boni & Liveright.

Kaplan, Charles (1982) Report on the Kassel University conference. *Sociolinguistics Newsletter* 13 (1), 15–18.

Kaplan, Robert (1983) Review of *Hunger of Memory* (Richard Rodriguez). *Language Learning* 33, 123–126.

Katz, Irwin (1967) Some motivational determinants of racial differences in intellectual achievement. *International Journal of Psychology* 2, 1–12.

Katz, Susan (2004) Does NCLB leave the U.S. behind in bilingual teacher education? *English Education* 36, 141–152 (this issue (36: 2) is devoted to the *No Child Left Behind* provisions).

Kautzsch, Alexander (2006) Review of *African American English* (Lisa Green). *Language in Society* 35, 149–152.

Keddie, Nell (ed.) (1973) *Tinker, Tailor... The Myth of Cultural Deprivation.* Harmondsworth: Penguin.

Kedourie, Elie (1961) *Nationalism.* London: Hutchinson.

Kellaghan, Thomas (1977) *The Evaluation of an Intervention Programme for Disadvantaged Children.* Windsor: NFER (National Foundation for Educational Research).

Kellaghan, Thomas (2001) Towards a definition of educational disadvantage. *Irish Journal of Education* 32, 3–22 (this issue appeared rather later than the indicated date; see also the other three papers in this number, papers that deal with disadvantaged children's reading achievements, their attitudes towards school, and some of the services made available to 'at risk' families).

Kirkland, David, Jeffrey Robinson, Austin Jackson and Geneva Smitherman (2004) From 'The lower economic': Three young brothas and an old school womanist respond to Dr Bill Cosby. *The Black Scholar* 34 (4), 10–15.

Kirkpatrick, Clifford (1926) *Intelligence and Immigration.* Baltimore, MD: Williams & Wilkins.

Kissau, Scott (2006) Gender differences in motivation to learn French. *Canadian Modern Language Review* 62, 401–422.

Klaus, Rupert and Susan Gray (1968) The early training project for disadvantaged children: A report after five years. *Monographs of the Society for Research in Child Development* 33: 4.

Kline, Wendy (2001) *Building a Better Race: Gender, Sexuality and Eugenics from the Turn of the Century to the Baby Boom.* Berkeley, CA: University of California Press.

Kochman, Thomas (1985) Review of *The Language Trap* (John Honey). *Language Problems and Language Planning* 9, 152–162.

Koopmans, Ruud, Paul Statham, Marco Giugni and Florence Passy (2005) *Contested Citizenship: Immigration and Cultural Diversity in Europe.* Minneapolis, MN: University of Minnesota Press.

Kozol, Jonathan (2007) The big enchilada. *Harper's,* August (315: 1887), 7–9.

Kretzschmar, William (1998) *Ebonics* (Special Issue of the *Journal of English Linguistics* 26: 2).

Krieger, Nancy and Elizabeth Fee (1994) Social class: The missing link in U.S. health data. *International Journal of Health Services* 24, 25–44.

Kristiansen, Tore, Peter Garrett and Nikolas Coupland (eds) (2005) *Subjective Processes in Language Variation and Change* (*Acta Linguistica Hafniensia* 37).

Kymlicka, Will (1995a) *Multicultural Citizenship.* Oxford: Clarendon Press.

Kymlicka, Will (ed.) (1995b) *The Rights of Minority Cultures.* Oxford: Oxford University Press.

Kymlicka, Will (1998) Review of *We Are All Multiculturalists Now* (Nathan Glazer). *Journal of Multilingual and Multicultural Development* 19, 165–167.

Labov, William (1969) The logic of nonstandard English. *Georgetown Monographs on Language and Linguistics* 22, 1–31 (reprinted in Keddie (q.v), from where the citations here are taken).

Labov, William (1972) Some sources of reading problems for Negro speakers of nonstandard English. In R. Abrahams and R. Troike (eds) *Language and Cultural Diversity in American Education.* Englewood Cliffs, NJ: Prentice-Hall.

Luke, Allan (1995) Text and discourse in education: An introduction to critical discourse analysis. *Review of Research in Education* 21, 3–48.

Luke, Allan (2004) Notes on the future of critical discourse studies. *Critical Discourse Studies* 1, 149–152.

Lupul, Manoly (1982) The political implementation of multiculturalism. *Journal of Canadian Studies* 17, 93–102.

Lupul, Manoly (2005) *The Politics of Multiculturalism*. Edmonton: Canadian Institute of Ukrainian Studies Press.

Lynn, Richard and J. Philippe Rushton (2006) Letter. *Times Higher Education Supplement*, 7 April.

Macías, Reynaldo (1989) *Bilingual Teacher Supply and Demand in the United States*. Los Angeles, CA: University of Southern California Center for Multilingual and Multicultural Research.

Mackey, William (1970) A typology of bilingual education. *Foreign Language Annals* 3, 596–608.

Mackey, William (1978) The importation of bilingual education models. In J. Alatis (ed.) *Georgetown University Round Table on Languages and Linguistics*. Washington, DC: Georgetown University Press.

Mackey, William (1981) Safeguarding language in schools. *Language and Society* [Ottawa] 4: 10–14.

Macnamara, John (1973) Attitudes and learning a second language. In R. Shuy and R. Fasold (eds) *Language Attitudes: Current Trends and Prospects*. Washington, DC: Georgetown University Press.

Majors, Richard and Janet Billson (1993) *Cool Pose: The Dilemmas of Black Manhood in America*. New York: Simon & Schuster.

Majors, Richard and Jacob Gordon (eds) (1994) *The American Black Male*. Chicago, IL: Nelson-Hall.

Maloof, Valerie, Donald Rubin and Ann Miller (2006) Cultural competence and identity in cross-cultural adaptation: The role of a Vietnamese heritage language school. *International Journal of Bilingual Education and Bilingualism* 9, 255–273.

Mann, Arthur (1979) *The One and the Many*. Chicago, IL: University of Chicago Press.

Manning, M. Lee and Leroy Baruth (2004) *Multicultural Education of Children and Adolescents*.Boston, MA: Allyn & Bacon.

Marenbon, John (1987) *English Our English: The New Orthodoxy Examined*. London: Centre for Policy Studies.

Marks, Gary (2006) Are between- and within-school differences in student performance largely due to socioeconomic background? Evidence from 30 countries. *Educational Research* 48, 21–40.

Marmen, Louise and Jean-Pierre Corbeil (1999) *Languages in Canada: 1996 Census*. Ottawa: Supply & Services Canada.

Martin, Renée (ed.) (1995) *Practicing What We Preach: Confronting Diversity in Teacher Education*. Albany, NY: State University of New York Press.

Martin-Jones, Marilyn and Suzanne Romaine (1985) Semilingualism: A half-baked theory of communicative competence. *Applied Linguistics* 6, 105–117.

Marwit, Samuel (1977) Black and white children's use of standard English at 7, 9, and 12 years of age. *Developmental Psychology* 13, 81–82.

Marwit, Samuel and Gail Neumann (1974) Black and white children's comprehension of standard and nonstandard English passages. *Journal of Educational Psychology* 66, 329–332.

Marwit, Samuel and Karen Marwit (1973) Grammatical responses of Negro and Caucasian second graders as a function of standard and non-standard English presentation. *Journal of Educational Psychology* 65, 187–191.

Marwit, Samuel and Karen Marwit (1976) Black children's use of nonstandard grammar: Two years later. *Developmental Psychology* 12, 33–38.

Marwit, Samuel, Karen Marwit and John Boswell (1972) Negro children's use of nonstandard grammar. *Journal of Educational Psychology* 63, 218–224.

Mason, Mary (1986) The deficit hypothesis revisited. *Educational Studies* 12, 279–289.

Mayr, Ernst (1968) Discussion. In M. Mead, T. Dobzhansky, E. Tobach and R. Light (eds) *Science and the Concept of Race.* New York: Columbia University Press.

McAllister, Gretchen and Jacqueline Irvine (2000) Cross-cultural competency and multicultural teacher education. *Review of Educational Research* 70, 3–24.

McBrien, J. Lynn (2005) Educational needs and barriers for refugee students in the United States: A review of the literature. *Review of Educational Research* 75, 329–364.

McCulloch, Oscar (1888) *The Tribe of Ishmael: A Study in Social Degradation.* Indianapolis, IN: Charity Organization Society.

McDermott, Ray and Kenneth Gospodinoff (1981) Social contexts for ethnic borders and school failure. In H. Trueba, G. Guthrie and K. Au (eds) *Culture and the Bilingual Classroom.* Rowley, MA: Newbury.

McDermott, Ray and Kathleen Hall (2007) Scientifically debased research on learning, 1854–2006. *Anthropology and Education Quarterly* 38, 9–15.

McDiarmid, G. Williamson (1992) What to do about difference? A study of multicultural education for teacher trainees in the Los Angeles Unified School District. *Journal of Teacher Education* 43, 83–93.

McDiarmid, G. Williamson and Jeremy Price (1990) *Prospective Teachers' Views of Diverse Learners: A Study of the Participants in the ABCD Project.* East Lansing, MI: National Center for Research on Teacher Education.

McIntosh, Carey (1998) *The Evolution of English Prose, 1700-1800: Style, Politeness and Print Culture.* Cambridge: Cambridge University Press.

McKinzey, R. Kim (2005) Too dumb to die: Mental retardation meets the death penalty. *Web Psych Empiricist.* On WWW at http://www.wpe.info/papers_table.html. [The original posting was in September 2003; the most recent posting, August 2005, includes three updates by McKinzey].

McLaren, Angus (1990) *Our Own Master Race: Eugenics in Canada, 1885–1945.* Toronto: McClelland & Stewart.

McLaughlin, Barry (1978) *Second-Language Acquisition in Childhood.* Hillsdale, NJ: Lawrence Erlbaum.

McMillen, Liz (1997) Linguists find the debate over 'Ebonics' uninformed. *The Chronicle of Higher Education,* 17 January, 16–17.

McNamara, Tim and Carsten Roever (2006) *Language Testing: The Social Dimension.* Oxford: Blackwell.

McWhorter, John (1997a) Wasting energy on an illusion. *Black Scholar* 27 (1), 9–14.

McWhorter, John (1997b) Wasting energy on an illusion: Six months later. *Black Scholar* 27 (2), 2–5.

McWhorter, John (2000) *Losing the Race: Self-Sabotage in Black America.* New York: Free Press.

McWhorter, John (2003) *Doing Our Own Thing: The Degradation of Language and Music and Why We Should, Like, Care.* New York: Gotham Books.

Meditch, Andrea (1975) The development of sex-specific speech patterns in young children. *Anthropological Linguistics* 17, 421–433.

Mehan, Hugh (1984) Language and schooling. *Sociology of Education* 57, 174–183.

Mehta, Ved (1971) John is easy to please. *The New Yorker*, 8 May, 44–87 (this essay is reprinted – with five others – in Mehta's *John Is Easy To Please: Encounters With the Written and the Spoken Word.* New York: Farrar, Straus & Giroux, 1971).

Menand, Louis (1994) The culture wars. *New York Review of Books*, 6 October (no. 41), 16.

Mercer, Neil and Derek Edwards (1981) Ground-rules for mutual understanding: A social psychological approach to classroom knowledge. In N. Mercer (ed.) *Language in School and Community.* London: Edward Arnold.

Mills, Sara (2003) *Gender and Politeness.* Cambridge: Cambridge University Press.

Milroy, James (1984) Sociolinguistic methodology and the identification of speakers' voices in legal proceedings. In P. Trudgill (ed.) *Applied Sociolinguistics.* London: Academic Press.

Milroy, James (1992) *Linguistic Variation and Change.* Oxford: Blackwell.

Milroy, James and Lesley Milroy (1985) *Authority in Language: Investigating Prescription and Standardisation.* London: Routledge & Kegan Paul (a second edition, 1999, has a new subtitle: *Investigating Standard English*).

Milroy, Lesley (1987) *Language and Social Networks* (2nd edn). Oxford: Blackwell.

Milroy, Lesley and Dennis Preston (1999) *Attitudes, Perceptions, and Linguistic Features* (Special Issue of the *Journal of Language and Social Psychology* 18:1).

Milton, John (1644/1958) *Prose Writings.* London: Dent.

Minaya-Rowe, Liliana (2002) *Teacher Training and Effective Pedagogy in the Context of Student Diversity.* Greenwich, CT: Information Age.

Mincy, Ronald (2006) *Black Males Left Behind.* Washington, DC: Urban Institute.

Mitchell, Linda (2001) *Grammar Wars: Language as Cultural Battlefield in 17th- and 18th-Century England.* Aldershot: Ashgate.

Mitchell, Rosamond and Florence Myles (1998) *Second-Language Learning Theories.* London: Arnold.

Molina, Natalia (2006) *Fit To Be Citizens? Public Health and Race in Los Angeles, 1879–1939.* Berkeley, CA: University of California Press.

Morrison, Joan and Charlotte Zabusky (1980) *American Mosaic: The Immigrant Experience in the Words of Those Who Lived It.* New York: Dutton.

Morton, Thomas (1800) *Speed the Plough.* London: Longman & Rees.

Moses, Rae, Harvey Daniels and Robert Gundlach (1976) Teachers' language attitudes and bidialectalism. *International Journal of the Sociology of Language* 8, 77–91.

Moss, Margaret (1973) *Deprivation and Disadvantage.* Bletchley: Open University Press.

Mossman, Douglas (2005) Capital punishment of the mentally disabled requires special consideration. In N. Fisanick (ed.) *The Ethics of Capital Punishment.*

Detroit, MI: Greenhaven, 2005 (originally published as 'Psychiatry in the courtroom' in *Public Affairs* 150, 22–37).

Mount, Harry (2006) *Amo, Amas, Amat... and All That*. London: Short Books.

Muello, Peter (2005) Rio's boneyard of bondage. *Globe & Mail* [Toronto], 29 November (the story was widely reported in newspapers around the world; the common wire-service story that most of them reproduced mistakenly rendered *cemitério* as *cemeterio*).

Mufwene, Salikoko, John Rickford, Guy Bailey and John Baugh (eds) (1998) *African American English: Structure, History and Use*. New York: Routledge.

Mugglestone, Lynda (1995) *'Talking Proper': The Rise of Accent as Social Symbol*. Oxford: Clarendon Press.

Murdoch, Stephen (2007) *IQ: A Smart History of a Failed Idea*. New York: Wiley.

Murphy, Christina (1975) Language, idiom, accent and literacy: An interview with John Edwards. *Irish Times*, 3 November.

Myhill, Debra and Frances Dunkin (2005) Questioning learning. *Language and Education* 19, 415–427.

National Association for Multicultural Education (2003) *Multicultural Education*. A definitional statement adopted by the Board of Directors in February. On WWW at www.nameorg.org.

National Conference of Christians and Jews (1994) *Taking America's Pulse*. New York: NCCJ.

National Conference for Community and Justice (2000) *Taking America's Pulse, II*. New York: NCCJ.

National Conference for Community and Justice (2006) *Taking America's Pulse, III*. New York: NCCJ.

Nature Genetics (2004) Genetics of the human race (Special Issue: a supplement to Volume 36: 11).

Nero, Shondell (ed.) (2006) *Dialects, Englishes, Creoles and Education*. Mahwah, NJ: Lawrence Erlbaum.

Ng, Sik Hung (2007) Language-based discrimination. *Journal of Language and Social Psychology* 26, 106–122.

Ngũgĩ wa Thiong'o (2004) Gikuyu: Recovering the original. In W. Lesser (ed.) *The Genius of Language*. New York: Pantheon.

Niedzielski, Nancy (2005) Linguistic purism from several perspectives: Views from the 'secure' and 'insecure'. In N. Langer and W. Davies (eds) *Linguistic Purism in the Germanic Languages*. Berlin: Walter de Gruyter.

Niedzielski, Nancy and Dennis Preston (2000) *Folk Linguistics*. Berlin: Mouton de Gruyter.

Nieto, Sonia (2004) *Affirming Diversity: The Sociopolitical Context of Multicultural Education*. Boston, MA: Allyn & Bacon.

Noel, Leroy (2005) Bernard Coard tells a mouthful. *Trinidad & Tobago News Bulletin Board*, 15 January. On WWW at www.trinidadandtobagonews.com/forum/webbbs_config.pl/noframes/read/2750.

Noels, Kim and Richard Clément (1998) Language in education. In J. Edwards (ed.) *Language in Canada*. Cambridge: Cambridge University Press.

Noguera, Pedro (1996) Confronting the urban in urban school reform. *Urban Review* 28, 1–19.

Novak, Michael (1971) *The Rise of the Unmeltable Ethnics.* New York: Macmillan (a revised edition, under the title *Unmeltable Ethnics: Politics and Culture in American Life,* appeared in 1996. New Brunswick, NJ: Transaction).

Nunberg, Geoffrey (1986) An official language for California? *New York Times,* 2 October.

[U.S.] Office of Management and Budget (2005) Revisions to the standards for the classification of federal data on race and ethnicity. On WWW at http://www.whitehouse.gov/omb/fedreg/ombdir15.html.

O'Connor, Carla (1997) Dispositions toward (collective) struggle and educational resilience in the inner city: A case analysis of six African-American high school students. *American Educational Research Journal* 34, 593–629.

Ogbu, John (1978) *Minority Education and Caste.* New York: Academic Press.

Ogbu, John (1982a) Cultural discontinuities and schooling. *Anthropology and Education Quarterly* 13, 290–307.

Ogbu, John (1982b) Societal forces as a context of ghetto children's school failure. In L. Feagans and D. Farran (eds) *The Language of Children Reared in Poverty.* New York: Academic Press.

Ogbu, John (1983) Minority status and schooling in plural societies. *Comparative Education Review* 27, 168–190.

Ogbu, John (1987) Variability in minority school performance: A problem in search of an explanation. *Anthropology and Education Quarterly* 18, 312–334.

Ogbu, John (1999) Beyond language: Ebonics, proper English and identity in a Black-American speech community. *American Educational Research Journal* 36, 147–184.

Ogbu, John (2003) *Black American Students in an Affluent Suburb: A Study of Academic Disengagement.* Mahwah, NJ: Lawrence Erlbaum.

Olneck, Michael (2000) Can multicultural education change what counts as cultural capital? *American Educational Research Journal* 37, 317–348.

Orellana, Marjorie, Lucila Ek and Arcelia Hernández (1999) Bilingual education in an immigrant community: *Proposition 227* in California. *International Journal of Bilingual Education and Bilingualism* 2, 114–130.

Ortego y Gasca, Felipe (1981) A bilingual childhood. *American Scholar* 50, 430–431.

Orwell, George (1937) *The Road to Wigan Pier.* London: Gollancz (the quotation is taken from the 1966 Penguin paperback edition).

Orwell, George (1940) England your England. In *Inside the Whale and Other Essays.* London: Gollancz (the quotation is taken from the 1964 Penguin paperback edition).

Osborn, Terry (2000) *Critical Reflection and the Foreign Language Classroom.* Westport, CT: Bergin & Garvey.

Osborne, Jason (1997) Race and academic disidentification. *Journal of Educational Psychology* 89, 728–735.

Ossorio, Pilar and Troy Duster (2005) Race and genetics: Controversies in biomedical, behavioral and forensic sciences. *American Psychologist* 60, 115–128 (this issue is devoted to 'Genes, race and psychology in the genome era' and, beyond the Ossorio and Duster paper, there are useful contributions from Audrey and Brian Smedley (q.v.) on race and racism, and from Robert Sternberg, Elena Grigorenko and Kenneth Kidd, and Richard Cooper, on race and intelligence).

Ousby, Ian (2000) *The Cambridge Guide to Literature in English*. Cambridge: Cambridge University Press.

Ovando, Carlos and Karen Gourd (1996) Knowledge construction, language maintenance, revitalization and empowerment. In J. Banks (ed.) *Multicultural Education, Transformative Knowledge and Action: Historical and Contemporary Perspectives*. New York: Teachers College Press.

Palozzi, Vincent (2006) Assessing voter attitude toward language policy issues in the United States. *Language Policy* 5, 15–39.

Pandey, Anjali (2000) *Symposium on the Ebonics Debate and African American Language* (Special Section of *World Englishes* 19, 1).

Pandit, Prabodh (1979) Perspectives on sociolinguistics in India. In W. McCormack and S. Wurm (eds) *Language and Society*. The Hague: Mouton.

Parekh, Bhikhu (2006) Fighting the war on dogma. *CAUT Bulletin* (Canadian Association of University Teachers), November.

Pastore, Nicholas (1978) The Army intelligence tests and Walter Lippmann. *Journal of the History of the Behavioral Sciences* 14, 316–327.

Pattanayak, Debi (1986) On being and becoming bilingual in India. In J. Fishman, A. Tabouret-Keller, M. Clyne, B. Krishnamurti and M. Abdulaziz (eds) *The Fergusonian Impact*. Berlin: de Gruyter.

Peal, Elizabeth and Wallace Lambert (1962) The relation of bilingualism to intelligence. *Psychological Monographs* 76, 1–23.

Pearce, Sarah (2005) *You Wouldn't Understand: White Teachers in Multiethnic Classrooms*. Stoke-on-Trent: Trentham.

Pearson, Karl (1914–1930) *The Life, Letters and Labours of Francis Galton*. Cambridge: Cambridge University Press (3 volumes in 4: Volume 1 (1914); Volume 2 (1924); Volumes 3a and 3b (1930)).

Penny, Laura (2005) *Your Call is Important to Us: The Truth about Bullshit*. Toronto: McClelland & Stewart.

Pennycook, Alastair (2001) *Critical Applied Linguistics: A Critical Introduction*. Mahwah, NJ: Lawrence Erlbaum.

Pérez Carreón, Gustavo, Corey Drake and Angela Barton (2005) The importance of presence: Immigrant parents' school engagement experiences. *American Educational Research Journal* 42, 465–498.

Peritz, Ingrid (2005) CBC in hot water after show guest says blacks have low IQs. *Globe & Mail* [Toronto], 30 September.

Perry, Theresa, Claude Steele and Asa Hilliard (2003) *Young, Gifted and Black: Promoting High Achievement among African American Students*. Boston, MA: Beacon.

Persell, Caroline (1981) Genetic and cultural deficit theories: Two sides of the same racist coin. *Journal of Black Studies* 12, 19–37.

Petrovic, John (2005) The conservative restoration and neoliberal defenses of bilingual education. *Language Policy* 4, 395–416.

Philippou, Styliane (2005) Modernism and national identity in Brazil, or how to brew a Brazilian stew. *National Identities* 7, 245–264.

Philips, Susan (1970) Acquisition of rules for appropriate speech usage. *Georgetown University Round Table on Linguistics and Language Studies* 23, 77–101.

Philips, Susan (1983) *The Invisible Culture*. New York: Longman.

Phillipps, K.C. (Kenneth Charles) (1984) *Language and Class in Victorian England*. Oxford: Blackwell (in association with André Deutsch).

Phillipson, Robert (1992) *Linguistic Imperialism*. Oxford: Oxford University Press.

Piaget, Jean (1952) *The Language and Thought of the Child*. London: Routledge & Kegan Paul.

Pichart, James and Richard Anderson (1977) Taking different perspectives on a story. *Journal of Educational Psychology* 69, 309–315.

Piché, Gene, Michael Michlin, Donald Rubin and A. Sullivan (1977) Effects of dialect-ethnicity, social class and quality of written compositions on teachers' subjective evaluations of children. *Communication Monographs* 44, 60–72.

Piestrup, Ann (1973) *Black Dialect Interference and Accommodation of Reading Instruction in First Grade*. Berkeley, CA: University of California, Language-Behavior Research Laboratory.

Pinker, Steven (1994) *The Language Instinct*. New York: Morrow.

Plant, E. Ashby, Patricia Devine and Paige Brazey (2003) The bogus pipeline and motivations to respond without prejudice: Revisiting the fading and faking of racial prejudice. *Group Processes and Intergroup Relations* 6, 187–200.

Plowden, Bridget (1967) *Children and Their Primary Schools* (Plowden Report). Department of Education and Science (London): HMSO.

Plowden, Bridget (1970) Compensatory education and the infant school. In T. Cox and C. Waite (eds) *Teaching Disadvantaged Children in the Infant School*. Swansea: University College.

Podhoretz, Norman (1985) Against bilingual education. *New York Post*, 8 October.

Poetter, Thomas, Joseph Wegwert and Catherine Haerr (2006) *No Child Left Behind and the Illusion of Reform*. Lanham, MD: University Press of America.

Ponting, Clive (1994) *Churchill*. London: Stevenson.

Poplack, Shana (ed.) (2000) *The English History of African American English*. Oxford: Blackwell.

Poplack, Shana and Sali Tagliamonte (2001) *African American English in the Diaspora*. Oxford: Blackwell.

Porcel, Jorge (2006) The paradox of Spanish among Miami Cubans. *Journal of Sociolinguistics* 10, 93–110.

Porter, John (1972) Dilemmas and contradictions of a multi-ethnic society. *Transactions of the Royal Society of Canada* 10, 193–205.

Portes, Alejandro and Rubén Rumbaut (1996) *Immigrant America* (2nd edn). Berkeley, CA: University of California Press.

Potter, Jonathan and Margaret Wetherell (1987) *Discourse and Social Psychology*. London: Sage.

Power, Sally, Peter Aggleton, Julia Brannen, Andrew Brown, Lynn Chisholm and John Mace (eds) (2001) *A Tribute to Basil Bernstein, 1924–2000*. London: Institute of Education.

Preston, Dennis (1989) *Perceptual Dialectology: Non-Linguists' Views of Areal Linguistics*. Dordrecht: Foris.

Preston, Dennis (ed.) (1999) *Handbook of Perceptual Dialectology: Volume 1*. Amsterdam: John Benjamins.

Preston, Dennis (ed.) (2003) *Needed Research in American Dialects*. Durham, NC: Duke University Press.

Pütz, Martin, Joshua Fishman and Jo-Anne Neff-van Aertselaer (eds) (2006) *Along the Routes to Power*. Berlin: Mouton de Gruyter.

Quiocho, Alice and Francisco Rios (2000) The power of their presence: Minority group teachers and schooling. *Review of Educational Research* 70, 485–528.

Radio-Canada (2005) Plaintes contre le Docteur Mailloux devant le CRTC et le Collège des Médecins. On WWW at www.radio-canada.ca/culture/.

Rafter, Nicole (1988) *White Trash: The Eugenic Family Studies, 1877–1919*. Boston, MA: Northeastern University Press.

Rainwater, Lee (1970) Neutralizing the disinherited: Some psychological aspects of understanding the poor. In V. Allen (ed.) *Psychological Factors in Poverty*. Chicago, IL: Markham.

Ramirez, J. David, Terrence Wiley, Gerde de Klerk, Enid Lee and Wayne Wright (eds) (2005) *Ebonics: The Urban Education Debate* (2nd edn). Clevedon: Multilingual Matters.

Rampton, Ben (2006) *Language in Late Modernity: Interaction in an Urban School*. Cambridge: Cambridge University Press.

Rampton, Ben (2007) Neo-Hymesian linguistic ethnography in the United Kingdom. *Journal of Sociolinguistics* 11, 584–607.

Rampton, Ben, Karin Tusting, Janet Maybin, Richard Barwell, Angela Creese and Vally Lytra (2004) U.K. linguistic ethnography: A discussion paper. On WWW at www.ling-ethnog.org.uk.

Rampton, Ben, Janet Maybin and Karin Tusting (eds) (2007) *Linguistic Ethnography: Links, Problems and Possibilities*. Oxford: Blackwell (*Journal of Sociolinguistics* 11 (5)).

Rao, Raja (1938) *Kanthapura*. London: Allen & Unwin.

Raven, John (2005) Lethal intelligence. *The Psychologist* 18 (2), 68.

Raven, John and John Stephenson (eds) (2001) *Competence in the Learning Society*. New York: Lang.

Reagan, Ronald (1982) *Public Papers of the Presidents of the United States: Ronald Reagan, 1981. Book 1: January 20 to December 31, 1981*. Washington, DC: United States Government Printing Office (Reagan's speech was initially reported in the *Democrat and Chronicle* (Rochester, New York), 3 March 1981).

Reagan, Timothy (2006) Review of *Second Language Teacher Education: International Perspectives* (Diane Tedick). *Studies in Second Language Acquisition* 28, 133–134.

Reagan, Timothy and Terry Osborn (2002) *The Foreign Language Educator in Society*. Mahwah, NJ: Lawrence Erlbaum.

Reyes, Luis (2006) The *Aspira Consent Decree*: A thirtieth-anniversary retrospective of bilingual education in New York City. *Harvard Educational Review* 76, 369–400.

Rich, F. (1997) The Ebonic plague. *Globe & Mail* [Toronto], 9 January.

Richardson, Brian (2005) *Tell It Like It Is: How Our Schools Fail Black Children*. London: Trentham.

Richardson, Elaine (1998) The anti-Ebonics movement: 'Standard' English only. *Journal of English Linguistics* 26, 156–169.

Rickford, John (2002) Linguistics, education and the Ebonics firestorm. In J. Alatis, H. Hamilton and A.-H. Tan (eds) *Georgetown University Round Table on Languages and Linguistics 2000: Linguistics, Language and the Professions: Education, Journalism, Law, Medicine and Technology*.

Rickford, John (2005) Using the vernacular to teach the standard. In J.D. Ramirez, T. Wiley, G. de Klerk, E. Lee and W. Wright (eds) *Ebonics: The Urban Education Debate* (2nd edn). Clevedon: Multilingual Matters.

Rickford, John and A. Rickford (1995/2005) Dialect readers revisited. *Linguistics and Education* 7, 107–128 (a two-page summary appears in J.D. Ramirez, T. Wiley, G. de Klerk, E. Lee and W. Wright (eds) *Ebonics: The Urban Education Debate* (2nd edn). Clevedon: Multilingual Matters, 2005).

Rist, Ray (1970) Student social class and teacher expectations: The self-fulfilling prophecy in ghetto education. *Harvard Educational Review* 40, 411–451.

Roberts, Mark (2008) *The Mark of the Beast: Animality and Human Oppression.* West Lafayette, IN: Purdue University Press.

Robinson, Philip (1976) *Education and Poverty.* London: Methuen.

Robinson, W. Peter (1965) The elaborated code in working class language. *Language and Speech* 8, 243–252.

Robinson, W. Peter (1972) *Language and Social Behaviour.* Harmondsworth: Penguin.

Robinson, W. Peter (1985) Social psychology and discourse. In T. van Dijk (ed.) *Handbook of Discourse Analysis, Volume 1: Disciplines of Discourse.* London: Academic Press.

Robinson, W. Peter (1998) Language and social psychology: An intersection of opportunities and significance. *Journal of Language and Social Psychology* 17, 276–301.

Robinson, W. Peter (2001) A tale of two histories: Language use and education in relation to social class and gender. *Journal of Language and Social Psychology* 20, 231–247.

Robinson, W. Peter and Howard Giles (eds) (2001) *The New Handbook of Language and Social Psychology.* New York: John Wiley.

Robinson, W. Peter and Susan Rackstraw (1972) A *Question of Answers.* London: Routledge & Kegan Paul.

Rocher, Guy (1973) *Le Québec en mutation.* Montreal: Éditions Hurtubise.

Rodriguez, Richard (1980a) Aria: A memoir of a bilingual childhood. *American Scholar* 50, 25–42.

Rodriguez, Richard (1980b) An education in language. In L. Michaels and C. Ricks (eds) *The State of the Language.* Berkeley, CA: University of California Press.

Rodriguez, Richard (1982) *Hunger of Memory: The Education of Richard Rodríguez.* Boston, MA: Godine.

Rodriguez, Richard (1993) *Days of Obligation: An Argument With My Mexican Father.* London: Penguin.

Roeming, Richard (1971) Bilingualism and the national interest. *Modern Language Journal* 55, 73–81.

Rogers, Rebecca, Elizabeth Malancharuvil-Berkes, Melissa Mosley, Diane Hui and Glynis Joseph (2005) Critical discourse analysis in education: A review of the literature. *Review of Educational Research* 75, 365–416.

Romaine, Suzanne (1995) *Bilingualism* (2nd edn). Oxford: Blackwell, 1995.

Ronjat, Jules (1913) *Le développement du langage observé chez un enfant bilingue.* Paris: Champion.

Roosevelt, Theodore (1919) Abolish hyphen Roosevelt's last words to public. *Chicago Daily Tribune*, 7 January.

Rosen, E. (1982) Epistle to Kaplan: Remarks on the ethno-inquiries. *Sociolinguistics Newsletter* 13 (1), 18–23.

Rosen, Harold (1972) *Language and Class: A Critical Look at the Theories* of Basil Bernstein. Bristol: Falling Wall Press.

Rosen, Harold (1978) Signing on. *The New Review* 5: 1.

Rosenthal, Robert and Lenore Jacobson (1968) *Pygmalion in the Classroom.* New York: Holt, Rinehart & Winston (see also the slightly enlarged edition – New York: Irvington, 1992).

Rosewarne, David (1984) Estuary English. *Times Educational Supplement,* 19 October.

Rosewarne, David (1994) Estuary English: Tomorrow's RP? *English Today* 37, 3–8.

Ross, Lee and Richard Nisbett (1991) *The Person and the Situation.* Philadelphia, PA: Temple University Press.

Rotberg, Iris (1984) Bilingual education policy in the United States. *Prospects* 14, 133–147.

Rushton, J. Philippe (1995) *Race, Evolution and Behavior.* New Brunswick, NJ: Transaction.

Rushton, J. Philippe and G. Young (1975) Context and complexity in working class language. *Language and Speech* 18, 366–387.

Rutter, Michael and Nicola Madge (1977) *Cycles of Disadvantage.* London: Heinemann.

Ryan, Ellen Bouchard (1979) Why do low-prestige varieties persist? In H. Giles and R. St Clair (eds) *Language and Social Psychology.* Oxford: Blackwell.

Ryan, Ellen Bouchard and Miguel Carranza (1975) Evaluative reactions of adolescents toward speakers of standard English and Mexican American accented English. *Journal of Personality and Social Psychology* 31, 855–863.

Ryan, Ellen Bouchard, Miguel Carranza and Robert Moffie (1977) Reactions toward varying degrees of accentedness in the speech of Spanish-English bilinguals. *Language and Speech* 20, 267–273.

Ryan, William (1971) *Blaming the Victim.* New York: Pantheon.

Sachs, Jacqueline (1975) Cues to the identification of sex in children's speech. In B. Thorne and N. Henley (eds) *Language and Sex: Difference and Dominance.* Rowley, MA: Newbury.

Sachs, Jacqueline, Philip Lieberman and Donna Erickson (1973) Anatomical and cultural determinants of male and female speech. In R. Shuy and R. Fasold (eds) *Language Attitudes: Current Trends and Prospects.* Washington, DC: Georgetown University Press.

Sacks, Harvey, Emanuel Schegloff and Gail Jefferson (1974) A simplest systematics for the organization of turn-taking for conversation. *Language* 50, 696–735.

Salkie, Raphael (2004) Blair's lessons in ethics of respect. *Times Higher Education Supplement,* 8 October.

Samelson, Franz (1977) World War I intelligence testing and the development of psychology. *Journal of the History of the Behavioral Sciences* 13, 274–282.

Samelson, Franz (1978) From 'race psychology' to 'studies in prejudice': Some observations on the thematic reversal in social psychology. *Journal of the History of the Behavioral Sciences* 13, 265–278.

Sampson, Geoffrey (1980) *Schools of Linguistics: Competition and Evolution.* London: Hutchinson.

San Miguel, Guadalupe (2004) *Contested Policy: The Rise and Fall of Federal Bilingual Education in the United States, 1960–2001.* Denton, TX: University of North Texas Press.

Sandiford, Peter and Ruby Kerr (1926) Intelligence of Chinese and Japanese children. *Journal of Educational Psychology* 17, 361–367.

Schank, Roger (2006) Thinking is no help in making the grade. *Times Higher Education Supplement*, 28 April.

Schatzman, Leonard and Anselm Strauss (1955) Social class and modes of communication. *American Journal of Sociology* 60, 329–338.

Schegloff, Emanuel (1997) Whose text? Whose context? *Discourse and Society* 8, 165–187.

Schlesinger, Arthur (1992) *The Disuniting of America: Reflections on a Multicultural Society.* New York: Norton.

Schneider, William (1992) After Binet: French intelligence testing, 1900–1950. *Journal of the History of the Behavioral Sciences* 28, 111–132.

Schwartz, Robert (2001) Racial profiling in medical research. *New England Journal of Medicine* 344 (18), 1392–1393.

Scott, Jerrie (1998) The serious side of Ebonics humor. *Journal of English Linguistics* 26, 137–155.

Scruton, Roger (2006) Values are not learnt through teaching. *Daily Telegraph*, 16 May.

Seligman, Clive, G. Richard Tucker and Wallace Lambert (1972) The effects of speech style and other attributes on teachers' attitudes toward pupils. *Language in Society* 1, 131–142.

Shafer, Robert and Susanne Shafer (1975) Teacher attitudes towards children's language in West Germany and England. *Comparative Education* 11, 43–61.

Shockley, William (1970) A 'try simplest cases' approach to the heredity-poverty-crime problem. In V. Allen (ed.) *Psychological Factors in Poverty.* Chicago, IL: Markham.

Shohamy, Elana (2001) *The Power of Tests.* Harlow: Longman.

Shurkin, Joel (2006) *Broken Genius: The Rise and Fall of William Shockley, Creator of the Electronic Age.* London: Palgrave Macmillan.

Shuy, Roger (1970) The sociolinguists and urban language problems. In F. Williams (ed.) *Language and Poverty.* Chicago, IL: Markham.

Siegel, Jeff (2006) Keeping creoles and dialects out of the classroom: Is it justified? In S. Nero (ed.) *Dialects, Englishes, Creoles and Education.* Mahwah, NJ: Lawrence Erlbaum.

Siegel, Jeff (2007) Creoles and minority dialects in education: An update. *Language and Education* 21, 66–86.

Sigall, Harold and Richard Page (1971) Current stereotypes: A little fading, a little faking. *Journal of Personality and Social Psychology* 18, 247–255.

Simons, Herbert (1974) Black dialects and learning to read. In Jerry Johns (ed.) *Literacy for Diverse Learners.* Newark, DE: International Reading Association.

Simons, Herbert and Kenneth Johnson (1974) Black English syntax and reading interference. *Research in the Teaching of English* 8, 339–358.

Simpkins, Gary, Grace Holt and Charlesetta Simpkins (1977) *Bridge: A Cross-Cultural Reading Program.* Boston, MA: Houghton Mifflin.

Simpkins, Gary and Charlesetta Simpkins (1981) Cross-cultural approach to curriculum development. In G. Smitherman (ed.) *Black English and the Education of Black Children and Youth: Proceedings of the National Invitational Symposium on the King Decision.* Detroit, MI: Center for Black Studies, Wayne State University.

Sirin, Selcuk (2005) Socioeconomic status and academic achievement: A meta-analytic review of research. *Review of Educational Research* 75, 417–453.

Skeels, Harold and Harold Dye (1939) A study of the effects of differential stimulation on mentally retarded children. *Proceedings of the American Association of Mental Deficiency* 44, 114–136.

Skidmore, Thomas (1974) *Black into White: Race and Nationality in Brazilian Thought.* Oxford: Oxford University Press.

Sleeter, Christine and Carl Grant (1987) An analysis of multicultural education in the United States. *Harvard Educational Review* 57, 421–444.

Slembrouck, Stef (2001) Explanation, interpretation and critique in the analysis of discourse. *Critique of Anthropology* 21, 33–57.

Slotkin, Richard (2005) *Lost Battalions: The Great War and the Crisis of American Nationality.* New York: Henry Holt.

Smedley, Audrey and Brian Smedley (2005) Race as biology is fiction, racism as a social problem is real. *American Psychologist* 60, 16–26.

Smith, Ernest (2001) Ebonics and bilingual education of the African American child. In C. Crawford (ed.) *Ebonics and Language Education.* New York: Sankofa.

Smith, J. (1988) Review of *Discourse and Social Psychology* (Jonathan Potter and Margaret Wetherell). *The Psychologist* 1, 109.

Smith, Madorah (1939) Some light on the problem of bilingualism as found from a study of the progress in the mastery of English among preschool children of non-American ancestry in Hawaii. *Genetic Psychology Monographs* 21, 119–284.

Smitherman, Geneva (ed.) (1981a) *Black English and the Education of Black Children and Youth: Proceedings of the National Invitational Symposium on the King Decision.* Detroit, MI: Center for Black Studies, Wayne State University.

Smitherman, Geneva (1981b) What go round come round: *King* in perspective. *Harvard Educational Review* 51, 40–56.

Smitherman, Geneva (1998) Ebonics, *King* and Oakland: Some folks don't believe fat meat is greasy. *Journal of English Linguistics* 26, 97–107.

Smitherman, Geneva (2006) *Word From the Mother: Language and African Americans.* London: Routledge.

Smitherman-Donaldson, Geneva (1988) Discriminatory discourse on Afro-American speech. In G. Smitherman-Donaldson and T. van Dijk (eds.) *Discourse and Discrimination.* Detroit, MI: Wayne State University Press.

Sniderman, Paul and Louk Hagendoorn (2007) *When Ways of Life Collide: Multiculturalism and its Discontents in The Netherlands.* Princeton, NJ: Princeton University Press.

Snow, Catherine (1982) Knowledge and the use of language. In L. Feagans and D. Farran (eds) *The Language of Children Reared in Poverty.* New York: Academic.

Sommers, Christina (2000) *The War Against Boys: How Misguided Feminism is Harming Our Young Men.* New York: Simon & Schuster.

Somervill, Mary (1974) Language of the disadvantaged: Toward resolution of conflict. *Journal of Negro Education* 43, 284–301.

Somervill, Mary (1975) Dialect and reading: A review of alternative solutions. *Review of Educational Research* 45, 247–262.

Somervill, Mary and John Jacobs (1972) The use of dialect in reading materials for black inner-city children. *Negro Educational Review* 23, 13–23.

Spearman, Charles (1927) *The Abilities of Man*. London: Macmillan.

Spearman, Charles (1937) *Psychology Down the Ages*. London: Macmillan (2 volumes).

Spearman, Charles and Llewelyn Wynn Jones (1950) *Human Ability*. London: Macmillan.

Spears, Arthur (1987) Are black and white vernaculars diverging? In R. Fasold, W. Labov, F. Vaughn-Cooke, G. Bailey, W. Wolfram, A. Spears and J. Rickford, *Are Black and White Vernaculars Diverging? Papers from the NWAVE-XIV Panel Discussion* (*American Speech* 62 (1), 3–80).

Speicher, Barbara and Seane McMahon (1992) Some African-American perspectives on Black English Vernacular. *Language in Society* 21, 383–407.

Spender, Dale (1980) Talking in the class. In D. Spender and E. Sarah (eds) *Learning to Lose: Sexism and Education*. London: Women's Press.

Spitz, René (1946) Anaclitic depression. *Psychoanalytic Study of the Child* 2, 313–342.

Spolsky, Bernard (1989a) *Conditions for Second-Language Learning*. Oxford: Oxford University Press.

Spolsky, Bernard (1989b) Review of *Key Issues in Bilingualism and Bilingual Education* (Colin Baker). *Applied Linguistics* 10, 449–451.

Spolsky, Bernard (1995) *Measured Words: The Development of Objective Language Testing*. Oxford: Oxford University Press.

Sroufe, L. Alan (1970) A methodological and philosophical critique of intervention-oriented research. *Developmental Psychology* 2, 140–145.

Stammerjohann, Harro (ed.) (1996) *Lexicon Grammaticorum: Who's Who in the History of World Linguistics*. Tübingen: Max Niemeyer.

Stanworth, Michelle (1981) *Gender and Schooling: A Study of Sexual Divisions in the Classroom*. London: Women's Research Centre.

Staples, Brent (1997) The last train from Oakland. *The New York Times*, 24 January.

Steele, Claude (1992) Race and the schooling of African-American Americans [sic]. *Atlantic Monthly*, May (269: 4), 68–78.

Steele, Claude (1997) A threat in the air: How stereotypes shape intellectual identity and performance. *American Psychologist* 52, 613–629.

Steele, Claude and Joshua Aronson (1995) Stereotype threat and the intellectual test performance of African-Americans. *Journal of Personality and Social Psychology* 69, 797–811.

Steigerwald, David (2004) *Culture's Vanities: The Paradox of Cultural Diversity in a Globalized World*. Lanham, MD: Rowman & Littlefield.

Stein, Gertrude (1937) *Everybody's Autobiography*. New York: Random House.

Steinberg, Laurence, B. Bradford Brown and Sanford Dornbusch (1996) *Beyond the Classroom*. New York: Simon & Schuster.

Steiner, George (1992) *After Babel* (2nd edn). Oxford: Oxford University Press.

Steiner, George and Cécile Ladjali (2003) *Éloge de la transmission: le maître et l'élève*. Paris: Albin Michel.

Stern, Alexandra (2005) *Eugenic Nation: Faults and Frontiers of Better Breeding in Modern America*. Berkeley, CA: University of California Press.

Stetson, George (1897) Some memory tests of Whites and Blacks. *Psychological Review* 4, 285–289.

Stewart, William (1972) On the use of Negro dialect in the teaching of reading. In R. Abrahams and R. Troike (eds) *Language and Cultural Diversity in American Education*. Englewood Cliffs, NJ: Prentice-Hall.

Stinson, David (2006) African American male adolescents, schooling (and mathematics): Deficiency, rejection, and achievement. *Review of Educational Research* 76, 477–506.

Stoller, Paul (1977) The language planning activities of the U.S. Office of Bilingual Education. *Linguistics* 189, 45–60.

Stone, Maureen (1981) *The Education of the Black Child in Britain: The Myth of Multiracial Education*. London: Fontana.

Strauss, Anselm and Leonard Schatzman (1960) Cross-class interviewing: An analysis of interaction and communicative styles. In R. Adams and J. Preiss (eds) *Human Organization Research*. Homewood, IL: Dorsey.

Stubbs, Michael (1983a) *Language, Schools and Classrooms*. London: Methuen.

Stubbs, Michael (1983b) *Discourse Analysis*. Oxford: Blackwell.

Stubbs, Michael (1984) Applied discourse analysis and educational linguistics. In P. Trudgill (ed.) *Applied Sociolinguistics*. London: Academic Press.

Stubbs, Michael (1986) *Educational Linguistics*. Oxford: Blackwell.

Sudnow, David (1972) Temporal parameters of interpersonal observation. In D. Sudnow (ed.) *Studies in Social Interaction*. New York: Free Press.

Swaffar, Janet (1999) The case for foreign languages as a discipline. *ADFL Bulletin* 30(3), 6–12.

Swann, Michael (1985) *Education for All: The Report of the Committee of Inquiry into the Education of Children from Ethnic Minority Groups* (Report). Department of Education and Science (London): HMSO.

Talbot, Margaret (2003) The executioner's IQ test. *New York Times Magazine*, 29 June.

Tannen, Deborah (1998) *The Argument Culture*. New York: Random House.

Tannen, Deborah, Shari Kendall and Carolyn Adger (1997) Conversational patterns across gender, class and ethnicity: Implications for classroom discourse. In B. Davies and D. Corson (eds) *Oral Discourse and Education*. Dordrecht: Kluwer.

Taylor, April and Sandra Graham (2007) An examination of the relationship between achievement values and perceptions of barriers among low-SES African American and Latino students. *Journal of Educational Psychology* 99, 52–64.

Taylor, Charles (1992) *Multiculturalism and 'The Politics of Recognition'*. Princeton, NJ: Princeton University Press.

Taylor, L. and Graham Skanes (1977) A cross-cultural examination of some of Jensen's hypotheses. *Canadian Journal of Behavioural Science* 9, 315–322.

Telles, Edward (2004) *Race in Another America: The Significance of Skin Color in Brazil*. Princeton, NJ: Princeton University Press.

Templin, Mildred (1957) *Certain Language Skills in Children*. Minneapolis, MN: University of Minnesota Press.

Tenenbaum, Harriet and Martin Ruck (2007) Are teachers' expectations different for racial minority than for European American students? A meta-analysis. *Journal of Educational Psychology* 99, 253–273.

Terman, Lewis (1906) Genius and stupidity: A study of some of the intellectual processes of seven 'bright' and seven 'stupid' boys. *Pedagogical*

Seminary 13, 307–373 (this, Terman's PhD thesis, was reprinted in 1975: New York: Arno).

Terman, Lewis (1918) The use of intelligence tests in the Army. *Psychological Bulletin* 15, 177–187.

Terman, Lewis (1922) Were we born that way? *The World's Work* 44, 655–660.

Terrill, Marguerite and Dianne Mark (2000) Pre-service teachers' expectations for schools with children of color and second-language learners. *Journal of Teacher Education* 51, 149–157.

Thomson, J. (1977) Social class labelling in the application of Bernstein's theory of the codes to the identification of linguistic advantage and disadvantage in five-year-old children. *Educational Review* 29, 273–283.

Throop, Rachel (2007) Teachers as language policy planners. *Working Papers in Educational Linguistics* (Graduate School of Education, University of Pennsylvania) 22 (2), 45–65.

Thurmond, Vera (1977) The effect of Black English on the reading test performance of high school students. *Journal of Educational Research* 70, 160–163.

Todd, Loreto (1997) Ebonics: An evaluation. *English Today* 13 (3), 13–17.

Tomlinson, Sally (1984) Home, school and community. In M. Craft (ed.) *Education and Cultural Pluralism.* London: Falmer.

Torrey, Jane (1973) Illiteracy in the ghetto. In N. Keddie (ed.) *Tinker, Tailor... The Myth of Cultural Deprivation.* Harmondsworth: Penguin.

Torrey, Jane (1983) Black children's knowledge of standard English. *American Educational Research Journal* 20, 627–643.

Tough, Joan (1977) *The Development of Meaning: A Study of Children's Use of Language.* London: Allen & Unwin.

Tough, Joan (1982) Language, poverty and disadvantage in school. In L. Feagans and D. Farran (eds) *The Language of Children Reared in Poverty.* New York: Academic Press.

Tough, Joan (1985) *Talk Two: Children Using English as a Second Language.* London: Onyx.

Trudgill, Peter (1972) Sex, covert prestige and linguistic change in the urban British English of Norwich. *Language in Society* 1, 179–195.

Trudgill, Peter (1975) *Accent, Dialect and the School.* London: Edward Arnold.

Trudgill, Peter (1979) Standard and non-standard dialects of English in the United Kingdom: Problems and policies. *International Journal of the Sociology of Language* 21, 9–24.

Trudgill, Peter (1984) Preface. In P. Trudgill (ed.) *Applied Sociolinguistics.* London: Academic Press.

Trudgill, Peter (1998) Review of *Language is Power* (John Honey). *Journal of Sociolinguistics* 2, 457–461.

Trudgill, Peter (2000) *Sociolinguistics: An Introduction to Language and Society* (4th edn). London: Penguin.

Trudgill, Peter (2002) *Sociolinguistic Variation and Change.* Washington, DC: Georgetown University Press.

Tucker, G. Richard and Wallace Lambert (1969) White and Negro listeners' reactions to various American-English dialects. *Social Forces* 47, 463–468.

Tucker, William (1994) *The Science and Politics of Racial Research.* Urbana, IL: University of Illinois Press.

Tucker, William (2002) *The Funding of Scientific Racism: Wickliffe Draper and the Pioneer Fund.* Urbana, IL: University of Illinois Press.

Turner, L.D. (Lorenzo Dow) (1949) *Africanisms in the Gullah Dialect.* Chicago, IL: University of Chicago Press.

Tusting, Karin and Janey Maybin (2007) Linguistic ethnography and interdisciplinarity. *Journal of Sociolinguistics* 11, 575–583.

Tutton, Richard (2007) Opening the white box: Exploring the study of whiteness in contemporary genetics research. *Ethnic and Racial Studies* 30, 557–569.

Tuveng, Elena and Astri Wold (2005) The collaboration of teacher and language-minority children in masking comprehension problems in the language of instruction: A case study in an urban Norwegian school. *Language and Education* 19, 513–536.

Tyson, Karolyn (2002) Weighing in: Elementary-age students and the debate on attitudes toward school among Black students. *Social Forces* 80, 1157–1189.

UNESCO (1953) *The Use of Vernacular Languages in Education.* Paris: UNESCO.

Unz, Ron and Catherine Snow (2002) Bilingual education: A necessary help or a failed hindrance? *Harvard Education Letter*, January/February. On WWW at www.edletter.org/past/issues/2002-jf/forum.shtml/.

Unz, Ron and Gloria Tuchman (1998) One homogeneous nation: The Unz initiative. On WWW at http://www.smartnation.org/unz.htm.

Valenzuela, Angela, Linda Prieto and Madlene Hamilton (2007) *No Child Left Behind and Minority Youth: What the Qualitative Evidence Suggests.* Berkeley, CA: University of California Press (*Anthropology and Education Quarterly* 38 (1)).

Van Dijk, Teun (1993) Principles of critical discourse analysis. *Discourse and Society* 4, 249–283.

Van Dijk, Teun (2001) Multidisciplinary CDA: A plea for diversity. In R. Wodak and M. Meyer (eds) *Methods of Critical Discourse Analysis.* London: Sage.

Varghese, Manka (2004) Professional development for bilingual teachers in the United States. In J. Brutt-Griffler and M. Varghese (eds) *Bilingualism and Language Pedagogy.* Clevedon: Multilingual Matters.

Varghese, Manka (2006) Bilingual teachers-in-the-making in Urbantown. *Journal of Multilingual and Multicultural Development* 27, 211–224.

Venezky, Richard (1970) Nonstandard language and reading. *Elementary English* 47, 334–345.

Venezky, Richard (1981) Non-standard language and reading: Ten years later. In J. Edwards (ed.) *The Social Psychology of Reading.* Silver Spring, MD: Institute of Modern Languages.

Verschueren, Jeff (2001) Predicaments of criticism. *Critique of Anthropology* 21, 59–81.

Vick, M. (1974) Relevant content for the black elementary school pupil. In J. Johns (ed.) *Literacy for Diverse Learners.* Newark, DE: International Reading Association.

Walker, Francis (1896) Restriction of immigration. *Atlantic Monthly*, June (77: 484), 822–829.

Wallen, Matthew and Helen Kelly-Holmes (2006) 'I think they just think it's going to go away at some stage': Policy and practice in teaching English as an additional language in Irish primary schools. *Language and Education* 20, 141–161.

Wallis, Claudia and Sonja Steptoe (2007) How to fix 'No Child Left Behind'. *Time*, 4 June (169: 23), 26–33.

Walsh, Catherine (1991) *Pedagogy and the Struggle for Voice*. New York: Bergin & Garvey.

Wardhaugh, Ronald (2006) *An Introduction to Sociolinguistics* (5th edn). Oxford: Blackwell.

Watts, Ronald (2003) *Politeness*. Cambridge: Cambridge University Press.

Wax, Murray and Rosalie Wax (1971) Cultural deprivation as an educational ideology. In E. Leacock (ed.) *The Culture of Poverty: A Critique*. New York: Simon & Schuster.

Weathers, John (2007) Privatizing schools. *Working Papers in Educational Linguistics* (Graduate School of Education, University of Pennsylvania) 22 (2), 67–93.

Webb, Nick (2005) *The Dictionary of Bullshit*. London: Robson.

Webster, Jonathan (ed.) (2005) *Language, Society and Consciousness: The Collected Works of Ruqaiya Hasan: Volume 1*. London: Equinox (two further volumes – *Semantic Variation: Meaning in Society* and *Language in Education: Social Aspects* are in preparation).

Wee, Lionel (2002) When English is not a mother tongue: Linguistic ownership and the Eurasian community in Singapore. *Journal of Multilingual and Multicultural Development* 23, 282–295.

Weinberg, Bernd and Suzanne Bennett (1971) Speaker sex recognition of 5- and 6-year-old children's voices. *Journal of the Acoustical Society of America* 50, 1210–1213.

Weinreich, Uriel (1953) *Languages in Contact*. The Hague: Mouton.

Wente, Margaret (2006) A+ for cultural capital. *Globe & Mail* [Toronto], 27 June.

Wetherell, Margaret (2007) A step too far: Discursive psychology, linguistic ethnography and questions of identity. *Journal of Sociolinguistics* 11, 661–681.

White, John (2005) Puritan intelligence. *Oxford Review of Education* 31, 423–442.

White, John (2006a) The religious origins of intelligence testing. *The Psychologist* 19, 360–361.

White, John (2006b) *Intelligence, Destiny and Education: The Ideological Roots of Intelligence Testing*. London: Routledge.

White, Karl (1982) The relationship between socioeconomic status and academic achievement. *Psychological Bulletin* 91, 461–481.

Wickett, John (1990) *The Evolution and Development of the Intelligence Testing Movement*. Antigonish, Nova Scotia: St Francis Xavier University.

Widdowson, Henry (2004) *Text, Context, Pretext: Critical Issues in Discourse Analysis*. Oxford: Blackwell.

Wierzbicka, Anna (2005) Universal human concepts as a tool for exploring bilingual lives. *International Journal of Bilingualism* 9, 7–26.

Wiese, Ann-Marie and Eugene Garcia (2001) The *Bilingual Education Act*: Language minority students and U.S. federal educational policy. *International Journal of Bilingual Education and Bilingualism* 4, 229–248.

Wigfield, Allan, Alice Galper, Kristin Denton and Carol Seefeldt (1999) Teachers' beliefs about former Head Start and non-Head Start first-grade children's motivation, performance, and future educational prospects. *Journal of Educational Psychology* 91, 98–104.

Wiggan, Greg (2007) Race, school achievement and educational inequality: Toward a student-based inquiry perspective. *Review of Educational Research* 77, 310–333.

Wiggen, Geir (1978) The use of dialects in the initial teaching of the written language: The Norwegian case. Paper presented at the *AILA* conference, Montreal.

Wiley, Terrence and Wayne Wright (2004) Against the undertow: Language-minority education policy and politics in the 'age of accountability'. *Educational Policy* 18, 142–168.

Wilkins, Roy (1971) Black nonsense. *The Crisis* 78 (3), 78.

Williams, Frederick (1970a) Language, attitude and social change. In F. Williams (ed.) *Language and Poverty.* Chicago, IL: Markham.

Williams, Frederick (1970b) Psychological correlates of speech characteristics: On sounding disadvantaged. *Journal of Speech and Hearing Research* 13, 472–488.

Williams, Frederick (1974) The identification of linguistic attitudes. *Linguistics* 136, 21–32.

Williams, Frederick (1976) *Explorations of the Linguistic Attitudes of teachers.* Rowley, MA: Newbury.

Williams, Frederick, Jack Whitehead and Leslie Miller (1972) Relations between language attitudes and teacher expectancy. *American Educational Research Journal* 9, 263–277.

Williams, Hugo (2006) Freelance. *Times Literary Supplement,* 28 April.

Williams, Robert (ed.) (1975) *Ebonics: The True Language of Black Folks.* St Louis, MO: Institute of Black Studies.

Wilson, Woodrow (1902) *A History of the American People.* New York: Harper Brothers.

Winfield, Ann (2007) *Eugenics and Education in America.* New York: Peter Lang.

Wiseman, Stephen (1968) Educational deprivation and disadvantage. In H. Butcher (ed.) *Educational Research in Britain.* London: University of London Press.

Wiseman, Stephen (1973) The educational obstacle race: Factors that hinder pupil progress. *Educational Research* 15, 87–93.

Wodak, Ruth (2006) Dilemmas of discourse (analysis). *Language in Society* 35, 595–611.

Wolfe, Tom (1970) *Radical Chic, and Mau-Mauing the Flak Catchers.* New York: Farrar, Straus & Giroux.

Wolfram, Walt (1969) *A Sociolinguistic Description of Detroit Negro Speech.* Washington, DC: Center for Applied Linguistics.

Wolfram, Walt (1973) Objective and subjective parameters of language assimilation among second generation Puerto Ricans in East Harlem. In R. Shuy and R. Fasold (eds) *Language Attitudes: Current Trends and Prospects.* Washington: Georgetown University Press.

Wolfram, Walt (1998a) Black children are verbally deprived. In L. Bauer and P. Trudgill (eds) *Language Myths.* London: Penguin.

Wolfram, Walt (1998b) Language ideology and dialect: Understanding the Oakland Ebonics controversy. *Journal of English Linguistics* 26, 108–121.

Wolfram, Walt (2005) Ebonics and linguistic science: Clarifying the issues. In J.D. Ramirez, T. Wiley, G. de Klerk, E. Lee and W. Wright (eds) *Ebonics: The Urban Education Debate* (2nd edn). Clevedon: Multilingual Matters.

Wolfram, Walt and Donna Christian (1989) *Dialects and Education: Issues and Answers.* Englewood Cliffs, NJ: Prentice-Hall.

Wolfram, Walt and Erik Thomas (2002) *The Development of African American English.* Oxford: Blackwell.

Wood, Gordon (1994) The losable past. *The New Republic,* 7 November (211: 19), 46–49.

Woodford, J. (2004) Bill Cosby, education, and the lumpenizing of the contemporary Black world. *The Black Scholar* 34 (4), 21–26.

Woodford, O. (1982) Interview on *Ebony* (BBC-TV), 17 November.

Woodhead, Martin (1988) When psychology informs public policy: The case of early childhood intervention. *American Psychologist* 43, 443–454.

Wright, Ian and Carol LaBar (1984) Multiculturalism and morality. In S. Shapson and V. d'Oyley (eds) *Bilingual and Multicultural Education.* Clevedon: Multilingual Matters.

Wright, Laura (ed.) (2000) *The Development of Standard English, 1300–1800: Theories, Descriptions, Conflicts.* Cambridge: Cambridge University Press.

Wright, Stephen and Évelyne Bougie (2007) Intergroup contact and minority-language education. *Journal of Language and Social Psychology* 26, 157–181.

Wright, Wayne (2005a) Scholarly references and news titles. In J.D. Ramirez, T. Wiley, G. de Klerk, E. Lee and W. Wright (eds) *Ebonics: The Urban Education Debate* (2nd edn). Clevedon: Multilingual Matters.

Wright, Wayne (2005b) *Evolution of Federal Policy and Implications of* No Child Left Behind *for Language Minority Students.* Tempe, AZ: Arizona State University College of Education.

Yancy, George (ed.) (1998) *African American Philosophers.* London: Routledge.

Yeung, Alexander, Herbert Marsh and Rosemary Suliman (2000) Can two tongues live in harmony: Analysis of the *National Education Longitudinal Study* of 1988 (NELS88) longitudinal data on the maintenance of home language. *American Educational Research Journal* 37, 1001–1026.

Yell, Mitchell and Erik Drasgow (2005) *No Child Left Behind: A Guide for Professionals.* Upper Saddle River, NJ: Pearson.

Young, R. (1983) A school communication-deficit hypothesis of educational disadvantage. *Australian Journal of Education* 27, 3–15.

Younger, Michael and Molly Warrington (2006) Would Harry and Hermione have done better in single-sex classes? A review of single-sex teaching in coeducational secondary schools in the United Kingdom. *American Educational Research Journal* 43, 579–620.

Zangwill, Israel (1909) *The Melting Pot: Drama in Four Acts.* London: Heinemann.

Zeichner, Kenneth (1994) Teacher socialization for cultural diversity. In J. Sikula, T. Buttery and E. Guyton (eds) *Handbook of Research on Teacher Education.* New York: Macmillan.

Zéphir, Flore (1997) Haitian Creole language and bilingual education in the United States: Problem, right or resource? *Journal of Multilingual and Multicultural Development* 18, 223–237.

Zéphir, Flore (1999) Challenges for multicultural education: Sociolinguistic parallels between African American English and Haitian Creole. *Journal of Multilingual and Multicultural Development* 20, 134–154.

Zientek, Linda (2007) Preparing high-quality teachers: Views from the classroom. *American Educational Research Journal* 44, 959–1001.

Zigler, Edward and Winne Berman (1983) Discerning the future of early childhood intervention. *American Psychologist* 38, 894–906.

Zigler, Edward and Victoria Seitz (1980) Head Start as a National Laboratory. Unpublished manuscript.

Zigler, Edward and Jeanette Valentine (1979) *Project Head Start: A Legacy of the War on Poverty*. New York: Free Press.

Zorn, Jeffrey (1982) Black English and the *King* decision. *College English* 44, 314–320.

Index

Although there is some overlap, this index generally omits entries for material that is clearly to be found under a heading shown in the table of contents. Thus, for example, the information covered in the 'Compensatory Intervention?' section of Chapter 5 is not referred to here in the 'compensatory programs' entry. Space constraints have meant that not all personal names have been listed here.